Kāma's Flowers

SUNY series in Hindu Studies

Wendy Doniger, editor

Kāma's Flowers

Nature in Hindi Poetry and Criticism, 1885–1925

Valerie Ritter

SUNY PRESS

Published by State University of New York Press, Albany

Printed in the United States of America

For information, contact State University of New York Press, Albany, NY
www.sunypress.edu

Production by Diane Ganeles
Marketing by Anne M. Valentine

Library of Congress Cataloging-in-Publication Data

Ritter, Valerie
Kāma's flowers : nature in Hindi poetry and criticism, 1885–1925 / Valerie Ritter.
p. cm. — (SUNY series in Hindu studies)
Includes bibliographical references and index.
ISBN 978-1-4384-3565-7 (hardcover : alk. paper)
ISBN 978-1-4384-3566-4 (pbk. : alk. paper)
1. Hindi poetry—19th century—History and criticism. 2. Hindi poetry—20th century—History and criticism. 3. Nature in literature. I. Title.

PK2040.4.R57 2011
891.4'3150936—dc22 2010031949

10 9 8 7 6 5 4 3 2 1

dedicated to
Gaynell Nevada Mixon Floyd
and
Betty Grace Newton Ritter

Contents

Preface

The title of this book refers to the God of Love, Kāma, the personification of the classical Sanskrit conception of desire and pleasure, one of the basic aims of human life (*puruṣārtha*). Kāma as a concept encompasses all things concerned with pleasure and refinement, including both enjoyment of the arts and erotics. It is of course the realm of life described in the famous *Kama Sutra* of Vātsyāyana. As a personified god, Kāma carries a bow and arrow with which he shoots victims of love and other pleasures; his arrows are said to be tipped with flowers. A story from the *Vāmana Purana* tells us more, describing how Kāma tempted god Shiva to leave off his austere meditations for carnal desire:

> When Śiva left the Pine Forest, Kāma tried to excite him once again, but Śiva saw him and looked at him with an angry glance, and burnt him to ashes as if he were a forest of dry wood. As his feet caught fire, Kāma dropped his bow, which broke into five parts, these turning into five trees and flowers, and, by the grace of Śiva, all his arrows turned into flowers and Kāma himself died.[1]

Thus, the god of love himself disappears, and his weapons suddenly sprout into trees and flowers. This story about Kāma, Pleasure itself, parallels what happened in the Hindi poetry in this period: the definition of refined pleasure changed such that the erotics inherent in poetics transformed into nature poetry—resulting in poems about flowers instead of lovers. These flowers—as all of the stuff of the nature poetry that emerged in Hindi in the modern era—held powerful resonances with both older poetics and new concerns with freedom, political and social. The flowers which formerly adorned Kāma's arrows, messengers delivering pleasure, desire, and lust, are now these arrows of desire themselves, reincarnated. The accoutrement has become the thing it had once ornamented, and love poetry becomes nature poetry, in the shift to

Hindi poetic modernity. In the end, of course, Kāma never really dies, in mythology, and in poetry.

This book examines poetry and criticism surrounding the representation of nature in Hindi poetry, concentrating on the extremely important but overlooked period of 1885–1925, known for its early nature poetry by Śrīdhar Pāṭhak and "Hariaudh" of the Dvivedī Era, and the early poetry of later avowed nature poets, Jayaśaṅkar Prasād, Sumitrānandan Pant, and "Nirālā," of the Chāyāvād (Shadow-ist) era. The analysis of works from this particular span of decades shows that writing literarily of nature was a multivalent strategy, to be innovative with new empirical perspectives and the invocation of sociopolitical concerns, but also to be creatively allusive to traditional poetics, most fundamentally Sanskrit's *śṛṅgāra* (the "erotic sentiment" of traditional poetics), newly problematized in the colonial era. The book describes the constituent elements of poetics for Hindi authors of this period, and complicates the usual ascription of modern Hindi nature poetry to Romantic influence. Addressing translations from English, Hindi criticism, both classics and little-known Hindi texts of the period, and the gendered aspects of the reform of *śṛṅgāra* as literary mode, the book serves as a guide to understanding the evolution and significance of a major theme of modern Hindi poetry.

The Subject of Nature

"Nature" (*prakṛti*) in Hindi poetry was a subject I came upon through Hindi literary criticism on Dvivedī era poetry. I found to my surprise that one of the seminal works of the era, which altered mythology and traditional poetic themes considerably, was considered a work of "nature poetry." I would never have predicted this; if the author had intended this to be "nature poetry," I thought, critics would surely deem that he had failed in his attempt. It was "mere description" in my view, and in a conventional Sanskritic mode replete with redundant terms for "beautiful," "charming," etc. that smacked of classical poetics in *mahākāvya*, but hardly brought Wordsworth to mind. To the contrary, I discovered that not only did the Hindi critics praise what they saw as the turn toward natural realism, but that the general Hindi-educated population could spontaneously recite the most famous so-called "nature-description" verses of this poem, and with relish. I met many people who had memorized the verses in school, but it was clear they also truly appreciated them. They all knew that these verses represented something new when they were composed, even though now they seem as traditional as modern Hindi could be, in Sanskrit meter no less. My curiosity was piqued. What exactly was this nature-in-poetry that the Hindi secondary literature always cited, and the inheritors of the Hindi canon perceived so clearly? Thus began my inquiry into the subject of this book, which led me through the twentieth-century Hindi literary critical establishment, to the poems themselves. It became clear that nature in Hindi poetry had much to do with the advent of poetic modernity for the authors of these poems and critical texts, but the story was extremely complex and multifaceted. It clearly had much to do with the reappraisal of literary erotics, qua "tradition," and confrontation with English poetic values.

Further, I began to suspect that nature in Hindi poetry has a significance that reaches beyond poetics per se, providing a window into the history of the present-day quotidian aesthetics of North India. In unpacking the high valuation of "natural description" and "love of nature" in Hindi poetics, I rethought what I considered the idiosyncratic decorative culture of North India, of posters of forest cottages, and advertising campaigns of bees on flowers. Even the cinematographic trademarks of Hindi films, close-ups of the single flower, panning the mountain vale, weaving through trees in wooded enclosures, fit in with the aesthetic world of this Hindi nature poetry. Clearly modern Hindi poetic nature of the early decades of the twentieth century was part of a larger cultural fabric.

One of the basic ways in which nature is readable in modern Hindi poetry and in the popular cultural images just described, is through the lens of *śṛṅgāra*, the category of erotic sentiment in classical Sanskrit poetics. Deeply intertwined with what we now call Hinduism, and in particular worship of Krishna and his lover-consort Rādhā, this Sanskrit poetics and theology has transmuted into the everyday *habitus* of North India, and forms part of a subconscious framework for thinking about human sexual love and erotics in the contemporary world.[2] Most certainly, *śṛṅgāra* has affected how love "looks" and "feels" in South Asia,[3] as a dominant strain in a complex symphony of cultural tropes. An abstracted erotics still flourishes, despite the dismantling of the institutional apparatus for this classical *śṛṅgāra*, the traditional poetics of learned Brahmans, and despite the fear of sexual decadence, which animated debates over poetry century ago and still grabs headlines today.[4]

In this book I do not simply make the argument that *śṛṅgāra* is a "survival," but rather that that the reinvention of *śṛṅgāra* in Hindi high culture accompanied the broader problem of how to be modern-but-Indian. Scholars often criticize the tendency to read *śṛṅgāra* overmuch in modern culture. Rightly, they have seen in this scholarly tendency a means of erasure of non-Sanskritic, Muslim, and folk cultures, or an

Orientalist fetishization of "timeless tradition." These points are well taken. However, the existence of particular *śṛṅgārik* tropes within genres self-consciously announcing their distance from such "tradition," and the particularities of these modernized *śṛṅgārik* tropes, demand attention. *Śṛṅgāra* is integral to the modern Hindi poetic nature, and indeed the ideals of beautiful natural spaces in general in modern India, and a history of it in the modern poetic context is part of the history of interactions between colonialism, aesthetics, and theology.

The semiotic potency of the natural images of poetry and popular culture contribute to something like Raymond Williams's "structures of feeling" in modern Hindi-speaking India.[5] We could say that the semiotic world of love in contemporary India is colored by a much older erotic poetics, the ideals of which are, as Lacan had observed in regard to courtly love in the West, "tout à fait concrètes dans l'organisation sentimentale de l'homme contemporain, et y perpétuant leur marche."[6] This situation is palpable in the Indian context, where these images are potent precisely because of their past lives, yet such natural images came to be understood as a feature of what was modern in modern Hindi poetry.

The nature in Hindi poetry can also inform us of the structures of feeling beyond the erotic, namely, the affect of Indian nationalism. Take for instance the name of the memorial at Gandhi's residence at the Sabarmati Ashram in Ahmedabad: Hṛday-kuñj, "Heart's Arbor." What accounts for this particular image of the arbor, of the conjoining of nature and love, in a place of national pilgrimage? The early poetry of modern Hindi will give some insight into this question. Hindi is not the originating source of these images, and not the only language to use them in these ways, but it is an important resource in considering how modern Indian literatures became so, and how national uses of nature are integrated into their larger cultural sphere.

Nature has become a topic of more and more interest in Asian Studies generally, specifically in the context of studies of the constitution of modernity. From these works it is clear that the phenomenon of Nature in rhetoric—political or literary—though linked with European contact, was not a uniform phenomenon across Asia. Julia Adeney Thomas has examined "Nature" as a principle in political theory in Meiji Era Japan (the rough equivalent, chronologically and culturally, to our period of 1885–1925 in North India). Her narrative explaining the creation of the "Japanese love of nature" is based upon a core conception of nature as a negatively valued antonym of culture, an idea that had little effect upon Hindi poetics, and when it did so, took on different significances. Thomas's conclusion that the Japanese iconized Nature became a chauvinistic, nationalist one in the early twentieth century has some parallel for Hindi, but with an entirely different story of how this came about.[7]

Chinese modern literary history, especially as put forth by Shumei Shi, holds some quite striking parallels for the subject of nature in modern Hindi poetry. Foremost among them is the "neoromantic" trend, which "conflat[ed] the discourses of biological evolutionism, literary movements, and the Chinese national character, . . . [with] heavy emphasis on the necessity of naturalism."[8] Further, the emphasis on a teleology of progress in Chinese literary history, leading to a Europe-defined modernism, also has distinct echoes in the Hindi context, as does the modernism Shi describes in the (albeit later) work of Fei Ming, which alluded to a "traditional lyricism embodying the poetic harmony between feeling (*qing*) and landscape (*jing*)" in ingeniously incorporating the aesthetics of Tang nature poetry into a modernist language and syntax of disjunction and fragmentation."[9] Though somewhat later than our chronological purview here, and following a somewhat different course, these Chinese developments mirror the Hindi, and indeed Indian situation regarding the negotiation of aesthetics within the "East-West culture debates"[10] of the late nineteenth and twentieth centuries. Literary nature, then, is ripe for discussion in a pan-Asian framework, and even more so, ripe for redress within the specific literary historical circumstances of North India.

The Watershed Era: 1885–1925

As the title of this book indicates, reforming poetics meant reforming the arrows of Kāma—the things that delivered aesthetic pleasure, which in nineteenth-century India included a foundational erotic poetics. Kāma's arrows then more literally—as incitants of sexual desire—then had to be reformed. Being modern in colonial India had much to do with consternation about sex, not only in terms of how "obscenity" applied to *śṛṅgārik* works, but in confronting English sexual mores and what they might mean in terms of "progress," a keyword of the times.[11] Here we can recall the dangerous, seductive character of Sandip in Rabindranath Tagore's *Home and the World* (1915) who teases his friend's wife Bimala about reading "an English book in which sex-problems were treated in an audaciously realistic manner," a book "of blunt things, bluntly put," which serves ambiguously in the novel as a symbol of social risk, yet also liberation into a world of "realism."[12] The years of 1885–1925 thusly saw much grappling with poetic values around the problem of erotics.

Authors in Hindi, dedicated to promoting and preserving Sanskrit cultural forms, and Hinduism itself, grappled with a systematized and theologized classical poetics that did not mesh well with the English literary values they had begun to value also. Foremost, the dominant category of *śṛṅgāra*, the erotic sentiment, flew in the face of all ideas of modern progress. Authors sought to disengage the subject matter of *śṛṅgāra* from its pre-modern moorings and use these images for description of their new poetic truths: "nature" and "emotion," and sometimes the social goals of "love of country," and "independence." In this we find a resemblance to Foucault's repressive hypothesis, in which sex became something "not simply condemned or tolerated, but managed, inserted into systems of utility, regulated for the greater good of all." Likewise, the transmutation of *śṛṅgāra* into less overtly sexual tropes could be interpreted as the "proliferation of discourses" that the sexual taboo ironically supplies. However, this book will present a different and complex aesthetic situation, in which the modern poetics of *śṛṅgāra* does not become something to be confessed, a secret to be discussed ad infinitum, as Foucault describes, but rather becomes a way for Hindi poets to engage with what they saw as modernity's trappings: ideas of science, nation, and liberty.[13]

This disengagement and re-purposing within the literary sphere has a history in the formation of modern national consciousness. The authors examined here had inherited the drive for Hindi as a national language, and in various degrees, the assumption that literature was an index of civilization and that, ergo, eroticism in literature was problematic. In the words of Jayaśaṅkar Prasād in 1909, in his benedictory essay at the beginning of his *Indu* magazine:

> It is universally accepted that literary progress (*sāhitya kī unnati*) is required for racial progress (*jātīya unnati*). And from looking at literature alone, the limit of racial progress can be shown or proven. As much progress as a race has achieved, correspondingly will its literature appear elevated.[14]

It is almost as if Thomas Babington Macaulay's racialized damning of Indian knowledge in educational policy—"a single shelf of a good European library was worth the whole native literature of India and Arabia"[15]—had taken root in India with a strict definition of literature itself, and specifically in the form of principle: literary progress—literally, *unnati*, "elevation"—had become a requirement of civilizational progress. The erotic decidedly did not represent progress, a progress that Indian people saw as leading ultimately to political Independence. The entity of "nature" seemed to these authors to hold huge positive potential, as the moral status of literature became paramount.

We know surprisingly little about this period of Hindi when these aesthetic changes were taking place. We know much more about the literary developments in Europe and Bengal: the classic novels of the British Raj by Rudyard Kipling and E. M. Forster, and the works of the famed Bengali Rabindranath Tagore dominate our knowledge of this era. Several scholars have addressed the important and basic topics of the language politics surrounding Hindi and Urdu in this era, and the public sphere created by Hindi print culture. But the questions remain: What was happening poetically, and aesthetically, in Hindi at this time? What about the evolution of *Hindi poetry*, the poetics of the language that would become the self-appointed scion of Sanskrit's glorious Hindu past? This book will approach answers to these questions, and will address specifically an important feature of the Hindi literary landscape ever since: the reformation of *śṛṅgāra*, the poetics of erotics, into the stuff of modern poetry on nature, love, and nation.

Outline of the Following Chapters

Chapter 1 describes the terms by which modern Hindi poetry is commonly understood, the constituent aspects of the literary world of modern Hindi poetry, and the complications of examining this literary field. Examining the historical and social context of these Hindi authors of the late nineteenth century, it becomes apparent that these terms "modern," "Hindi," and "modern poetry," were ambiguous and under contestation.

Chapter 2 shows that a veritable obsession with "nature in poetry" occurred in Hindi literary criticism in the twentieth century, which located the onset of modernity with changes in poetic nature, and linked this in turn to the influence of English Romanticism. I then give evidence that the surfeit of significations of nature and the natural for our polyglot poets complicates this narrative of English Romantic influence.

Chapter 3 addresses the question of what we might glean of the "influence of English" in terms of Hindi adaptations of English poetry in the late nineteenth century, and how these have influenced the conception of English "nature" in the Hindi context. To this end, I analyze two very prominent translations from English into Braj Bhāṣā of eighteenth-century verse, one Śrīdhar Pāṭhak's 1889 translation of Oliver Goldsmith's *Deserted Village*, the other Ratnākar's 1897 translation of Alexander Pope's *Essay on Criticism*. From these we see that certain features of English nature remained significant in their Hindi translation, and that a particular vocabulary was emerging for writing of nature.

Chapter 4 examines both poetry and criticism in Hindi from 1900, in reference specifically to nature, surveying the relevant works of the famed editor of modern Hindi, M. P. Dvivedī, and the most famous original work by Śrīdhar Pāṭhak, "Kāśmīr Suṣumā" (The Beauty of Kashmir). Here we find various reactions: an uncomfortable clash of values of realism and political import with the aesthetics of *śṛṅgāra*; the integration of *śṛṅgāra* with geographic nationalism; and a rhetorical device for describing landscape in a realist and Sanskritic mode.

Chapter 5 addresses the critical aesthetic maneuver of early twentieth-century Hindi: the freeing of the natural objects of Sanskrit metaphor from their former bodily referents. Specifically I look at Hariaudh's *Priyapravās*, and several poems from the young Jayaśaṅkar Prasād, 1909–1918, that exemplify the phenomenon of what I call "object-poems."

Chapter 6 addresses the perspectival sleights of hand in the writing of two authors of the younger generation, Prasād and Rāmanareś Tripāṭhī. Here we find elaboration of Nature as principle, with theological overtones; nature as an alternative to the normal social world of love also emerges, which implies a coincidence of nature with freedom, personal and political. Finally, I describe in brief the entrenchment of nature subsequently in the quotidian poetry of the early twenties.

Chapter 7 steps back to examine the gender politics of poetics in this era, as the erotic mood *śṛṅgāra* was reformed. Pointing out that cultural authenticity claims in the Hindi sphere impinged upon literary depictions of women, I examine in detail some criticism and poetry on the problematic *śṛṅgāra* and on women as poetic subjects, showing that despite rejection of Braj poetry for its eroticism, Khaṛī Bolī poetry retained some features of heroine-description. I close the chapter with an examination of the scientization of the theory of *śṛṅgāra*.

Chapter 8 returns to the problem of nature-in-poetry per se, examining the first major critical essay addressing the import of nature in Hindi, "Natural Scenes in Hindi Poetry" (1923) by seminal critic Rāmacandra Śukla. In a close analysis we find a realist landscape Śukla identifies with Indian identity through the ages, and ultimately with Indian political independence. A materialism of nature supersedes the poetic apparatus of *rasa* for inspiring emotion. Śukla enunciates the shift in nature in poetry in terms of the rhetoric of "independent" nature and the sublime effect of aggregated natural objects.

Chapter 9 looks at the early years of the Chāyāvād (Shadow-ist) generation, the poets identified with the first "successful" modern poetry in Hindi, with avowed inspiration from the late English Romantics. The term "personification" came to the fore as natural objects appear as hero and heroine. *Śṛṅgāra* appeared safely naturalized, philosophized, and even nationalized. Here I show that along with their innovations, Chāyāvād poets wrote in clear consonance with their Dvivedī era forebears in regard to nature.

In the Concluding Remarks I summarize my observations on the poetic traits incurred through this turn to nature. Nature was not reinvented by Chāyāvād poets along Romantic lines, I argue, but rather the Chayavad poets developed further an already established strategy treading the ground in between the world of *śṛṅgāra* and the world of scientific and political *yathārth,* "commensurate reality," as defined in decades previous.

On Reading Hindi Poetic History

The form of this book, with its voluminous translations, explication du texte, and unusual chronological scope, requires some explanation. There is inevitably the feeling of a survey in this work because of the burden of explication of a lesser-known part of literary history, lesser-known even to native Hindi readers. The reader will find many translations of critical and poetic texts, most of which have never been published previously in Western languages. This fact, and my critical goal of historicizing poetic tropes have both conspired to shape this book into a monograph with multiple functions: a literary historical analysis of a particular trope within a particular body of poetry, along the lines of the thousands of such monographs on Western literature, and a venue for translations of the poetic and critical works the book analyzes, for an audience that may be familiar with the great figures of Indian literature and history, but not with the full range of texts I present and analyze. The result is this hybrid sort of work, which has the predictable shortcomings of such experimental endeavors. My hope is that by publishing this study, replete with its many translations, I can speed along the future era when—as in studies of English, Spanish, or Russian literature—scholars can assume their readers have access to and familiarity with Hindi texts examined.

In regard to my critical stance: I am unapologetically eclectic in my approach to these texts. I present this study as an effort in the vein of post-colonial studies, purely in the sense that this work considers the colonial context of this aesthetic world to be essential to understanding it, and seeks hard evidence as to how Hindi poetry evolved vis-à-vis English literary values. This work is informed by an academic style of close reading born of New Criticism, but in orientation quite new historicist. The book ultimately addresses questions about the work of poetry and culture to which structuralist semiotics speaks—what happens when a sign, a trope, a word, takes on a new life? With no conscious stake in any one particular school of method or ideology that informs literary history and criticism, this is what I intend to illustrate for the particular time, place, and linguistic world described in *Kāma's Flowers*: What happens to a changing sign in British India, within the deeply felt and deeply cherished realm of poetry? What happens when we historicize poems themselves, and trace the reifications and circulations of tropes by observing them at work, and avoid the broad generalizations that have preoccupied so many literary historians of Hindi? In the end we will know more about what and how a poem signified in early twentieth-century India, and about how poetry functions in contexts of acute cultural self-consciousness.

This book seeks to reframe the terms of engagement, addressing the immediate aesthetic pre-history of Chāyāvād in the Dvivedī era, and only the very beginning of the emergence of Chāyāvād, through 1925. The benefits of this framework are manifold: we can historicize the tropes of Hindi poetry more completely, rather than taking the typical strategy of considering an author or movement's work in a wide swath of decades. For example, it is rare to find any study of the major Chāyāvād poets Prasād, Pant, and Nirālā, without reference to their poetry of the thirties and beyond. Here, with the delimitation of 1925, we can see the poetic world of the late nineteenth and early twentieth centuries much more clearly, and are in a position to reassess the usual, normative ascription of Romanticism, and all that implies, to the rising Chāyāvād generation. In taking this approach to Hindi poetry, and Hindi literary history generally, I am somewhat renegade. Some, especially those steeped in the deeply ingrained literary historiography of Hindi and Bengali, may find my arguments contrary to conventional wisdom, which as conventional wisdom, certainly has a point. However, I believe Hindi poetry deserves no less than the careful attention I have given it.

Acknowledgments

I owe my primary debts to those who shepherded me through my graduate work several years ago, from which the kernel of the idea of this book was born. Foremost has been Michael C. Shapiro, to whom I am grateful for years of intellectual guidance, professional advice, and good etymological jokes. I thank Sagaree Sengupta for taking me under her wing early on.

Due thanks go to Wendy Doniger for approving the inclusion of this book in the series. Thanks also go to the Fulbright Foundation for dissertation research in India, and to the Universities of Virginia and Chicago, for research and travel monies for India and England. I also thank the University of Washington Department of Asian Languages and Literature, which supported the seed of this project with support for graduate study. I also thank the U.S. Department of Education for the Foreign Language and Area Studies Fellowships I received for many years of my graduate studies.

The manuscript has benefited from presentations at the Annual Conference on South Asia (UW–Madison), the American Academy of Religion, the University of Chicago Franke Institute, University of Virginia South Asia Seminar, the European Conference for Modern South Asian Studies, the American Oriental Society, the Association for Asian Studies, the University of Pennsylvania South Asia Seminar, and the University of Florida CHITRA (Center for the Study of Hindu Traditions) lecture series.

I thank Orient Blackswan for permission to reprint, in Chapters 1, 3, and 5, parts of my article "Networks, Patrons, and Genres" in their *Hindi and Urdu Before the Divide* (F. Orsini, ed., 2010). I thank Permanent Black for permission to reprint, in Chapters 3, 4, and 5, revised and expanded portions of my articles in the anthology *Nationalism in the Vernacular* (S. Nijhawan, ed., 2010). I thank SUNY Press for reprinting in Chapter 5 parts of my article for their volume *Alternative Krishnas* (G.

Beck, ed.; 2005). I thank Johns Hopkins Press for permission to publish an expanded version of my article "The Proper Female Subject" (Copyright © 2010 Johns Hopkins University Press) as Chapter 7, "Women Problems." This article first appeared in the *Journal of Women's History* (22:1, Spring 2010).

For their comments, advice, and support in the formulation and execution of this project, and my academic career, I thank Frank Conlon, Alan W. Entwistle, John Stratton Hawley, Naseem Hines, R. S. McGregor, Francesca Orsini, Heidi Pauwels, Frances Pritchett, and Mira Srivastava, as well as the anonymous readers of the book manuscript. For their important practical assistance, I thank the staff at the United States Educational Foundation in India and at the American Institute of Indian Studies. In the vital matter of fonts, I heartily thank Sean Pue and Andrew Glass for their help over the years. For their efforts in the final publication stages, I thank Uday Prakash and Sanjeev and Priti Vidyarthi for their advice in copyright matters. Finally, I heartily thank Louise W. Seiler for painstakingly indexing this work.

For their help and insights in locating and analyzing these texts, I thank Dhirendranāth Siṁh, of the *Aaj* newspaper, and dedicated scholar of early modern Hindi literature; Lakṣmīdatt Vyās of the Bhārat Kalā Bhavan at Banaras Hindu University; and Dayārām Gupta of the Hindī Sāhitya Kuṭīr, Varanasi, publisher of Hariaudh's works since 1940. I also sincerely thank the administrations and staffs of the Nāgarī Pracāriṇī Sabhā Library in Varanasi, the major repository of Hindi poetry before 1910; the Hindī Sāhitya Sammelan library in Allahabad; the Nehru Memorial Library of New Delhi; and the Banaras Hindu University library, Varanasi.

For their suggestions and insights, I thank Vasudha Dalmia, Lindsay Harlan, Janice Leoshko, Gail Minault, and Rupert Snell. For their moral support and camaraderie over the span of years of this project, I thank Amy Bard, Joan Burnside, Erin Douglass, John Farrell, Jason Grunebaum, Timothy Lenz, Pamela Lothspeich, Jason Neelis, Ellen O'Brien, Tracy Pintchman, August and Otto Ritter, Todd Scudiere, and Ravi Singh.

I must also thank others more personally. My heartfelt thanks go to Kelly Herrick, who has seen me through it all, and to the inspiring Riley Lemire. Finally, I thank my parents, Kurt and Ellen Ritter, for their support in this unlikeliest of endeavors.

Transliteration Conventions and Abbreviations

Terms not found in the *Oxford English Dictionary* will be given in transliteration. Transliterations will largely follow the diacritical conventions of *The Oxford Hindi-English Dictionary*, edited by R. S. McGregor, 1993. In quotations from other authors in English, I will retain their transliteration; because of this there may be some variance from my scheme.

I will retain word-final *'a'* in citations from poetry, but not in titles of poetic volumes, in prose, or in the spelling of names. I will retain the word-final *'a'* in non-poetic contexts when it is commonly pronounced (e.g., *sāhitya*, not *sāhity*). For clarity, word-internal *'a'*s will always be given, despite the fact that they are not always pronounced.

Terms from and invoking Sanskrit and classical poetics, as well as names of classical Sanskrit authors, will be transliterated with the word-final 'a' (e.g., *śṛṅgāra rasa*, not *śṛṅgār ras*; and Jayadeva, not Jayadev). Certain surnames will appear with word-final 'a' according to English convention (e.g., Gupta, not Gupt). Names of the few authors well-known in English and certain terms-of-address-cum-surnames will be cited with their conventional English spellings (e.g., Tagore, Premchand, Mukherjee, Chatterji).

For place names, whenever possible I will use the current standard English names and spellings, regardless of the name used in the text, and without diacritical marks (e.g., Allahabad, not Prayāg; Azamgarh, not Āzamagaṛh). I transliterate terms from Bengali and Urdu as best approximated within this Hindi transliteration system.

Note on Translations

This book presents many translations of Hindi literary texts in the literary dialect of Braj Bhāṣā, and in other varieties of spoken and textual modern Hindi, sometimes in the spoken standard of Khaṛī Bolī, and sometimes highly Sanskritized. Many of these translations are of poetry, much of which was written in meter. These facts present several quandaries for translation which I will address here briefly.

Some translators believe in translating rhyme into rhyme; some have attempted to capture the flavor of Braj Bhāṣā poetry in particular by producing rhyme and using antiquated English (K. P. Bahadur's translations of Keśav Dās and Bihārīlāl come to mind). I do not produce rhyme in translation (except fortuitously on occasion), and I use modern American English norms at all times. While in the case of Braj especially, a literary dialect distinct from normal standard speech, this may create a false sense of linguistic immediacy, we can solace ourselves with the fact that until at least circa 1910 most of the Hindi literary audience would have understood Braj quite easily. Its "flavor" may be lost in translation, but its devotion and often courtly refinement will hopefully remain in my renderings.

Poetry in modern Hindi presents a more straightforward translation problem. Here I have had to dispense with rhyme, but when possible tried to retain assonance and alliteration, with an unselfconscious conception of "how poetry sounds." Certain turns of phrase will undoubtedly seem infelicitous and strange in American English; such is a symptom of poetry's singular opacity-in-clarity among the genres. Especially for the highly referential poetry of South Asia, steeped in multiple poetic systems and mythologies, translation will often present a trope utterly foreign to a Western audience. I see no point in naturalizing myth, especially—e.g., making Kāma, the god of love, into Cupid (although they both carry bow and arrow, this equation obscures too much). There will remain an element of foreignness that should only buttress my claims of the power of Hindi poetics in colonial India.

In sum, my translations are generally rather literal, but also more than merely literal. While avoiding the theoretical problem of how to translate the poetic qualities of poetry, suffice it to say that what is not literal has to do with presuppositions of poetics. In the words of Michael Riffaterre, "No literary translation . . . can ever be successful unless it finds equivalencies for . . . literariness-inducing presuppositions. . . . [T]he translator must transpose presuppositions."[1] Indeed, the project of this book is to analyze some of the presuppositions that comprise the base poetics of the modern Hindi world.

Abbreviations

HSS — *Hindī śabdasāgar* (*The Hindi Ocean of Words*), Śyāmasundar Dās, et al, eds. (11 vols.; 1929; Rev. and enl. 9th ed., 2nd printing, Varanasi: NPS, 1986)

NPS — Nāgarī Pracāriṇī Sabhā

OED — *The Oxford English Dictionary* (2nd ed. 1989; *OED Online*; Oxford University Press)

OHED — *The Oxford Hindi-English Dictionary*, R. S. McGregor, ed. (Oxford: Oxford University Press, 1993

Chapter 1

Terms of Engagement

A Guide to the Assumptions of Hindi Poetics

To approach the subject of this book, several basic questions need to be addressed, both for the uninitiated reader of Hindi texts, and for the scholar of Hindi who is reading the poetry of 1885–1925 anew. These questions are: What was the poetic background out of which Hindi poets composed? What would the term "modern Hindi poetry" signify at the beginning of this period? What is conventional wisdom about the period as a whole, especially in regard to Hindi nature-in-poetry? The bulk of this chapter will address each component of the term "modern Hindi poetry," to establish basic premises for understanding the world of the Hindi poet, and point to particular features within the idea of "modern Hindi poetry" that inform the nature poetry within it. The latter two sections will address how the literary eras are configured, and how nature has figured in these precepts of conventional wisdom of the decades following. Altogether, these sections will equip us with the literary and cultural logic that has informed the nature-phenomenon in Hindi poetry.

There are many constituent parts comprising the entity of "modern Hindi poetry." We must address the basic impinging terms and circumstances in order to establish points of reference for the particular period (1885–1925), genre (poetry), and theme ("Nature") analyzed in this book. To do this, I will parse this phrase "modern Hindi poetry" in the manner of a Sanskrit compound, and start the story with the last, or head word, "poetry," then proceeding to the vexed terms "Hindi" and "modern." This introduction will thusly rehearse some of the basic literary history familiar to scholars of Hindi, and also provide a context specifically for engaging with the concept of poetic Nature.

Definitions and Ideals for Poetry in Nineteenth Century North India

A functional definition of poetry held special difficulties in the late-nineteenth century poetic context.[1] It was the end of a century that had seen the displacement of the old elite poetic norms and the partial inculcation of new edicts and models for poetry from Britain. Sanskrit literature, to which Hindi poets often looked for inspiration, had boasted one of the most developed and complex poetics in the world. It possessed the category of *kāvya*, poetry per se, using something called *vakrokti*, "crooked speech," of which *mahākāvya*, the "great *kāvya*," demonstrating features of meter and subject, and length, was an archetype. Features from the highly developed poetics of Sanskrit would surface in the other genres as well, cropping up in the *Ramayana* narrative, or appearing in tandem with the explication of a "scientific" topic. Shorter *kāvya* forms often merged with song, and this was de rigueur for much of the devotional poetry of the second millennium CE which were usually performed as songs, or at least possible as such. For nineteenth-century poets, for whom the classical and devotional traditions were quite alive and well, verse remained something for performance, but became more textual as demands for a printed modern canon grew. With the addition of the novel form, the lack of which many Indians bemoaned, poetry became more a category of the past than of the future, which the novel and essay commanded.

The Hindi poet of the late nineteenth century was caught in a bind between varying poetic worlds: on the one hand he would have complex and intimate knowledge of Sanskritic and Persian poetic traditions, and on the other, some kind of familiarity with the much more foreign English poetic world, in original or translation from English, which represented the new worldliness, and knowledge of which had become a standard for the new gentlemanliness. Authors of the preceding twenty years had broached this basic conflict, but without a satisfying hybrid solution. The question of how to integrate past and present poetic ideals remained an open question of the day. We will consider first English, then Sanskrit, and the vernacular poetries of Braj Bhāṣā and Urdu, to highlight the complexity of the question of poetics in this context.

English Poetics in Colonial India

The question of the variegations of influence of English on the poetics of late nineteenth-century India is a complicated one that scholars have not adequately researched as yet. In assessing the English influence on Hindi poetry, we have to first consider the extreme stratification of access to English and ideas of "Englishness." While certain Indians would have been privy to the latest in British poetry, depending on their relationship to education, profession, financial means, and their own literary interest, others saw only certain English books, or read only translations from English in periodicals, and even then may have had deep interest in things English and felt variously committed to the cosmopolitanism they represented. Thus, there was a wide spectrum of engagement with English literary mores, and this does not even account for the very real "lag" in time and space, in getting English literature into India at this time.

Of course, the educational literary canon, in laboratory in India, as Gauri Viswanathan has shown in her *Masks of Conquest: Literary Study and British Rule in India*,[2] took a preeminent place in the imagining of English poetry and what it had to offer. While a thorough study of the dissemination of English poetry in India has yet to be done, we can get glimpses of the nature of this poetry from the *Education Reports* and the *Statements on Registered Publications*, of which the latter shows several guides for English literary readers.[3] We can also consult the extant syllabi of English-medium colleges and other testing institutions.[4] Besides what one might glean from extant educational records, we can also assume that a component of English poetry floating around India consisted of the most "popular" type: poetry in popular anthologies, illustrated gift books perhaps, and magazines. Thus, along with the famous poems of Indian English education, such as Gray's "Elegy," and Wordsworth's "Daffodils," a mish-mash of other English poems would have appeared in tandem in the North Indian publishing market.

A sense of competition and confrontation with English literature underlay much writing in Hindi, and in the early twentieth century poetry was becoming overshadowed by the perceived "English" genres of prose—the novel, the essay, the story—as representing modern citizens, their concerns, and their preoccupations. Both imported English novels and Indian novels tended precisely toward social concerns, and ultimately themes of morality, which Priya Joshi has argued formed a transcendent world of principles in literature, in contrast to the subjugation of colonial life for an Indian.[5] Indeed, we find this trait of moralization across Hindi genres, poetry as well as prose, throughout the period we address here.

As Frances Pritchett described the poetic world of nineteenth-century Urdu poets, English influences were manifold and "floating in the air," and therefore extremely difficult to pin down or quantify.[6] This largely holds true for those writing in Hindi as well. As for the nineteenth-century Urdu poets, the new dominance of English political, economic, and educational institutions had induced a sense of cultural loss of their previous "golden era," and a concomitant sense of current cultural decadence, but English literature also represented some truly hopeful cultural possibilities in their view. From the writings of Hindi poets and others, we can see clearly that many accepted the idea that moral decay brought about Indian subordination. Brought up on British histories of the Roman Empire, as well as indigenous ideas of fallen times, from the Islamicate one described by Urdu poet Alṭāf Ḥusain Ḥālī (addressed in the following chapter), to the *kali yug* (age of destruction) of Hindu thought, many educated Indians likely found such an argument of a decadence-induced fall from glory familiar, if not simply logical. In the words of Marathi author Viṣṇu Kṛṣṇa Cipaḷūṇkar (1850–82), analyzed by Sudhir Chandra in *The Oppressive Present*, Indians found themselves "crushed by English poetry," and sought to revivify a glorious past—"inventing tradition" in the classic Hobsbawmian sense—believing they were culturally inferior to the English in the present. Further, according to Chandra, poetry functioned as both a synecdoche for the entirety of colonial hegemony, and a cause of the current political cum cultural state. In Cipaḷūṇkar's words, "Crushed by English poetry, our freedom has been destroyed. . . . [and] under their laws we have become bankrupt."[7] Knowing English poetry held weighty cultural import, as a sign of an individual's elite education and "progressivism," and also a sign of Indian cultural/political loss.

Furthermore, for many Hindi authors, English did not truly offer the "last word" in terms of defining poetry. Deeply attached to their own poetic pasts, these poets had to find a way to reconcile their understanding of the valuable parts of indigenous poetry with their understanding of what English poetry could offer them. While "taking light from English lanterns,"[8] certain tropes and theories from English came to the fore that would take on lives of their own as markers of the modern in the Hindi poetic context. The adoption of English literary values did not replicate the English literary situation; the meaning of poetry for our authors could not have been that of the contemporary London scene, but the world of classical Sanskrit, the centuries-old Hindi dialect of Braj Bhāṣā, and contemporary Urdu poetics, mixed with avant-garde Bengali experiments with Western styles, and the English poetry of canon and popular anthologies.

So from whence did the Hindi poetics of 1885 come? *Rasa*, *bhāva*, devotional idioms (in turn derived from the latter), and an Indo-Persian allusive world of love and longing, war and lament, all appeared in the foreground, as poetic choices for the Hindi poet to brandish expertly, reform, or reject. The values of English poetry would somehow mix in with these supposedly less "modern" native forms, and Bengali, Gujarati, Marathi, and Urdu authors had already begun such syncretistic experiments.[9]

Classical Sanskrit Poetics

By far, the most referenced poetic theory by the Hindi poets of the late nineteenth and early twentieth centuries was the concept of *rasa*, cornerstone of classical Sanskrit aesthetics. Other scholars have delineated *rasa* (lit., juice, essence) in great depth, and from its earliest known sources.[10] Here it will suffice to say that this theory of aesthetics deriving at least from the tenth century, from Bharata's work on dramatics, the *Nāṭyaśāstra*, categorizes aesthetic experience according to emotional categories that are presented in the dramatic work, and then inspired in the educated audience. These emotional categories ordain particulars of subject matter and setting of the dramatic, and by extension poetic, work. *Rasa* is an all-encompassing abstraction that defines the aesthetic experience, and according to Edwin Gerow (upon whose works we will rely for standard and brief explications of these matters):

> a medium of experience, emotional awareness, "taste" that is first and foremost in or of the audience . . . [*rasa*] is a mood, an emotional consciousness, wherein all the disparate elements of the play, language, gesture, imitations, scenery, coincide, and are understood after all not to be disparate. . . .[11]

Importantly, *rasa* is ultimately an abstraction of the experience portrayed, which is shared among the connoisseurs of the audience. The self-conscious "feeling of a feeling" of the *rasa* theory bears some resemblance to modern thinking on aesthetic perception by I. A. Richards (by the late 1920s a favorite of Hindi critics), J. Wood, Langer, Gassett, and the "synaesthetists," as Gerow has noted.[12]

Conventionally *rasa* falls into eight categories,[13] and the category which dominates them all as the topic of poetry and drama is that of *śṛṅgāra*, the "erotic sentiment" or "mood of love," known as the "king of *rasa*s." Other *rasa*s can appear as subthemes within a *śṛṅgārik* work.[14] While the *rasa* system is at root prescriptive of character, setting, plot, etc., art within the *rasa* aesthetic world is intended to create an effect that apotheosizes the particular abstracted emotion as an end in itself. *Bhāva*, the "feeling" induced by a *rasa*, similarly becomes an end in itself. As Abhinava interpreted in the eleventh century:

> . . . the drama, the poem . . . generalizes the conditions of emotion and consequently generalizes or abstracts emotion itself—makes it into something essentially shared. This is Abhinava's *rasa*, emotion turned inside out—determining its conditions (the fictive play) rather than being determined by them (the real world)—and thus free of its conditions. Abhinava interprets this inversion as the experience of the possibility of experience itself, an experience that both cancels the boundaries separating men and kindles in them a desire for the essentially similar experience of liberation . . . the Advaita [monistic] inversion of cognitive point of view: the precondition of being is understood as more real than the particular manifestations of being.[15]

Such abstraction of emotion, and its role as determiner of conditions, "rather than being determined by them (the real world)," is important to remember as we consider how Indian authors in the nineteenth century grappled with incorporating Western poetics. But more practically speaking, *rasa* meant supplying a particular apparatus of *bhāva* ("feeling," the concrete experience of the *rasa* in question), *anubhāva* ("after-feelings," or "consequents," such as gestures indicating a feeling), *uddīpana* ("incitants," one of the category of "determinants," such as objects in the setting that encourage the experience of the *rasa*), and other conditions that would determine the features of the work. These were most elaborated over the centuries in relation to *śṛṅgāra rasa*, such that the presence of a *papīhā* bird, a night-blooming lotus, a creeper on a tree, etc., would ergo signify a theme of love.

Another stream of criticism elaborated the many sorts of *alaṃkāra*, "ornament," comprising poetic speech. These ornaments were conceived as belonging to the categories of sense and of language, as *arthālaṃkāra* (ornament of sense/meaning), e.g., various types of simile, and *śabdālaṃkāra* (ornament of language/phoneme/sound), e.g., alliteration, assonance. The Hindi authors of the nineteenth century would have studied to some considerable degree this science of verbal ornament originating from the late seventh-century authors Bhāmaha and Daṇḍin. This tradition included even "natural" or "direct" description (*svabhāvokti*) as an ornament among the others (which surprisingly held only minor interest for our Hindi poets emulating the language of speech and realism). This *alaṃkāraśāstra* and the ongoing theory of response that was *rasa* remained pertinent for all those trained in Sanskrit belles lettres, and writing in the vernacular genres emulating Sanskrit, well into the twentieth century.

Uniting the *rasa* of dramatic theory and *alaṃkāra* was the concept of *dhvani*, exposited in the ninth-century text *Dhvanyāloka*, by Ānandavardhana. *Dhvani*, literally "echo" or "sound," is then "interpreted as an expressive function inherent in language," and in more concrete terms, an "other meaning" that arises from a poetic utterance within the rubric of *rasa*: "as system of meaning in which the signifier is fixed but its corresponding signifieds theoretically infinite."[16] This location of multiple signification in language ultimately served both the apparatuses of *rasa* and of *alaṃkāra*:

> The denotative level [i.e., the *vibhāvas*, etc., of *rasa* theory, and the *alaṃkāra* of poetry per se] persists and is not cancelled; a further "content" is suggested via that denotation, which suggestion turns out to promote primarily the stable *rasa* as well.[17]

Thus *rasa* is often referred to as *rasa-dhvani*, with *dhvani* as the suggestive, "echo"-function of language to take the auditor's thoughts to further significations within the context of the understood *rasa*. As we shall see in the following chapters, the concept of *dhvani* would have been a viable, even desirable one, for the innovating Hindi litterateur of 1885–1925, but surprisingly, the term was rarely elaborated or even used in reference to contemporary poetry of this modern era. It remained by and large an understood component of the functioning of *rasa* in poetry.[18]

Along with *dhvani*, the concept of *aucitya*, appropriateness or decorum, a term found in Bharata, Ānandavardhana, and the works many others, persisted quietly in Hindi poetic world of the nineteenth century. This *aucitya*, which had ordained conventions of propriety in poetry's subjects and language, would be a key element of Chāyavād rebellion; less so for the poets of the preceding decades we examine here, who experimented more subtly.

Beyond the basic premises of *rasa* (essence, sentiment, relish, "feeling of a feeling"), *śṛṅgāra* (the erotic sentiment, "king of *rasas*"), *dhvani* (echo, suggestion), *alaṃkāra* (ornament), and *aucitya* (propriety), the developments of the sixteenth century are of prime importance in understanding the vernacular poetry in North India. This century witnessed the explicit integration of aesthetic experience and religious experience in influential Vaishnava sects devoted especially to Krishna, in his forms as an infant and as a seductive cowherd among the gopis (cowherdesses) in the pastoral region of Braj.

> A completely new turn to the *rasa* theory (in its dramatic context) was given by the Vaishnava theologians of Bengal,

> notably Rūpa Gosvāmin [in his *Bhaktirasāmṛtasindhu*] who took the preeminence of *śṛṅgāra* among the *rasa*s and boldly identified that *rasa* with the sentiment of the worshipful Krishna bhakta, thus in effect turning the real world of religious concerns into a drama, wherein everyone enacts the play of Krishna and the gopis.[19]

The sixteenth century aesthetic turn in Krishna theology, found most apparently in adherents of Caitanya, as Rūpa Gosvāmin mentioned above, would profoundly affect poetics in the North Indian vernaculars, and especially that of Braj Bhāṣā, to which we will now turn.[20]

Braj Bhāṣā into the Nineteenth Century

Braj Bhāṣā, the dialect associated with Krishna's home region of Braj, and the language of the legendary poet saint Sūr Dās (fl. late 15th–16th c.), became widespread in Hindu and Mughal courts, transforming into a pan-regional vernacular with cosmopolitan associations. The development of Brajbūlī, a mixture of Braj and Bengali, among devotees of the Bengali guru Caitanya, whose followers made Braj a pilgrimage place, attests further to the interregional nature of Krishnaite religiosity and the languages of its poetry, based often on the variety of Hindi in the Braj region. Braj Bhāṣā poetry, which soon developed a literary standard independent of its spoken dialect, most often addressed Krishnaite subjects, but in the courtly context, the relationship of Rādhā and Krishna merged with the ostensibly secular classical Sanskrit exposition of *śṛṅgāra* via the taxonomy of the hero and heroine (*nāyak* and *nāyikā*), and the modes of their relationship. In regard to the *nāyikā-bhed* (taxonomy of heroines) genre, R. S. McGregor has written that Nand Dās (fl. sixteenth century) wrote his *Rasamañjarī*, a text often illustrated in miniature paintings, with the idea that "the *nāyikā-bhed* theory [is] the key to an understanding of the nature of divine love."[21] Other sects that established themselves in the pilgrimage region of Braj "are described as *rasik* because they concentrated exclusively on the emotional experience (*rasa*) generated by contemplation of the love-play of Krishna and Rādhā."[22] Along with the merging of courtly aesthetic theory with bhakti theology, some Braj religious institutions held quasi-political status with the Mughal powers in nearby Agra, receiving some degree of royal patronage; in turn, some devotional idioms took on a strong courtly cast,[23] while bhakti devotion itself remained defined as a movement of more rough-hewn cultural origins. In this, Braj poetry merely resembled Indic arts generally, all over the subcontinent, in this inextricable court-temple aesthetic connection.

This courtly poetry, often called *rīti*,[24] or *rīti*-era poetry, would often be indistinguishable from the explicitly devotional and folk bhakti poetry on Krishna and Rādhā, in a mutual interdependence of content and idiom. As Braj courtly poetry used devotional idioms and references, so Braj bhakti poetry would use the *alaṃkāra* of high poetics. The importance of *śṛṅgāra* to Braj Bhāṣā poetry cannot be underestimated, as the sentiment of erotic love appeared in Braj renditions of Sanskrit works, and also devotional poetry on Krishna. Not unlike the European pastoral, such poetry on Krishna and the gopis in Braj often took the form of an urbane idealization of the non-urbane, in a kind of "staged pastoralism."[25] On the other hand, the body of poems on the pastoral loves of Krishna merges with those referencing the urbane (*nāgara*, lit. of the city/town, sophisticated) Krishna, whose identity shifts to one like the courtly hero in his love play. Braj poetry thus cultivated a double persona for Krishna and his lover Rādhā: on one hand simple village youth, on the other sophisticated characters in the roles of *śṛṅgāra*'s taxonomy of love.

The content of this Sanskritic tradition, in the medium of Braj Bhāṣā, consisted then of the two poles of high Sanskritic imitation and simple folksy songs of devotion, and all points in between.[26] Common to all of this poetry was a preoccupation with love for Krishna, on the part of the gopis, of Rādhā, or the author of the poem itself, all serving the idea that all-consuming, ecstatic and sometimes painful love approximates love for god. In certain respects then, this vernacular tradition resembles the troubadour poetry of Europe, but with more elaboration of its formal poetics, and a much longer life in popular culture. These literary dialects of Hindi were languages of courtly pastoral, as well as languages of "the street" and its living religious devotion. This latter feature would remain—today, too, Braj Bhāṣā bhajans are sung—but the high literary use of Braj would wane considerably in the early twentieth century.[27]

To illustrate the folk-poetry side of this poetic situation, see the following verse from blind saint-poet Sūr Dās, who legendarily spurned the summons of Emperor Akbar, but was adopted by the Vallabha sect that worshiped Krishna with courtly pomp and circumstance. This famous verse was found in a booklet for the use of devotees, sold among the many small, colored books of the bazaar and the stalls outside temples[28]:

> Night and day our eyes rain [tears]
> The rainy season remains with us always
> Since Śyām departed.
> Night and day our eyes rain [tears].
> The kohl doesn't stay on our eyes,

Our hands and cheeks have gone black.
Our bodice-cloth never dries,
Rivulets flow in between our breasts.
We are awash with tears down to our feet
The whites of our eyes flow away
Sūr Dās says, Braj is immersed
And no one can be saved.

Here a situational irony delivers the poetic pleasure: the rainy season—the season of love—stays with the gopis when their lover Krishna is absent. The refrain itself reinforces the irony of having the pain of separation, *viraha*, in the season of union, as the beginning of the line, *nisi din barasata* (night and day rain . . .) delays its subject, *naina hamāre* (our eyes), creating a momentary expectation of rain as rain, only to reverse the import of this sign. The irony doesn't stop here: the latter two lines declare that Braj is irretrievably immersed in this flood of tears, but signifies in fact a happy circumstance. *Ḍūbata*, drowned or immersed, commonly verbalizes the state of engrossment in and enjoyment of *rasa*, a liquid essence after all, and thereby signifies the positive effect of this pain of love: to helplessly long for god is the point of devotion, and like the women of Braj, the devotee should wish to be in such a dire but perhaps delicious plight of being steeped in love for Krishna. To be in this state, where "no one can be saved," is in fact to achieve salvation through Krishna from the ocean of existence. The hyperbole (rivulets between the breasts, etc.), possibly even humorous, only further suggests the ultimately happy subject of this image. This type of poem is most certainly a song; the refrain "day and night our eyes rain [tears]" would be repeated at the end of each verse, and its plain-spoken diction falls in a memorable AABA rhyme scheme. Like much of the Sūr oeuvre, here complexities of rhythm and rhyme impart semantic force.[29]

Another kind of verbal virtuosity characterized high courtly poetry in Braj on exactly the same themes. Take the following example from Keśav's *Rasikapriyā* (Beloved of the Connoisseur), a work delineating the types and interactions of a hero and heroine couple, identified as Krishna and Rādhā. This verse exemplifies "Rādhikā displaying the *viraha* (pain of separation) of *karuṇa rasa* (the pathetic mood)." The original text interspersed will indicate the highly alliterative and punning quality of this work, which many consider an epitome of courtly *rīti* style.

Looking upon (*herata*) the green green field (*harita harita hāra*),
 it steals (*harata*) my heart,
  I am exhausted (*hārī hauṁ*), I who have deer (*harina*) eyes; I
   don't find Hari anywhere.

Upon the densely forested Braj (*banamālī*), a line of clouds (*banamālī*) rains
How can I bear the sorrow that the one wearing the forest flower garland (Banamālī) is far away, O Keśava?
In the lotus of my heart, seeing the eyes of the Lotus-eyed one (Kamalanaina)
I will become [his,] the woman of the Lotus-eyed one (*kamalanainī*[30]), what more can I say?
You yourself, O Cloud-dark one (Ghanaśyāma), just like the clouds (*ghanahiṁ se*), you are like an anvil (*ghana*) weighing upon me heavily (*ghane*).
How can I remain in these days of the rainy season without Ghanaśyāma?[31]

The Hindi interposed here gives good indication of the poetic goals of this text: alliteration, assonance, and overall, poetic gaming with pun and double-meaning. Each couplet uses alliteration heavily in the first three feet, and then in the last quarter shifts away from this technique to direct exclamation. We find examples of what is classically termed *yamaka*, the repetition of a word in its various meanings, and *śleṣa*, "double-meaning." Each line plays upon an epithet of Krishna; thus Keśav cleverly repeats the name of god.

No less devotional than Sūr's poem above, still we might say that Keśav's poem is the inverse of Sūr's. Keśav's poem seems lighter in tone because of its very elaborate wordplay; when his Rādhā points out the irony of having the rainy-season *ghan* (clouds) without Ghanaśyām (Krishna), it is primarily a quandary based on words. Sūr's poem uses the more emotionally intense tactic of associating the pain of love with its own season, alluding to theological truths and possibilities more than accruing dazzling double entendres. Taking the latter Keśav poem to represent broadly the literary specificities of court, we may attribute to this courtly Braj poetry an even more judicious and allusive use of formal poetics than found in most songs attributed to a bhakti poet par excellence like Sūr. Keśav's poems held a more puzzle-like pleasure, and a concern with sound at a more minute level, such that they are aesthetic first and foremost, as well as conducive to devotion. Such were the classical models of Braj, at the micro-level of practical poetics, to which our late nineteenth-century authors looked.

Urdu Poetics

Indubitably the dominant vernacular poetic form known to our Hindi poets of the late nineteenth century was the Urdu *śer*, a highly developed and beloved form from the eighteenth century, performed in poetic gatherings in and out of court. In a language more similar to the pan-regional lingua franca speech style than Braj (see discussion below), the Urdu *śer* held an epiphoric pleasure for its audience, who would exclaim at the repetition of the shared line-final or couplet-final syllables that bound verses together in a ghazal. Often inspired by its Persian forebear, the ghazal intimated the refined world of court as it simultaneously spoke plainly yet elliptically of pain and love. An example from eighteenth-century Dakhini Urdu, by Sirāj can serve as an example here:

> I have seen my beloved without a veil
> I think I have seen a dream.
> . . .
> In the manuscript of beauty,
> I have seen your stature as a line of choice verse.
> . . .
> Ever since the army of Love came,
> I have seen the land of the heart laid to waste.
> . . .
> O Siraj, in the fire of love
> I have seen my heart [burn like] a kebab.[32]

The repeated final phrase "have seen" joins the couplets, but the wordplay in fact comes just before that, with each line presenting a different word ending in –āb: first "dream" (*khvāb*), then "choice" (*intikhāb*), and then a dramatic flourish with "ruined" (*kharāb*), and even more drama—or perhaps humor—but at any rate, surprise, with "kabob" (*kabāb*). In language quite direct and resembling (even in this southern style of Urdu) the language of speech, these verses are yet highly wrought, and based upon wordplay both entertaining and poetically intensifying. The early poets of the modern Hindi canon most definitely read every form of Urdu literature and criticism of their day; only in the 1920s did the Hindi-Urdu divide begin to take effect at the level of textual literacy.[33] Thus Urdu poetics—however briefly it can be discussed here—was fundamental to the poetic world of the Hindi author.

The general educated public of North India functioned in the Urdu medium in the nineteenth century—Urdu was indeed the official language of court and administration in the North-West Provinces, Bihar, and part of the Central Provinces by 1837. Unsurprisingly, Urdu poetry was a crucial element of the learned social sphere. Urdu poetry, its poetics, and its poetic terms held high esteem with many of these Hindi poets, who sometimes had styled themselves as Urdu poets in their youth (e.g., Ratnākar, described in Chapter 3). The dominance of Urdu poetics was likely most prominent in regions renowned for Urdu poetry, namely the former Nawabi Oudh, in the heart of the "Hindi belt," and the Mughal capital cities of Delhi and Agra, the latter located next to the region of Braj. We can in fact index the poetic dominance of Urdu in a Hindi courtly publication of 1894, by the Maharaja Pratāpanārāyaṇ Siṁh of Ayodhya in Oudh. This massive *Rasakusumākār* [Rasa in the Form of a Flower] *or A Book on Rhetoric*, had its many Sanskritic terms for metaphor, etc., glossed in their Persian/Urdu equivalents, suggesting that he saw need to educate or bring about a Braj audience.[34] Not only did the text give evidence of its Persianate literary context, but also its British one: the Maharaja described *śṛṅgāra rasa* and its constituent parts with a diagram, a practice which he described as "the English style" of explanation, as opposed to the norm of verse explication. That such an exposition was necessary, and in "the English style," testifies to the varied poetic world of Braj Bhāṣā's public.[35]

Definitions and Ideals for the Hindi Language in the Nineteenth Century

One unique feature of any attempt to define Hindi in the late nineteenth century was the sociolinguistic situation: the language(s) we now call Hindi and Urdu, write in very different orthographies, and associate with Hinduism and Islam, respectively, were for centuries profoundly intertwined, and fluidly crossed boundaries of sect and script. The Hindi belt was the location of historical centers of Urdu—i.e., Persianate Nastaliq-script literature. The center of Urdu was in a sense everywhere, as it was the language of courts generally, and among the Hindu public, especially those of communities associated with court, e.g., Kayasths, and Khatris. Hindi authors of the late nineteenth century, newly committed to the use of one script over the other, were friends and colleagues with Muslim authors in Urdu, despite increasing Hindu/Muslim social segregation. They spoke grammatically the same language, and shared the same "Ganga-Jamuna" composite culture, of the cultural "rivers" of Sanskrit/Hindu and Perso-Arabic/Muslim traditions, which merged like the rivers Ganges and Yamuna in the center of North India. They interacted in the many new publishing houses, cultural institutions in themselves. Indeed, the Naval Kishore Press of Lucknow, one of the most important presses of India in the last half of the nineteenth century, published in both Hindi and Urdu, "defying the ongoing dichotomization of Hindi and Urdu."[36] At the same time, a history of Hindi excluding Urdu-script literature and foregrounding Hindu and classical Sanskrit themes began to be conceived and reproduced in essays and anthologies.[37] Thus, Hindi poets wrote in the midst of a paradoxical world: a dichotomizing sociolinguistic context, and yet a still unified intellectual sphere.

Poetry in the script of Hindi—that is, in Devanāgarī, a dominant script of Sanskrit—was, grammatically speaking, most all in the Braj dialect until the 1870s. The very choice to compose poetry in modern Hindi, most especially in the style of speech, was not only experimental, but contained a social agenda implicit in the rhetoric of "natural language" in colonial India: to write in Kharī Bolī was to demonstrate a belief in "progress" toward "modernity" and a sort of "democracy" of demotic speech, a belief serving the merchant classes of the towns, not the elite of traditional court or English power structures. Writing in Braj Bhāṣā had little of the cachet of modern progress, but would still serve to support the Hindi/Hindu equivalence. The transition was slow, and around the turn of the century the grammatical line between Khaṛī Bolī Hindi and Braj Bhāṣā in poetry increased somewhat. The idea that modern poetry should be in the language of speech escaped no one, no matter which side of the fence they were on. For those supporters of Khaṛī Bolī, there was then a subsequent definitional problem, linguistically and culturally: how should this Khaṛī Bolī—speech style—Hindi in the Devanagari script be differentiated from its twin in the Nastaliq script, and what would make its poetry poetic, without the meters or vocabulary of Braj, Sanskrit, or Persian? In the words of the famous Hindi essayist Pratāpanārāyaṇ Miśra in 1888, besides casting it in Braj or Persian meter or that of current popular song (*lāvanī*), "to use any other meter in [Khaṛī Bolī poetry] would be like putting a coat and boots (*koṭ būṭ*) on a tender-limbed beauty (*komalāṅgī sundarī*)."[38] Heartfelt wrangling over these matters would persist through the early decades of the Hindi movement and into the 1920s.

THE CULTURE OF THE HINDI MOVEMENT

The authors examined in this book belonged to the "Hindi movement," a phenomenon of language politics that formed the cultural background of Hindi writing of our period. The Hindi movement essentially began as a movement against the use of Perso-Arabic script, and very shortly evolved into a movement to Sanskritize not only lexicon, but culture at large. Essayist Pratāpanārāyaṇ Miśra's slogan, "Hindi, Hindu, Hindustan," although ironically a lament for Hindi's losses, has stuck as a catchphrase for the religio-political import of the Hindi movement, a nationalist identity-based movement seeking to align the future Indian state with

"Hinduism." In regard to this, Christopher King has cogently elaborated the Hindi movement's role in "multi-symbol congruency," which Paul Brass had brought to the discussion of language and nationalism.[39] Vasudha Dalmia and King, among others, have given detailed accounts of the beginning of the Hindi movement in the nineteenth century. Dalmia has described extensively the writings of Bhāratendu Hariścandra, the Father of Modern Hindi, as its first major publicist and promoter. She has also delineated the precise ways in which definitions of Hindi were made to align with Hindus and their political agendas, through education reform and political battles over the language of government.[40]

Agitation for Hindi as a language of government and education had begun in earnest in the 1870s, and had achieved some success in the Central Provinces and Bihar, while the North-West Provinces and Oudh, the origin of the authors discussed in following chapters, remained Urdu-medium. It was only in 1900 with the Nagari Resolution in the United Provinces that Hindi attained equal status with Urdu in "a largely symbolic victory."[41] However, the Hindi movement thrived in the city of Varanasi, where three graduates of Queen's College founded the Nāgarī Pracāriṇī Sabhā in 1893, The Society for the Promotion of Nagari.[42] The NPS dedicated itself to Hindi in the midst of communal rioting in the region surrounding the Cow Protection movement, and in a general atmosphere of Hindu militating against a perceived anti-Hindu Muslim population and indifferent British authority. The NPS, as major organ of the Hindi movement, arose as part of the larger fabric of Hindu-Muslim conflict, and became an institution unto itself; virtually all of the Hindi authors mentioned in the present study were known members of the NPS, and many in fact served as *sabhāpati* at their annual meeting, giving the keynote address.

The Society's position on what exactly constituted Hindi remained somewhat murky, but consistently it linked "Hindi" to "Hindu." Devakīnandan Khattrī's Nagari-script novels, which nevertheless were replete with Persianate vocabulary, were condoned (but not promoted) by the Society,[43] and Braj Bhāṣā poetry on Krishnaite and national themes continued apace in the publications of the Society's members. But from its beginning, the idea of cultural reform, really a sort of cultural "cleansing" of non-Hindu, "foreign" words and cultural tropes, animated its projects. As King has elaborated, the Society's committees performed this even retroactively, in their manuscript searches in order to create a Hindi literary canon in Nagari script Braj, Avadhī, etc. that would give the appearance of a Hindi tradition partitioned from Urdu completely. What manuscripts they found in Persian scripts, by Hindu authors on Hindu themes, were presented merely as sad artifacts of "foreign rule" by Muslims. The vitriolic controversy of the years leading up to and shortly following the 1900 Resolution, was part and parcel of the Hindu intellectual world. Speeches, poems, and dramas were written on the topic, often embodying Hindi and Urdu as females—the good housewife and the seductive whore, respectively, in the usual scheme of the Hindi-proponent author.

At this point we can prospectively look to the Hindi Sahitya Sammelan (Conference on Hindi Literature), founded in 1910, another organization dedicated to Hindi. This Allahabad-centered institution "formed a bridge between Hindi intellectuals and Congress politicians,"[44] and would profoundly affect the dissemination and definition of Hindi literature with its own examination program in Hindi and its publication series on canonical pre-modern and modern Hindi authors. The hashing out of what sort of Hindi should be ordained as the national language was done largely in the public conferences held by the Sammelan in the twenties and thirties.[45] The political project of making Hindi a national language was thus intertwined with the Sammelan and the NPS, and informed their literary and educational projects.

The linking of Hindi with Hindu partisanship is a legacy that still lives on. Indeed, many works of the early period of Hindi literature used Hindu epics for their subject matter (often for anti-colonial purposes), giving Hindi literature Sanskrit's imprimateur, and linking this literature with Hindu nationalism, which itself referenced and self-validated with Hindu epic and Puranic themes. Further, there is no denying that the Hindi movement was coeval with the violence of late nineteenth-century communalism. The Hindi movement has come to represent a North Indian imperialism and oppressively homogenizing cultural impulse, denying the multilingual and multicultural past in a "majoritarian drive for one national culture."[46] It was by and large successful: by 1950, Hindi was a national language of independent India, the Nagari script was in use in much of the educational system, and a literary canon for this Hindi was well established. These organizations of the Hindi movement also established canon quite effectively, and have to some extent preserved rare Hindi texts for posterity. Thus, to write in Hindi during the period of foment of the Hindi movement associations was ipso facto to be part of its politico-cultural movement and its set of political and cultural agendas, which our authors took extremely seriously.[47]

THE LINGUISTIC NOVELTY OF MODERN HINDI

Writing in modern Hindi, the "speech-style" of Khaṛī Bolī, and writing in Braj on "modern" subjects, were both essentially experimental endeavors in the nineteenth century. In the former case, this involved the question of how to linguistically define this Hindi language, and differentiate it from Urdu. The linguistic basis of the situation is complex and has been much discussed already. Rather than repeat this complex history here, which others have broached and continue to research,[48] I will put forth a mere thumbnail sketch of the linguistic thinking on "Hindi," with a view toward the particular novelty writing in modern Hindi presented to the poet, addressing at length the characterizations of the linguistic situation of Frederic Pincott in his 1889 *Khaṛī Bolī ka padya: A Poetical Reader of Khaṛī Bolī*, a work of critical importance in Hindi poetic history.[49]

Linguist Colin Masica describes the relationship of Hindi and Urdu as "different literary styles based on the same linguistically-defined subdialect," which colloquially "are virtually identical" but "at formal and literary levels, however, vocabulary differences begin to loom much larger . . . to the point where the two languages/styles become mutually unintelligible."[50] The Hindi-Urdu distinction is therefore profoundly sociolinguistic, and is especially problematic to define because of the many and varied terms for Hindi/Hindavī[51] from the thirteenth century onwards.[52]

The most telescopic view of the linguistic history of Hindi is as follows: This language Hindi or Hindavī was a lingua franca based on the composite dialect of the Mughal capitals of Delhi and Agra of the sixteenth century, and it incorporated into its lexicon words from Persian, Arabic, and Sanskrit sources in a New Indo-Aryan grammatical frame. A native tongue in the region of Meerut, near Delhi, it became the language of the bazaar across wide regions, and the language associated with Agarwāl traders.[53] Various names have been attached to this language, in attempts to capture its various uses and breadth of lexical range. The term "Urdu," literally the "language of camp," emerges in the late eighteenth century, specifically referencing the Muslim/Mughal usage of this local language.[54] Another term, "Hindustani," is found commonly from the nineteenth century, but now has fallen into disuse. This type of Hindi, which would be most likely written in the Urdu script, was used unselfconsciously with regard to etymological provenance. This "Hindustani," written in Nagari script, later became a point of great contention in the Hindi movement, as its proponents, like Gandhi himself, fought with those favoring a more Sanskritized, ergo more Hindu-identified Hindi, within the literary/political sphere of the Hindi Sāhitya Sammelan.[55] Now the lingua franca that was called Hindustani in the British era is found as the language of present-day mundane speech, evidenced in the bazaar and in entertainment media. The term "Khaṛī Bolī," identical at root to this lingua-franca concept of

Hindustani, arose among Hindi promoters of the nineteenth century, which term gradually came to represent a less Persianized and more Sanskrit-inclined lexicon.

In the end, we can summarize that in the nineteenth century, under pressure from a variety of sociohistorical influences, "Urdu" came to represent in the early 1800s a term for the local "Hindustani" with a Persian lexical bias, which bias would be epitomized in certain heavily Persianized Urdu poetry. "Hindi" on the other hand would represent a Hindu-identified version of Hindustani, in a Sanskritic script (Kaithī, Mahājani, or Devanagari), and often using a Sanskrit-derived, if not outright Sanskritized lexicon. During 1885–1925, the years under study here, many definitions of Hindi were flying about, but the distinction between Hindi and Urdu was made primarily on the basis of script, etymology, or sociological import of the content. Those who strove to be Hindi poets did so with a Hindu-identified stance; writing in Hindi meant not only a certain choice of script, but also a certain degree of distance from the genres and tropes of Urdu, the "other," yet intimately close, register of educated speech and thought.[56]

The linguistic perplexities and sheer novelty of writing poetry in modern spoken-style Khaṛī Bolī Hindi for the late nineteenth-century poet can be elucidated from a text published in 1889 by Fredric Pincott, *Khaṛī Bolī ka padya: A Poetical Reader of Khaṛī Bolī*. An editor at W. H. Allen, Fredric Pincott was a self-taught scholar of Indian languages, and member of the Royal Asiatic Society.[57] This volume was edited by Pincott, who wrote its lengthy introduction, but the text itself was one compiled by Ayodhyā Prasād Khatrī (1857–1904), of Muzaffarpur, a teacher and collector's agent in Ballia, who is remembered by early literary historians as a man for whom "the promotion of Khaṛī Bolī became his life's purpose," who "would always discuss Khaṛī Bolī with every writer he met,"[58] and in order to disprove the naysayers who alleged that Khaṛī Bolī was unfit for verse composition, he personally collected handwritten examples of Khaṛī Bolī poetry in a notebook.[59] He had published a grammar in 1877, and a book entitled *Khaṛī Bolī Āndolan* (The Khaṛī Bolī Movement) in 1888. The volume published in London and edited by Pincott was comprised of a lengthy introduction, and collated specimens of Khaṛī Bolī poetry from the eminent authors of the day, apparently culled from periodical and book publications, and presumably Khattrī's abovementioned notebook.

Pincott's introduction explained in no uncertain terms the experimental quality of writing proper poetry in this former "uncourtly idiom of the vulgar":

> Concurrently with the evolution of the Urdu language,[60] the non-Islamitic form of Hindi (which is technically known as *Thenth* Hindi, "pure Hindi," or *Kharī Bolī*, "correct speech") has gradually developed into a flexible and expressive language, the vesture of an extensive and scholarly literature, now rapidly expanding. The progress of *Kharī Bolī* has, hitherto, not been so marked as that of Urdu, because it has had to rely on its natural strength. . . . It has lacked the fostering hand of Government patronage, and has been generally neglected even by the natives themselves, as they esteem it the uncourtly idiom of the vulgar. During the last twenty years, however, it has steadily forced itself more and more into attention, as its flexibility, terseness, strength, vigour and richness have become more clearly recognized by scholars.[61]

The athleticism of Pincott's rhetoric—flexibility, terseness, strength, vigour, as it "steadily forced itself . . . into attention"—belies the atmosphere of competition with Urdu and the Muslims it purportedly represented, and perhaps also with the "tradition" represented by Braj.

The work outlines the particular challenges facing those defining a modern literary "Hindi" in 1889. In his preface Pincott outlined five "kinds of language in the North-West of India": (1) the "Hindustani of literature and official life," (2) a "poetic form of Urdu," (3) the "cultivated Kharī Bolī of literature generally," (4) "the poetic, or Braj, form of Hindi," and (5) "colloquial forms of speech," noting that the first two usually take the Urdu script, the third and fourth the Nagari-type script, and the latter either, but generally a Nagari-type script. The editors of this volume of verse further parsed Kharī Bolī into "*ṭheṭh* Hindi" (the "*thenth*" Hindi Pincott refers to), and two other categories classified with the English word "style": the "munshi-style" (*munśī-sthāil*),[62] and the "pandit-style" (*paṇḍit-sthāil*). In this couplet, then, we can see an exemplification of the aspirations and ironies of writing Hindi poetry in the late nineteenth century.

Pincott explains that Khatrī seeks

> to induce his countrymen to abandon the use of the archaic Braj dialect in their poetic effusions, and to persuade those who favour Urdu to use Nagari. . . . In fact, he proposes a compromise: one party is asked to abandon a cherished dialect of their language, and the other party to give up a customary method of writing it.[63]

This program, Pincott opines, would "remove the greatest obstacle to the intellectual development of Northern India. The absurdity of talking and writing prose in one language, and poetry in what is virtually another language, is beginning to make itself felt." After comparing the Braj/Khaṛī Bolī situation to writing English poetry in the Dorset dialect, and prose in the London dialect, Pincott finds that the use of Braj as a medium of poetry forms an "anomaly" that is "inconvenient," and therefore "Babu Ayodhya Prasad is endeavouring to confer a substantial boon on his countrymen, by inducing them to clothe all their ideas in one common form of speech, written in one common character."[64]

The use of Braj for poetry was symptomatic of a larger problem, according to Pincott—a problem of intellect created by a bad verbal logistics that would separate speech and poetry. "Inconvenience," "anomaly," and so forth are in the eye of the beholder; the linking of the persistence of poetic Braj to issues of cultural failure, so to speak, characterizes his position. In the words Pincott used to characterize the position of Khatrī (who remains voiceless in this preface), the "spread of ennobling ideas" and "purification of the mental and moral aspirations of Hindustan generally" can effect "the unification and modernization of the poetic medium of the country," and this in turn would unite Indians together.[65] To support his point that this unifying language of speech-style Nagari creates modernized or at least "better" poetry, Pincott states that the subject matter of the poems of the volume indicate progress: "[they] are excellent in tone, and they manifest a love of nature, a reverence for sacred things, and a desire for the best interests of humanity, the whole of which affords good evidence of the progress India is now making." These traits alone made the volume commendable for its efforts to "raise the character of Indian literature."[66] Underlying these comments is an unmistakable judgment, and back-handed reference to the erotic sentiment or other "Oriental unreality." Pincott's attitude was typical of those who supported the cause of Khaṛī Bolī; for them, linguistic change in poetry contained an implicit moral agenda toward "progress" in content as well as form.

Despite the enumeration of types, kinds, and styles, and the valuation of "tradition" as worn-out and possibly harmful, which characterize this cultural moment, still Hindi poetry mixed the old and the new, and "Urdu" with "Hindi." As an example, we can look at the beginning of the section for the latter pandit-style category of Khaṛī Bolī. The compiler Khatri added a Braj *dohā* couplet, presumably his own, indicating his advocacy for this pandit-style, and punning such that he connected established custom to vice, and innovation to virtue: "The carriage goes along the beaten path, the bad son goes to vice / Without a *līka* ["beaten path" or "vice"] go these three, the poet, the hero, and the good son."[67] Here we must note that despite its intent to promote Khaṛī Bolī, this *dohā* was written in precisely the "well-worn path" of Braj, and although it prefaced the section for the Sanskritized "pandit-style" Khaṛī Bolī Hindi, nevertheless it included the Urdu/Arabic term for poet, *śāyar*. The conceptual divisions between Khaṛī Bolī and Braj, and Sanskritized Hindi and Hindustani/Urdu, were not completely in force in poetry itself. Further, the very idea of Khaṛī Bolī poetry rankled even among promoters of Khaṛī Bolī prose. In his advance review of the work, Pratāpanārāyaṇ Miśra wrote pointedly on what he saw as the folly of poetry in Khaṛī Bolī. The resemblance of Khaṛī Bolī poetry to that of Urdu was both an accomplishment to brag of, and a danger, in his view. He countered the universal comprehensibility argument with his own: Would everyone understand Khaṛī Bolī more readily than Braj? And is such clarity the point of poetry anyway? "If the project is only to explain to everyone then go right ahead and write prose."[68] Thus, the experiment of Khaṛī Bolī Hindi in poetry was at the convergence point of debate over the meaning of modernity for poetry, and the Hindi-Urdu debate itself.

HINDI AS REPRESENTATIVE

In a sense the Hindi movement launched an "upstart" language, with theretofore unrealized pretensions to match any other national language in the world in its utility and symbolic value. In poetry, this meant that authors strove to equal the great poets they knew and loved in Urdu and whom they read in Bengali. Hindi aspired to the cosmopolitanism of a language of power, as Urdu already was. Further, its promoters also saw Hindi as a democratic medium, representative of the less urbane masses left out of the halls of power inhabited by elite Muslims, westernized Bengalis, and the British. Thus Hindi's supporters presented its very existence with a certain proletarian undertone, since support for it came from lower ranking clerks and the merchant castes, sometimes wealthy but not of highest social status.[69] On the other hand, the cultural import of Hindi was also dialogically shaped in contrast with Bengali, even as it borrowed Bengali's already pre-Sanskritized lexicon.[70] As Orsini has noted, "the English educated bilingual middle class of Calcutta had no real equivalent in North India," where English-bilingual Indians were much more scarce, and colonial presence much less entrenched in everyday life. Hindi-*wallahs* felt this difference from Bengal—and especially the Calcuttans—very keenly.

This much is clear, that Hindi authors of the late nineteenth century felt that the Bengali babus from Calcutta were "more modern" Indians, and they resented the measure of social power these "modern" Bengalis possessed in the colonial state. On the other hand, Hindi authors sometimes spurned Bengali modernity as mere mimicry (as Homi Bhabha has elaborated), as a sort of cultural deracination. The developing Hindi public sphere in which the "project" of modernity was played out, to use Sanjay Joshi's model, situated the Hindi middle-class reader as not only in the middle between the poor low-castes and the English-speaking elite,[71] but also in the middle between the "traditional Indian" of pre-colonial and village India—an image concretized by colonial discourse—and the modernity of the Calcutta Bengali—to many Hindi-*wallah*, transgressively progressive "mimic men," who aped the English without thought. Regional politics thus complicated the idea of what Hindi, and its literature, should represent.

Hindi built itself out of difference, but formed a kind of doppelganger of Urdu in the sheer fact of their shared grammatical/lexical base, and of Bengali in its bold modern aspirations. However, Hindi was differentiated by its association with the "Hindu masses." It was positioned by its promoters as the language of a Hindu culture that was being dispossessed and decaying, whose members would eventually reign triumphant. Ultimately, the idea of Hindi for these authors of 1885–1925 presented the possibility of giving voice to some of the "mute inglorious Miltons"—to quote Gray's elegy—of the smaller principalities and districts, and the possibility of establishing a language and set of genres that would represent the non-elite classes of Hindus, relatively apart from the ambit of English education.[72]

The Problem of Defining the Modern

"Modern" is an adjective that has defied easy historicization or definition in the Indian context; the meaning of the term in various languages, as "modern," *ādhunik* (in Hindi and Bengali), *jadīd* (in Urdu), and so on, has yet to be extensively empirically analyzed. Obviously, modernity has denoted much more than mere chronology. Contemporary scholars have written extensively on the subject of modernity outside of Europe and North America. "Alternative modernities" has emerged as a central term, with "colonial modernity" specifically forming another locus of research.[73] Others have argued that ideas of modernity in South Asia predated colonialism.[74] The task of investigating what constituted modernity in North India a century ago among those on the fringes of the colonial enterprise, the readers of the poems in a Hindi magazine—women perhaps—who never aspired, nor were chosen by the colonial state to be "English in taste, opinions, morals, and intellect,"[75] is difficult to accomplish.

Fundamentally, we know that at least for the nineteenth-century Indian, a major component of the idea of the modern came "packaged" with the cultural difference of the British themselves.[76] The basic connection of modernity with Englishness is absolutely palpable in the Hindi printed texts of the late nineteenth century and beyond, most basically in their portrayal of a *habitus* of certain material accoutrements and social practices derived from Europe,[77] in various "contact zones."[78] Viswanathan has convincingly argued that "modernity," missionary Christianity, and the abstraction of Englishness merged in the educational policies of British India. Technology and modernity similarly structure another equation, still common today, the history of which has been addressed by Gyan Prakash's *Another Reason*.[79] The phenomenon of Orientalism, which Edward Said formulated in his eponymous and groundbreaking book, reified conceptions of the binary of tradition and modernity that still populate the popular imagination today. In truth, the precepts of this Orientalism—East as mystical, inscrutable, childish, and female; and West as rational, scientific, advanced, and male—have been constantly under scrutiny, and utilized variously, by Indian thinkers. In the words of Vasudha Dalmia, in response to Said, "the 'orientals,' with a highly developed cultural apparatus of their own, did not remain silent, nor merely resistant, but articulated their own stand in view of the changed cultural-political situation."[80] The enunciation of these stands in view of the idea of modernity per se, a concept which by the late nineteenth century was inextricably tied to the racialized power-differential of colonialism, is a matter of continuing scholarly work, and in need of ever more historical precision.

An idea of "being modern" hung in the atmosphere surrounding everyone involved in the Hindi movement and writing on new literary subjects and/or in the new poetic medium of Khaṛī Bolī. What exactly this "modern" meant is difficult enough to gauge for the contemporary scholar, but complicating this, the literary historical narrative developed in the twentieth century looked at the literary shift to modernity in Hindi through very particular lenses, which need to be critically appraised themselves, lenses which merge the standards of the colonists' teleology of progress with a Marxist dialogism that regarded "tradition" and literature itself in limited ways. While the idea of an unstinting "tradition" in binary relation to "modernity" has been revaluated by contemporary academics, still this binary permeates popular thinking even today, handicapping real understanding of the literary world of Hindi in the late nineteenth century. As Sudhir Chandra has written,

> The modernity-tradition polarity introduces a serious perceptual limitation: the dichotomy is projected back to explain and categorize even those actions, attitudes, beliefs and values that did not rest on, or stem from, such a polarity. . . . people can—as often happened in nineteenth-century India—view the phenomena designated "modernity" and "tradition" without opposing them to each other.[81]

We can see most clearly Hindi authors' vexed relation to modernity through their qualities that distinguish them from Bengali especially: Hindi authors held a closer grip on pre-colonial forms—the verse genres of Braj Bhāṣā and Avadhī, Sanskrit meters, or just generic *mātrik* meters, and the concomitant subject matter of these—all of which Bengali poets had already begun to leave behind by the late nineteenth century (see Michael Madhusudan Dutt's *payār* meter approximating Miltonic blank verse, and Rabindranath Tagore's interest in free verse). Both Bengali and Hindi poets looked to the poetry of the saints, especially Kabir, whose god did not have the bodily sensuousness of Krishna poetry, but Hindi authors did not follow exactly the same path to modernist abstraction trod by the famed Tagore and others. They did so with a commitment to older forms that lingered into the twenties, and defined a distinctly Hindi vision of poetic modernity, where the formal poetics of the Sanskritic and Bhāṣā past remained between the lines along with the critics' proclamations of progress.

The Literary Eras and the Language of Hindi Poetry, 1885–1925

Any discussion of Hindi literature necessarily refers to the critical estimation of literary eras, and in fact, it has been the critical force of these eras' characterizations that have made the period of 1885–1925 one less-studied and less-loved than those following. What follows is an outline of the contours of the Hindi literary eras, and an explanation of what they have meant for understanding the poetry addressed in this book. The purview of this study of the "nature" that emerged in modern Hindi poetry spans three of the conventional "eras" of Hindi literature, beginning in 1885, the year of the death of Hariścandra, the father of modern Hindi, encompassing the Dvivedī Era, named for its stern standardizer of Hindi prose, Mahāvīraprasād Dvivedī, and for its stern idealism and didacticism. Finally, the book ends in 1925, at the first full bloom of the young Chāyāvād "Shadow-ist" poets, who have left the most palpable legacy of all of these poets. The Chāyāvādī poems still rouse a crowd in poetic gatherings today. They represent a modern yet quaintly florid poetic style of the past, and still clearly influence amateur and famed poets alike. It is not uncommon to meet people now who claim their own poetic inspiration comes from Chāyāvād, at least in part. Chāyāvād represents the baseline of conventional poetic practices for Hindi writers, famed and amateur alike. It is universally acknowledged that the first successful modern Hindi poetry is found in the Chāyāvād poets in the early 1920s.

The preceding generation of Hindi poets, of the decades before the twenties, has been buried by Chāyāvād fame, remaining in the shadow of the "Shadowists." The critical reception of the Chāyāvādīs as the beginning of "successful" modernity in Hindi poetry is problematic, having to do with a literary critical need to create a particular kind of narrative of development, and a general discomfort with the poetical "ground" out of which these poets wrote. This book will redress the overlooked pre-Chāyāvād years of modern Hindi poetry, and thereby redress the literary critical tradition which has built a certain apt but obfuscating categorical apparatus to explain it. In keeping with the critical tradition's own developmental and historical model, understanding what happened to poetry in these early decades of its self-conscious "modernization" will help us read later aesthetic developments.

Any discussion of Hindi literary history must begin with the narrative propounded by Rāmacandra Śukla,[82] who with his 1929 *History of Hindi Literature* (Hindī sāhitya kā itihās) in its expanded 1942 edition, along with certain of his critical essays, has dominated subsequent Hindi literary critical thinking profoundly.[83] Leaving aside his exposition of the emergence of Hindi in the early centuries of the second millennium, what is pertinent here is his theme of a fall from ancient glory, in which Śukla articulates a distinction between earlier devotional (*bhakti*) and later courtly (*rīti*) poetry that had not previously mattered much, if it existed at all. Sūr and Keśav, as I have presented here, became mascots of opposing poetical schools, the pure devotion of Sūr being superseded subsequently by the "decadence" of what Hindu nationalists still call a dark age of courtly culture under Muslim rule. Hence, in Śukla's influential estimation, the "good" pre-modern Hindi poetry was devotional, cementing the association of Hindi with Hinduism, which had been at the basis of the Hindi movement itself.

The critics' epoch-making continued within the modern period: the Hariścandra Era, named for Banaras litterateur Bhāratendu Hariścandra (1850–1885); the Dvivedī Era, named for editor Mahāviraprasād Dvivedī, who ruled the most influential Hindi journal from 1900–20, and the Chāyāvād (Shadowist) Era, beginning after World War I, and in earnest by the early twenties. This schema has set the terms for how we speak of the Hindi literature today, as evidenced in plenteous publications organizing literary history around just these eras. Later; the most important literary critics after Śukla, i.e. Hazārīprasād Dvivedī (1907–79) and Nāmavar Siṁh (1926–) both adhered to this model of progressive improvement through the generations, into the progressive and experimental eras. In poetry, this progress was found notably in regard to "nature" (*prakṛti*) and "women" (*nārī, strī*). Below some elaboration on these eras is in order, and on their lives as discrete entities in literary criticism as well.

The Hariścandra Era

The Hariścandra era denotes a period in which the idea of "modern Hindi" began to form, largely due to Hariścandra's very public efforts to promote the use of the Nagari script in education and government, as Vasudha Dalmia has outlined in detail in her book on this subject. As the period of modern Hindi's emergence, this era has been studied mainly for its Hindu-identified proto-nationalist claims, and Hariścandra's own innovative dramas and essays. Hariścandra wrote presciently of bringing the standard of natural speech—*svabhāvokti* ("natural description" in Sanskrit)—to Hindi poetry, a trait that he found in Sūr Dās.[84] Poetically speaking, however, Hariścandra and his literary circle composed in Braj Bhāṣā and Urdu more than in Khaṛī Bolī.[85] Although Hariścandra died young in 1885, Śukla and many others have extended the Hariścandra era to the turn of the century, with the rationale that Hariścandra remained a figure of significant influence and emulation to be equaled only by Mahāviraprasād Dvivedī who came on the scene circa 1900.

In general, the poetic scene in Hindi—whether Khaṛī Bolī or Braj—began to diminish with the emergence of prominent essayists (e.g., Pratāpanārāyaṇ Miśra [1856–94], Bālamukund Gupta [1865–1907]) and the flourishing of literary dramas, many of them written from Sanskrit dramas, and incorporating Braj poetry with Khaṛī Bolī Hindi. Prominent among these dramatists was Lālā Sītārām (1858–1937) of Ayodhyā, who wrote Khaṛī Bolī prose and Braj verse translations of Sanskrit dramas and Shakespeare. Some poetry did appear in periodicals and books, such as that collated in Pincott and Khattrī's anthology of 1889, discussed above. Translations of poetry from English increased as well, most notable among them those of Śrīdhar Pāṭhak of Goldsmith, and Ratnākar's less noted, but important translation of Pope in the inaugural issue of the *Nāgarī Pracāriṇī Patrikā*, the magazine for the Society for the Promotion of Nagari (these will form the subject of Chapter 3). Many literary translations of the late nineteenth century were from Sanskrit. Raja Lakṣmaṇasiṁh found acclaim for his Braj version of the *Cloud-Messenger* (*Meghadūtam*) of 1882, one among many such renditions. Topics of original and translated poetry did turn somewhat toward nature, the subject Pincott found so edifying. While the *Meghadūtam* itself fit that bill, others modified traditional subjects with new foci. For instance, the Raja Jaganmohan Siṁh composed a poem describing the "beauties of nature" and also giving a history of his native state of Vijay-Raghogarh in the conventional manner. In sum, a mixture of Braj and Khaṛī Bolī appeared in print in these early years, with both understood as "modern" in topic or in intent. However, at the same time Braj began to be cast as a "medieval dialect" for religious use, the elderly "mother" of a young, vigorous, perhaps even "masculine" Khaṛī Bolī Hindi, the domain of new topics of literature.

The Dvivedī Era

Coming to the Dvivedī Era, we find that it is reckoned variously, and accounted for rather simplistically. Its dating would seem to depend on the leadership of Mahāviraprasad Dvivedī, but in fact the NPS dates the era to the founding of its own organization in 1893, before Mahāviraprasad Dvivedī emerged on the U.P. literary scene.[86] Most have dated this era from either 1900 or 1903, when Dvivedī took over the editorship of the *Sarasvatī* journal in Allahabad, the preeminent Hindi magazine until the 1920s. Dvivedī indisputably affected the course of the development of modern Hindi, although the changes he encouraged did not occur in monolith form, particularly in poetry, which often retained Braj linguistic features in his journal.[87] The fact that the "Dvivedī Era" can conceivably extend backward into the 1890s demonstrates also that he was not isolated in his cause; in many ways Dvivedī continued the project of reform and modernization of Hindi begun in previous decades.

As editor of *Sarasvatī*, a literary-cum-general-interest magazine named for the goddess of speech, arts, and learning, Dvivedī is credited with standardizing Hindi through his editorial hand and his articles on grammar. He brought to the Hindi public sphere a larger regional consciousness, and a vision of the future wide reach of the Nagari-script, Sanskritized "Hindi" in the Hindustani-speaking regions. His literary values of patriotism and didacticism were the distinguishing features of the era, and embodied most fully in Dvivedī's protégé, Maithilīśaraṇ Gupta (1886–1964), whose poetry often delivered political messages in a Sanskritized Khaṛī Bolī medium. Several poets of this era were designated later as part of the *svacchandatāvādi* strain, those who literally "had freedom," and more literally, "had their own bounds" or "meter," determined by themselves, not convention. These poets were known for elaborating "the grandeur of the forest, the examination of nature, [and] the portrayal of love in the free (*svacchand*) expressions."[88] Originally a term meaning "free, unbound, unrestricted" and used poetically—perhaps describing pollen or the like[89]—this term *svacchand* by the 1930s had come to be the calque for the English term "Romantic."[90] The poets of *svacchandatāvād* are considered the precursors to the next Chāyāvād generation, which did indeed revolutionize the use of meter and conventional subject matter. In general, however, the Dvivedī era is associated strongly with Dvivedī himself and his stern edicts. The era named for him is commonly considered to end either with World War I, or at the end of his editorship in 1920, at which point this next generation of poets began to supersede the Hindi literary stage.

The Dvivedī era has never been one that has captured the imagination of scholars or students as much as either Hariścandra himself, or the Chāyāvādīs following. However, Dvivedī era literature is usually considered respectfully in Hindi literary histories. The most famous poet in its ranks, Maithilīśaraṇ Gupta, is reverently regarded as a national hero of sorts, as his verse work *Bhārat-bhāratī* (Voice of India) became an essential text of Hindi language nationalism. However, in general it is certain that the Dvivedī era has a negative reputation overall in regard to its poetry. This reputation is primarily due to the perceived failure of poets of this era to go beyond didacticism, and the strange nature of their language, which was often Sanskritized in unwieldy ways. Retrospectively, only a certain strain of Marxian interpretation has truly valued the Dvivedī era for taking Hindi out of its alleged medieval torpor of courtly decadence and religious superstition and into "useful" subjects in the "language of the people";[91] otherwise, the Dvivedī era is seen as an adolescent, interstitial developmental period, or only part of dialectical progress toward a "real" poetic modernity.[92]

Western scholarly monographs on Hindi literature, which have heretofore discussed the Dvivedī era only in passing, have often taken up the stance of mid-century Hindi critics who found in Chāyāvād the glorious emergence of Hindi modernity after an embarrassing period of stiff uninspired poetic lessons in the Dvivedī Era. Some observations of Dvivedī era style are well-taken: there was in fact an element of "insipid didacticism" in some of this poetry, and a "ball-and-chain" effect of "monotonous conformity to standard Hindi prose style."[93] No doubt the dismissal of the Dvivedī era poetry has something to do with the fact that Bengali poetry of the same period seems so much more "modern," so much more what Yeats, sometime fan of Tagore, and what we, twenty-first century Western readers, would expect from the early twentieth century; Tagore's poetry simply fit in with the current international stage of world literature more than did Hindi poetry of the same era. The Chāyāvādīs, when they emerged in the twenties, did present a poetic modernity more familiar to Western norms that some even consider lifted from Tagore and his poetic bent for abstraction.[94]

What needs to be remembered, as we delve into Dvivedī era poetry, a region where most others have feared to tread, is that Hindi poets before Chāyāvād were experimenting with their own sort of modernism, one which they constructed out of a sense of difference from Bengali, and out of what they very much considered specters of their decadent Braj and Urdu past. Hindi poetic modernity was thus an exercise in negatives: poetry that was not Urdu in lexicon, not Braj in morphology, and not Urdu, Braj, or Bengali in content. Examining Dvivedī era Hindi poetry, and the broader period of 1885–1925, sheds light on self-conscious experiments with literary modernity among those seeking a specifically Hindi cosmopolitanism that represented the *jana* ("the people") rather than the colonial modernity they saw in Calcutta. The inquiry into the beginning of modern Hindi poetry found in this book will inform the interpretation of Chāyāvād poetry, which in fact grew quite organically out of earlier Hindi poetic themes and forms, despite its clear Tagorean influence. Rather than look at Hindi poetry as a latecomer to literary changes led by Bengal, let us consider the Hindi literary community as actors creating a modern poetics for themselves. These discomfiting literary ventures of the Dvivedī Era, I would submit, are embedded memories within later Indian literary developments.

Nature, Romanticism, and Modern Hindi Criticism

Within this ubiquitous and mostly unquestioned exposition of eras,[95] which led to Chāyāvād through a value-laden teleology of development—*vikās*[96]—certain other interesting patterns are evident in Hindi literary criticism. For one, a set of critical categories has obtained a semi-permanent status in the hundreds of literary critical publications on Hindi, namely: social context, woman, and nature. Social context and the "status of women" seem rather understandably concomitant, inter-referencing indices in a historical narrative. But "nature" demands closer attention as an equally perennial category to index modernity, sometimes in reference to works that would not seem to the Western reader to have much to offer in terms of the subject of nature to begin with.

Comprehensive surveys and encyclopedias of Hindi literature discuss nature in poetry (and not in prose) as a matter of course. Three books on Hariaudh's *Absence of the Beloved* (*Priyapravās*) alone contain entire chapters on "nature description" in Hindi poetry, and its presentation in the work. "Nature description" is the subject of at least a dozen books on Hindi literature of all periods, modern and pre-modern, or both. Premodern nature-in-literature studies have often had the intent of finding a "science," empiricism, or naturalism that predates British presence, or proving the "utility" of the poetry in question. Here, Raghuvaṁś's *Prakṛti aur Hindī kāvya (madhya-yuga)* (Nature and Hindi poetry [in the middle ages]) of 1948 and *Prakṛti aur kāvya (Samskṛt khaṇḍ)* (*Nature and poetry [Sanskrit volume]*) of 1951[97] are prominent, and others of lesser scope have appeared since. As in Raghuvaṁś's Sanskrit volume cited above, interest and praise for Sanskrit poetry with the modern valuation of "nature-in-poetry" has become commonplace. In the introduction to one of M. Kale's many editions of Kalidasa's works, he states, "It is a principle recognized by all modern critics that 'Nature must be the life and essence of poetry'; and in respect of this, Kālidāsa may be said to be essentially a poet of Nature."[98] Thus, nature has become a literary value of vaster proportions than Hindi alone, as a standard applied anachronistically to Kālidāsa. Nature as a topic of book chapters, of sections within entries of literary histories, and as a desideratum of Indian literary histories thrives even today. The particular outlines of this nature-phenomenon in Hindi criticism are complex.

In Hindi criticism, "Nature" in modern poetry of both the Dvivedī and Chāyāvād Eras, was often analyzed in contradistinction to poetry of the *rīti-kāl*, the era of courtly poetry of the sixteenth to eighteenth centuries, the so-called "Madhya-yug" (middle age). Critical comparisons, and usually lengthy and elaborate ones, between Chāyāvād poetry and *rīti* poetry were common in the works of prominent twentieth-century critics such as Hazārīprasād Dvivedī, Nāmavar Siṁh, Rambilas Sharma (1912–2000), and Rāmasvarūp Chaturvedī (1931–2003), among others, and continue in the present only. This continuing ghost of *rīti* was quite present in the 1920s, due to the continued presence of old-style erotic verse, but also a peculiar flattening of the past; the beginning of modernity seemed embarrassingly recent, and it was always struggling to smother a non-modern and erotic mannerism. The evaluation of this *rīti* poetry as "mannerist" obliterates its other features, such that in the contemporary Hindi literary world, *rīti* signifies merely its negative connotation of hackneyed convention, that is, *mere* mannerism.[99] Hence, the term *rīti* now represents bad literature *in toto*, damning what it describes, and its overcoming is often described in terms of nature—its description, its foregrounding, or its positioning as poetic subject in itself. The Hariścandra and Dvivedī Eras take their places as progressively less-stilted literary eras, shedding *rīti* convention for nature-description, leading to the Chāyāvād era in which nature went beyond naturalism to display a more Romantic modernity, having received the boon of influence from Bengali and English. Nature has thus become integral to Indian descriptions of the constituent qualities of modern Hindi literature, and a critical narrative has been established in which the Chāyāvādī poets, qua Romantics, presented the first substantial nature poetry in Hindi. The narrative resolves with the flowering of nature poetry, which (along with other formal and thematic features) made Chāyāvād the first truly modern poetic movement in Hindi, indeed the savior of a languishing Hindi poetics.

But what constituted this redeeming nature in criticism and the poetry itself, across the periods? A complex of meanings, centered around the concept of the phenomenal world, including science but not technology, including agglomerations of physical and visible organic material, and including animals, people, and the forces that drive their creation, in the basic sense of the Sanskrit/Hindi term for nature, *prakṛti*. For our purposes here, *prakṛti* as this literary nature *does not include "nature" in the sense of the essence or intrinsic qualities of something.*[100] Instead, it is resolutely the material and phenomenal world, in its range of implications from the realm of scientific inquiry to theological entity.

Summary

This chapter has presented a rough guide to the assumptions of Hindi poetics: the precedents, models, and historical/political context within which which the Hindi poets of 1885–1925 approached their composition; and the assumptions of the critical sphere since then about the nature of literary history as progress, and as critically indexed to Nature, itself considered a bequeathment to Hindi poetry that was ultimately Western in source. "Modern Hindi poetry" within the confines of the late nineteenth and early twentieth centuries was a pursuit that was at first experimental, and remained a continuing subject of discourse, as issues of language, genre, and ultimately "Hindiness" were debated by critics and poets. The literary-historical teleology that crystallized in the late twenties has defined a developmental scheme through which this poetry has been viewed: the Hariścandra era as the seed of modern Hindi, the Dvivedī era as its uncomfortable adolescent years, and the Chāyāvād era as its first coming of age, its young adulthood, an image that coincided with the image of Chāyāvād—and with it Swadeshi—as a youth movement. Finally, we have been introduced to the particular subject of poetic Nature, in its conception as the phenomenal world, which has held special purchase in the narrative of modernization of Hindi literature, and has been linked specifically to Western influences. While critics have indexed nature with Westernization, from naturalism to Romanticism, and in fact linked nature specifically with a Romantic conception of personal and political freedom (as the following chapter will describe), we can alternatively find an older, more semiotically compact explanation for the dominance of nature-in-poetry as a sign of the modern. The following chapters will delineate this multivalence of Nature in the Hindi poetry of the late nineteenth and early twentieth centuries, a Nature which has become such a beloved element of Hindi modernity.

Chapter 2

Critical Nature

> But now this Krishna, Nature, has shown its grand form to Arjuna.
>
> —Nāmavar Siṁh, *Chāyāvād* [Shadow-ism], 1955[1]

Nature is a category of literary criticism in Hindi that has been surprisingly constant and of surprisingly vast ontological proportions. It is the subject of many chapters and entire books within Hindi literary studies, and appears countless times in Hindi literary criticism as a signal of literary modernity, and a signal of progress toward realism, away from the literary past, the verses of Braj and Urdu so denigrated in the colonial era. This chapter examines the surfeit of meanings of nature-in-literature—a theme implying the cultural significance of nature, but not explaining which nature, or whose nature is so important, and why. Here we will begin with analysis of criticism characterizing nature-in-poetry in Hindi, and then move to indigenous modes, and then to nineteenth-century modes, in English, Urdu, and Bengali, of literary nature and "the natural," in criticism and in practice.

The Nature of the Modern and Modern Nature

"Nature" in Hindi poetry demands closer evaluation, as a perennial category of inquiry in Hindi literary criticism (along with "social context" [*sāmājik sandarbh*] and "woman" [*nārī*]). Likewise, the subject of nature is a desideratum of academic writing into the present day: comprehensive surveys and encyclopedias of Hindi literature discuss "nature" in the various eras of Indic poetry as a matter of course. This often takes the form of a discursive catalogue of the passages with reference to plants and animals, and natural phenomena such as dawn, rain, and so forth, the critic finds in the text at hand, often with the implicit message that the poet had a capacity to present the truth of nature. Perhaps ironically, a shift to the personification (*mānavīkaraṇ*) of these objects is also often noted as a shift to "nature" and "the modern" in the twentieth century. With this *mānavīkaraṇ,* calque for the English "personification," we see a turn away from the realism that nature-in-literature implied, toward poetic fancy, subjective truths, embodiment, and ultimately, the familiar, older erotics. How did this contradictory situation emerge and become such a dominant theme of Hindi discourse?

Certainly Western critics have written substantially on the subject of nature in literature (mostly pre-1950), but "nature" seems to take an even more prominent place in assessments of late nineteenth- and early twentieth-century Hindi poetry. This discourse is not unique to Hindi among South Asian languages. Frances Pritchett has noted this nature-phenomenon in Urdu and connected it to English per se: "the icon of 'natural poetry' . . . has never been decisively dislodged from its niche" in Urdu literary criticism and "stands as a monument to a time . . . when the English owned nature."[2] This icon is clearly even more entrenched in the Hindi literary critical world, in which "nature description" (*prakṛti varṇan*) appears as the subject of at least a dozen Hindi literary critical works, surpassing the quantity of similar works in the other Indic languages.[3] This strong critical belief in nature as a sign of progress toward realism, and the influence of English Romanticism, exists even though the Hindi poets in question (and even more, their audience) did not, in Francesca Orsini's words, have "the kind of 'cultural bilingualism' we find in the Bengali *bhadralok,* at ease in both the English and 'vernacular' world."[4] There seems to be something very "Hindi" about "nature-in-poetry." There is no obvious impetus for the sometimes mind-boggling scope of such discussion of nature in Hindi, by which authors have repeated rehearsed Indic philosophical bases of nature (*prakṛti*) and traced its presence in texts from the Vedas onward through time. The fullest expositions of nature-in-poetry in Hindi occurred in the decade after Independence, which may hint at a nationalist background for this concern, and at the passing of the glory years of the Chāyāvād generation, so influenced by the British Nature Poets.[5] The category of "nature poetry" endured however: it was even the focus of a 1960 anthology, including the young poets of the day, by experimentalist poet Sachchidanand Vatsyayan "Agyeya."[6]

The critical urge to identify "nature in literature" appears to be English at its source, but its manifestation occurred in Hindi through modes of transmission we do not yet fully understand. For one thing, the term "landscape" per se, which looms so large in art and literary criticism in England, is more difficult to pin down in Hindi criticism, which uses the terms "nature" and "nature-description" most amply. However, the English "landscape" may be the source of the term "natural scene" (*prākṛtik dṛśya*) used commonly in early twentieth-century Hindi criticism. The Hindi "landscape" thus evoked an ontological "Nature," *prakṛti*, and the perspectival artifice of a "scene" in ways that the English term "landscape" did not. The path of this transmission and seeming revision is not clear; while Bengali would have been a source of criticism invoking *prakṛti*, and Urdu critics introduced nature as a poetic subject per se from the 1870s at least, these facts do not account for the pervasive and continued presence of the critical category of "nature-in-literature" in Hindi criticism.

Nature has clearly signified both Romanticism and modernity for critics and to some degree certainly poets, and critics have gone to pains to show how very Romantic the Hindi poets of the twenties were. The Chāyāvād poets thus are seen to embody a healthy modern turn in Hindi's aesthetic progress. Nature—and clearly a Romantic Nature—had to do a lot of work in this literary critical landscape. English ideas of "nature" were received and absorbed in *transformatively* eclectic ways.[7] We can reasonably surmise that by the late nineteenth century various culturally-loaded, overlapping, and sometimes contradictory ideas of the English term "nature," and its rough equivalent in Sanskrit, *prakṛti*, were mutually influential upon colonial North Indian authors, English-educated or otherwise. Clearly, ideas of English "nature," including any combination of the post-Enlightenment empirical physical world, the innate propensities of men and beings, or the divine landscape of the European Romantic poets, interacted with indigenous literary natures.[8] The task at hand is to parse out what components have interacted, and account for the fact that Hindi Chāyāvād poetry, as much as it is labeled Hindi Romanticism, is simply very different from the poetry of the English Romantics, which it is supposed to resemble. So which "nature" and whose "nature" has entered so thoroughly into Hindi literary discourses? The inadequacy of the English term "nature" in reference to Indic philosophies and literary motifs bespeaks the immense complexity of this moment of cultural exchange, in which Hindi poets sought to incorporate into a modernist aesthetic, on their own universalistic terms, this very over-determined English nature of scenic views, science, social critique, and divine system of "the real."

As mentioned in the previous chapter, comparisons between Chāyāvād poetry and Braj *rīti* poetry, to the detriment of *rīti*, have been de rigueur among critics into the present, and among prominent twentieth-century critics. The articulation of Hindi poetic modernity in fact depends on the foil of this Braj *rīti* poetry, and interestingly, its lack of a "complete" nature. In the words of Siṁh, in his 1955 work on Chāyāvād,

> Earlier poets did not see this grand form of nature. They only saw the *kokil* (cuckoo) bird, the *cātak* (pied cuckoo) bird, the peacock, the full moon, the rainy season, the *ṭesū* (flame-of-the-forest) flower, the mango, and on and on. In this way they only saw nature in parts. Only the modern poet has obtained a vision of that whole/unbroken nature that is hidden within these parts. Just as . . . Arjun understood Krishna to be his charioteer, . . . the earlier poets, ignorant of the greatness of nature, used it in very common ways. But now this Nature, like Krishna, has shown its grand form to Arjun.[9]

Significantly here, the vision of the objects of comparison that define the non-modern—the sweet-voiced *kokil* bird, the *cātak* bird that longs like a lover, etc.—within an integrative reframed whole, unbroken (*akhaṇḍit*) Nature signifies the modern. Further, nature's integrative whole is itself a revelation of the divine, evoking Krishna's own statements in the *Bhagavad Gita* that he is suffused in all the things and creatures of the world.[10] The views of mid-twentieth-century Hindi literary critics had concord with a global trend to view modern thought as unifying or encompassing formerly disparate things; however, the matter of the Sanskritic nature had a much more significant life as the poetic entities of metaphor (*upamā*) and mood-incitant (*uddīpana*). For this reason, Siṁh's statement reflects not only a shift in perspective that has defined the modern, but a shift in poetics away from things as the metaphorical signifiers of old, toward the things-in-themselves aggregated in Nature. The new nature-in-poetry would be resonant of the older tropes, but with more possibilities to refer on one hand to the "real" empirical and social world, and on the other, a universal, macrocosmic, and spiritual Nature, itself equally an expression of true reality for these poets. The old nature somehow did not suffice for these purposes.

Within Siṁh's model of development, the Dvivedī era is cast as having only a partial, paradoxically traditional, modernity. Its poetry is disdained for its inability to shed the bonds of pre-modern poetic conventions, in attempts at modernity that resulted in awkwardly didactic and/or prosaically descriptive content. This castigation of Dvivedī era poetry as "*itivṛttātmak*" ("matter of fact," as Śukla glosses it[11]) and the accompanying glorification of Chāyāvād poetry often take place in the context of nature description itself. Certain Dvivedī era poets, especially Śrīdhar Pāṭhak and "Hariaudh," are lauded for their initial attempts away from "bounds of convention"[12] in the direction of "natural description." Nature has thus become critical to Indian debates about the nature of modern Hindi literature and the Hindi poet, the alleged immorality or decadence of pre-modern Indian culture, and the nature of modernity itself, peculiarly wedded to the narrative of British Romanticism.

Furthermore, the narrative of nature-in-poetry has been linked with the language of individual liberation, as in English Romanticism: "If on the one hand, the modern poet's desire for social freedom and personal development was expressed in the form of opposition to ancient conventional restrictions, on the other hand it was expressed in love of nature [*prakṛti prem*]."[13] Further, Siṁh posits, "the feeling of love for country arose from love of nature alone," a "liberated space [*unmukt kṣetra*]."[14] Before Siṁh, Hazārīprasād Dvivedī had attached social freedom to literary nature as well—a freedom both in the space of nature itself, and in a sense of self, personal freedom. The Chāyāvād poets would epitomize these, but according to him the poets of 1900–20

> did important work preparing the environment of love of nature (*prakṛti prem*), the independent stream-of-love (*svacchand premadhārā*), and personal freedom. Śrīdhar Pāṭhak's poetry gave nourishment to nature-love and the independent love [again, *svacchand premadhārā*] and Rāmanareś Tripāṭhī's *Milan*, *Pathik*, etc., [also] developed the inclination of freedom. . . . Today we have forgotten the importance of these poems. They are called prosaic (*itivṛtātmak*) and forgotten. But in fact they laid the groundwork for Chāyāvād, now considered the glory of Hindi poetry.[15]

Hindi critics have taken British Romanticism à la Wordsworth as the master narrative, and linked the ethos of personal freedom explicitly with the movement toward political freedom—here, in the Indian context, Swadeshi. Critics have likewise exalted the Chāyāvād as a youth movement that saw freedom in "the kingdom of nature," while in previous societal conventions they lost their identity [*vaiyaktikatā*], were constrained by the family, and experienced a "lack of solitude." They could develop personally in nature, but also saw equivalence between personal and societal development and freedom. Siṁh finds historical corroboration of growing individualism in the Chāyāvād era, which he locates in the break up of the joint family, bourgeois capitalism, and nationalism.[16] The term *svacchandatā* (freedom, unboundedness) as a calque for the English Romanticism, which was used to characterize Chāyāvād poets and certain of their precursors, denotes the high symbolism of liberation in the breaking of what were characterized as "bonds" of metrical convention. Many strands of thought—poetic, political, and historical—merge in this narrative about Hindi poetic modernity.

In the language of Hindi criticism, in the modern era, Nature emerged "in independent form" (*svatantra rūp se*), echoing a term for Swadeshi, and the abovementioned early twentieth-century individualism. Again, Siṁh gives voice to the oft heard narrative of Hindi poetic modernity, that the youth saw nature scientifically, which accounts for nature's "independent form," stripped of *rīti-kāl* conventions.[17] Hence, Chāyāvād reinvented pre-modern metaphors, and in essence reinvented them in a more "scientific" or at least "realistic" way, even as they created a kind of "symbolism" for *upamānas*.[18] Chāyāvād "freed" nature, as the rhetoric goes, from being portrayed as *uddīpanas* and *upamānas* alone; but certainly, Chāyāvād poets often used the echoes of *uddīpanas* and *upamānas*, and transposed the figures of pre-modern poetry into a more macrocosmic Nature.[19] Along with a putative "scientific" perspective, then, came a particular modern "fancifulness" that "got at the soul" of the objects of previous "nature description."[20] This mystical, somewhat symbolist quality of Chāyāvād poetry remains one of its continuing allures.

The following sections survey possible models for literary nature for the Hindi poet. Some may find this exercise overwhelmed with detail. However, one simply cannot discuss Hindi literature without ample reference to these multilingual and multicultural connections and contexts. The world of these poets was a polyglot one, indeed overwhelmed with the details of several highly developed and culturally potent literary value systems. In presenting these various natures, I will address the possibilities of reading a literary nature in Hindi beyond that of English poets. All too often scholars ask these questions in an English center of intellectual gravity in which colonial Indians merely react or borrow. I hope to foray into the territory of those people for whom the power of English, poetic or otherwise, was a factor of secondary importance, and re-center the focus on colonial India as place where cultural production encountered "the English" among many other realities.

Indigenous Literary Natures

It is difficult, and indubitably anachronistic, to speak of "nature poetry" in the pre-colonial Indian context for the simple reason that such an idea, with all the connotations of this phrase in English, did not exist as such.

While certainly descriptions of nature and nature's constituent objects *appeared* with abundance in poetry, there was little theorization of this appearance as a literary end unto itself. To consider the cultural ground with which colonial poets embraced the natural ideal, we will have to start with a new epistemological beginning, trace the appearance of the objects or spaces assignable to the category of the English term "nature" in various influential literatures, and then imagine the perspective of the colonial poet who felt a desire to interpret pre-colonial Indian texts in terms of this clearly English-inspired "nature" in poetry. If "landscape is a natural scene mediated by culture," that is, landscape is both signifier and signified, represented and presented, as Mitchell has suggested, then what happens when the mediated vision of English nature is re-mediated in the Indian context?[21]

Like English "nature," the term *prakṛti* from Sanskrit is extremely complex.[22] Originally a term of grammar and ritual, it has accrued meanings expressing interpretations of the physical world as an illusory, entropic, female entity that is nevertheless the necessary embodied counterpart to the *puruṣa* (lit. "male/man," the passive and inert "spirit-principle" "for the sake of which *prakṛti* evolves"[23]). A cursory look at the term's etymology shows that it derives from the root *kṛ*, "to make, produce," etc., and signifies literally " 'making or placing before or at first,' " thence "the original or natural form or condition of anything. . . ." It carries meanings of "cause, original source," and "nature, character, constitution, temper, disposition," in the ancient *Mahābhārata* epic and other texts.[24] In reference to philosophical systems, Monier-Williams notes the Sāṅkhya *prakṛti* as "the original producer of (or rather passive power of creating) the material world (consisting of three constitutive essences or *guṇas* . . .)," and then glosses it in a binaristic manner in reference to Vedanta: "distinguished from purusha, Spirit as Maya [illusion, matter] is distinguished from Brahman [soul, spirit] in the Vedanta." Elaborating these, he cites "the . . . producers . . . which evolve the whole visible world. . . .[25] Thus, *prakṛti* as both "Nature" and "nature" existed in a semantic position defined by these commonplace binaries, and its modern religious vogue perhaps lent a universalistic philosophical bent to modern "nature" in Indian poetry. Monier-Williams cited also a personified and gendered, deified form of *prakṛti*: "a goddess, personified will of the Supreme," the active principle of creation.[26] Later readings of this term identify *prakṛti* with shakti (power), the primordial energy, essential yet possibly destructive, also gendered as female, and/or embodied as a goddess, in multifarious contexts. For our purposes, the site of the connection between pre-colonial and colonial or "modern" nature will be best articulated by the term "organic"—those things generated "naturally" and ranging in scope from a flower or animal (cultivated or wild), to a landscape, to an abstraction encompassing the material world. The negative, dangerous aspects of nature as a primal, liminal space of "not-culture," as we know them through the Latin *natura* in the West, do not pertain as much to this powerful and inexorable *prakṛti*. Rather, here nature appears more abstractly, as the necessary counterpart to *puruṣa*; its alluring and sometimes dangerous power remains more of a philosophical point about femaleness.[27]

In terms of the constitutive elements of this material world, as manifested literarily, we find in traditional conceptions of organic spaces, the arbor, the country road, the mountains, the jungle, and large-scale swaths of topography, which were arcadian in particular culturally inflected ways, involving religious asceticism, sensual pleasure, the "play" (*līlā*) of the god Krishna, and conventions of ideal love and longing-in-love. The ashram of the mendicant is conventionally in a remote corner of the forest. The love-play of the god Krishna and the cowherd-girls (gopis) takes place in semi-enclosed, semi-decorative spaces of arbors, groves, bowers, and he extorts their curd along a deserted country road. Indeed, a particular denomination of devotees who meditate upon Radha and Krishna's "love-play of the bower" (*nikuñj līlā*), with songs like the following, which detail how Krishna dances with the peacocks, the birds sing along with the drumming of thunder, and Krishna's very name is Kuñjabihārī—he who sports in the bower.

> Śyām [Krishna] dances with the peacocks and delights the enchanted Śyāmā [Rādhā];
> Just so the black cuckoo sings a prelude, the pied crested cuckoo accompanies it, just so the thundering of the clouds plays a drum;
> Just so the dark dense cloud is black like night, just so the lightning flash presents a lamp;
> Haridāsa's sovereigns are Shyāmā [Rādhā] and Kuñjabihārī [Krishna, "who sports in the bower"]; delighted, Rādhā smiled and embraced him.[28]

Here natural objects of a "pastoral" *śṛṅgāra* are linked, not uncharacteristically, with the trappings of court, describing a sort of happy situational irony: Rādhā and Krishna may sport in a rural arbor, but their divinity makes them king and queen of all. The dual nature of this pair as the cowherd folk of Braj and simultaneously divine royalty, or at least merged with the courtly ideals of hero and heroine, is repeated in myriad contexts. We might note that miniature paintings would sometimes depict a blue Krishna with Rādhā (or another paramour) within a natural setting clearly contained *within* a royal compound. Idioms of devotional practice in the Krishna pilgrimage center of Brindāvan likewise furnish more evidence of idiomatic crossover between worship of the cowherd Krishna and worship of an imperial king in the immediate pre-colonial era. Thus the pastoral feature of Sanskrit and vernacular poetry on *śṛṅgāra* often includes or strategically invokes its complement, the court.[29] Indeed, Krishna and Radha in their arbors and bowers often appear in poetry with the epithet *nāgar/ī*, "sophisticated, of the city." The urban and the man-made are not excluded from or opposed to these landscapes, but often contiguous or contained by them.

Along with the semiprivate natural spaces, weather events and seasons have a conventional place in Sanskritic literatures. Rain and and its coming suggest romance, and even Krishna himself, his body being "rain cloud-dark." Further, a woman watching the rain without her lover is assumed to be in pain with longing. The seasons themselves are literary objects (and even musical modes, i.e., *rāg basant*, the raga of spring), and likewise integral to the interactions of hero and heroine. The urban and the man-made are not excluded from or opposed to these landscapes, but often contiguous or contained. Indeed, Krishna and Radha in their arbors and bowers often appear in poetry with the epithet *nāgar/ī*, "sophisticated, of the city."

A theorization of literary description of natural objects, if not as "Nature" per se, had already emerged in the formulation of the famous Keśav Dās' treatise on poetics, *Kavipriyā* (*Handbook for Poets*) of 1601. Here this famous poet of the *rīti* era in his classification of "general" poetic ornaments (*sāmānya alaṃkāra*), lists "splendor of the earth and of court" as two among four categories of poetic ornaments.[30] Canto Seven is dedicated to description of the ornaments of the earth (*bhūmi-bhūṣaṇ-varṇan*), which as with the other categories detailed, gives a veritable catalogue of objects of a landscape, natural and man-made, and two varied scales of locality, region/country (*des*) and town/city (*nagar*): "*desa, nagara, bana, bāga, giri, āśrama, saritā, tāla/rabi, sasi, sāgar, bhūmi ke bhūṣaṇa ṛitu saba kāla*" (Region, town, forest, garden, mountain, ashram, river, lake/Sun, moon, ocean—[all these are] ornaments of the earth—seasons [and] all the times [of ritual]).[31] A *dohā* couplet and *kavitta* verse follows for each of these items, some describing archetypes, as in the description of the six seasons famed from Sanskrit poetry, some describing the specific item in the kingdom of Orccha, and most in turn listing objects found along with these objects or phenomena. A certain drive toward realism is evident in Keśav's reference to Orccha's Tuṅgāraṇya forest, Betwa river, the courtesan Pravīn Rāy's garden, and the enumeration of structures and people. However, incorporated with this realia, the idealized, mythological, and love-infused scenes of nature appear just as often.

Sanskrit poetry has used natural objects and scenery allegorically and metaphorically as stock devices. Objects of nature function as stimulants (*uddīpanas*) to the erotic sentiment, *śṛṅgāra rasa,* and natural objects or events can sympathetically or ironically refer to human romantic events. The objects of comparison of Sanskritic similes and metaphors (*upamā* and *rūpaka*) often overlap with those very "stimulants" that remind the audience of love, such as the rainy season, moon and moonbeams, the *cakora* and *cātaka* birds, lotuses of various nomenclatures, and other natural objects that would suggest a scenario of love between the hero and heroine to the knowledgeable audience of connoisseurs (*rasikas*). Such natural objects and animals were standard comparisons expressing physical beauty: lotuses, leaves, the moon, moonlight, flocks of bees, and other animals and plants are rampant in Sanskrit poetry. Beauty demanded the comparison of body parts with various natural objects. For instance, this poem from the eleventh century Vidyākara anthology of Sanskrit courtly poetry demonstrates the "organic" body aesthetics of classical India.

> Their lips, though delicate as leaves,
> wilt not when bitten many a time;
> their limbs as soft as flowers
> still bear the wounds of nails.
> the tender creepers of their arms
> tire not in tight embraces;
> inexplicable
> is Love's way with women.[32]

In this manner, natural objects had suchy currency as metaphor for female beauty that Kalidasa describes Umā in the *Kumārasambhava* as "a collection of all things that are natural / similes for beauty, each one in its right place, / fashioned by the universal creator . . . / as if eager to see all beauty in a single form."[33]

While nature sympathizes with the heroes and heroines, reflecting their love-lorn state or their ideal appearance, *uddīpanas* of *śṛṅgāra* also cause pain to these characters when perceived by one separated from his/her beloved, as in the lovelorn woman who feels burned by the cool moonlight, and the madness of the bereft lover, perceiving his beloved in natural elements around him, or in a classic example, talking to a cloud. A verse by Dev (1673–1745 CE) exemplifies the powerful emotion that "nature"—the wood, the birds, and the clouds—can trigger:

> The *papīhā* bird cries out *"kahuṁ piva,"* and hearing this

sound she runs off to find him
The peacock calls out, says Dev, and clouds surround and cover all around
The woman has lost her mind, looking at the beautiful forest land there
Her throat filled with sighs, her eyes filled with tears.[34]

The natural elements that comprise the background of the *śṛṅgāra rasa* prescribe the emotional state of *śṛṅgāra*, in any of its situational possibilities. Hence, we might make the general statement, along with modern Hindi literary critics, that nature (comprised of flora, fauna, remote places, and weather) was fundamental to the affective qualities of *śṛṅgāra* poetry and drama, both as an incitement to feeling in the audience, and as an incitement to emotion for the characters within the poem or drama.[35]

And natural objects could take other, more allegorical roles. Braj Bhāṣā poet Bihārī Lāl used the metaphorical prop of the bee[36] and the flower-bud in this couplet about human desire: "no pollen, no sweet nectar, no blossoming yet; / if the bee is caught up with just the bud, what will happen later [when it blooms]?"[37] Rasalīn in *Rasa-prabodha* (*Awakening of rasa*), an eighteenth-century Braj rendition of the established Sanskrit poetic genre, the *ṣad-ṛtu-varṇan* (description of six seasons), continues this concept in Hindi, as he imagined seasons as female heroines (*nāyikās*) within the romantic scenes of *śṛṅgāra rasa*. Here the spring appears as a handmaiden, and monsoon is likened to a *prauṛhā*, the "experienced woman" found in *nāyikā-bhed*, the classification of heroines.

Here she brings blooming flowers, there she stirs the wind;
Here she spreads out the moonlight, the handmaid (*dāsī*) of the season of honey [Spring], as she comes.[38]
Filled with flower fragrances, slow and gentle blows the wind;
like an accomplished lover (*prauṛhā*) the monsoon wind enwraps the heart and steals the mind[39]

The seasons themselves were thus integrated into the relational typology of *śṛṅgāra nāyikā-bhed*, and *ṣad-ṛtu varṇan* genres. Not merely a courtly conceit, this connection of seasons with moods of love figures in folk genres also, the *bārah-māsā* (poems or songs of the twelve-months, in the voice of the pining woman) being a prime example, and contemporaneously, the generic association of rainy weather with love in Hindi film. Indeed, the arcadian settings of Hindi films during romantic songs evoke much the same set of *uddīpanas*.[40]

Urdu poetry, the literary ground out of which modern Hindi

poets emerged, drew additionally from Persian sources, and likewise, entailed a somewhat enclosed world of signifiers for love, its actors and objects. Persian-derived "nature-in-poetry" had some similar traits, but the Hindi authors at issue here rarely invoked it. In fact, the rose, cypress, and desert landscape of Lailā and Majnūn were intentionally disengaged by many early modern Hindi poets, as part of anti-Urdu and anti-Muslim sentiments. Still, several motifs do merit consideration as silent background to the generally Sanskritic nature of the Hindi poets: the Islamic Paradise as a beautiful garden with beautiful women; the garden itself (manifested physically in the famous Mughal gardens dotting royal landscapes across India); and the setting of the hunt. Intellectual traditions brought from Persia also comprise the epistemic world of the nineteenth-century Hindi poet. Certain genres of historical writing, such as the *nāma*, the "account," and other Persian narrative verse genres, would have been models for poets interested in "describing the real" or the "natural world." A binary distinction between the real/spiritual and the artificial/temporal, *haqīqī* and *majāzī*, may have complicated thinking about poetry "about reality" in the nineteenth century, as the "realities" of allegorical/metaphoric objects were a mask for the spiritual truths of Sufi verse romances.[41] Rāmacandra Śukla characterized the sixteenth-century *Madhumālatī* by Mañjhan as incorporating "descriptions of nature" to express "spiritual love" (*ādhyātmik premabhāv*).[42] Certain of these Persian motifs can definitively be located in Hindi poetry, up to the present day: the rose with thorns as an object of poetic description, and as a symbol of the imperfection or difficulty of the world; birds, caged or free; and reference to verses or poems themselves as flowers, gathered in collections which constitute flower-beds, gardens, etc. The breeze, for example, would have a great presence in modern Hindi poetry, as the male counterpart to the female blooming bud, and as a messenger of love analogous to that of Kalidasa's cloud. Finally, the ghazal form that dominated Urdu courtly poetry in the eighteenth century used a poetic vocabulary that foregrounded the beloved before any natural setting. As American Urdu scholar Frances Pritchett has stated, "in the ghazal world it is always the beloved who creates the beauty of 'nature,' rather than the other way around."[43]

The pre-colonial poetic landscape was in a basic way landscape-focused, but perhaps more correctly, oriented toward an enclosed, rather isolated space of a garden or small forest, in which natural objects paralleled, enhanced, sympathized with, or exacerbated the love emotions of humans. Furthermore, these scenes were built out of components of the natural world—metaphorical objects for an idealized desirable body and the lovers' desires, or "props" for love—that would altogether, mosaic-like, refract the poetic truth of the *śṛṅgāra rasa* upon the audience. Rather than "nature description," description *by means of* natural objects characterized the referential contents of courtly poetics, ornament, and genre. Indigenous literary nature encompassed a verbal art that conceived of nature as entwined with emotion, as a creeper to a tree.

Nature and the Real in Nineteenth-Century Indian Poetics

Keeping in mind these (albeit roughly outlined) indigenous hermeneutical frameworks for "talking about nature" either empirically or literarily, we can now turn to the nineteenth century to address the question of "how English is modern Hindi nature?" The answer is not simple. However, we see clearly in the hermeneutical shifts of the nineteenth century a turn toward nature as both a principle and as subject matter in itself, and a reassessment of older literature in these terms.

By way of introduction to the vernacular poetic thinking on "nature," we will examine an instance of how Sanskrit poetics also came within this critical purview, which included concomitantly both the sublime and emotion. Pandit Pramadā-dās Mitra,[44] former instructor at Benares Sanskrit College, and translator with James Ballantyne of Kavirāja's *Sāhityadarpaṇa,* found a consonance between Sanskritic *rasa* and *bhāva* and certain of the sentiments of English critical vocabulary:

> Where . . . is the element of passion in the description of inanimate nature, or of irrational creatures? A little reflection would show that, in order to be poetical, it must have the colouring of emotion; it must, to use Indian phraseology, call forth one of the permanent sentiments by an exhibition of a part at least of the three-fold cause of its manifestation. Thus, the Sublime and the Beautiful in nature must come under one or other of the Relishes [*rasa*s] enumerated. First, the objects described may be contemplated with wonder as the prevailing sentiment, and the Marvellous will be the Relish of such poetry. Or, secondly, the poet may rise from the contemplation of Nature to Nature's God, reverence being the prevailing sentiment in such a case. . . . Shelley's celebrated "Hymn to a Skylark," for instance, is throughout coloured with wonder or admiration.[45]

By permanent sentiments Mitra means the *sthāyī bhāvas*, which would then feed into the logic of *rasa*, also cited. But his world of poetics did not stop there: Mitra goes on to quote John Stuart Mill on the poetic description of things "as they appear, not as they are," "seen through the medium and arrayed in the colors of the imagination set in action by the feelings." As Mitra quotes Mill on how a poetic description of a lion is not as a naturalist would have it, but through imagery which "might occur to a mind contemplating a lion, in the state of awe, wonder, or terror, which the spectacle naturally excites,"[46] one is struck by the resonance with the meta-emotive states of *rasa*. Mitra does not elaborate this convergence of poetics, East and West, but simply presents Mill as a modern corroboration of the aesthetic mode of the *Sāhitya-darpaṇ*. Description thus had an ambiguous status in colonial poetics, as a mode linked to modernity and empiricism, but also a poetic mode requiring more than simply empiricism.

What might be called emotion, or *rasa*, as found in Shelley or Kavirāj, arose here in answer to the question of what makes poetry poetical, i.e., what distinguishes it from merely the description of things, "the description of inanimate nature" or "described objects," without any "contemplation with wonder" or "reverence." Here, as in other contexts, the material world of nature figures as the material of description that on one hand is merely "stuff," and on the other is the stuff-of-the-sublime. The question here, which we might make paradigmatic of Indian colonial poetics, has shifted to the problem of "described things," and how to determine whether their description is poetic or not. "Description of things" is valued positively in contrast to "fancy," the alleged bane of Oriental verse; but the subjectivity and fancy of a natural description would compare positively to mere description, because such subjectivity or fancy signifies the genre of poetry, distinct from the prosaic or simply banal. Here the colonial intellectual's poetic problem comes into focus: the problem of the ambiguous import of the material "stuff" of the poetic world—it should be nominally "realistic," and therefore "modern," but also not lacking an extra-material, dangerously "fanciful" element, beyond discursive descriptive skill alone and exciting the feelings, as both *rasa* theory and Mill would have it.

Contemporary literatures at this same time were looking to the Sanskritic past for inspiration, while turning toward the subject of nature in criticism and verse. Below we will examine the place of the literary concept of "nature" in three key fields: English literature as experienced by the colonial intellectual, Urdu criticism and poetry that our Hindi authors surely read, and the well-known Bengali poetry of the day.

"Nature Again Asserts Her Dominion": English

Ideas of the "natural," encompassing concepts of realism, demotic language, and the picturesque, were perhaps the major aspect of Western literature received by nineteenth-century Indians. As explained above, it is now conventional wisdom that Indians "received" literary values such as realism and Nature from English, and this fact heralded Indian aesthetic modernity. Finding concrete evidence of this transmission is more difficult. We can be sure that ambitious young English-educated men valued the emulation of English poetry. In a 1933 festschrift for famed editor Dvivedī, the revolutionary and journalist Sant Nihal Singh wrote an English article on his own English literary education in the Panjab. For him, English literature entailed a profound epistemological problem of both reception and creation: how could one appreciate "realistic" description of something never personally sensed? He seems to suggest that a "true" sensory experience of English nature was impossible for the vernacular student:

> The sensuous appeal [of English prose] failed to enrapture: for the scenes depicted were torn from a book of life with which we were totally unfamiliar—the nuances employed in description were of a nature that the Punjabi eye had not learnt to distinguish—the scents conjured up were such as to fail to secure any response from the Indian nostrils, unacquainted with them, as they were. . . .

But despite this, Singh writes that the English-educated Indian author in fact valued what he did not understand or know: "to sing the praises of the English spring (even when the singer's eyes had never feasted upon those glories) was the height of Indian ambition."[47] Singh goes on to describe the change of later decades toward Indian subject-matter (casting off of the net of the "Macaulay maya," as he puts it, referring to Macaulay's famous indictment of Indian thought), but he focused illustratively on nature description, as that which stood out as a major element of the perceived influence of British poetry in India.

The attribution of nature in poetry to the English influence was so common in colonial India as a whole that it would be difficult to track down every source demonstrating this phenomenon. One particular example, a speech in 1886 Lahore given by J. N. Muzumdar on Bengali literature, can serve to epitomize this widely-held opinion on the part of the English-educated class of Indians. Muzumdar began with the idea that English has had a nourishing, maternal influence upon Bengali, and has ameliorated the lack of nationality—perhaps fellow-feeling, perhaps nationalism—in Sanskrit-derived literatures. But ultimately the problem is with convention and lack of realism:

> Art has mastered nature, and everything has become convention. There are certain well-known grooves in which most of our thoughts must revolve. If a heroine is to be described, she must have moon-like face, gazelle-like eyes, pomegranate-like teeth, cuckoo-like voice and sound. . . . Then there is the same spring, the same separation, the same heartless Cupid. . . . Heroes and heroines move before you like automatons.

Muzumdar's characterization then takes on the cast of the familiar bodily and gendered rhetoric of colonialism:

> Western literature is strong, robust, and full of energy; while Oriental literature is languid, weak, and moves as artificially as a nautch girl. Coming under the healthy influence of English literature, Bengali literature has avoided one of the greatest defects of Eastern literature. Nature has again asserted her dominion, and art has once more become subordinated to it.

Muzumdar then immediately connects modern literary nature—induced by English, evident in Bengali—with the specific character of India.

> It is not my intention to say that everything is defective in Oriental literature. . . . India, with its snow-clad mountains, its silvery Ganges, its blue Jumna, its numerous lakes, forests, plains, springs, and waterfalls, having a climate varying from that of the torrid to that of the frigid, has been fitly termed the epitome of the whole world. In the beauty, variety and sublimity of natural sceneries, she yields to no other country in the world: it is emphatically the land of the poet and the devotee; and we have those feelings in abundance which such scenes are calculated to give rise to in our minds. . . .[48]

Thus, the influence of English is one of eugenic improvement for the cultural index of the *belles lettres*. English has taught that where there is the dominion of nature, there is truth and knowledge; and as it happens, India possesses a surfeit of "natural sceneries," a sort of poetic birthright that Indians simply need to claim. Hence, while English brings to light the defects of the mother Sanskrit, and the crass display of the nautch girl of the vernacular literatures, it also presents nature as a way to modernity uniquely appropriate for India.

Virtually every modern Indian literary or cultural history addresses the profound effect of British literary models that displayed "realism," were "historical," or had the "scientific spirit." "Nature description" and then "love of nature" appear as poetic corollaries of these values. Historians generally place the presence and influence of British Romantic poetry (especially Wordsworth, Coleridge, and Shelley) in India in the late nineteenth and early twentieth centuries. In Hindi, Romantic poetry in translation, along with English writing of most other types, is found in a steady trickle in late nineteenth- through early twentieth-century periodicals.[49] Much of the translation in periodicals seem to have been culled from other periodicals, including English ones, and English poetry was clearly accessed through anthologies such as Palgrave's *Golden Treasury*, English readers like the *Royal Reader*, and publications of Macmillan and Longman's Publishers, both well-established in colonial markets.[50] I emphasize here the fact that tracking what "English nature poetry" meant to the Indian reader is an extremely complex question of transmission because of the eclectic nature of the consumption of late Romantic poetry, despite its institution as canon by the late nineteenth century.

The connection between British literature and British cultural power has been well-explored in Sudhir Chandra's discussion of nineteenth-century Indian intellectuals.[51] Gauri Viswanathan's seminal *Masks of Conquest: Literary Study and British Rule in India* addresses the importance of English literature in the colonial project, and the educational ideologies that injected literature into curricula. It is well known that many of the authors she cites from English curricula, such as Addison, Bacon, Hume, Locke, Mill, and Smith, later entered the non-English public sphere in periodical translations. Shakespeare and Milton figure as giants of the colonial literary education; translations of works with religious and moral themes such as Bunyan's *Pilgrim's Progress*, and Johnson's *Rasselas* appeared from the early nineteenth century onward. Later, translations of the novels of Collins and Reynolds (many in Urdu) became quite popular and indeed influential upon later Hindi prose authors.[52] Meenakshi Mukherjee's *Realism and Reality: The Novel and Society in India* addresses the constitution of realism in prose. Urmila Varma has analyzed the influence of British poetry on Hindi poetry in imagery, meter, and diction, concentrating mainly on the influence of British Romantic poetry on Chāyāvād poetry. She concentrates mostly on nature and personification in Chāyāvād poems from the late twenties onward—a field beyond the scope of this book, which seeks out the "back story" of this well-known English Romantic influence upon Chāyāvād poetry. Before the full bloom of Romantic influence appeared in Chāyāvādī poets, and in the midst of the colonial educational enterprise, even in the poetic context, "nature" was linked inextricably to discourses of "realism" and "morality," and these literary values certainly derived from the undeniable cultural effects of colonial education, still being theorized today.

"A Flower for the Coat": Urdu

Hindi literature developed in a quite dialogic fashion with other regional Indian literatures, and an examination of the "nature phenomenon" in Urdu and Bengali (at least) is necessary.[53] In terms of the nature question itself, Frances Pritchett has addressed the degree and type of influence of English poetry on Urdu poetry, in *Nets of Awareness: Urdu Poetry and Its Critics*, and especially in Chapter 11, "Natural Poetry."[54] Her discussion of "the historic" and "the natural" as poetic standards for Urdu litterateurs Muḥammad Ḥusain "Āzād" (1830–1910) and Alṭāf Ḥusain "Ḥālī" (1837–1914) remains highly relevant to Hindi letters, since Hindi authors were subject to the very same literary milieu. As of 1875, Āzād and Ḥālī, the famous Muslim reformer Sir Syed Ahmad Khan, and British government officers, had all promoted the specific term, "natural poetry," not so much Herder's *Naturpoesie* as more "realist" poetry in the linguistic register of speech. Colonel Holroyd, Director of Public Instruction of the Panjab, who attempted to reform the Urdu mushairas (poetic gatherings for recitation) of the nineteenth century, promoted such literary goals as writing "from Nature," as in writing in a manner with less poetic ornamentation or literary allusion, and more descriptively and realistically, "aiming at moral instruction, and presenting a natural picture of our feelings and thoughts,"[55] as opposed to the symbolic universe of unrequited love at the heart of the Urdu ghazal.

Sir Syed Ahmad Khan (1817–98), famous educationist who founded what would later become Aligarh Muslim University, and led what became the reformist "Aligarh movement," was the foremost Urdu public intellectual of his time, and a thinker both loyal to and critical of the British. As founder of a scientific society and the "Muslim Cambridge" of the Anglo-Oriental Muhammaden College and employee of the East India Company, Sir Syed had ample exposure to English thinking on nature as an object of scientific inquiry and otherwise. In the words of critic Sadiq, if his use of the term "nature" was English, then it was an eighteenth-century term for the real:

> He does not use ["nature"] in the sense of the simple and primitive as opposed to the cultured and sophisticated, as used by Rousseau. Nor does he interfuse it with a spiritual significance like Wordsworth. In his use of it, he is more akin to the eighteenth-century English writers who use it as the opposite of whatever is far-fetched, remote, or unreal: and it is probably that he may have picked up the idea from the writings of the Augustans, presumably from Addison. [56]

The proposition that Khan's nature was an eighteenth-century English one, positioned as a corrective to the "far-fetched," etc., is further buttressed by his essays (largely translations), intended to "wage war against the licentiousness, vulgarity, ignorance, superstition, and the false taste of his age in poetry, very much as it was Addison and Steele's function to expose the loose morality of Restoration life and literature."[57] Sir Syed's nature, at least somewhat Addisonian, and linked to his mission to reform licentiousness, formed the intellectual background of the seminal Urdu critical work of the nineteenth century, Āzād's *Water of Life* (*Āb-e-ḥayāt*) of 1880, to which we will turn now, which was vitally concerned with "nature in poetry."

A text written in a hybrid genre of biographical compendium of poets (*tazkira*) and English-style literary history, Āzād's *Water of Life* (*Āb-e-ḥayāt*) of 1880 is rife with the terms "nature" and "natural" (both the Urdu *kudrat/kudratī* and the transliterated English terms "nature"/"natural") as standards of aesthetic worth, and as the litmus test for good Urdu poetry, of any era. Indeed, he expressed his philological view with an organic metaphor: "although Urdu grew in the ground of Sanskrit and Bhāṣā, it has flowered in the breezes of Persian."[58] Along with such florid characterizations, Āzād both apotheosizes Urdu poets and laments Urdu's ostensible decline from an overabundance of Persian-style overly-fanciful comparisons. While "to show the style of beauty the beloved has in the hot season, they will say that . . . the sweat of dew began to drip from the cheeks of the flower," produces a relatively "delicate" and "subtle" effect, overmuch of this alienates the non-Persian reader, and furthermore "in presenting our thoughts, we . . . suppose lifeless things to be alive—or rather, . . . to be human."[59] Such criticism of fanciful personifications, and similes and metaphors, "the well-used handkerchiefs of our ancestors for hundreds of years," echoed in the Hindi context of Braj Bhāṣā and Khaṛī Bolī poetry in Sanskrit idioms, although we will see that personification was reinvented for modern Hindi poetry in the coming decades, especially the forest flower and the rain cloud.

Āzād in his *Water of Life* sounds like any nineteenth-century Englishman in his praise of poems in the simple and affecting style of women's folk songs for the rainy season: "Look at these words and thoughts—how they are immersed in Nature [*nechar*]! How very genuinely they present the natural thoughts and heartfelt longings of women and girls!"[60] Thus while such words of love remained valued, their aesthetic qualities were framed in their positions as ethnographic artifacts of the real and the natural.

The critical framework of nature and the natural seems to have remained quite attractive to colonial-era poets for some time, much like many other Western commodities. Pritchett notes,

> [Āzād] continued to urge radically Westernizing approaches to poetic problems: "Just as English arts and sciences are improving our clothing, houses, conditions, thoughts, and knowledge, in the same way English literature too goes on giving *islāh* (correction) to our literature."[61]

By extension, we might surmise that the colonial poet considered "nature poetry" an extension of the social and technological "development" brought by the colonizers. Āzād evokes the disciplinary social ramifications of this interchange pointedly—now English standards are the *ustād*, the teacher, who gives *islāh* to Indian poetry. Āzād may have imagined his colonial culture in the image of his description of the incorporation of Persian into Braj Bhāṣā:

> the radiance of the victor's ascendant fortune gives everything of theirs—even clothing, turban, gait, conversation—such a glow and luster that they appear desirable. . . . And people do not merely adopt them, but are proud of doing so. Then they bring forth, by means of rational arguments, many benefits of having done so.[62]

Āzād portrays the colonial cultural situation as a type of familiar cosmopolitanism, in which poets will take up foreign tropes for their poetry as they pick flowers in a garden, "And they made [the flower/a foreign trope] into an ornament—if not for their turban, then for the collar of their coat [a transliteration from English, and signifying the English style of dress: *koṭ*]."[63] Or perhaps "nature poetry" functioned as an implement, along the lines of Geeta Kapur's analysis of the "surrogate realism" of European-trained Indian artist, Raja Ravi Varma: "Just as prose fiction, especially the novel . . . comes to be regarded in India as per se realistic . . . , representational painting in oils [was] construed to mean *an enabling technique that stands for an accredited realism.*"[64] Such an "accredited realism" seems a likely aim behind the critical term "nature description" which later inundated the Hindi literary critical vocabulary, even when the nature description in question displayed a high Sanskritic idealism or non-realist features such as personification.[65]

Āzād described the "general principles" of English literature as such: "whatever situation and inner state you write about, you present it in such a way that you cause the same feeling or the same mood . . . as would be aroused by experiencing or seeing the thing itself." Then in short order, he compares Urdu writing, which "attracts the ear" with its "colorful words and subtle themes," but does not create an "effect in the heart." Āzād invokes the example of the poetic garden, in the familiar enumerative cadence, and seems to object to a lack of a certain kind of visual semblance in Indic poetic descriptions:

> In praising a garden we will sometimes scar [with jealousy] the heart of the green garden of the skies [Paradise]. . . . In fact, we'll blacken many pages praising, in all different styles, its each and every flower and leaf. But the swaying of its greenery, the radiance of its flowers, its sweet smells, the rippling of flowing water, its well-pruned trees, the blooming of the flowerbeds, the scent of the air, the call of the parrot, the cry of the *papīhā* (pied crested cuckoo, which calls for its lover), the voice of the *koyal* (the black cuckoo, messenger of spring) that affects the human heart with spiritual joy—we don't describe [the garden] in a way that portrays [it] before the reader's eyes.[66]

Nor, in his assessment, does an Urdu description of a battle (a topic of a popular elegy genre, the *marsiya*) inspire patriotism. The "enjoyment" that English thoughts and themes produce cannot be accomplished in Urdu, he wrote, and this should provoke shame over the weakness of the language. This can be understood as the result of an indexical relationship: "a people's literature corresponds to that people's condition, and its thoughts correspond to the state of the country and the country's education." Here Āzād makes a claim about the nature of English democracy, which was "established through its people's participation" and dependent on widespread education and the process of debate.[67] "We ought to reflect on what kind of power their speech (*bayān*, account, narrative, description) has," he submits, in contrast to India, where "in our language, if anything was achieved, it was the volumes of some poets praising the victorious fortune of a king, which are only suitable for diversion and amusement. . . . That true essence (*jauhar*, also excellence, worth) was not achieved. . . ."[68] Āzād carries the linkage of political power and rhetorical power further, and into the poetical realities of his time:

> . . . the wretched themes of beauty and love, the beloved's downy cheek and beauty spot, and the words about the springtime in the garden— . . . If we want to say something, first we have to banish these things from our minds, then . . . bring forth . . . similar novel metaphors, new similes, innovative constructions, and sophisticated verbal forms. . . . The lack of courage that has become the sovereign ruler of our people—can we ever have a better chance to stop it from affecting us than by doing this?[69]

Clearly, this lack of courage, personified as a sovereign ruler, serves as the emblem of Urdu-knowers' political subjecthood; we see here that British sovereignty actuated a crisis of poetic meaning that encompassed the psychological and political. A literary, rhetorical, or linguistic locus of political weakness was likely never previously supposed in South Asia before the nineteenth century. This theme of feudal decadence as the ruin of both poetry and of political dynasties was an influential one; taken up by famous Urdu critics such as No'mānī Shiblī in the late nineteenth century,[70] it is now a commonplace of Marxist criticism in both Urdu and Hindi. The old metaphors, and the need to change them, had thus begun to have a deeply political gravity in modern criticism across the Urdu-Hindi spectrum.

Ḥālī's later *Muqaddamah* of 1893 took up related topics of the reform of Urdu poetry, and has remained a classic of Urdu literary criticism. By an author representative of the Aligarh generation of Muslim reformists, already famous for his polemic verses on the degradation, moral, cultural, and political, of contemporary Muslims, in the *Musaddas-e-Ḥalī* of 1879,[71] this work argued that poetry is linked fundamentally to morality and society, and should function to benefit these. Among several overlapping statements on the features of good poets and poetry, including imagination, proper diction, and acquaintance with poetic forebears, we find emphasized the observation of the physical world: "In order to become a poet, the first thing is a previously existing capability; and then, the examination of nature;" for example, "mountains, forests, and his own inner self."[72] This set of principles for natural poetry—both in method and in subject—was put forth as remedy to what he saw as the solipsistic world of the Urdu ghazal, which like Sanskrit literature, as described above, had begun to seem "artificial" in a negative way, despite the fact that the ghazal tradition had never aspired to naturalism in the first place. When Ḥālī famously presented three qualities of poetry given by Milton—"simple, sensuous, and passionate" in the original English—he took the "sensuous" into the particular semantic realm of realism. No doubt treating it as a concept literally signifying "of the physical senses," Ḥālī glossed it as *aṣliyat par mabnī*, founded on truth, or reality.[73]

What explains this turn of critical judgment against older themes of poetry and toward this avowedly naturalistic method and natural subject? Pritchett finds that Ḥālī seemed to be writing the *Muqaddamah* as a counterpart to Wordsworth's "Preface to the Lyrical Ballads," and that "Āzād and Ḥālī's whole relationship with their own heritage is haunted by the invisible presence of Wordsworth. . . ."[74] And he is indeed invisible, as he is never mentioned by name. Pritchett is forced to conclude that there is no definitive answer to the question of influence: "Scholars who play find-the-sources for Āzād and Ḥālī soon discover that most of their ideas floated in the Victorian air," and that British sources may have been received from several multilingual sources, perhaps only in part, and perhaps only in faulty translations. "Ḥālī was operating within a larger Victorian literary milieu, in which possible sources were legion, and influences and parallels even more so."[75] It is similarly hard to "play find-the-sources" for Hindi poets, but we know certainly that many read Āzād and Ḥālī. Dvivedī himself based his well-known essay "The poet and poetry" ("Kavi aur kavitā") (1907) on Ḥālī's 1893 *Muqaddamah*,[76] and imparted the dicta that "the work of poets of learned and civilized countries . . . is to describe real events, . . . not clusters of flowers falling from the sky,"[77] and "to observe closely the development of nature" and (in seeming corollary) examine "the nature (*svabhāv*) of man," which are the special purview of the poet, and measure of his worth.[78] Like Ḥālī, he invoked a Hindi/Urdu version of Milton's three qualities of poetry—simple, sensuous, and passionate—as *sādagī* (simplicity), *asliyat* (reality), and *jos̈* (emotion/fervor).[79]

However, poetic realism within the Urdu poetic tradition had an uneasy relationship to propriety and decorum. The critics Āzād and Ḥālī had in fact largely ignored one poet earlier in the century, who was known precisely for the quality of realism they promoted: Nazīr Akbarābādī (1740–1830). "A Bohemian by temperament," who "did not take kindly to the etiquette and formalism of courts and declined to attach himself to the rulers of the day," Akbarābādī was an Agra poet known for his minute observation, sensuousness, and his occasional use of uncouth vocabulary.[80] Aditya Behl has written evocatively of his poetic iconoclasm, reaching "beyond the hypertrophied aestheticism of the accepted topoi of roses and nightingales, the paradise-like garden and its flowers, and the longing for wine," to "poems about the feel and texture of *everyday life*: desciptions of items of daily use, of what it is like to slip in the mud in the monsoon, to go swimming in the Jamuna, to enjoy the ordinary pleasures of north Indian life."[81]

The curious exclusion of the author from the early critical works on Urdu literary history perhaps speaks to the centrality to realism in this era of a certain decorum of subject matter, despite the exhortations to record the world without the hindrance of old metaphors. The Urdu poets' difficulty of incorporating mundane realism into their works was not lost on the English proponents of such. In the words of S. W. Fallon, writing in 1879, the contemporary critics have missed the true value of Akbarābādī:

> The poetry which he has evolved from common things—as no other Hindustani poet has condescended, or been able to do—is ignorantly regarded by native scholars as the surest proof that he was no poet. "He has written," they say, "on such common subjects as flour, and *dal* (pulse), flies and mosquitoes." . . . His poems are a picture gallery in which may be seen speaking pictures. . . .[82]

And of course, Fallon goes on to say that "Nazir had a keen sympathy with nature, and with every form of humanity."[83] Leaving aside his sympathy with humanity—and indeed impolite society—plenty of nature-description can be found in his verses, not uncommonly in the Sanskritic vein, and sometimes descriptions of nature "for its own sake," or "interpenetrated with humanity," in the words of critic Muhammad Sadiq, translator of the following lines:

> There is an unbroken trickle of eavesdrops from the
> thatched roof of a cottage
> Right up to the middle of the mountain the grass is
> waving.
> Steadily the rain falls and runs into streamlets.
> The birds and animals all bathe together.
> The frogs croak, the cricket chirps.
> The cranes in thousands line the sky

The koel and the sparrow-hawk break into shrill cries
And the intoxicated peacock screams like the cuckoo.[84]

These lines on the rains are clearly indebted to some extent to the vocabulary of Sanskrit poetics, but as was the wont of this eccentric poet, the natural scene is presented in an almost prosaically descriptive fashion, and in Sadiq's words, as "a townsmen's poetry of nature; of its remote and wild aspects he has no knowledge"[85]—basically the same view as that of Sanskrit poetry, generally speaking, as discussed in the previous chapter and below. The Urdu critics' anxiety about Akbarābādī, and his concurrent resuscitation as a realist in the late nineteenth century by Fallon and then others, are signs of this particularly loaded moment in poetic taste, where realism—and nature as a large part of that realism—began to reign, albeit ambiguously, as a precept of taste.

Generally speaking, in the secondary literature since, the role of nature in Urdu literature has been discussed primarily in reference to these Victorian texts of Āzād and Ḥālī, and indeed Nature in Urdu poetry itself in the nineteenth century had basic connections to the experiments with realism encouraged by both these critics and borrowings from English genres. Examples of such ranged from the "graphic pictures of Indian sights and scenes" of educational writer Muhammad Isma'il[86] to Āzād's rather forced descriptions of the seasons.[87]

However, another Panjabi author, Muhammad Iqbāl (1879–1938)[88] would lead the vanguard of Urdu poetry in the twentieth century, such that his writings, philosophical and poetic, have been ordained as the outcome of the cultural strivings of the Aligarh school. In the words of Muhammad Sadiq, "the breakaway from the Middle Ages, which found its first characteristic expression in the writings of the Aligarh school, reached its apogee in the philosophy of Iqbāl. In him the old values are all transvalued."[89] His early poetry was concurrent with that of our Hindi authors examined in subsequent chapters, and they were surely aware of his writings, if not actually reading them. Iqbāl's Nature very likely impinged upon that of the Hindi authors, even as the sociocultural distinctions simultaneously widened between Hindi and Urdu.

Iqbāl had studied at the Scotch Mission College in his native Sialkot, Panjab, at Government College in Lahore, and as protégé of Sir Thomas Arnold at Cambridge and Munich; and as someone who indubitably read his forebears' works on the beneficial influence of nature and reality on poetry, it is not surprising that he would be inspired to some sort of nature poetry, directly inspired by the European poetry he encountered in person, more profoundly than most. Of his early poetry, one linked nationalism and landscape and became an unofficial national anthem. "Tarāna-e Hindī" ("Anthem of India"), was first published in 1904 in the literary magazine *Makhzan*, with the title "Hamārā Deś" (Our country), and is well known today as its opening refrain in song form, "Sāre jahāṁ se acchā . . ." (Best in all the world . . .).[90] The imagery was familiar both for its citation of Urdu's Islamic paradise, and for its reference to the Himalayas and the Ganges, representing the subcontinent's geography and cultural icons. The sentiment of the poem places the audience within this Hindustan, as nightingales in a garden. Amid the description of a "highest mountain, neighbor of the sky," and "thousands of streams" in its lap, and Iqbāl's appeal to an Indianness bridging religious differences ("Religion does not teach us to be enemies . . . We are Indians; our homeland is our India"), he also appeals to a sense of historical decay, which India has defeated: "Greece, Egypt and Byzantium have all been erased . . . / . . . our existence is never erased. . . ."[91] Here the rhetoric of the destruction wrought by time, familiar in the works of earlier Urdu writers, is victoriously denied in the case of Hindustan. Paradoxically, the destruction of past glory would soon dominate his poetry, but this time with the paradisial garden in ruin, in his famous *Śikvā* (Complaint) of 1911 and *Javāb-e Śikvā* (Answer to the Complaint) of 1913. Here the sad state of the Islamic world is imagined as a desolate natural scene, and the nightingale laments:

> The turtle-doves have left the cypress and from its branch
> flown
> Flowers have shed their petals which are at random strewn.
> The beaten paths of the garden lie desolate and forlorn;
> Branches are stripped of leaves that they once had worn.
> But his [the nightingale's] spirit alone has remained free
> from the prison of the seasons.
> If only there was someone in the garden to understand his
> lament![92]

When Allah responds, in Iqbal's *Answer* of 1913, he likewise analogizes for a hopeful Islamic future: "Soon buds will sprout on the branches . . . / Weeds and brambles will be swept out . . . / And where martyrs' blood was shed red roses shall bloom. / Look, how russet hues have tinged the eastern skies! / The horizon heralds the birth of a new sun. . . ."[93] Thus, for Iqbāl, the nature in poetry was on one hand an affective symbol of homeland, like the garden of Hindustan, best in the world, or the Himalaya mountain peaks, but the garden was itself a powerful metaphor for Iqbāl's historical sense of loss.

In general, we can surmise that Iqbāl could have composed poetry with a European Romantic frame of reference along with an Urdu or Persian one. His familiarity with and inspiration from the English Romantics is well known; one can find in his poetry the stray phrase in clear resonance with Shelley as much as the typical rhetoric of the garden. The bulbul of his gardens could be that of older Urdu poetry, or the immortal bird of Shelley's "Ode to a Nightingale." Further, one of his Persian works was a response to Goethe, and this fact, along with his time in Germany, suggests a Romantic influence beyond merely that of the English. In the final reckoning though, we are on our own to decipher what influences he may have imbibed. As Shamsur Rahman Faruqi has written, Iqbāl did not seem to have a conscious poetic to work from and was a "romantic who avoided Romanticism." Faruqi finds Iqbāl's Nature in the early poem "Man and the Company of Nature" (Insān aur bazm-e qudrat) to be merely his "own theological self,"[94] and while one can find in some of these early poems a nature that is "an open harmony, a joyful companionship," and in Urdu style, in it "everything . . . is intoxicated with the wine of being,"[95] still, Faruqi opines that Iqbāl's "social and official self led him into dreary deserts of . . . moralizing. . . . This was Iqbāl's dilemma and he could never resolve it."[96] In short, Iqbāl has the legacy of being a philosophical poet more than anything else, but his affective geography and allegorized landscapes—doubly allegorized with the despair and hope of Urdu poetics, and of the state of Islam—must have held considerable inspiration for Hindi poets.

By and large Iqbāl's nature in the 1924 *Bāng-e-darā* is quite similar to that of the Chāyāvād authors following, and this is only appropriate, considering the timing of publication, just slightly before the Chāyāvād authors begin to flourish. Like them, he commonly personifies natural objects or phenomena, which form singular subjects of the poems; buds and breezes appear very often, and commonly with shades of Urdu love poetry. Ultimately, however, the poetry of this contemporary of our Hindi poets here, in our purview of 1885–1925, was more dedicated to philosophizing on Nature, and the place of the self within it, than were the Hindi poets. While certainly such themes did emerge for Hindi poets, the persistent dramatic voice of the poet within the poem—a demanding interlocutor in the first-person "I," much like what C. M. Naim would call the "pseudo-dramatic" strategy of Iqbāl's poems—differentiates him from the particular poetic habits of the Hindi poets we examine in the teens and early twenties.[97] Clearly though, the slight differentiation from convention with the natural poetic objects in Iqbāl's early poems, and the macrocosmic, and sometimes Sufism-inflected Nature evident in his verse, must have played a role in contemporary Hindi poets' experiments with modernism, which used quite similar poetic strategies.

"Hail to the Mother": Bengali

Contemporary Bengali poetry, reflecting a more Anglicized culture of the upper classes of Calcutta, was most certainly central to the development of modern poetry in Hindi. The composition and cultural obsessions of the "middle class" Bengali *bhadralok* hardly need another rehearsal here, nor does the Hindi-belt characterization of Calcutta and Bengalis as Westernized (for good or ill) and therefore more "modern." The critic Hazārīprasād Dvivedī claimed that Bengali novels freed Hindi from the "web of illusion" of "overly passionate" *aiyyārī* (fantastical) and *qissā-goī* (adventure-romance)[98] novels in Hindustani and Urdu, and that Bengali brought *komal bhāvanāeṁ* (tender feelings) and *sukumār kalpanāeṁ* (delicate imaginings) to Hindi.[99] Below, selected poetic writings on and about nature will form our subject, by Baṅkimacandra Chatterjee and Rabindranath Tagore, authors well-known to the Hindi audience of the time.

Landscape and nationalism had of course merged aesthetically via India-as-goddess, with the song "Bande Mātaram" ("Hail to the Mother") in a quasi-Sanskrit mantra form, from Baṅkimacandra Chatterjee's 1880 novel *Ānandamaṭh*. Linking the landscape with an embodied, female India in the form of the mother goddess Durgā, the song does not so much elaborate the Mother's fierceness but rather her association with the natural elements and ideals of Sanskrit poetry, traits that would characterize later Hindi nature-descriptions as well: "[The mother of] sweet water, sweet fruits, / [of the] cool south wind, / dark with crops, // [of] the thrilling nights of the radiant moon / [of] the splendor of flowering, leafy trees / [of] smiling, sweet words."[100] Notably, English translations of this song have drawn the land/nationalism connection more strongly than the original lyrics, which in fact suggest this more obliquely within the original's Sanskritic conventions of ideal beauty, in compounds that do not explicate their relation to the subject, the Mother, nor identify this mother explicitly as a place, e.g., the mother of the wind. Compare the following translation into English of M. Dvivedī: "Land of the glad white moon-lit nights, / Land of trees with flowers in bloom."[101] The degree to which the Bengali original expressed a "motherland" per se versus a "mother goddess" was in dispute at first,[102] but the song since metamorphosed into a recognizably nationalist sentiment, figured not only in the Goddess, but the natural images also. Hence, in the years between 1880–circa 1900, the conception of Sanskritic poetic language for talking about nature was considered variously, and seemed to be in a state of theoretical flux: is poetic nature a discursive project, or one of innuendo and inference as of old?[103]

In 1861 Michael Madhusūdan Datt wrote of nature in rather conventional ways in his otherwise iconoclastic *Meghanādabadha-kābya*.[104] By 1883, Rabindranath Tagore had been writing poetry on cosmic themes that seemed to allude to a grand systemic universe, but even then in a rather conventional, religious way, that was more "modern" in style than in its content (e.g., "Brahma, Vishnu, Shiva"). His oft-quoted stanza from "A Half-Acre of Land" (Dui bigha jami) of 1896 consists of iterations of the "contents" of landscape, and recalls the vocative refrain of Baṅkim's "Hail to the Mother": "I bow, I bow to my beautiful motherland Bengal! / To your river-banks, to your winds that cool and console; / Your plains, whose dust the sky bends down to kiss; // Your leafy mango-woods, where the herd-boys play; // Your sweet-hearted women returning home with water. . . ."[105] By 1900, he had written in the idiom of the gopi/devotee, with "real" natural objects of comparison forming a macrocosmic backdrop to the familiar affect of the lovelorn woman, in "Love's Question" (Praṇaya-praśna): "Is this true? // That the dawn surrounds me with light from delight in me, // That the touch of my hot cheek intoxicates the breeze, // That daylight hides in the dark of my hair." The poem moves toward the universal, in a double gesture toward irony—of the lover's hyperbole—and toward an *advaita*-like theology—"That the earth can be wrapped in the end of my sari // That the universe is nothing but me and what loves me, // That for me alone your love has been waiting / Through worlds and ages awake and wandering."[106] In a maneuver that will reappear in Hindi Chāyāvād, we see an identification of the self with the divine-as-universe, a trope that will take on more concrete natural imagery in its Hindi renditions.

Further, Rabindranath Tagore wrote critical essays that took up the topic of "nature" in discussion of Kalidasa, especially, and Śakuntalā most of all. In a 1902 essay comparing Kalidasa's *Abhijñānaśākuntalam* (The Recognition of Śakuntalā) with Shakespeare's *The Tempest*, Tagore extols Śakuntalā's familial connection to the plants and creatures of the forest, and points to a relationship with nature as one of the defining features of Indian culture:

> Nowhere except in Sanskrit literature, I believe, has mute nature been given such a central and essential place in drama. One can write an allegorical play by personifying Nature and putting words on her lips; but to keep nature natural, yet make it so living, so immediate, so pervasive, so intimate, to make it perform so many dramatic functions—we have not seen this anywhere else. Where external nature is regarded

> as something distant and alien, where humanity raises walls around itself to create divisions throughout the world, such creations of literature are impossible.

The Tempest, in contrast, exemplified for Tagore the conflict between humankind and nature, and between men.[107] Tagore in this and many other of his writings positioned the Sanskritic literary nature as a national feature, and one which contributed to his construction of a spiritual, peaceful, and pastoral "East," morally superior to the material, violent, and industrialized "West." Tagore's visions of literary nature would reappear in Hindi by the early 1920s in subtly but importantly different forms: the description of this natural universe would have stronger links to the Sanskrit poetic past, and sympathy for nature could even sometimes indicate an Marxian sort of materialism. Subsequent chapters will illuminate these links and indications.

In summary, the possible models and sources for the Hindi poet in English, Urdu, Sanskrit, and Bengali, for nature-in-poetry and criticism of such, were very much in abundance. Assessments of Indian poetry's engagement with Nature in these respective languages formed the background of modern Hindi poetic self-definition. From the excerpts given here, and the following chapters, it is evident that the burden of identity fell heavy upon Hindi authors' shoulders, as their particular "anxiety of influence." Taking inspiration from these several sources, Hindi poets carved out a niche of "Hindi-ness" for themselves, which included the complexly drawn vision of literary Nature that forms the subject of this book.

Conclusions

All critics agree that Chāyāvād represents, to some degree or another, a Hindi version of Romanticism through the lens of Tagore, and that the preceding Dvivedī era poets introduced particular precepts of "Romanticism" such as "natural language" and "natural description" (although in an incomplete, ultimately unsuccessful way, according to the critical narrative). These characterizations have become iconic, such that most people take as self-evident truth that "Chāyāvadīs are Romantic Nature poets," and in so doing, either dismiss them or misread them; moreover, the modern Hindi poetry preceding them is ignored.

However, a more nuanced picture is possible by looking closely at the terms of critical engagement in this conventional literary history. "Romanticism" and the modern were collapsed together for Hindi literary critics, who saw Romanticism as modern, and nature was a way to "accomplish" this Romanticism and thereby accomplish some degree of modernity. Additionally, the Hindi critical enterprise has recreated the teleology of English literary history: Dvivedī era poets represent rationalism with strong neo-classical themes, description of nature without sufficient Romantic recognition of its import, and an incomplete foray into literary subjectivity; Chāyāvād poets are foremost aesthetes, who feel identification with nature and express a heretofore suppressed individual subjectivity. This standard assessment appears myopic in at least two ways: it assumes an absolute impossibility of subjectivity within pre-modern poetic conventions, and it ignores the resoundingly neo-classic character of the reputedly "liberated" poetry of Chāyāvād. Moreover, this dominating category of "nature," and its description or love for it, subsumes or elides virtually all other qualities ascribed to European Romanticism. In this manner, Nature begins to represent poetic modernity so completely, and its valuation appears so utterly linked to a colonialist teleology of progress, that it simply demands redress. We must look past this "liberation narrative" of what Chāyāvād brought to Hindi modernity for the epistemological richness informing nature-poetry and writing about it. Hence the special place of "nature-in-literature" in the Hindi critical context derives from particular readings and adaptations of European enlightenment thinking, enmeshed with familiar pleasures—poetic and theoretical—of the poetic menagerie of *cātaka* bird, Spring, the flower, and the bee.

Chapter 3

Nature in Translation

> In poetry, as in scenes of nature, what enchants the heart
> Is not the beauty of each separate part.
>
> —Ratnākar, translating Pope[1]

What did colonial authors *make* of English literature? This is a question essential to any examination of the part that English literary Nature played in Hindi's own transforming literary Nature, and critical assessments of it. The question of what Hindi authors took, or not, from English literature is a deeply complex question. The history of translation in the colonial era is long and complex, and arguably the English canon was never more successfully fetishized than among the elite segments of the colonial Indian public; on the other hand, far more colonial-era Indians responded to or cognized English literary norms in ways we still have not examined. This is an attempt to reckon with the large question of how for the Hindi-consuming public in the late nineteenth century interpreted English literature.

It is tempting to gloss over the story of reading English in the colony, on one hand, as a tragic story of the imposition of British cultural aspirations, and on the other, a mine of possible traces of "resistance," "sly civility," and other bywords of post-colonial theory. Indeed, in the theme of Nature we see both imposition of a British literary value, and as we shall see below, an emergent politics in its Hindi reinvention. But why should we leave it at this? How did such processes of imposition, reception, and re-valuation occur at the ground-level of texts, their aesthetic features, and literally, their words? This chapter presents in detail two late nineteenth-century Hindi (that is, Braj Bhāṣā) translations of English literary texts that are important to Hindi literary historiography for two reasons: first, both of them were among the early translations of long English poetic works and had achieved considerable public prominence as such; second, they were both translations not of Romantic poetry, as we might suspect, but rather eighteenth-century works of Oliver Goldsmith and Alexander Pope. The first of these translations was published in 1889 by Śrīdhar Pāṭhak, of Goldsmith's *Deserted Village* (1770). The second was published in 1897 by Jagannāth Dās "Ratnākar," of Pope's "Essay on Criticism" (1711).

The continued interest in eighteenth-century authors has already been noted in passing by Gauri Viswanathan and Sudhir Chandra. Viswanathan noted "the preponderance of eighteenth-century neo-classical writers in the government curriculum in the mid-nineteenth century, as opposed to the Romantic writers in the missionary curriculum," and observes that while in England the two streams were fused together, in India the imagery of the Romantics happened to better serve the Christian cultural mission.[2] Neither of these Hindi translators attended Christian schools, and therefore may have had little exposure to the high Romantic poets, according to Viswanathan's theory. Further, Harish Trivedi has commented that among the earliest works translated from English into Hindi from the 1870s,

> were not only plays by Shakespeare . . . but also somewhat surprisingly assorted works of the eighteenth century. It would appear that, with the notorious Arnoldian devaluation of the classics of eighteenth century English poetry . . . it was the body of neo-Augustan classics which still constituted the latest glories of English literature whose reputation was safe and whose place in the canon assured.[3]

Trivedi's assessment of the power of canon for the colonial translator certainly seems correct. One also wonders how much our translators, trained in Braj poetics, felt more formal affinity with the pre-Romantic, Augustan classics, replete with end-stopped heroic couplets, rather than with the more foreign, amorphous metrics of the late Romantics. At any rate, the older sections of the English canon clearly took substantial hold of the Hindi literary imagination, perhaps even more so than in other Indian languages.[4] It is the transmutation of these texts and their particular lexicons that will concern us here, especially in relation to the aestheticized realm of the pastoral landscape and the question of critical standards of poetic truth—that is, nature as a place of social memory and subsequent alienation and loss, and Nature as an aesthetical ontology.

Śrīdhar Pāṭhak's Ūjaṛ gām (The Desolate Village)

Śrīdhar Pāṭhak (1859–1928) was considered the first "nature poet" in Hindi, to whom literary histories have ascribed the values of "Romanticism" and a concomitant love for one's homeland.[5] Rāmacandra Śukla, arguably the most influential literary critic in Hindi, stated in his *History of Hindi Literature* that Pāṭhak is "the true founder of *svacchandatāvād (romāṇṭisizm)*" in Hindi.[6] Hazārīprasād Dvivedī wrote that Pāṭhak "gave nourishment to the love of nature (*prakṛti-prem*)."[7] A Brahman from the Braj region near Agra, from a family of practicing Vaishnava pandits, Pāṭhak received some traditional education in Sanskrit at home, and attended educational institutions in Arts and Law set up by the British, in both vernacular and English mediums. In fact, his English was excellent, and he perhaps was the most English-inclined of the renowned Hindi poets of his generation. As a young man he published poetry on devotional themes, but from the beginning had an inclination toward "natural" genres of the description of the seasons, in Braj Bhāṣā,[8] and also published several poems on social themes and patriotic topics. He published frequently in the burgeoning periodical press of the day, in both Braj and Khaṛī Bolī Hindi, and only a smattering in English.

He published an early didactic quasi-Khari Boli poem in 1887, *Jagat sacāī sār* (Digest on the truth of the world) on finding god in nature and deducing truth, in an apparent attempt to ameliorate superstition.[9] Thus, his engagement with "nature" in poetry seems to have been in an exposition of god-in-nature along the lines of Romantic poets reading the divine in the landscape, as well as through precepts of scientific method. Notably, he exhibits an enumerative style we will find perennially in later decades of "nature description," as he explains, "[God's] presence and power you will know only in things": "All of these types of birds, all colors of flowers / These swaying creepers in the forest. . . . / These rivers, these lakes and ponds, the humming of the bees on the flowers / In sweet tones in the arbor of dense and wonderful trees," and so on. In these, he concludes, "appears the lila of god, wondrous and unsurpassed." Finally, he labels all of this as material nature, in the Persian and Sanskrit terms: "Some call that nature (*kudrat*), which some call maya.[10]

Nature is described as an amassment of *things* or perhaps subjects, as in the subject matter of a literary work (*vastu*). These natural objects are the handiwork of God, and also thereby a part of God's play (lila), which is evocative of the play of Krishna. The objects themselves are familiar ones, enumerated in a variety of Sanskritic contexts, although not so compactly. Although this poem is really a minor entry in the annals of the Hindi canon, it gives an early example of several potent tropes of the later, more universally recognized "nature description" in Hindi poetry and its pointedly enumerative technique.

Pāṭhak's longtime career with the British government[11] allowed him to travel extensively to the British hill stations of Nainital, Simla, and Mussoorie, and locations in the Himalayan foothills form the subject matter of much of his poetry. English portions of his diary indicate he used the English vocabulary of natural beauty: he saw "grand wild scenery" and took a photograph "at a romantic site."[12] His long poems "Beauty of Kashmir" (1904) (discussed in Chapter 4) and "Dehra Dun" (1915) received acclaim as early travel/nature description poetry in Hindi. After a personal conflict with an English official in Simla, Pāṭhak resigned from government work altogether, and dedicated himself to literary concerns, hosting many salons in his Allahabad bungalow. Notably, in the 1910s his poetry turned quite nationalist in tone, despite rather loyalist statements in the same period.[13] Pāṭhak figures in literary histories primarily as a translator of Goldsmith and writer of "nature poetry" on "natural scenes," and thereby as an exemplar of "Romantic influence," which in turn entailed a "love of nature." Śukla wrote that "Pāṭhak described nature the most among the poets of his era, and because of this he is called a worshiper of nature. . . ."[14] In the words of a widespread biography, "At the foundation of his independent style was his love of nature,"[15] and in a significant conflation of "Romantic" and "English," "Pāṭhak was a poet of Romantic tendencies. For this reason, his attraction to the English poet Goldsmith was natural."[16]

Pāṭhak published his translation of Goldsmith's "The Hermit" in 1886, under the title *Ekāntavāsī yogī* (The Solitary Yogi), a work hailed as the beginning of Romanticism (*svacchandatāvādī dhārā* or "stream of the movement of freedom") in Hindi.[17] Śukla, writing in 1929, would consider it a radical break from convention, as a work inspiring the Khaṛī Bolī movement, "a love story whose touching quality is similar to that found in the songs of illiterate women," and a story of universal appeal among "men and women of all countries and classes."[18] Goldsmith was counted among the most translated authors of late nineteenth-century India;[19] he was an established author in the English curricula on the subcontinent[20] and would remain so into the coming decades.[21] He had been translated at least once before in Hindi, in a collection of his *Deserted Village* and *Traveller* with Parnell's *Hermit* and other verse in 1881.[22] In contrast to this now obscure 1881 translation of Goldsmith, Pāṭhak's somewhat loose and expanded translation of *The Hermit* in a folksy metrical style met with a positive reception among the literati, including favorable reviews in the *Indian Magazine* and *Homeward Mail*. Several gushingly positive reviews of *The Solitary Yogi* cited its salubrious injection of "Nature" itself into Indian literature, and framed the significance of Goldsmith in translation in terms of realism, rationality, and corollary material gain in the world. Conversely, Indian poetry was portrayed as in dire need of corrections of its pathologies, namely extravagance and an absence of the correct sympathies.

> It is obviously an attempt, on the part of an observing man, to lead his countrymen from the extravagance of romance, and to induce them to realise the more satisfying beauties of Nature. Such an effort . . . would be most beneficial to India. The exuberance of hyperbole which disfigures Oriental verse and legend lifts the mind into the clouds of dreamland, and weakens the practical virtues which make a people great. The simplicity of Nature, on the other hand, . . . keeps the mind within the range of fact and probability. . . . he will really benefit his country by inducing Indians to take delight in the realities of Nature.[23]

Pāṭhak, here condescendingly referenced as the "observing man," likely took inspiration from this sort of praise to continue on to translate *The Deserted Village* and *The Traveller* in 1889 and 1902, respectively, though it is uncertain to what extent he saw these projects as ones to "benefit his country." "Delight" was indubitably a familiar pursuit for him, but finding its inspiration in "realities" per se—with all the connotative weight of science and truth of the term—surely entailed an epistemological flexibility, if Pāṭhak did indeed define his task in this way. By 1900, critics in Hindi had sung his praises for his realism and his putative political underpinnings for his translations. "Like Carlyle or Malthus, he tries to take the minds of the readers toward real and burdensome things, and with this intention he has translated English poetry also," wrote the Miśrabandhu brothers, who also lauded his avoidance of *śṛṅgāra* and "obscenity" as found in traditional poets.[24]

Goldsmith's original subject matter in *The Hermit* would have appealed to an Indian audience, already familiar with hermit ascetics, women proving their love through vows (*vrat*) of penance (e.g., the myth of the Hindu god Shiva and goddess Pārvatī, who performs her own austerities in order to win Shiva's affections and thereby seal their union, the practice of women vowing to undergo hardship for the sake of their husbands, etc.), fantastic disguises, and coincidence (e.g., epic and bardic narrative traditions of all types). The Hermit's welcome of the stranger would resonate with pre-colonial images of the hospitable priest at the ashram in the jungle (e.g., *Abhijñānaśākuntalam, Rāmāyaṇa*), and of exile in the forest (*Rāmāyaṇa*); his vegetarianism no doubt seemed uncannily familiar to the audience.[25] Angelina's description of pastoral love ("And when, beside me in the dale / He caroll'd lays of love / His breath lent fragrance to the gale / And music to the grove," etc.) would easily translate into the landscape of the flute-playing Krishna's amours with the cowherdesses, and this is exactly what occurs in Pāṭhak's translation, which contains several unmistakable allusions to Krishna poetry. The pastoral clearly translated well.

Delving again into Goldsmith, Pāṭhak published his translation of *The Deserted Village* in 1889, with the title *Ūjaṛ gām* (*The Desolate Village*), connoting not only a village bereft of people, but laid waste in ruin. The poem was dedicated to his friend Frederic Pincott,[26] whose letter on Pāṭhak's previous poem, *Solitary yogi*, was included in the preface. Pincott wrote, "Your verses, I trust, will direct the Indian mind to the beauties of nature and to the tender feelings of the heart. Extravagance of language and artificiality of sentiment characterize and disfigure Oriental Verse. . . ."[27] Thus, Pāṭhak's translation of Goldsmith was seen as an exercise not just in "disciplining," "extravagance," and "artificiality," but a project to create a new kind of superior taste, a taste for authenticity through "nature" and "feeling." As for Pāṭhak's intentions for this translation, he states little in the English Preface, but indicates an unease with the cultural gap between the original and translation: "the subject being purely English and the rendering, for the greater part, closely literal, I do not know how far the present work will prove acceptable to the non-English knowing reader, although no pains have been spared on my part to make it interesting."

In his Hindi verse introduction, however, he suggests another perspective, in which he sees Goldsmith's poetry as something resembling more than a "purely English" subject, but something to be adopted, and in some sense consumed. Addressing his words to the supporters of Hindi, *rasik* gentlemen, "always tasting anew the nectar of the pleasures of verse / bees drinking the honey of new poetry, lovers of new flowers," he admits, conventionally, to the faults in his work, and then urges them in closing, "Take this up with a compassionate heart; O! embrace it; / consider this as something of 'one of your own,' and make it your own." Here his diction suggests a sense of collective identity: this Hindi translation is an "item" or "product" (*vastu*, literally "thing"), of "one of your own" (*apane jana*, your own people). His appeal might also suggest that the translated content of this Hindi text, and metonymically English poetry, *should be* their own. Whether Pāṭhak meant for his audience to realize some fraternal relation with Goldsmith's poetry or to strain to embrace this foreign work, we cannot know.

Entirely absent was any indication of Pāṭhak's perceptions of the work's political significance. While from our contemporary perspective, Goldsmith's *Deserted Village* is a work with radical political potential, Pāṭhak and the critics, who have vaunted the Goldsmith translations as the beginning of nature poetry in Hindi, have remained silent on the politics of the work per se. It is as if the critical tradition in Hindi picked up precisely the critical currents of nineteenth-century England, in which (in the words of a recent literary historian) "critics' focus on literary and biographical matters . . . concealed the poem's politics and replaced the political with the pastoral Goldsmith."[28] In Hindi criticism as well Goldsmith clearly represented the pastoral (and by extension, for them, Romanticism generally), but it may be possible to see how this "nature poetry" retained some of its political force in Hindi translation, through the examination below.

The poem was written in a somewhat modified version of the literary dialect Braj Bhāṣā.[29] To use literary Braj Bhāṣā itself was to participate in a sort of rural nostalgia established since the sixteenth century. For older authors, its nostalgic possibilities ironically compounded with the arguments for its unsuitability for modern literature. Pāṭhak pointed out in the preface to the third edition that it was only natural that he had used Braj Bhāṣā, which approximated the deserted village itself[30]—indeed, Braj Bhāṣā was to be supplanted by the style of speech, Khari Boli, as the dominant register of Hindi poetry circa 1910.

However, the nostalgic possibilities, per se, of the landscape portrayed in Goldsmith's original *Deserted Village*—as in the words of Goldsmith, "These were thy charms—but all thy charms are fled"—are here transfigured in Pāṭhak's Indianized *Desolate Village*. The landscape for Pāṭhak partakes of the theological status of Braj's nature, perpetually "present" as lila. Pāṭhak imparted this landscape through a lexicon familiar to an audience that heard and read of the setting of Krishna's romances, which creates striking differences from Goldsmith's original. Compare Pāṭhak's first two stanzas (in rather literal translation) with Goldsmith's one[31]:

Pāṭhak's Ūjaṛ gām	*Goldsmith's Deserted Village*
O Dear Auburn, best of all villages,	Sweet Auburn! loveliest village of the plain;
Where hard-working farmers reside, happiness and plenty complete.	Where health and plenty cheered the labouring swain,
Where the delightful season of spring comes early,	Where smiling spring its earliest visit paid,
	And parting summer's lingering blooms delayed:

And at the time of going, the flowers and fruit linger late.
The very lovely handsome arbors of greenery,
Full of splendor, beauty, pleasure, masses of happiness all.
Pleasing to the hearts of the innocent and carefree,
The lovely spots of the meeting places of my youth.
Just the thought of "sport" itself was dear to us,
All the happy time passed by with bliss.
How many times have I wandered about in your green lands,
Where all scenes appeared to my heart dear with the happiness of the humble.
How many times have I stopped, gazing towards the beauty;
Here a shaded cottage, there the beauty of farmland.
The spring flows always, the moving water-mill shines;
Upon the nearby foothill a church pleases the heart.
The shade of the "Hawthorn" bush in which
There is a row of stools of various coverings.
Where the talkative elders gossip,
And the lover speaks his affection to the ear of his beloved.

Dear lovely bowers of innocence and ease,
Seats of my youth, when every sport could please,
How often have I paused on every charm,
The sheltered cot, the cultivated farm,
The never-failing brook, the busy mill,
The decent church that topt the neighbouring hill,
The hawthorn bush, with seats beneath the shade,
For talking age and whispering lovers made!

At first glance, Pāṭhak's translation not only doubles the length of this initial scene, but exaggerates the terms of beauty. In fact, these terms that appear redundant merely reflect the surfeit of synonyms for "beautiful," etc., in common poetic descriptions of the visual excess of beauty, common in Sanskritic literature generally, and often driven by metrical demands. To our point here, several of these terms are culturally loaded in particularly

Indian ways, reflecting how beauty "operates" in a Sanskritic context: the visual elements of this village scene possess *rasa,* "shine," "please the heart." This latter phrase, from the verb *moh-*, "to intoxicate," would lead the audience further toward a reading of the landscape as one of Krishna's lila, as would the particular verbs of *ḍol-* (to wander), and *nihār-* (to gaze, as upon a beloved, etc.). Indeed, lines 5 and 6 could be taken straight from Braj Bhāṣā poetry on Krishna frolicking among the arbors of Braj with his lady-loves.[32] "Splendor, beauty, pleasure, masses of happiness" hardly mimics Goldsmith's original; rather, Pāṭhak recasts the scene according to another poetic standard, which requires the expansion of Goldsmith's "lovely" and "charming" scene into one more intensely so, with words whose emotional connotations do more than merely supplement[33] the nostalgic intention of the original, but rather redefine it as a quite familiar space of pre-colonial love. A panoply of other figures in the poem appear Indianized as well, more or less co-opting Goldsmith's bucolic village and its inhabitants to the Indian setting.[34] Certain similes translated comfortably into Hindi, despite their foreign source, and Goldsmith's statements concerning the meaninglessness of wealth and desire also translated easily into the Hindu context. In fact, Pāṭhak demonstrated in his notes following his even greater intent to transcreate. His notes include several "alternative verses," which are even more Braj-ified, and in one case labeled a "description of the village pleasures of our United Provinces."[35] Although in the middle of the poem, Pāṭhak retains a reference to "England" as the location of the poem, despite this ambiguity of place, Pāṭhak's project was clearly one seeking consonances between Goldsmith's English/Irish village scene and an Indian one.

Goldsmith's village is, of course, oft described with evocative descriptions of natural decay: "no more thy glassy brook reflects the day / but choked with sedges, works its weary way";[36] "Sunk are thy bowers in shapeless ruin all, / And the long grass o'ertops the mouldering wall";[37] "Thy glades forlorn confess the tyrant's power. / Here, as I take my solitary rounds, / Amidst thy tangling walks and ruined grounds, / And . . . return to view / Where once the cottage stood and the hawthorn grew."[38] These phrases are in fact rather inert in Hindi translation, accurately enough rendered but without the emotional effect of those verses idealized as the Braj landscape, and without the emotional effect of wistful nostalgia that Goldsmith must have intended. The particular pastoral of Goldsmith's original was thus altered a bit in its overall effect in Hindi, to be less evocatively gloomy.

This is not to say that the plight of the village was also lost in translation. As is well known, Goldsmith's pastoral, in *The Deserted Village* and other works, was inherently political. How we might read the political import of Goldsmith's poem in this Indian context is a question for which there is no straightforward answer. Goldsmith's original text was one of some controversy: in its political position bemoaning the fruits of agricultural capitalism, and its apparent amalgamation of the English and Irish village. In his dedication of the work to Sir Joshua Reynolds, he indicated that his description of the village was debatable in his own time, as his ascription of the cause of its ruin to luxury.[39] The work inspired much debate and even parodies, while becoming a standard of curricula and anthologies. Decades later, T. B. Macaulay wrote that Goldsmith fell victim to another logical sin, of "describing ill," i.e., that the poem is an amalgam of "the happy days of a true English village," but in its decay, an Irish village. "The felicity and misery which Goldsmith has brought close together belong to two different countries, and two different stages in the progress of society. . . . [H]e has produced something that never was and never will be seen in any part of the world. . . ."[40] The question then remains: what did Pāṭhak make of the politics of this poem, and what did he intend with his Indianized translation of it? Further, what does all of this mean for a Hindi conception of nature?

Pāṭhak's "desolate village" was described in a manner like Goldsmith originally intended, that is, of a place that combined both pastoral ideals and negative realities, and an archetype that represented all villages, whose condition reflects upon national political morality. In keeping with the "representative" nature of Goldsmith's Auburn for "the village," Pāṭhak's choice of Braj Bhāṣā for the language of the text evoked Indic pastoral poetry of Krishna's frolics in Braj, but did not necessarily denote the particular geographic area of Braj, since the dialect was a cosmopolitan vernacular for poetic use; at most we can assume the delineation of the United Provinces, as his postscript verses indicate. While it is reasonable to assume that Pāṭhak was interested in discourse of the day surrounding the state of Indian villages, it is unclear to what extent and how Pāṭhak saw the conditions described in Goldsmith in his Indian surroundings. For instance, a "deserted village" would have been difficult to find in United Provinces in 1889.[41] Goldsmith's description of tenant evictions ("His seat . . . / indignant spurns the cottage from the green"[42]) and emigration ("thy children leave the land"[43]) would not seem in themselves terribly compelling topics for Pāṭhak; Goldsmith's land alienation differed from the North Indian experience substantially, and Pāṭhak himself was fairly removed from the social groups and regions experiencing emigration to the West Indies, which furthermore did not create population depletion. The threat of famine certainly was present, but had not been so extreme at that time to be an obvious contemporary Indian reference for Pāṭhak's transcreation. It therefore may be no accident that Pāṭhak's village is not "deserted" as in Goldsmith's original, but rather ūjaṛ, uprooted, overturned, in distress.

What does ring true in the U.P. (United Provinces) context is Goldsmith's characterization of evil landowners, known for exorbitant rent demands and usurious credit lending in the late nineteenth century. As an agrarian historian has written of this social world: "the zamindar-creditor, . . . with his concentration of local power, . . . [lived] for immediate returns, . . . all the more desirable in view of the constant need to spend lavishly on ceremonial and the law courts in order to win prestige and deter competitors."[44] Analyzing the agrarian political economies of Goldsmith and Pāṭhak's respective locations and eras is obviously beyond the scope of this study; nevertheless, at the level of rhetoric it is easy to construe the relationship of this zamindari—a category overlapping with heredity nobility and its concomitant courtly pomp—to the ruinous luxury described by Goldsmith: "Ill fares the land, to hastening ills a prey, / Where wealth accumulates and men decay;" "along the lawn where scattered hamlets rose, / Unwieldy wealth and cumbrous pomp repose."[45] However, while this limited rhetorical analogy may be drawn, it would not translate to any especial sympathy for the peasantry on the part of a man like Pāṭhak, as in Goldsmith's lamentation of the demise of "a bold peasantry, their country's pride."[46]

Here it is useful to look at a verse exemplifying the work of "tyrants" upon the land:

Pāṭhak's Ūjaṛ gām	*Goldsmith's Deserted Village*
Amidst those bowers where so much splendor spread, The harsh hand of injustice appears. Where glimmeringly shone the dense pretty greenery, Now has become barren, its goodness ruined. Fallen into one hand, all your beautiful earth The plough fields yield half, the land remains all waste.[47]	Amidst thy bowers the tyrants' hand is seen, And desolation saddens all thy green: One only master grasps the whole domain And half a tillage stints thy smiling plain.[48]

Here in the Hindi there is no "tyrant" per se, rather the "harsh hand of injustice." The translation contains within its vocabulary the monetization of "tillage": "plough fields," *jot,* can signify by extension the rent paid by a cultivator; the term for "half" here, *adhūrā*, more generally signifies "incomplete"; hence, this line can be read as a comment more directly on the financial distress of cultivators: "the rent produced is half" rather than "the fields yield half."

Further, we can also read anti-colonial intimations in the linkage of this landowning wealth with "trade's proud empire," and "trade's unfeeling train," which might "dispossess the swain" in a "rage of gain." The British themselves could quite easily fill out the metonym of "Trade" that Goldsmith decried. While the exact relation of these two entities, the zamindar and the British, is not clarified in Pāṭhak's text, it is reasonable to see the latter as exacerbating the former's rapacious demands, as supplying the new à la mode goods of the former's mansions and palaces. Hence, the zamindars, both of old and of the present, could represent the agents of luxury and downfall, and the British could represent trade, gain, empire—the supplier of luxury.

In a passage that strongly implies a political and cultural critique, Pāṭhak writes the following, translating Goldsmith's critique of Luxury:

Pāṭhak's Ūjaṛ gām	*Goldsmith's Deserted Village*
How does your bombast [*mada*], which appears at first as a deceitful happiness Spread pleasure, in the end to destroy? Kingdoms keep being enlarged by you, to a sickly uplift [*unnati*] Exercising a prideful power they don't possess.[49]	How do thy [luxury's] potions, with insidious joy, Diffuse their pleasure only to destroy! Kingdoms by thee, to sickly greatness grown, Boast of a florid vigour not their own.[50]

Most critical is the term *unnati*, translated here as "uplift," and a very particular rendition of Goldsmith's term "greatness," for which many other more literal translations would be possible. Instead of one of the many terms for "greatness" found in Sanskrit, Pāṭhak chose *unnati*, a contemporary word, and an exceedingly loaded word in its time. This *unnati* usually functioned as a calque for English terms like "progress," and "uplift" (as in "social uplift"), and later "development." Hariścandra himself had used the term in his motto about the "progress of one's own language" ("progress in one's language is the source of all progress") in his famous appeal for the expansion of Hindi,[51] and it would become a veritable byword of the times, as Pratāpanārayaṇ Miśra wrote in his wry 1893 essay, "The Great To-do about Progress (*unnati*)."[52] It was, in other words, a term integral to ideas of reform among Indian intellectuals, and precisely a term that exemplified the English colonizer's vision of their moral and cultural purpose in India. That Pāṭhak chose this reading of "greatness" cannot have been accidental; *unnati* would necessarily signify more than mere "greatness." Possibly this *unnati* signified technological development—this greatness is after all that of "Luxury." In alluding to the dangerous intoxicating potions of luxury, and false claims to power, Pāṭhak could be mocking the invocation of *unnati* as "progress" by those zamindars and royalty who were slaves to luxury. However, there is a distinct possibility that Pāṭhak intended this amalgam of luxury, intoxication, and progress to represent England herself, as of 1889 a most important agent of trade, which Goldsmith had accused of usurping the land and dispossessing its people with its "unfeeling train." While Goldsmith's allusion to land evictions did not translate into Pāṭhak's Indian context, the feeling of injustice wrought by usurpation and dispossession certainly did.

As Goldsmith turned to Poetry in an apostrophe near the end of the text, Pāṭhak transforms these to words suitable for the current climate of criticism for Braj poetry, of *śṛṅgāra*, of the "extravagance of romance" and for "Oriental poetry."

Pāṭhak's Ūjaṛ gām	***Goldsmith's Deserted Village***
And you, poetry, the sweet most beautiful maiden	And thou, sweet Poetry, thou loveliest maid,
Always the first to abandon the land of sensual pleasure	Still first to fly when sensual joys invade;
You, powerless in these fallen sinful times	Unfit, in these degenerate times of shame,
To obtain good fame or affect hearts	To catch the heart or strike for honest fame;
O! heart-enchanting goddess!. . . .[53]	Dear charming nymph!. . . .
. . .	. . .
Explain again that the kingdom which is possessed of its own strength	Teach him, that states of native strength possest,
Although totally penniless, is still a place of happiness.[54]	Though very poor, may still be very blest.[55]

Fittingly in this Hindi context of consternation on language and literature, Poetry will proclaim the integrity of her people.

Surely Pāṭhak was well aware of the historical context underlying Goldsmith's *Deserted Village*, and he likely did not consider his translation as purely an academic exercise. Indian feeling of commonality with the Irish was palpable in the 1880s and beyond.[56] Pāṭhak's own diary testifies to his interest in 1894 in Dadabhai Naoroji, promoter of self-rule and recently elected Member of Parliament.[57] Very likely he knew of the political controversies surrounding Goldsmith's depiction, and even Macaulay's faulting of the poem for its geographical/historical liberties. Indeed, perhaps Pāṭhak felt freer to use the trope of the village for an ideological point because of Goldsmith's free use of the deserted village as a locus for ideology, even if ultimately a mostly aestheticized enunciation of such. With a plethora of lexical options before him, and despite metrical demands, Pāṭhak chose words cloaked in pointedly extra-textual connotations, located in his own social milieu.

If "nature description" for Pāṭhak is somewhat subsumed by questions of social relations, this feature might also pertain to the political undercurrent of Goldsmith's "Village." What then could explain the fact that *Ūjaṛ Gām*, Pāṭhak, and Goldsmith's *Deserted Village* have become so identified in Hindi literary criticism with "nature poetry" per se? Given that Pāṭhak's nature appears as consonant with the pre-colonial nature of Braj and Sanskrit, what then constitutes modern "nature description?" It seems plausible that the generically divinized character of the English Nature of the eighteenth century and the idealized Braj landscape merged into a landscape of emotional excess, the other-worldly (*alaukik*) "sublime" and unremittingly beautiful paradisiacal space of Vaishnava lila, elaborated bit by bit in devotional poetry, and through the wide-scope lens of nostalgia for the countryside.

Nature as a place of ruin—"The desolate village" notwithstanding—did not recur often in Hindi poetry (at least until the 1940s). Nor did the terrifying aspects of nature so integral to the Romantic sublime have much truck in the Hindi poetic world (until circa 1935, the date of J. S. Prasad's famous *Kāmāyanī*). It is perhaps significant that one of Pāṭhak's few *English* poems *does* contain such a "gloomy" and "stern" view of the Himalayas: "Where to the groaning winds stern thunder speaks; / And Heaven's orbs are longest lost in gloom. / And nothing reigns but vapour, blast and boom."[58] However, the critic Śukla, in 1929, was correct in qualifying Pāṭhak's nature as one apart from realism: ". . . it is necessary to say here that [Pāṭhak's] worship [of nature] was limited to only those forms that are pleasing and joyful to man, or grand and beautiful."[59]

In contrast, early Hindi versions of literary Nature seem to emphasize not only a pleasure of both Indic and English provenance, but to link natural and/or geographic spaces with the *lok* or *jana* ("the people"). This phenomenon might be linked to poems such as Pāṭhak's *Ūjaṛ Gām*, which politicize through their nostalgia, and provide further evidence of the truism in English studies that poetic nature and its social form as the rural, can create nationalist sentiment. While this phenomenon did travel to colonial India, as part of a "global Romanticism,"[60] in which "the East" was necessary for such potent national idealizations, the poetic nature and the *social* poetic nature of Hindi literature arrived at its politics differently, and in an aesthetically quite complex fashion.

Ratnākar and His "Samālocanādarś" ("An ideal of criticism")

In rather different circumstances about a decade later, a traditional cosmopolite of Varanasi also translated English verse into Braj Bhāṣā, and not merely verse, but a work of poetic theory, Alexander Pope's "Essay on Criticism." Jagannāth Dās "Ratnākar" was born at the center of the elite literary life of Varanasi in 1866.[61] He was the great grandson of a court-connected gentleman of Lucknow with ancestral links to the Mughal court of Delhi. His father, Puruṣottam Dās, was a wealthy Agaravāl merchant of Varanasi and a friend of Bhāratendu Hariścandra, the "father of modern Hindi literature." Thus, Ratnākar literally grew up within the literary ferment of the United Provinces elite, amongst Hariścandra's social circle. Ratnākar studied English (and presumably Bengali) at the Bengali *ṭolā* high school, and then later at Queen's College. He passed his BA in English, and began an MA in Persian and a law degree, both unfinished. As would be expected, he was well-versed in Urdu poetry. He began to write in Braj and Braj alone around 1890, around the time of his brief work as secretary for the Raja of Awagarh in the Etah district near Agra. Ratnākar thus emerged from a cultural milieu of a merchant class of growing economic and cultural power, which embraced high cultural forms of many varieties. These included not only the company of poets and circulation of texts in Braj, Urdu, and Persian, but British-style public organizations for educational or scholarly pursuits.[62]

Ratnākar was also intimately connected to the burgeoning print culture of the era and its literati. Ratnākar was an active member of the Nāgarī Pracāriṇī Sabhā, the first and for thirty years the premier organization promoting Hindi (i.e., most any form of Hindi-Urdu in the Devanagari script, and later Sanskritized Hindi) in political and cultural spheres. This association was natural not only because of his social position, but also due to his interest in collecting old manuscripts, an enterprise carried out by the NPS under the direction of Śyāmasundar Dās. From circa 1888–89, Ratnākar had pursued the acquisition of older Braj Bhāṣā *rasik*, Vaishnava, and Sikh-oriented manuscripts through his social connections with courts in other regions.[63] Ratnākar became personal secretary to the Raja of Ayodhya in 1903, a man with literary interests himself. Later Ratnākar assisted his widow, the Maharani, who commissioned and rewarded him for his 1921 *Gaṅgāvataraṇ*, which reward he donated to the Nāgarī Pracāriṇī Sabhā for an annual prize for Braj Bhāṣā poetry for "the advancement [*unnati*] of Braj." The work was based on the story from the *Rāmāyaṇa*, but valued by later critics for its "nature description." He is commonly considered the "last great Braj poet" and verses from *Century of verses on Uddhav* (Uddhavaśatak,1929) remain common in university curricula. Much of Ratnākar's poetic output was published only in periodicals during his lifetime, and in these works we find a number of *kavitta* verses on topical themes of nationalism, filtered through the lens of *vīra rasa*. Until shortly before his death in 1932, he worked in Varanasi on the *Sūrasāgara* critical edition project for the NPS.

Ratnākar published a translation of Alexander Pope's "Essay on Criticism" in 1897 in the first issue of the magazine issued by the Nāgarī Pracāriṇī Sabhā. As its Hindi title, "Samālocanādarś," indicated, Ratnākar considered the "Essay" an "ideal," "exemplar," or perhaps even a "classic" of criticism, as the term *ādarś* would imply, echoing the seventh-century Daṇḍin's famous *Kāvyādarśa*, a treatise on poetics. This was not a literal translation; he used Braj Bhāṣā verse,[64] which required some alteration of sense, and he altered the proper names to those of Indian—and Sanskrit—origin. Furthermore, Ratnākar stopped short of finishing the "Essay," and instead appended several of his own verses, which contained his dicta for contemporary Hindi poets.

It is unclear exactly where and how Ratnākar read Pope's "Essay on Criticism," but very likely, he read an excerpt for his English MA curriculum.[65] There is no foreword or other text explicating his intention in this translation, or the motivation to include this "Essay" in the very first issue of the NPS magazine, but from its inclusion and its interpolated verses we can safely surmise that Ratnākar thought Pope's essay to be relevant to the current state of Hindi/Braj Bhāṣā poetry, in the midst of change from the poetic forms of old to new. While Pope had been characterized in MA-level anthologies as representative of the Augustan poets composing with a polish "sometimes degenerating into effeminacy" and possessing an "enervate grace" in contrast with preceding Restoration majesty and subsequent Romantic feeling,[66] Pope's verse was still praised as a key to English, and even universal, literary precepts, as well as for its virtuosic density of meaning and craft. The famous phrases of his *Essay on Criticism* though merely "conventional truisms, the ordinary rules of composition, and which are taught to boys as part of their prosody," according to Ward,[67] likely seemed valuable information to Ratnākar, and the epigrammatic form familiar, similar to the prosodic dicta of Sanskrit and Braj, metrically rendered in sloka and *dohā* couplets. Pope's production of "striking couplets which have lodged in all our memories," in Ward's words, would have seemed a quite naturally worthy critical-poetic goal to an author like Ratnākar, proponent of Braj poetic forms.[68]

What interests us here is not so much Pope's arguments in the original "Essay" of 1711, but rather how certain values and abstractions steeped in British Enlightenment thinking were translated and renegotiated in an Indic context. Some common Indic literary terms stood in good stead: *rasāsvādan* (tasting *rasa*) (5.2) for Taste; *sahṛday* (having heart, sympathetic) stands for Critic; *samālocanā* (examination, viewing comprehensively) for criticism (24.3). Characters also approximated the originals, though with a more religious cast. The embodied Greece is Sarasvatī (23.1), the goddess of the arts; Vālmīki, author of the epic *Rāmāyaṇa*, stands in for Homer, creating more religious overtones, which are further carried through in the "*gunau dhyāna dhari*" ("meditate on his virtues") of following line (29.7). Kalidasa appears as young Maro, Virgil; the land of Bhārat (India) as Rome (31.1). Bharata, famed ancient theorist of *rasa*, figures as Aristotle (32.6, 60.3); Timetheous appears as dramatist and theorist Bhavabhūti, and Dryden as poet Padmākar. Walsh, Pope's literary mentor, appears as Hariścandra, who had likewise encouraged the young Ratnākar. Certain redolent images in the English version, such as the "shapeless rock or hanging precipice," fall rather flat in the Hindi version, and seem to have held little interest for Ratnākar as tropes of any "natural sublime" of the English variety.

Certain equivalences in this translation hint at lives of their own in this context and suggest a certain contemporary richness. The ideal and standard of "Nature," our primary interest here, is translated directly, with *prakṛti*, throughout the text, and is used as if in itself an unproblematic term for poetics, though fundamentally associated with philosophical discourses largely disconnected from Indic poetic theory. The foregrounding of Pope's Nature in this late nineteenth-century translation was indeed a bit ironical, since in English criticism Pope had been criticized broadly many decades earlier for (among several reasons) being *un*-natural, in what was a defining controversy of the Romantic movement.[69] The opinion of the English high Romantics, thought to be so influential in the colonial Indian poetic world, here seems to have no import. Pope's "Essay" was translated by Ratnākar for the NPS magazine's inaugural issue, presumably to bring Nature and other English literary values into dialogue with Hindi poetry aficionados.

Upon examination, Pope's terms surrounding the use and function of this "Nature" appeared somewhat altered and emphasized in Ratnākar's translation. Given the many lexical choices at hand, which might have rendered these particular verses more literally, Ratnākar's translation clearly represents an interpretation, and one tailored to the Hindi audience. For example, consider the new cast Pope's original takes in Ratnākar's version of the following verse:

Ratnākar's "Samālocanādarś"	***Pope's "Essay on Criticism"***
First improve your thought, looking at the effect/influence of Nature, By her method of assessing, which is always the same *rasa*/ homogenous:[70]	First follow Nature, and your judgment frame By her just standard, which is still the same:

Ratnākar's translation of "looking" to the "effect/influence of Nature" (*prakṛti-prabhāv nihāri*) was quite straightforward, in comparison to his translation of Nature's purpose to "frame" and set a "same" "standard," which he translated with the more morally loaded act of "improving,"[71] and the concrete term referring to a scientific inquiry and testing or assessing, *jāñc*. The "sameness" of this standard is rendered not with the more obvious Hindi gloss of "to remain unchanged," or "the same as before" or such like, but rather with the interesting *ika-rasa-vārau*, a term for "homogenous," having a more aesthetic connotation of something unified as one *rasa*, the aesthetic emotion at the basis of Sanskrit poetics. Pope's dictum is here made more didactic—"improve"—and more scientized—"assessing, testing"—and yet linked with an idea of a prosaically homogenous constancy that implies an eternality of aesthetic pleasure.

Similarly, Pope's "to copy Nature is to copy [ancient rules]" is rendered with some excess of meaning that is still on target for a Braj/ Hindi audience:

> Hence, learn to sing the praises of ancient precepts,
> To go down those paths is to go into the fold of devotees
> of [i.e., to follow] nature.[72]

The original "learn a just esteem" has morphed into a religiously marked *guṇa gāvana*, to sing the praises or describe the qualities of someone (often a deity), and the concept of "copying" is transformed in a way that is true to Pope's intent, but powerful and strange in Hindi for other reasons: *panth*, a term for a group of (usually religious) followers, fellow-travelers on a path, is attached to Nature itself. While Ratnākar may not have meant to infuse a religiosity into this translation, the idiom that he uses to project these hortatory statements makes use of the idiom of devotion, both familiarizing the foreign text and creating newer hybrid concepts that demanded the audience to ponder new and unlikely concatenations.

Certain concepts in Hindi serve multiple uses in translation of Pope. *Niyama*, the term for "precept," "method," "practice," etc., and related to *nīti*, "moral precepts" (a genre of courtly literature in Sanskrit and the vernaculars), glosses "maxims," "law," and other more differentiated terms in the English original, with the general effect of creating a more discipline-oriented stance. *Kavitā*, poetry itself, stands in for both the Muses and Wit, thus flattening the effect of the original, but avoiding the complication of defining Wit versus genius, which would present special difficulty in Hindi. Furthermore, this choice makes the text more explicitly, concretely about poetics, which may indicate Pāṭhak's intention for this essay in the first place. "Nation" is translated as "*nara-jāti*" in 46.5, meaning "race of men" more concretely and perhaps more faithfully to Pope's sense of "race of men."

In the Hindi literary context, certain of Pope's references become concretized in historically specific ways, which foreshadow literary trends for Hindi's future. The allegedly deleterious effects of *śṛṅgāra*, embodied particularly in the *nakha-śikha varṇana* (toenail to head description),[73] seem to rise as a specter over Ratnākar's rendering in verse 55. Pope's denial of the "exactness of peculiar parts" for the "joint force" is contextualized into a more explicit idea of bodily description, with use of *aṅgani*, parts or limbs, which are *suḍaula*, well-formed, both terms more common for bodies than "parts" per se.[74]

Ratnākar's "Samālocanādarś"	***Pope's "Essay on Criticism"***
In poetry, as in scenes of nature, what enchants the heart, Is not the beauty of each separate part.[75]	In Wit, as Nature, what affects our hearts Is not th'exactness of peculiar parts;
What we call beauty we do not consider the lip and the eye, But we call it the mixed effect, the result of all.[76]	'Tis not the lip, or eye, we beauty call, But the joint force and full result of all.

These translated verses more concretely invoke bodily descriptions; however, taken as a whole, the lines certainly engage the more theoretical senses of "separate parts" and "exactness," *aṅga* being equally idiomatic in physical and metaphysical contexts, and *suḍaula*, regularly "well-formed," standing in for "regular" in a nearby verse (57.4). Interestingly, the first line of the passage is well-colored with Braj Bhāṣā idioms of poetic/

devotional pleasure (*mana moh-* evoking Krishna's captivating presence, for "what affects our hearts"), and Pope's "Nature" is amplified as "scenes of nature," such that Ratnākar's translation seems to be teaching a new way of seeing, or "scene-ing." We can surmise here that Ratnākar saw Sanskritic landscapes as produced in "parts," with couplets recited on particular flowers, particular lips, and the comparisons therein, and that he saw the injunction of this English poet as one toward aggregation of parts into whole, the gathering of "peculiar parts" together for "joint force," "separate beauty" into a "mixed," indeed "joined" effect. The translation of this "Nature" forced Ratnākar to name what he perceived as immanent in the original, and less than obvious to the Braj/Hindi audience: that modern poetic Nature came packaged in visual scenes, named in the Hindi as "scenes" as such, and representing systematized universal truths.

The narrative of cultural decadence and decay found easy translation in 116.15–16, where the "modest fan" became the veil, symbol of female modesty, and the modest woman's blush took on the culturally inflected shyness of "*lajānā*" (to be ashamed, shy, embarrassed). In 42.1, Pope's "figures," "monstrous and mis-shap'd" become *rūpaka*s, a term technically exact in translation, meaning "something possessing a form," but commonly denoting "metaphor." As it happened, the metaphor-laden tendencies of Sanskritic and Persian poetic schools had also long been under critical attack; thus the criticism of monstrousness, likely struck the audience as one directly relevant to the oft-referenced "flights of fancy" of Oriental poetry. Unsurprisingly, Pope's remarks on Conceit are easily converted to the poetic ornament of *utprekṣā*[77] (63.1, 70.2); *alaṃkāra* itself figures as an exact translation of "ornament," the subterfuge of the bad poet:

> Poets, like painters, thus unskill'd to trace
> The naked nature and the living grace,
> With gold and jewels cover ev'ry part,
> And hide with ornaments their want of art.

In this strange coalescence of Augustan and colonial literary criticism of vernacular literary "fancifulness" and decadence, "ornament" had more concrete and political import in Braj/Hindi in 1897 than it did in English in 1711. The prevalent colonial criticisms of Indian poetry, in this chapter exemplified by Pincott's reference to disfigured Oriental verse, strongly echoed Pope's sentiment here, in this work deemed important enough for the NPS magazine's inaugural issue.

A few of Ratnākar's phrases suggest philosophical sea-changes in poetics, which are yet not fully invested in—or perhaps abjure—the vocabulary of Pope. The idea of a new kind of "real," concomitant with the Nature of Pope, inspired Ratnākar to terminology that paralleled what became the term for literary realism in Hindi literary criticism in the twentieth century—*yathārthavād*.[78] We find versions of *yathārtha* in "Samālocanādarś" used for Pope's "fit" (17.1–2, 63.3, 70.3), and *prakṛti jathāratha rūpa* for "the face of nature."

Further interest is shown in the idea of the "subject."

Ratnākar's "Samālocanādarś"	*Pope's "Essay on Criticism"*
Know the way of going of the good gait of the ancients;	Know well each Ancient's proper character;
Their songs and their use of that-which-is-described (*barnya prayojana*) in every line,[79]	His Fable, Subject, Scope in ev'ry page;

Rather than use the metrically appropriate and customary term for literary subject, *vastu*, in compound with *prayojan* (the use of), Ratnākar chose to use the adjective *barnya*, seemingly as a nominative: that which is describable, that which is to be described, that which is worthy of description. This choice seems significant, among these other bits of mounting evidence that poetic nature, as Ratnākar read Pope, was integrally related to ideas of description of the real.

In regard to Pope's theorizing on poetic license, Ratnākar's translation suggests that poetic and political theorizing do go hand in hand. In the first instance, we find that Nature as well plays a role, as in the famous line on "nature methodiz'd":

Ratnākar's "Samālocanādarś"	*Pope's "Essay on Criticism"*
Those rules of old discovered, that are not devised	Those Rules of old, discover'd, not devis'd
Are Nature, but Nature bounded, within a limited path.	Are Nature still, but Nature Methodiz'd.
Nature is but like Independence restrained	Nature, like Liberty, is but restrain'd
By the very rules she herself created.	By the same Laws which first herself ordain'd.

Those "Rules of old" are those of "Unerring Nature," "source, end, and test, of Art" of the previous verse. Pope presents these rules as not contrived or constructed, but discovered within Nature. An analogy ensues with Liberty, which is ambiguously political, both in the original and in

Hindi translation. Here Ratnākar's "Independence" (*svatantratā*), translating Pope's "Liberty," is a term that decades later became part of the anti-colonial vocabulary—the *svatrantratā sangrām* (Independence struggle) of current parlance.[80] Liberty here signifies a kind of self-sufficiency, which as Pope describes, is characterized by its acting within laws ordained by itself. The analogy with Nature, as a source of rules, and ruled by its own rules, then follows as a support for Pope's argument for his own conception of the rules of good art. Ratnākar's *svatantratā* as Liberty does the job handily, as a term that imparts the independent agency the term denotes, and also by happenstance, echoes what would become a byword of India's political Independence from the British.[81] In fact, we might consider the use of *svatantratā* as this abstract Liberty as part of the semiotic world from which its nationalist meaning emerged by the 1930s, and importantly, in the poetics of the coming decades, this term *svatantratā* remained linked with Nature.

This *svatantratā*, "independence/self-rule" also serves for Pope's License. In 35.3–4 Ratnākar translates "lucky Licence" with interesting results:

Ratnākar's "Samālocanādarś"	***Pope's "Essay on Criticism"***
If somewhere a rule is not able to be realized (*na samartha yathāratha*),[82]	If, where the rules not far enough extend,
(After all, the method for enacting all rules is to follow through to their purpose)	(Since rules were made but to promote their end)
There is a desired independence, readied and auspicious,	Some lucky Licence answers to the full
Then independence itself wields the rules of this land.[83]	Th' intent proposed, that Licence is the rule.

Svatantratā, earlier signifying Pope's Liberty, here translates Licence perfectly well. This *svatantratā* does not "answer to the full / Th' intent proposed," but is rather readied and waiting, not to be the rule, but to wield the rules, *birājai*, over this land, *tā thala*, over which other's rules cannot extend. Although Ratnākar was hardly an anti-colonial nationalist, it seems the exhortation to *yathārth* in poetry merged into a statement of Indian particularity and right to power: where British rule was not coextensive with Indian reality, Independence was "ready" to "answer in full" and to rule. The translation of Pope's original with the addition of the concrete "this land" here suggests that this very notion of Licence/*svatantratā*—poetical or philosophical—seemed to the vernacular poet to be political at its core. The subtleties of such vocabulary have to be taken into account in assessing the influence of English poetics cum politics, and especially the politics of Romanticism. The example of Ratnākar's "Samālocanādarś" does not refute such a link but complicates it. Rather than assume blithely that the poetry of English Romanticism imbued Indian youth with a revolutionary spirit, rather I would submit that this Hindi revisioning of Licence and Liberty of the pre-Romantic Pope, in an ostensibly poetic context, suggests that English texts, even poetic/critical ones, were *read* as political, at some level by Indians, and implemented for quasi-political purposes. It was eighteenth-century literary texts, and the complexities of their translation, which laid a background for the aesthetics of the full-fledged nationalism of the twentieth century.

The penultimate six verses compress Pope's original ones significantly, and translate his scenario into a post-classical Indian one, in which there is no chase of the Muses from Latium by impious arms, but "A current voice was found again in Prakrit language(s)," referring to the reputed "fall" of Sanskrit and rise of vernaculars in North India around 1000–1200 CE. The subsequent emergence of Braj Bhāṣā as dominant courtly vernacular (approximating "Thence Arts o'er all the northern world advance"), is then characterized with its familiar colonial criticism:

> Much expertise in arts spread all around;
> Pleasing poetry began in Braj Bhāṣā,
> For a long time it concealed a lack of self-restraint. (148)

Subsequently, in place of a translation of France's "Critic learning," Boileau and Horace, Ratnākar expands in a different direction.

Ratnākar's "Samālocanādarś"	*Pope's "Essay on Criticism"*
There was a breed without Sanskrit which knew nothing	But Critic learning flourish'd most in France:
And to read what they wanted of it, they encountered much difficulty;	The Rules, a Nation born to serve, obeys,
Sanskrit proponents considered *bhāṣā* abhorrent	And Boileau still in Right of Horace sways.
They recited, "*bhāṣā* is as *bhāṣā* does, . . ."	But we, brave Britons, Foreign Laws despis'd,
And the proud *bhāṣā* poet creates poetry as he likes	And kept unconquer'd and unciviliz'd;

according to the refined ways. (149)	Fierce for the Liberties of Wit, and bold, We still defy'd the Romans, as of old.

Here Pope's "Critic learning" bears little resemblance to Ratnākar's translation; instead of Pope's taunt to the French,[84] Ratnākar gives us a scene depicting (it seems) the beleaguered circumstances of vernacular (i.e., Hindi) poetry, both by those who knew little of Sanskrit, and those who did. Who these people were who knew little of Sanskrit—Muslims? the English?—is unclear. However, "We, brave Britons" in Pope's original is transformed into the indomitable "proud *bhāṣā* poet," writing poetry as he likes. Then, following Pope, Ratnākar praises the Braj Bhāṣā, or vernacular poets generally, who "restor'd Wit's Fundamental Laws," or "established firm the eternal principles of poetry and art," which derive from the ancients, and Nature:

Ratnākar's "Samālocanādarś"	***Pope's "Essay on Criticism"***
But some of them became the circle of intellectuals, Who, of diminished pride and increased knowledge, Who become brave proponents of ancient truth, And established firm the eternal principles of poetry and art. (150)	Yet some there were among the founder few, Of those who less presum'd and better knew Who durst assert the juster Ancient Cause And here restor'd Wit's Fundamental Laws.

Thus for Ratnākar, Pope's "Essay" spoke to the vernacular poet's sense of being in between literary ideals—"only" vernacular, but proudly singing poetry "as he likes," and still following "eternal principles of poetry and art."

After two more verses, Ratnākar leaves off the Pope original with his own six verses in closing. These final six verses are rather more straightforward, and blatantly hortatory in purpose, clearly linking the message of this translation of Pope to Ratnākar's own: that neo-classicism in Braj, rather than experiments in Khaṛī Bolī, is the preferred path for modern Braj/Hindi poetry.

> But alas, now how many have become destroyers of truth in this way,
> Both the poet and the appraiser (*jāñcaka*) are indifferent to the experience of *rasa*,

There is no knowledge in the heart of the poetic ornaments
of sound and meaning,
Not a scrap of talent, skill or knowledge. (154)

Writing without talent and critiquing without
discrimination,
Going around full of egoism, puffed up always, day and
night,
Mixing and matching, someone puts together a literary work,
Here nonsense, there contradictions. (155)

Not knowing what are *ativyāpti, avyāpti,* and *asambhava,*[85]
He props himself up as a litterateur, sui generis.
One becomes crazy for Khaṛī Bolī,
Another gets mixed up with writing poetry without rhyme.
(156)

Those in whose hearts are harsh restrictions on *anuprāsa,*[86]
Why don't they give up these poetic restrictions and write
prose?
Anuprāsa never diminishes the power of a good poet,
But in truth gives rise to new perceptions in the heart. (157)

Those who write Braj Bhāṣā and *anuprāsa* insipidly,
They ask the Creator for a kind hearing from men.
On behalf of these people I desire humbly from [goddess of
the arts] Sarasvatī
Somehow, put the bad understanding of their hearts to
flight. (158)

To those who are delighted by these pleasure-giving forms,
And don't always stubbornly lead others astray
Let the poet and the pleasure-giving art of poetry be true
again,
May an abundance of progress [*unnati*] remain forever in
India. (159)

Here we can see the translator taking on the poetic trends of the day of Khaṛī Bolī and (more radically) free verse, and refuting them for conventional poetic values: the happiness or pleasure, *sukh,* that poetry gives us; *rasa;* Braj Bhāṣā, not Khaṛī Bolī; the distinctions of Nyāya logic; and the basic necessity of poetic ornament, *alaṃkāra.* Integrating and summarizing his claim is Indian *unnati,* a term for "progress" or social "upliftment," inextricable from the discourses of utilitarianism and Christian mission, and by then a byword of Indian nationalist thought.

What might we surmise of Ratnākar's intent in this translation? And what might we surmise of the meaning of such a translation in his particular context? Clearly Ratnākar sees this translation as an opportunity to impart poetical and critical values to his public, a point which he directly addresses in his last verses. Further, among the poetical values Ratnākar brings forth with this translation is Pope's conception of Nature as a source of ancient eternal truths, and a source for contemporary poetic expression as well: Nature is to be followed; it produces a "joint effect" of beauty; it is not overly-ornamented. Pope's portrayal of the reign of Nature alluded to political philosophy, and specifically the power of action, and self-rule: Nature is its own dominion, like *svatantratā* itself (Liberty or Licence), which steps in to rule where others cannot. The translingual connotative shifts (to borrow Lydia Liu's term[87]) effected here in Hindi strongly suggest that Pope's "Essay on Criticism" and its philosophical underpinnings were seen as platforms for political innuendo as well as literary critique. At the very least, Pope's words translated here in Hindi signify that (a) Nature as *prakṛti* is an ideal mode, if not subject, for art, and (b) that Nature in itself is an entity ruled by its own eternal and true laws. This rational and separately sovereign quality of Nature—self-regulating, governed by the truth it represents—would imply not only the scientized nature of empiricism, but also the political possibilities of such talk of Liberty/License/*svatantratā*.

The merging of village with landscape in assessments of the meaning of Pāṭhak's *Ūjaṛ Gām* in Hindi criticism illustrates the convergence in this period of the sociopolitical with nature as an aesthetic object. The loss that is at the heart of Goldsmith's poem is more subtly implied by Pāṭhak's work, which perhaps evokes a certain modern "nostalgia" through the pastorals of Braj Bhāṣā genres, while resuscitating them for appeals to political realities or empirical reality. Ratnākar's "Samālocanādarś" suggests that he found the edicts of British eighteenth-century poetic modernity in harmony with, and usefully innovative for, the project of modern Hindi poets. Concretized as the "natural scene," as a source of eternal truths, and as a measure of fitness or commensurability—*yathārth*—, "Nature," by way of Pope, appeared implicit in his message to Hindi poets.

Chapter 4

Realizing Classical Poetics

Studies of landscape painting and poetic description in nineteenth-century Britain and its colonies have linked perspective and frame with power. The picturesque, more than simply a pleasing view, has been shown to be an object of a sort of Lacanian gaze: to frame a landscape was to dominate it. More importantly in our context here, the mimetic quality of the production of visual and verbal landscapes, striving for depth and detail as much as idealization of idyll, joined with sentimentalism for place. In the Indian context, such visual and verbal representations had entered vernacular forms via English art training and the sort of poetry addressed in the preceding chapter, thought by colonials and Indians alike to bring an "independent," even botanical, perspective to Indian poetry. In the visual arts, Raja Ravi Varmā emblematizes the Indian renditions of realism in figure and landscape, as he utilized techniques of perspective with an intention of verisimilitude previously unimportant to most Indian artists, resulting in images strikingly different from Indic predecessors in their more photographic rendering. On the other hand, this realist Indian painting took on a certain pre-Raphaelite-like haziness; "European realism" per se was used in specific ways, in certain doses, to an effect the scholars still ponder.

Hindi poetry in general was less revisionist of previous norms than Ravi Varmā's paintings. However, change comes with the emergence of "nature description" as a dominant critical directive, and the manner in which this nature description becomes thought of as realism, while its execution is much more complex than any discursive "description." The ideological ramifications of "nature in poetry" as "nature description" and the results of the part/whole distinction found in such discussion will form the focus of this chapter. What will emerge is a tripartite complex:

a persistent semiotics of *śṛṅgāra* in politicized, realist landscapes; a separation of the objects of Sanskrit metaphor from their subjects, to become "independent" subjects of poetry; and finally landscapes described in poetic prose with enumerative rhetorical features derived from Sanskrit and implying a kind of aggregative materialist power of nature and of India. Through the works of two seminal authors, Mahāvīraprasād Dvivedī and, again, Śrīdhar Pāṭhak, here we will examine the first of these themes: the convergence of classical poetics with contemporary concerns with realism, liberty, and national identity.

Mahāvīraprasād Dvivedī, His Poetry, and His Edicts for Poetry

While Ratnākar took a hiatus from publishing his Braj poetry while he worked for the Maharaja of Ayodhya, and Pāṭhak continued writing both in Braj Bhāṣā and Kharī Bolī, Mahāvīraprasād Dvivedī (1864–1938),[1] the namesake of the next literary generation, came to prominence in Hindi letters at the turn of the century. In what is now deemed the early "Dvivedī Era," circa 1900–10, and specifically in the writings of Dvivedī himself, "nature description" emerges as a literary critical topic of primary importance.

For Dvivedī, poetry was in one sense a science. In his first important essay, "Kavi-kartavya" ("The duty of the poet") of 1901 in *Sarasvatī*, Dvivedī compared proper poetic diction to the judicious practice of chemistry, and asserted that "to speak one language and use another in poetry, that is against natural law (*prākṛtik niyam*)." On the next page, he mandates that description should recall real, i.e., *yathārth*, commensurate, experience (of a scene, a feeling, etc.), and make this experience manifest in the readers. In fact, the poet should feel an identity (*tādātmya*) with the subject described, be it a human emotion or an object. But this experience is ultimately one of the world outside the poet; accurate description or account, rather than ornamented thought, is paramount:

> While writing a natural description there should be such a firm impression (*saṃskār*) within the poet that he is actually in front of the river, mountain or forest being described, seeing its glory. When the poet becomes closely connected in this way with the describable subjects of his soul (*ātma*) then his description is real (*yathārth*), and then reading his poetry, the same feelings are arisen in the hearts of the readers. In making poetry, in our thoughts, we ought not to bring in

> poetic ornaments (*alaṅkār*) by force. In the throes of description of a subject, whatever comes out of our mouth, we should let remain . . . taking that which comes with natural feeling (*prakṛtibhāva*). . . .[2]

The verisimilitude of a natural description may be paramount, but the line between subjective and objective here blurs: the poet describes the subjects, *viṣay*, with which his soul identifies, and this description can replicate the experience of the presence of the objective thing in the readers. Corollary to his belief that the language of poetry and prose should be the same, i.e., in speech style Khaṛī Bolī, so poetic description should have the transparency of prose; the poet's description should be direct, not needlessly ornamented. Is this description then "objective" and analytical, or a description of subjective experience? Dvivedī was no Romantic proponent of the freewheeling subjective voice: "the subject of poetry should be entertaining and instructive (*manorañjan* and *upadeśajanak*)," he pronounced, much like Horace made a precept of *dulce et utile*. Poetry should also not be obscene or uncouth. Ultimately, the replication of experience is at the heart of Dvivedī's aesthetics, and this is where a moral imperative toward the real, both as it is and as it should ideally be, appears.

Like Plato, Dvivedī saw a danger in the replicative powers of poetry on wrong, uninstructive subjects. A case in point was the *śṛṅgāra* typologies of women in the *nāyikā-bhed*. Although he posits that such a genre originally had a utilitarian purpose of educating young men with realistic depictions of the types of women, providing a warning against the worst kinds, and advice on which were most suitable for love, Dvivedī claims the genre now is mere stultifying convention:

> There is no longer any need to write a work on the *parakīyā* (the woman who belongs to another man) to explain the enigma of one's own woman's comings and goings . . . why is it that . . . a poet considers the outer limit of his poetry the description of the gestures of women? It is only unthinking and blind tradition.

Even traditional *alaṃkāra* are disposable: "what benefit is there to seeing the definition and illustration of *helā hāv* (lovers' flirtations)? And what use is there in knowing the subtlest of the subtle differentiations of the *dīpaka* ornament?" Instead, Dvivedī advocates poetry on natural objects, men and in sweeping scale, and with reference to infinite horizons: "animals, from the ant to the elephant; men, from the beggar to the king;

water, from a drop to an ocean; the endless sky; the endless mountains; poetry can be on all of these."[3] Beyond the reaches of poetry, this scope of subjects could be seen as his goal for the journal *Sarasvatī* during his editorship. His own articles and others included science writing, ethnographic topics, and topics of social concern, from social reform agendas to politics. His drive to incorporate the world in *Sarasvatī* seems to have mirrored his pronouncements on poetry here, that it should encompass all, from science to art and politics.

Dvivedī's own poetry, which has never received much acclaim, did not take up topics of sweeping grand scale as he promoted above. Instead, we can identify in it representative themes of poetry in general around the turn of the century, albeit more Sanskritized than most. When his verse did address "natural" themes, it presented them with a mixture of familiar classical modes of Sanskrit poetry and current-day propriety. Like most poets of his generation, he had begun writing poetry on *śṛṅgārik* themes, often with a devotional cast and often in translation of famously erotic Sanskrit authors, such as Jayadeva and Bhartṛhari, although he managed to evade some of the more embodied images through circumlocution.[4] His Braj Bhāṣā "Description of the seasons" (Ṛtu-taraṅginī) of 1891, based on Kalidasa, was groundbreaking for its use of Sanskrit meters, a practice he had observed in Marathi. He translated Kalidasa's famous *Kumārasambhava* into Khaṛī Bolī Hindi verse (published in book form in 1902), and wrote several negative reviews of the "*Bhāṣā*" Kalidasa translations of Lālā Sītārām, publisher and enterprising translator of the day of both Sanskrit and English literary classics. He thus established himself among proponents of classical poetics in modern times.

In translating Kalidasa, Dvivedī thus partook in a literary trend fueled by the colonial and elite Indian interest in nature-in-poetry as a form of science writing. The previous decades had seen many new versions of the *Cloud-messenger* (Meghadūtam) and other classical *kāvya* and dramatic texts. This trend toward Kalidasa in particular was much reinforced by British philological interest and their reading of Kalidasa as "nature poetry" or at least reflecting some kind of geographical reality. As Lālā Sītārām wrote (in English) in the Introduction to his 1893 translation of the *Cloud-messenger*,

> The path which the Cloud is directed to take is the one "marked out for it by the eternal laws of nature," but the poet, as Monier Williams has remarked, has made it a convenient pretext for displaying his knowledge of geography, and I would add history, mythology and the principles of natural science. All this is "described with the true poetic pencil which

> by a few happy touches bring the subject of the description vividly before the mind's eye."[5]

Thus, the ancients wrote of nature with an intrinsic knowledge of the laws the moderns seek, and Sītārām adds that Kalidasa's work further demonstrates scientific and historical knowledge, and vividly replicates the perception of the given subject. Terms of engagement with Kalidasa here have turned to the empirical: laws of nature, geography, history, and principles of natural science, all buttress the worth of Kalidasa. Even mythological knowledge has some value here, seemingly as another body of texts to master. The poetry of Kalidasa becomes merely "a few happy touches of the pencil," whereby a vivid, accurate picture of the subject emerges for the reader. Kalidasa was thus writing nature and writing "description" in Dvivedī's context, "description" that succeeded as literature because it provided a verisimilar experience of perception.

Classicism characterized Dvivedī's early poetry in Sanskrit with Khaṛī Bolī prose glosses, but he also often integrated the topical into his verse. Of note here is "The moonlight's words to the cloud" (Meghamālām prati candrikokti) (comp. 1898–1900) in which the protagonist, the cooling moonlight, berates the clouds for withholding water. She complains, "you plead your water from the ocean" but withhold it, and "without food and water, countless people . . . have died," citing the sad state of Gujarat, Malwa, and Bihar. Shifting away from this timely reference to the drought of 1899, she chastises the clouds for moving to reveal the moonlight, foiling lovers' nighttime trysts under the cover of dark. Thus classical modes of "talking about nature" were implemented in a manner meant to be of contemporary concern. "Cloud poems" in Sanskritic style were extremely prevalent in Hindi poetry at the time, and Dvivedī used the trope in a pointed way, to incorporate "current events," perhaps even to speak to the politics of famine in British India.[6]

More strictly neoclassically, the Sanskritized Hindi gloss of his "Description of dawn" (Prabhātavarṇanam) (1902? comp. 1896) reads like prosaic modernist imagism, but also as Sanskrit epigrammatic verse through and through, where neat emotional allegories describe natural scenes.

> "My end will come soon." As if pondering like this in her heart, the night, envying the redness of the dawn, took on whiteness out of grief.
>
> . . .
>
> Look at the destruction of that dark young woman who was worshipped constantly for twelve hours; it seems to

> me that this moon, so distressed with grief, drowned in the western sea.

He doesn't shrink from personifying his natural entities as women—in the latter verse Dvivedī himself notes that his term *śyāmā* can mean "night" or "a woman," either a woman of sixteen years, or Rādhā herself, lover of Śyām. But this is hardly an erotic scene of *śṛṅgāra* in union—Dvivedī's classical women tended to be *virahinīs*—ladies pining for their beloveds—rather than women enjoying and being enjoyed. However, by and large the themes here were perfectly consonant with the surfeit of "natural" subjects, such as the seasons, flowers, clouds, and so forth, which dominated the Braj and Khaṛī Bolī Hindi in publication through the 1920s. Dvivedī, as the gatekeeper of the preeminent Hindi journal in this period, whose influence among Hindi poets was profound, may have affected poetry's shift toward the more "real" subjects of nature as much as he contributed to the development of the Khaṛī Bolī linguistic register.

In his next important essay on the subject of poetry, "Poet and Poetry," of 1907, Dvivedī borrowed liberally from Hali's *Muqadammah*, the Urdu text that presented a mixture of Miltonian poetics with other advice for how to write modern poetry.[7] Through this essay, Dvivedī integrated certain English terms into the Hindi literary critical vocabulary, sometimes via Urdu, with the Urdu terms' rough equivalents in Sanskrit. Other Sanskrit terms he reinterpreted for the modern context. For example, Dvivedī uses the term *kalpanā* (imagination) for the English "imagination," and declares this the greatest quality of the poet. This was by no means already a stable and standardized term or concept in Hindi print at the time. One of the NPS founders, Śyāmasundar Dās, had recently glossed "imagination" as both *kalpanā* and *bhāvanā*, which latter connoted more perception, desire, and feeling, in his *Hindi Scientific Glossary* of 1904. "Romantic," on the other hand, Dās glossed as "full of *kalpanā*," and tellingly, "full of *rasa*."[8] Thus, Dvivedī's "Poet and Poetry" essay appeared in a time of varying terminology for Hindi modern poetics, and presented a new position on how to read modern poetics for the project of Hindi, culling from English, Urdu, and Sanskrit sources, directly and indirectly.

Dvivedī's essay approaches the problem of realism in poetry with a political bent, such that literary ornament appears as artifice born of oppression of thought:

> Just as things appear in the world, so the poet should describe them. There shouldn't be any kind of hindrance or restric-

> tion in this. The poet's light dims from oppression . . . when he fearlessly expresses in a poem a feeling born sui generis in his heart, then the poem has total and complete effect on people. . . . Poetry is ruined by artifice. . . . An obstacle arises in telling the true thing because of the restraint of subjection (*paratantrayata*) or the bid to receive a prize or something; if the poet doesn't have the strength to speak his heart, then the *rasa* of his poetry of course diminishes. . . . There should be no hindrance for the poet . . . it is right for the river, lake, forest, mountain, flower, leaves, summer, winter, etc., to satisfy him.[9]

The exact identity of the oppressors remains ambiguous here. The reference to prizes could refer equally to British cultural projects as much as any courtly honor, but then the British did encourage poetry on the "unhindered" subjects of "the river, lake, forest." However, Dvivedī continues, linking political oppression specifically with bad courtly poetry: "In the era of flattery poetry attained a bad state. Those poets who were in service of kings, nawabs, and *bādshāhs* . . . had to flatter them . . . the task of the poet is to describe . . . real events, not flowers falling from the sky."[10] Thus, artifice and subjection are linked, and the truths of the poet's inborn feelings and the natural objects of river, lake, forest, and so on, align with freedom. In reading poetry as evidence of political economy, Dvivedī refers to the genres of the past rather than the present; his subsequent criticism of Urdu *āśikānā* (amorous, erotic) poetry and deity-tarnishing Sanskrit poetry would support this appearance of disowning past courtly genres.

Soon, however, Dvivedī paraphrases from Oliver Goldsmith's *Deserted Village*, (although not Sridhar Pāṭhak's Braj translation of it). The lines come from the end of the work, addressed to Poetry:

> I have to remain ashamed in assemblies and among company thanks to you. But when I am alone, then I take pride in you. Remember, your ascent (*utpatti*) is natural (*svābhāvik*). Those people who believe in their natural strength (*apane prākṛtik bal*), can live happily even if penniless. But pride on the basis of unnatural strength (*aprākṛtik bal*) will surely someday be crushed.[11]

These lines approximate Goldsmith's Poetry, who is "My shame in crowds, my solitary pride" (l. 412), but then Dvivedī turns in a different direction. His Poetry's ascent may refer to Goldsmith's invocation to Poetry to "Aid slighted truth with thy persuasive strain" (l. 423); Dvivedī's opposition of natural strength and monetary power alludes to what, in the Goldsmith, Poetry teaches:

> Teach erring man to spurn the rage of gain;
> Teach him, that states of native strength possest,
> Tho' very poor, may still be very blest;
> That trade's proud empire hastes to swift decay,
> As ocean sweeps the laboured mole away;
> While self-dependent power can time defy,
> As rocks resist the billows and the sky. (ll. 424–30)

Dvivedī then directs the reader toward the idea that this passage demonstrates that innovating poets should stay their course, despite criticism.

The exact meaning of Dvivedī's "natural strength" remains indeterminate. Although *prākṛitik bal* is a fair translation of Goldsmith's "native strength," how is the term *prākṛtik* differentiated from *svābhāvik,* that abstract "natural" characterizing poetry's inevitable resurrection? Is this *prākṛtik* a more material "natural," or one derived from a distinction from artifice? Dvivedī's induction of an "unnatural" power correlating to "trade's proud empire" would seem to allude to poetic artifice, in keeping with the gist of his previous argument. But why would Dvivedī use an example so clearly referential to colonial empire building, and being on the losing end of it, to make a point about authenticity in modern Indian poetry? Perhaps Dvivedī meant to semiotically associate artifice with technology, and authenticity with material nature, artifice with political oppression and the authentically natural with the victim of such, who seeks self-determination. Could this have colonial referents, even if the perpetrators of artifice were Indians? Dvivedī may be using this charged passage of Goldsmith as a springboard for elaborating the narrative of cultural decay of "Muslim dominated India," or he may use this passage with intent to speak of the lack he perceives in his present colonial culture. At the very least, the terms Dvivedī introduces next imply a homology between political self-determination and poetic iconoclasm: "the task of the poet is to express his heart's emotions independently (*svādhīntāpūrvak*)." Additionally, the old forms of verse are a hindrance to this self-determined, independent (*svatantratāpurvak*) expression, and hence innovation would be necessary.[12] Both of these terms for "independence" would soon be used in anti-colonial contexts, if not already in the lexicon of incipient Swadeshi.

Shortly thereafter, in seeming apposition to this poetic independence he advocates, Dvivedī introduces "Nature" in particular in regard to the special status of the poet: "the task of the poet is to attentively observe the development of nature." His comments clearly resonate with generic Romanticism, yet also invoke a Hindu infinite and wondrous lila, the otherworldly "state of play," along with a utilitarian view of the educative benefit for all of the knowledge of this type of poet:

> The task of the poet is to attentively observe the development of nature. . . . It is endless. Nature plays wondrous games. In one little flower she displays amazing skill . . . not noticed by ordinary men. . . . But the poet is able to see well the handicrafts of nature with his subtle vision, and can describe them, and gets many kinds of instruction from them; and by means of his poetry he brings benefit to the world. The more knowledge of seeing and understanding natural scenes and nature's handiwork a poet has, the greater poet he is.[13]

Dvivedī's foregrounding of "seeing and understanding natural scenes" as a way to develop the poetic faculty suggests a perspective deeply influenced by the "nature study" and "object lessons" of colonial curricula. The "river, lake, and forest, and so on," provide the intellectual fodder for modern poetry.

In corollary to physical nature, the nature of man also comes within the purview of the poet. "Besides observing nature, the poet should practice examining the nature of man (*mānav-svabhāv*)." Dvivedī argues that the poet must write from experience, from "real knowledge" (*yathārth jñan*) of emotion. "That poet who doesn't have enough knowledge of the impulses of the heart and natural things can never be a good poet." As examples, he cites two verses on autumn, one in Urdu, and another in Kalidasa's *Raghuvaṁśa*, concluding about the Sanskrit that, as it involves "the poor farmer" and "a real event," "this is solid evidence of Kalidasa's examination of nature." Hence, the "nature" of Dvivedī's essay entails not merely the visible non-human world, but the psychological, social, and evidentiary description of the "real event." This type of realism, even if psychological, is predominantly visual: "In the description of an emotional state (*manovikār*) words should be firmly placed in such a way as if they have drawn a picture of the described subject before the eyes of the listener."[14]

Thus, "independent" poetry adheres to visual, social, and scientific reality. But Dvivedī has some caveats. In explaining Milton's simplicity (which he terms *sādagī*), he avers that poetry should not describe coarse realities; rather than an unattractive by-way, poetry should describe a pastoral one with "flowering trees, . . . resting places . . . and new glimpses of natural scenes pleasing to the eyes." Nor should poetry be mistaken as a kind of history or account (*itihās*), or slavishly present "the truth of every matter"; however, it should not be "baseless" (*bebuniyād*) either. It should be based on rules of nature and emotion (*manovikār*), and never leave off its connection to *svābhāvikatā*, naturalness. "Poets who take up reality can say what they want freely (*svatantratāpūrvak*); they can put the real thing in a new form and fly here and there; but without leaving connection with reality." He concludes the essay with a statement that demonstrates the benefit to the polity of injecting reality into poetry: "the best test of good poetry is if upon hearing it people immediately say 'that's true.' . . . that poet is blessed, and the country of that poet is blessed."[15] This idealistic realism would characterize Hindi poetic subjects well into the future.

Dvivedī's 1911 essay, "The necessary means of becoming a poet" (Kavi banāne ke lie sāpekṣ sādhan), also expressed this ideal of description of the real in poetry. Dvivedī speaks to a growing audience of poets: "These days Hindi poets have gained a lot of strength. You find poets everywhere. You find poetry everywhere. The poet-factory is running day and night." Dvivedī mentions how publications encourage various sorts of poetry writing, but offers his reading of eleventh century Kṣemendra and his principle of *camatkār* (amazing-ness) as a model, which I would argue he interprets similarly to the Urdu term *'ajā'ib*, applied in the day to topics of popular science and "wonders of the world." Following the classical poets, he wrote, a poet needs to know the world: "the poet needs to have knowledge of the entire creation of God—whatever there is in the world, he ought to acquire knowledge of it. He ought to look himself at natural scenes and be acquainted with the nature (*svabhāv*) of living beings also."[16] Rather than merely read any particular poetics text, he argues, such knowledge of the world, natural and otherwise, serves the poet. After all, Kṣemendra for instance instructed that the poet should know something of gems, minerals, men, and all gentlemanly arts, and the ancient poets show us what they know of these things in their poetry.[17] Dvivedī published this essay in the midst of a series of articles on works by Sanskrit authors, and especially Kalidasa, linking Hindi with the Sanskrit literary tradition explicitly; hence his allusion to knowledge of nature and men comes with a validating classical framework, itself further validated by its evidence of natural knowledge in the gems and minerals of *kāvya* description.

Several years later in 1913, Dvivedī published an anonymous essay in poetic prose, which he bluntly entitled "Natural scene" (*Prākṛtik dṛśya*), that concretely connected "nature-description" and politics. The political overtones of the essay may account for Dvivedī's use of a pseudonym, "Kuñj," a term for the arbor where Rādhā and Krishna might frolic.[18] The essay consists of several pages of description of a natural scene by an unnamed subjective voice, which waxes poetic on god, the scene, and impending change in the air, like monsoon after the heat.

> It was summer. Harsh sun shone down all day. One's entire body burned all day from the raging hot wind; even at night the wind didn't rest at all. . . . But who knows why, today the time appears to be changing. Like the relieving fall season, who knows why today, there is a radiance. Today the sky is not covered with dust like other days . . . the lila of the Creator is astonishing.

While no aesthetic masterpiece, this essay is quite striking for its mode of extended description, in very Sanskritic language, and its "socialized" nature. The sun is exhausted from his labors, "because of his relentless labors all day his face was becoming red . . . [and] from a surfeit of happiness, [at the end of the day and his work], his face became even more red." On one hand a very concrete metaphor personifying the red setting sun, the imbuing of natural objects and the land with such personal qualities serves a political point. Dvivedī bursts into exclamation and a repetitive sort of deixis of the "scene":

> What a new, yet unseen scene! . . . What a wondrous, pleasing, beautiful, charming [*nayanarañjak, citākarṣak*] scene is visible today. . . . Come, look again at this scene closely, such scenes do not come over and over again. Who knows if there is some other subtle meaning in them. . . . Look at that, in the place where the sun sets a group of rays of the sun are emerging upwards. Gradually they spread over the entire sky. The sky becomes colored with red, yellow, green, blue, pink, purple, and so on. Then those rays gradually getting closer to each other, in the end in the east become gathered together. As if giving this lesson, that the lowest of the low peoples are able to ascend to the highest of the high peaks of civilization. And . . . slipping from that place, in the end obtain lowness; and . . . the name of this people is cut from the names of the

> living races and they become submerged in the terrible darkness of eternal forgetting.[19]

Dvivedī engages with his audience ("Come, look . . .") and points out the "other subtle meaning" in such a beautiful scene, a "lesson" that has to do with a people—Indians or all people of the East—who have risen and sunk, according to the inexorable principle of the setting of the sun. Although the allegory would suggest another rise, Dvivedī does not lead the reader to that explicitly, but in his subsequent philosophizing on finding meaning in such scenes, and the practical meaning of their import, resolves on a Gita-like stance that "we should remain engrossed in selfless actions"—a sentiment from the Gita invoked often then in nationalist contexts—and that worldly sovereigns rise and fall in balance like the planets.[20] It seems the Indian people need simply to do their duty (selfless actions) and wait for their inevitable rise. In yet another allegorical twist, Dvivedī links the international political situation to the competition of the planets Śukra and Bṛhaspati, Venus and Jupiter. "But," he notes, "it is not that there is no other competitor with them," referencing the pole star:

> Is any man who stands in one place ever able to get ahead of one going by quickly? Never—impossible! That is to say, India is an agrarian country. And this is also to say that if India were to stop sending its rice to England then the people there would start to die of hunger. But will the Indian farmer, using those very ploughs even today with which ten thousand years earlier at the beginning of creation his fields were plowed, ever be able to surpass those American farmers, who are becoming rich and prosperous by means of the invention of new machines and new research in agricultural science? I say forcefully—never.[21]

India is thus a pole star, a constant, which is not a positive allusion to ancient greatness as much as an expression of being left behind, while its competitors Venus and Jupiter move forward. Whoever bears responsibility for this lag in India's agriculture, etc., Dvivedī does not name.

In the remaining paragraphs the allegory becomes more complex and obscure. There is redness in the western sky at moonrise, which Dvivedī describes with imagery familiar for the moon-lineage avatars of Vishnu: "The red round face of the moon is so handsome! What a wondrous scene! What an otherworldly splendor! [that will] set afloat the flower-hearts of his lovers on the stream of the ocean of pleasure. . . ." The moon-king, younger brother of the sun, is at first red with anger at the smaller kings'—stars?—thoughts of liberty (*svatantratā*); then, "protecting the royal classes," he calms, takes on a white color (*śukla*), and thinks of Ram-*rājya*, the Hindu ideal reign of good. After references to paradoxes—that the moon is cooling despite receiving its light from the sun, and that both god Ram and demon Rāvaṇa studied the same Vedas—Dvivedī presents a resolution:

> . . . in the auspiciousness of the moon god's kingdom everyplace became the home of peace, Everybody became involved in their own progress [*unnati*] . . . only then do eternal enemies . . . Venus and Jupiter . . . peacefully spread the light of their knowledge. And because of the enmity in the east, although they are in different corners of the sky even now, still they glitter more or less equally.

A final sentence concludes enigmatically: "Come, let us all together greet the lord of the world who shows us this indescribably pleasing scene." We can search the political events in Europe or the colonies for the key to this allegory, but at the least we can recognize that Dvivedī uses the scene—including its astronomical facts—as a platform for talking about Indian political realities. This essay may demonstrate the linkage of the concept of "nature-description" with political fact, both concerned with "what is true," and further the expansion of "nature-description" beyond flora and fauna, to the workings of the universe. This natural scene had little to do with arbors and creeper-vines, but rather functioned as an inspiring "natural scene" by virtue of its instruction in the principles of the world.

By 1920, we find Dvivedī's ideas on nature-in-poetry quite changed. Perhaps under the influence of dire political crises, or of the younger cohort that would soon be called the Chāyāvādī, "Shadow-ists," Dvivedī wrote in "The future of poetry" (Kavitā kā bhaviṣya) of 1920 of nature in poetry as a steppingstone toward poetry on the nature of man. This new poetry would be based on material experience of the world, and also elucidate the eternal principles:

> After the external world, the poet turns his gaze to his inner world. Then in literature, the form of poetry changes. The distinguishing feature of poetry becomes man. Tearing his eyes from the world [*saṃsāra*], the poet concentrates on man. Then he knows of the mystery of the soul [*ātma*]. He finds

> the infinite in the finite and the reflection of boundless light in the material body.
>
> The focus of the poet of the future will be toward this. Up to now he has not wanted to make his poetic heroes the farmers smeared with dirt and the dirty laborers coming from the factory. He remained engrossed in praise of kings (*rājastuti*), heroic ballads (*vīr-gāthā*) and description of nature (*prakṛti-varṇan*). But now he will see the greatness of those low ones and then alone will the mystery of the world be apparent to all.[22]

Here "nature description" is on the side of the past, along with encomium and epic. Further, Dvivedī speaks with prescience of the preoccupation with paradox of the Chāyāvādīs, and the social concern of the Progressives. This turn toward transcendent principles is rooted in a kind of material or empirical vision of man, indeed a vision of the low classes of men who constitute the "productive forces." Further, this binary of "looking at the world" and subsequent "looking within" conjoins with an aesthetics of liberal Romanticism: Like the new poets will know the Soul from looking at Man, "will find boundless light in the material body," they will find greatness in the material humanity of laborers, and indeed uncover the "mystery of the world." The toiling laborers for Dvivedī represent the material embodiment of a transcendent, unknown reality of the soul. Indeed, within ten years, the agricultural laborer would come to embody early twentieth-century Hindi prose, with Premchand at its helm. Hence, Dvivedī's comments here are surprisingly in concert with the concerns of the later Progressivists of prose.

Beyond the Romantic aesthetics that entered Dvivedī's thoughts, we might read Dvivedī's evolution toward "those low ones" as literary subject as a subjective turn that follows from, or lies inherent, in his high valuation of empiricism. This is on one hand an obvious evolution—to write of things as they appear necessitates abandoning idealism—but for Dvivedī, this turn has more knotted roots in his valuation of empiricism as a tool for creating sympathy. In his earliest conception of 1901, he spoke of realist verisimilitude as the identity of the viewer's soul with the viewed, which then can take an unmediated expression, and recreate a sympathetic emotion in the reader. While this may be an aesthetic sympathy in the subject of nature, in the subject of humanity the sympathy takes on a progressive political bent.

Dvivedī's modern poetics of realist nature, and identity of the subjective poet with his described object, evolved to encompass more openly political and spiritual ends. Dvivedī theorized modern poetics as a combination of realism, identity, and sympathy, modes we can identify as empiricist, Romantic, and liberal, respectively; and from our perspective in the twenty-first century, this seems like rather "old news." For Dvivedī and his many readers, however, this roughly twenty-year span of theorizing on modern literary-ness had turned the usual pleasures of poetry on their head. The poetic Nature that at first was an object lesson in salubrious realism had become a political field as well, and finally for Dvivedī, a secondary genre in the greater pursuit of a spiritual, political sympathy; and he did all of this without abandoning the semiotic world of Indian poetics.

Śrīdhar Pāṭhak's "Beauty of Kashmir" (Kāśmīr suṣamā)

Some poems take on lives of their own; the "Beauty of Kashmir" was one of these, which would come to exemplify the geographic nationalism well known from Mother India posters, while encompassing much more, including critically complex turns in the narrative of how classical poetics became modern. We turn again to Śrīdhar Pāṭhak, well-known poet and friend of Dvivedī, who steadily published poetry on natural and national themes, many in distinctly Sanskrit diction, if not meter, and many in Braj Bhāṣā. The lengthy Pāṭhak-Dvivedī correspondence, especially on Pāṭhak's Goldsmith translations, testifies to their mutual influence. Dvivedī clearly admired Pāṭhak greatly, as an 1899 poem honoring him attested. However, Pāṭhak's most famous original poem, "The Beauty of Kashmir" of 1904, was relatively unmarked by the kind of natural realism Dvivedī had outlined in his first famous essay. In Pāṭhak's poem, beyond its features of "natural description" of objects within the landscape, the reader finds Nature embodied as beautiful woman, a description of the city of Srinagar in classical style, and an encomium of Pratāp Siṁh, Raja of Kashmir. Although steeped in a courtly mode, Pāṭhak's poem may also represent an early poetic example in Hindi of the nationalist iconicization of Indian geography. Always cited as an early example of the modern nature poetry in Hindi, "The Beauty of Kashmir," in its full original form, commands our attention here.

Pāṭhak's previous reputation as a "nature poet" was based on his translations of Goldsmith, and his poetic descriptions of mountain locales. The latter were, on the one hand, stock-in-trade in poetry in the Sanskritic tradition. On the other hand, Pāṭhak's locations were sites of colonial retreat and summer administration: Kashmir, Shimla, Dehra Dun, Mussoorie, Nainital. By the turn of the century, Indians of means had long traveled to the hill stations for vacation or employment; authors from various parts of India had published accounts of their travels, most of which followed the model of English prose travel literature. Hence, the idea of a verse "description" of Kashmir would seem à propos to an author like Pāṭhak, and for whom the Sanskrit accounts of landscape in *mahākāvya* would have also held great appeal. A Kashmir poem would speak to both literary genres at once. Pāṭhak had traveled to Kashmir on holiday, after a position with the Irrigation Commission in Shimla, and this holiday likely inspired this Braj Bhāṣā poem of 1904. The poem is most often cited as an early example of the Romantic source of nature poetry as "nature description" and because of its "personification" of nature, a technique considered more modern, imaginative and "Romantic" than the traditional Indic poetic nature.

As Harish Trivedi has pointed out recently, Pāṭhak wrote of nature as an attractive thing-in-itself, putatively stripped of its associations with human love. Most have considered this turn toward "the real" essentially linked to English poetry and the English picturesque:

> . . . [Pāṭhak was] the first Hindi poet whose work bore the clear impress of his having read the English Romantics and their eighteenth-century precursors. He wrote a large number of poems on nature, treating it not as a quarry for suitable or fanciful similes for human beauty, as Sanskrit and Hindi poets had traditionally done, but often reversing the poetic procedure by personifying nature and ascribing to it human attributes. Nature was seen in his poetry as a source of attraction in its own right, and not as a universal presence but as wearing different aspects in different locations. Pāṭhak wrote in particular about the hills and mountains . . . regarding such places not as holy or divine (in the tradition of Kalidasa . . .) . . . but in a new, British or Western light, in which they were attractive for their climate and aesthetics. . . .[23]

Trivedi also notes that Pāṭhak implemented a Westernized nature poetry in nationalistic ways, such that "it is nature in India, and not nature as such, that is so beautiful," and some of his poems

> participate in a pan-Indian nationalist poetic discourse beginning to develop in many languages around this time: the geographical shape of India is personified as Bhāratmātā, Mother India, with the Kashmir Himalayas in the north being the resplendent crown on the head of the human figure.[24]

Thus, a certain equivalence appears in Pāṭhak's poetry between Nature and India, both of which appear as beautiful and ideal females, when not described discursively as the rivers, lakes, or forests, etc. (to allude to Dvivedī's phrase), that make up their parts.

This poetic reversal, in which Nature has become the center of gravity of the poetic world, was on one hand an Enlightenment value that permeated the colonial cultural mission. On the other hand, this purported desire to uncover an objective nature, and reject the idea of nature as a "quarry for . . . fanciful similes," was achieved by Pāṭhak with an equally fanciful personification of a Lady Nature. This maneuver, which foreshadowed the future of Hindi nature-in-poetry, has been taken to be a decisive modern turn to the Hindi literary world. As poets made their nature more real, in rejection of the poetics of the past, their nature became more unrealistically embodied. In the modern seeing of this nature "as it is," "independently," poets wrote of it with fanciful similes folded in, often the very sort of *śṛṅgārik* similes to which moderns objected. When nature entered Hindi poetry as a thing-in-itself, it came along with the poets' proudly subjective reading of appearances. Their readings display a phenomenology indebted to *śṛṅgāra* as much as to the ruminations of Wordsworth.

The sixteen-verse poem begins with repeating benediction upon Kashmir, with images of Aryan antiquity so popular among the Hindu public.

> Blessed be the land of Kashmir, captivating and charming.
> . . .
> Blessed be the site of the most ancient seat of the Aryan
> religion.
> . . .
> Blessed be the famed abode of old, the delightful
> incomparable beauty.
> Earth that is twin of heaven, the master poets are defeated
> in its description. (1.1, 3, 5–6)

The second verse continues with the praises, and extends its clauses to include an enumeration of various components of its natural scenery, in high Sanskritic vocabulary.

> Blessed are the white snowy peaks, high, exalted, and
> lovely to behold.
> . . .

The cool pleasing breeze, the pure place of the Vitastā river
bank.
Blessed are the arbors, gardens, forest paths perfumed with
flowers,
Bloomed in various colors, drawn by the hands of Nature.
(2.2, 4–6)

Here Pāṭhak adds local color, citing with Kashmiri terms the regions "Gandhar bal," "Gagarī bal," and the "Ḍal" lake of Srinagar. Verse two ends with the first hint of the central conceit of the poem, the personification of Nature as a beautiful woman: "From each pretty lake, reflections abound, / As if mirrors for the Goddess Nature to gaze at her own beautiful form." (2.14–16)

Verse three of the poem continues in the vein of a paean, and in addition to the natural features of Kashmir, and "all living beings here, of water, earth, and sky," the people of Kashmir are also blessed, its women described in compound-laden terms redolent of Kalidasa's description of sophisticated ladies: "urbane deer-eyed women" (*nāgari mṛgalocani*), "moon-faced ideal beauties" (*padmini vidhuvadani*), "who inspire passion for love (*madana-sadmini-mada-mocani*).[25] Verse four then ushers in a classically-inflected sort of urban ecphrasis, reminiscent of Kalidasa's Himalayan city, "beautiful even in its defenses, circled by the flowing of the Ganges, / with walls that are enormous jewels, / and glowing herbs to light up the ramparts," of which the townsmen, trees, and women are subsequently described.[26] Similarly, Pāṭhak proceeds:

The blessed sophisticated Srinagar gleams on the banks of
the Vitastā.
The reflection of the mansions at the bank, the splendor of
the water enchants.
The seven "*kadala*"[27] bridges shine, the undulating boats bob
by.
A beautiful cluster of men and women frolic in the water.
The king's palace, Śeragaṛhī [the Lion Fort], shines
beautifully on the bank of the river.
Looking at the light of the glimmering lamps (*bijju-dīpa-duti*),[28] Purandara hides in his heavenly city.[29]
There is the gilded Gadādhar ju Krishna[30] temple
Attached to the royal house, a firm pillar of the royal
family's praise to God.
From the top of the mountain, the beauty of the city seems
quite amazing.

The houses, very splendorous, form rows.
They shine all around, all together, as if one great
congregation of handsome homes,
The midst of it adorned with the Vitastā's flows, like a pure
glowing line. (4)

Like Kalidasa's city, Srinagar glows with lights and glimmers with water, its fort and inhabitants also beautiful elements of the scene. Pāṭhak continues, listing various pilgrimage spots and rivers. While this scene evokes classical forebears, to write of the city of Srinagar in 1904 must have signified to Pāṭhak, at the same time, a project of geographical specificity and the touristic Western picturesque. Pāṭhak seems to strive for both aesthetic effects, as here the sort of bird's-eye view of Kalidasa's flying monks appears undifferentiated from the gaze-from-above of an English poet, or one beholding a scene both historical and real, yet timeless and sublime.

Then briefly, Pāṭhak inserts a verse in praise of a guru. He had taken initiation in tantra while in Srinagar, and in this verse gives mention of both his guru and interestingly, his guru's wife. The fact of Pāṭhak's interest in tantra proves the deep complexity of this poet's world-view, a poet both well-versed in English but equally committed to a religiosity utterly foreign to the British culture in which he circulated. Pāṭhak's interest in tantra may prove that his Nature was as much that of the philosophical and gendered *prakṛti* as that of scenic English literature.

Immediately following, Pāṭhak moves to another living figure, the king of Kashmir, and the political state of this land:

Blessed are the people, beloved to their king, and the
beneficent king, beloved to the people.
Blessed is the auspicious morality of the king, preserver of
the path of love.[31]
No difference is apparent between the law of the Muslim
[*yavana*] and Aryan.
Everyone sleeps peacefully, blessing their own king.[32]
Blessed is this unity among people of different beliefs [*mata*],
Guided by pure justice, leadership, intellect, character,
strength, and wisdom. (7)

Blessed is the king who is the ornament of the solar Dogra
lineage.
Protector of the Brahmins, glowing praise of him has
increased.

Blessed be the lord of faith engaged in good works, the
leader of devotion to Hari
Sri Pratāpasiṁha, sage of kings, Purandar [Indra] of
Kashmir. (8.1–4)

Thus, Pratāp Siṁh Dogra (r. 1885–1925) appears prominently in "The Beauty of Kashmir," a fact often overlooked in discussion of this poem. The aforementioned Śeragaṛhī was his recently built Grecian-style summer palace. This Pratāp Siṁh was the Hindu king of the Dogra lineage, which had ruled Kashmir and Jammu as an independent princely state from 1846 at the Treaty of Amritsar. At the time of this poem's publication, Pratāp Siṁh would have already handed over his rule 1889 to a Council of Regency under the British Resident, although he remained involved in the political workings of administration from 1891, including conflicts over Muslim education.[33] Such a paean for Pratāp Siṁh may bespeak a friendship between Pāṭhak and the Dogra ruler, and Pāṭhak's explicit mention of Pratāp Siṁh's happy rule over both "Aryan" and "*yavana*" alludes to conflicts in its very denial of it. Pāṭhak's mention of the king's favorable attitude toward Brahmins, the influential Kashmiri Brahmins from which the powerful Nehru clan emerged, also might indicate Pāṭhak's allegiances in the politics of the time, both in Kashmir and in Allahabad. We could also read Pāṭhak's praise of Pratāp Siṁh as a reflection of public support: in 1905, the year following Pāṭhak's "Beauty of Kashmir," the Council was abolished and Pratāp Siṁh regained certain of his powers, with apparent support of "native sentiment."[34] This poem may give evidence of such sentiment that objected to the assumption of power by the British Resident.

Suddenly then, Pāṭhak moves to what later became the most famous image of this poem. In telling apposition, the poetic subject shifts from the heroically styled king of Kashmir, to a heroine, Nature:

Nature sits alone here and adorns her beauty.
Moment by moment she changes her costume, moment by
moment she takes on new splendor.
She gazes at the reflection of her face in pure river-water mirrors.
Enchanted with her own beauty, she blesses herself[35] with
body and soul.
. . .
She frolics, full of various sports, imbued with the passion
of youth.
All made up, she longs, shouts in delight, thrills, gazes,
delicately dances.

She scatters her store of splendor, her sweet lovely beauty,
in the forest groves.
She glances, delights, laughs, lolls about,[36] smiles, steals
your heart. (9.1–4, 7–10)

This verse is mannerist (*rīti*) through and through, thoroughly Braj in its diction and grammar, *śṛṅgāra* in sentiment, and a model of the alliteration and assonance that fascinated courtly Braj poets (e.g., the last three lines, *Lalakati, kilakati, pulakati, nirakhati, thirakati, bani thani / madhura mañju chavi puñja-chaṭā chirakati bana kuñjana /citavati, rijhavati, hasati, dasati, musikyāti, harati mana*). Nature's juxtaposition with the Dogra king seems only appropriate; like any hero, he has his beautiful heroine-consort, which is Nature herself, his divinely beautiful possession. *Śṛṅgāra*, in its sense of physical adornment, appears personified also and in the various natural objects that adorn the landscape of Kashmir:

Here is beautiful Śṛṅgāra [Adornment], taking on various
kinds and forms
Lake, river, mountain, peak, the sky, a wood, a tree,[37] grass,
To fulfill his purpose, the desire of his own heart,
He keeps on serving the lotus feet of Nature. (10)

Another round of Kalidasa-esque natural description then ensues, culminating in the allusion to an embodied India:

All around, snowy mountain peaks, as if a crest of
diamonds in a crown.
The pure current of the river flows by, as if her golden
moon-necklace.
That diffused beauty of the blooming splendor of the wood
and grove
Arose as if from the womb of the earth, a trove of jewels.
That beauty of the snowy peaks, rivers, lakes, and woods,
as a whole,
Pervades the sphere, graces the four directions,
As if the shape of a brilliant jeweled crown garland,
A necklace strung of priceless orbs and tied on the head of
India.[38] (11)

Immediately following, the poem enters a passage of highly Sanskritic ornamentation with the *sandehālaṅkāra*, the "ornament of doubting"[39]—was it this or that, which made Kashmir?

In various ways, seen and unseen, with skillful artistry, a shelter
Covered this natural treasure-trove, as if Brahma[40] had made a fortress.
That is, he constructed a firm coffer, to keep hidden
The pure mass of the entire beauty of the world.
Did this conjurer's bag, full of the magic of the world,
Fall open in play, and spread out on top of the peaks?
Then did the *rasa* of youth [i.e., *śṛṅgāra*] come to male Spirit and female Nature?[41]
Did they adorn the pleasure-palace for the surges of ecstasy of love-play?[42]
Was this the palace garden of Head-queen Nature in bloom,
Or her open jewelry box, full of ornaments?
Is it a flowerbed in this luxuriant garden of Brahma,
That the king of yogis created here with his yogic powers?
Or was it that a circle of Tantrists [*bhairavicakra*] with their wares
Resolved upon it, and raised up their offering trays to Śakti?
Or did the Creator raise up to the head of India[43]
A bouquet of flowers created by gardeneress Maya?
. . .
Did it appear as a curtainless stage for the dancer Nature?
Or did the *Shiva-tantra* and its commentary open up, gleaming, on the dais?
Is it the ascetic's bowl full of the power[44] of the three worlds?
Or the sacred diagram of the wealth of splendor of the world produced from the surfeit of ascetic fervor?[45]
(13.3–18, 27–30)

Though elaborate, this verse displays a remarkable compactness in its allusions, all of which have to do with geographical space of the Himalayas: Tantrists and other ascetics with magical powers, and Shiva, the greatest of ascetics. In her turn, Prakṛti as Nature functions as a "head-queen," a heroine in the royal *śṛṅgāra* mode, but representing an archetypal *śakti* as well. This philosophical Prakṛti informs the image of the open Shiva-tantra text on the dais, but does not impede a Romantic reading of landscape as divine text. Here Kashmir embodies both the principle of Nature and a text.

Pāṭhak begins his denouement with a conundrum, an oft-cited passage on the merging of real and ideal in Kashmir. The resolution lies in the very collapse of the metaphor of "Kashmir as heaven":

> Which is the more beautiful, between the two, the divine world or Kashmir?
> Which is the home of splendor, which is an ocean of beauty?
> Who has any simile fit to give them?
> Is Kashmir a simile for the divine world, or the divine world for it?[46]
> The simile for Kashmir is that one alone, which delights with enchantment.
> You will never see another place in Creation equal to this.
> This alone is heaven, the divine world, this alone is the beautiful garden of the gods.
> Here alone is the home of the immortals, right here somewhere resides Purandar. (15)

This seeming hyperbole on Kashmir's perfection, and possible second reference to Prātap Siṁh as Purandar, still does not fully demonstrate the reality Pāṭhak describes. In a mode redolent of devotional poetry, he caveats: "the giver of *rasa* of the cloud of love [Krishna] remains in Śrīdhara's eyes / But the descriptions have not the power to intoxicate with the real [*yathāratha*] glory." He continues in the manner of the pleasure-taking connoisseur, outdone by beauty:

> [Kashmir is] the place of *rasa* for connoisseurs, our life-breath, our all, our life's riches,
> over Nature's forest for gamboling in frolicsome play.
> O finest among gentlemen connoisseurs, look indeed upon Kashmir.
> With heart intoxicated, like mine, covetously take the boon of its sight.[47] (16.7–10)

The poetic modes of classical connoisseurship, devotion, and the *śṛṅgārik* personification of a Lady Nature that are evident here suggest that the "realism" of describing nature as a thing-in-itself happened in a manner deeply influenced by earlier poetic modes. When an allusion to the real appears, it does so in the cloak of a typical expression of devotional ineffability: beauty beyond description. Still, Pāṭhak's "Beauty of Kashmir" seems to insist that the purpose of the poem is precisely this, to describe and replicate the object of the beauty of Kashmir, such that the description and the reality are merged, as does the ideal of heaven with the earth of Kashmir—both can be the metaphor for the other. This description then ends with a certain self-consciousness of this poetic act: the inimitable desirous gaze of the devotee-*rasik* for Lover Nature, *prakṛti preminī*. If this poem, with its paean, poetic ornament, and personification, is the beginning of "nature poetry" in Hindi, then what sort of nature in poetry emerges thenceforward? What peculiar resonances would nature hold then, as a continued object of poetic description, and object of critical attention, following Pāṭhak's lead?

Conclusions: Realizing Classical Poetics

Pāṭhak's "Beauty of Kashmir" seems to have only a little commonality with his friend Dvivedī's thoughts on nature in his article "The Duty of the Poet," what with its Lady Nature, and elaborate *sandehālaṅkāra*. The poem hardly spans from ant to elephant, beggar to king. Any injection of subjectivity of experience, and description of the author's *tādātmya*, his "identity" with it, comes at the end, in the manner of a colophon in bhakti poetry. The identity of poet with poetic subject, which Dvivedī advocated for natural description, is that of the loving devotee for what here seems a Goddess Nature. Dvivedī may have appreciated Pāṭhak's timely support for the controversially displaced Dogra king, arguing for his catholicity (e.g., "no difference . . . between the law of Muslim [*yavana*] and Aryan"); but this support appears in the form of fairly standard encomium (e.g., "the Purandar of Kashmir"). What we might identify as a sweeping scope of subject takes the form of the repetitive listing of items in the landscape, including "local color" but also the cityscape, as in Sanskrit *mahākāvya*. This notwithstanding, and also while in the garb of *stuti*, with its "blessed be . . . ," Dvivedī must have found this poem sufficiently *dulce et utile*. Even the Braj Bhāṣā medium did not bother Dvivedī. We can read this as a signal of the subtlety of poetic change; the mixture of Braj, Sanskrit, praise, description, politics, classical verbal ornament, and *śṛṅgāra* may have sufficed for Dvivedī's vision for poetry in 1904. Both authors, however, moved toward more political and Khaṛī Bolī renditions of landscape as the years went on. As Dvivedī described the political landscape of a "Natural Scene" in 1914, Pāṭhak's poems "Praise of Nature" (Prakṛti-vandanā) and "The Land of India" (Bhārat-dharaṇī) of 1918, among other similar poems, linked Nature or the earth with the idea of Indian nationhood, in Sanskritized Khaṛī Bolī.[48]

Both implemented an idea of the classical and the real for self-consciously modern literary purposes, sometimes to ironically adverse ends. In Dvivedī's critiques, inserting realism into classical poetics was a moral imperative, asserted in cultural self-critique, using arguments from various English and Urdu sources. Still, he never abandoned classical aesthetics. Pāṭhak clearly saw in his "Beauty of Kashmir" a modern undertaking of nature-description with a political, or at least identitarian valence in its queenly Kashmir, crowned with peaks. But ultimately, the geographic nationalism of Pāṭhak's "Beauty of Kashmir" is only truly comprehensible through the very fancifulness (and erotics) Dvivedī condemned. The empirical world, the map, and Nature, remain in these works the reference point of reality—not the doings of gods or lovers.

Chapter 5

Independent Subjects

Modern Modes of Nature as a Literary Subject

> Literature is the result of the coming-to-light of independent nature (*svatantra prakṛti*) and genius. It cannot stand anything's being subject (*paratantratā*) to something else.
>
> —Jayaśaṅkar Prasād, 1909[1]

This chapter will address the poetry of two members of the Dvivedī and Chāyāvād generations, respectively: Hariaudh and Jayaśaṅkar Prasād. Both wrote contemporaneously in the 1910s, the former as a middle-aged man, the latter as a somewhat renegade youth. The juxtaposition of these two poets will strike some as odd—most people dissociate the two, seen as representatives of vastly different mentalities: one under the pall of a constraining tradition, the other a Hindi Romantic breaking old bonds of meter and subject. However, here I will look at the aesthetic feature of Nature, newly emerging as a subject unto itself, as it developed in both of these authors' oeuvres, which overlapped thematically and historically in the 1910s. Despite their obvious differences in poetic values, we can see clearly their shared interest in reframing poetic nature.

The "Dvivedī Era" has always been defined by the disciplinarian mode of the editor Dvivedī himself and the nationalist concerns of its authors and the Hindi movement generally. The "Chāyāvād Era" has been defined in contradistinction to this; in typically modern form, Chāyāvād has been posed against a past of tradition and constraints of all kinds, from social to moral. Chāyāvād has represented freedom and individuality—in poetry, in love, and obliquely, in politics. There is no denying that Chāyāvād constituted a distinct cultural shift in Hindi poetics; many critics from Rāmacandra Śukla onward have demonstrated this, and the Hindi literary press immediately registered the Chāyāvād innovations throughout the twenties. The categorization of "eras," as Dvivedī and Chāyāvād, however, obscures the reality of the contemporaneousness of all of these poets; Dvivedī and Chāyāvād "generations" expresses the situation more accurately. Recognizing the distinction between generations—roughly twenty years apart in age—but also the consonances between them, before the more radical innovations of Chāyāvād in the 1920s, in this chapter I present two poets of these two generations, and specifically works published between 1900 and 1918, presenting the trope of nature in poetry as it was actually available to the Hindi-language consumers of 1900–1920. Hence we will examine a part of the story of Hindi's modern Nature that has been overshadowed by the many subsequent years of Chāyāvād nature-poetry, a part of this literary history where both elder and younger poets experimented with making old metaphors into new subjects.

Hariaudh and Natural Objects as Subjects

Ayodhyāsiṁh Upādhyāy "Hariaudh," along with Ratnākar and Pāṭhak, was a Braj Bhāṣā poet of some renown at the turn of the century. Unlike these two poets, and also unlike Dvivedī, he came from circumstances more removed from the cities and centers of colonial activity. Rather, he was a traditionally trained pandit from the district town Azamgarh, about a hundred kilometers north of Banaras, a rather isolated outpost of the colonial administration, but nevertheless a busy center of local trade and culture. Hariaudh's family, along with several others in his natal Nizamabad village, traditionally maintained what would now be called a "Sikh" appearance, i.e., turban and beard, due to their connection with a local gurdwara founded in connection with the longstanding Nanak-panthī community there, of which Hariaudh's family is supposed to have been an important member. The gurdwara, right next to Hariaudh's house, hosted informal poetic gatherings, where Urdu *shā'irī*, Braj, and Avadhī verse would be recited. Hariaudh reputedly proved himself in this company with his exegesis of a Kabīr verse while still a boy. Hariaudh attended the local school, passed the Hindi intermediate exam, and in 1879 received a scholarship to Queen's College in Banaras. He returned home after only six months, being unable to manage by himself in the city, and he continued studying with his uncle, a pandit who instructed him in Sanskrit, Panjabi, prosody, and astrology. Hariaudh also studied Persian with a maulvi, to the point that his Persian abilities equaled his ability in Sanskrit. His most important literary mentor was one Baba Sumerasiṁh Sāhabzāde, *mahant* of the gurdwara at Patna and also native of Nizamabad village. Sumerasiṁh traveled in literary circles all over the United Provinces, a friend of Hariścandra and later Ratnākar, and connected to the major Khaḍgavilās publishing house of Patna that put out Hariścandra's and Hariaudh's works, among many others, and served as a kind of salon and library for Hindi authors and its Anglo supporters.[2]

After a short career as a schoolteacher in Azamgarh, he was appointed as a subdistrict *qānūngo* in 1891, and from then on his writing career began to flourish. While based in Azamgarh, he would publish over twenty works, mostly poetry and criticism, before his retirement in 1923. Azamgarh being a district town and center of handicraft industry, Hariaudh did not lead an insular life, although his location was clearly somewhat remote from the cultural hubs of Varanasi and Patna. At least, Hariaudh would associate somewhat with the well-known local Urdu scholar Shiblī Nu'mānī, and presumably other Urdu litterateurs of Azamgarh. An Englishman supervised Hariaudh at the District Collector's Office in Azamgarh town, the Nizamabad gurdwara had pilgrims from the Panjab, and a local postmaster tutored him in Bengali. Hence, the traffic through Azamgarh was not insubstantial, and like the *sarāy*s that dotted the district roads, this town formed a real, though underestimated site of exchange for intellectual goods.

Well-known as a Braj poet and translator by the turn of the century, his fame catapulted with his 1914 *Priyapravās* (*Absence of the Beloved*), discussed below. Although an acquaintance of Mahāvīraprasād Dvivedī, he kept relatively separate from the Dvivedī circle, although he clearly agreed with Dvivedī on many poetic matters, and probably took some influence from Dvivedī's writings. After his retirement, he took an unpaid position at the Banaras Hindu University upon the invitation of founder Madan Mohan Mālaviya himself, and sat in the Hindi department with other famous litterateurs of his generation. When quite elderly, he taught in the Women's College. As a sort of elder statesman, he oversaw the development of the Chāyāvād generation of poets, attending gatherings in Banaras, Allahabad, and many other locales; his poems appeared often in journals ranging from Dvivedī's *Sarasvatī* to the more general interest *Māryādā* of the 1920s.

Verses from Hariaudh's 1914 *Absence of the Beloved* often follow those of Pāṭhak's "Beauty of Kashmir" in accounts of nature-description in literature, and this nature-description figures in virtually every assessment of Hariaudh's poetic contribution. In this section, I will examine Hariaudh's references to nature as a poetic subject, and his quite self-conscious implementation of natural scenes in his circa 1906 novel, *Adhakhilā phūl (The Half-Bloomed Flower)*. Then, I will examine both the canonized "nature description" of *The Absence of the Beloved*, and the uniquely transparent poetic sleight of hand of the climactic epiphany in the penultimate canto, a climax in which natural objects become the subjects, in the eyes of Rādhā, the god Krishna's lover.

For Hariaudh, the "useful" and the "real" as literary values implicated also use of nature, to form either descriptive realia, to imply an intellectualized religiosity (as we will see in *The Absence of the Beloved*), or to supply a scientific defense for *śṛṅgāra* (as examined in Chapter 7). He clearly felt that nature, along with other themes, represented the future of Hindi poetry, in contradistinction to the poetry he himself knew, loved, and composed in Braj Bhāṣā. In the Introduction to his 1909 volume *Garden of Verse* (Kāvyopavan),[3] he described the literary changes of the last decade, and reflects with some nostalgic poignancy on the waning currency of his beloved Braj medium.

> In ten years there has been a strange change in the taste of the people of this region. At this time there is not the previous . . . glory of Braj Bhāṣā, today in the field of poetry Braj is incompetent to support the royal umbrella of our own political power. Day by day it is falling from its place—and silently Khaṛī Bolī is gradually taking its place. In contemporary magazines, articles on ways to remove Braj Bhāṣā are being written even today—but where are the people protesting it? . . . the current of the times is not in accordance with Braj Bhāṣā . . . in taste, subject matter and feeling (*bhāv*)also, there is a difference. . . . Now people have enthusiasm especially for description of natural scenes (*prākṛtik dṛśya*), psychological[4] portraits (*svabhāv citra*), the promotion of love of country, means of uplift (*unnati-sādhan*) for the *jāti*, country, and society . . . ; *śṛṅgāra* poetry is also seen, but is very rarely met with.[5]

This grouping of natural scenes with psychological portraits and patriotism implies a congruence of all of these subjects, which we can locate in the ideology of realism, empirical and political. Parallel to this ideology, we might read the waning of Braj Bhāṣā as a poetic medium as part of the same realist movement. Several years earlier Dvivedī had announced his opinion that "in civilized society" [*sabhya samāj*] the language of prose should enter poetry; to have separate spheres was a sign of cultural impoverishment. Thus natural scenes, psychology, and patriotism were seen as congruent with the use of Kharī Bolī—all were new poetic idioms.

All of this contrasted starkly with the contents of the *Garden of Verse* volume itself. Hariaudh admitted that the poetry collected in it was mostly in Braj, and mostly *śṛṅgārik*, but he offers as a redeeming feature that it will "shed light" on "incidents" of his own life. Besides, he wrote, "even now there are such gentlemen who respect Braj Bhāṣā and read *śṛṅgāra rasa* poetry, taking pleasure."[6] Additionally, he writes in his introduction of the work itself as a garden, a common conceit for titles of nineteenth- and twentieth-century poetic works in Hindi.[7] However, he elaborates the garden metaphor extensively, making statements about nature, both physical and psychological, which might explain literary pleasure itself.

> You all must have gazed at one beautiful garden after another. You must have seen the garden's many creepers, vines, and beautiful fruits and flowers, must have heard the sweet sound of many sweet-voiced birds there, the unsurpassed beauty of the trees full of green must have been apparent. Today set foot in this garden too—

Using this garden metaphor, Hariaudh performs his traditional apologies for his poetry, and invokes ideas of Nature with a distinctly Romantic cast:

> . . . it is possible that its creepers are not that charming, that its chosen flowers are not that intoxicating and rare, its birds are not so sweet-voiced . . . and the leaves of its trees also may not hold the power of enchanting vision as they ought, but even so, this is a garden—you all will certainly find something or other as an object for your entertainment. Where will I find the amazing painter's brush of Nature, where will I find the ability to portray amazing pictures equal to it, . . . how could I be able to compete with a garden adorned by the hands of Nature? . . .

His standard is thus as if a painting by Nature's brush, so his verses are both the garden itself and an aspiring replication of Nature's beauty. He injects the audience into this natural scene as well, with the bee of

Vaishnava poetry: ". . . you all, like bees that have gotten juice, roaming about in the garden, might sometimes grace this garden with your presence as well. . . ."

In carrying on with his self-effacing message, Hariaudh invokes the principle of nature to explain imperfection. His poetry may not equal Nature's hand-painted portrait, but its shortcomings themselves illustrate natural law. Fortunately, the bees, as his ideal readers, do not pay much notice:

> It is the natural order (*naisārgik niyam*) that in flowers there are thorns, in the beds of creepers and jasmine there are marigolds and *gulamehadī* also. The trees' unsurpassable greenery, in which mass of leaves there are juicy (*saras*) things, there are also *niras*, dry, misshapen leaves also. It is principled naturalness (*niyamit svābhāvikatā*) that no thing is without fault in all ways . . . this much is my entreaty, that you all, making an example of "like a bee, he took the good qualities," will be so kind as to grasp its good qualities in all respects. . . .

While his garden of verse may approach the Edenic ideal in places, its failings can be understood as merely natural, the humble flowers mixed in. The garden in disrepair, an image common enough from Ḥālī's poetry on Islam in modern India, here figures as a realist metaphor for imperfection. The bees, traditionally the symbol of a pleasure-seeking connoisseur, or Krishna himself, here use their greed to find Nature's best, as critics in Hariaudh's imperfect garden of verse. Hariaudh thus has turned an idealized landscape common in poetry, Urdu and otherwise, into a realist metaphor based on non-ideals, and biological principles.

Natural scenes beyond the scope of traditional poetry also appeared in Hariaudh's earlier novel, *The Half-Bloomed Flower*, of circa 1906. These descriptions of natural scenes occurred at the opening of roughly half of the chapters, often in an unnamed subjective and exclaiming voice, and mostly would resolve in an analogy to a character's inner state or a turn of the plot.[8] Among these scene-descriptions, which were integrated with the setting of the plot, and which ranged from that of a bee in a garden, to a windstorm, to a forest, we can take as an example that of Chapter 4:

> How beautiful is the moon, how rare is its beauty, how lovely are its cool rays! When it spreads its light in all directions in the blue sky and seems to rain down *rasa* beautifully, at that moment who doesn't go mad seeing it? . . . It seems to the

> heart that some ambrosia is coming down from above, the directions begin to laugh, the leaves of the trees open. The entire world is joyful, as if it is being immersed [in *rasa*]. In such a moon, such a pleasing and lovely moon, why are there dark spots? Can anyone divine the answer!!! Aha! These big lotus-like eyes are so beautiful [*rasīlī*]! Its simple and sweet glance is so lovely!!

The narrative then begins to describe a day of shifting sunlight and clouds, relating to the emotional state of the heroine. Hardly divorced from the ideal beauty associations of the moon-as-face, this passage presents the referent as the moon itself. As a result, the moon, which commonly served as a metaphoric object or reminder for the beautiful face, here is the subject, as "real" phenomenon, not accessory. In turn, this passage highlights the subjective reading of it, now personified as a face. This turn toward the empirical thing-in-itself in these poetic-prose passages would foreshadow Hariaudh's use of "nature-in-poetry" in his famous *Absence of the Beloved,* which we will turn to next.

Hariaudh's most famous work, *Priyapravās* (*The Absence of the Beloved*), is usually included in the modern Hindi canon along with famous "epic" poems *Kāmāyanī* and *Sāket* by later Chāyāvād poets Prasad and Gupta; *Absence* predated the completion of these latter works, and also distinguished itself from them with its more complete neoclassicism and Krishnaite theme. Published by the Khaḍgavilās Press of Patna, publisher to the late Hariścandra, it appeared in book form first in 1914, in a Braj Bhāṣā-flavored Khaṛī Bolī in Sanskrit meters, with virtually no words of Persian origin.[9] Beyond its experiment with lexicon and meter, the work gained fame for its revisionist story of Rādhā and Krishna, which on one hand displayed a literarily conservative bent, and on the other recast Rādhā as a woman who vows herself to virginity and social service after an epiphany while looking upon nature.

The most cited and still memorized lines of *The Absence of the Beloved* are those reputed to illustrate Hariaudh's nature-description, which are situated at the very beginning of this long work, and have remained virtually identical throughout the many revisions of this work. While the description does appear somewhat naturalistic, his natural scenes conform quite thoroughly to an idealized vision of the holy landscape of Krishna's lila. In contrast, the nature descriptions of the rest of the work are not very distinguishable from previous renderings of nature in Braj or Sanskrit. However, the first verses are considered to display a realistic description of the red hues of twilight, using some images less common in "traditional" poetry. The importance of this passage in the

Hindi poetic canon might be gauged by the fact that it is still common for people to recite from memory the first verse, "*divasa kā avasāna samīpa thā / gagana thā kucha lohita ho calā/taru-śikhā para thī aba rājatī / kamalinī-kula vallabha kī prabhā.*"

> The end of day was near.
> The sky had become blood-reddish.
> On the peaks of the trees shone now
> The light of the sun, the beloved of lotus [*kamalinī*] clusters.
> In the middle of the forest grove, a flock of birds'
> Beautiful sound swelled.
> The flock of various kinds, full of tones,
> Was flying in the midst of the vault of the sky.
> The redness of the sky increased.
> The horizon all around became red with love.
> The greenery of the mass of all the trees
> Became as if bathed in redness.
> Also on the banks of the river began to glitter
> The redness of the sky's surface.
> On the water of rivers and lakes
> A very beautiful reddish-brown color.
> Upon the mountain peaks climbed
> A ray wandering among the heads of the trees.
> The disc of the sun became concealed
> In the middle of the vault of the sky, slowly, gradually.[10]

These verses are hardly heretical or of foreign cast. In the stately pace of the *drutavilambita* meter, accommodating the modern Hindi grammar but providing a distinctly classical difficulty in comprehension, the first verse contains a double entendre on the lotuses and the sun, which commentators have noted belies a subtext of Krishna-oriented *śṛṅgāra*—as the *kamalinī* lotuses love the sun, so the beautiful *kamalinī* type of women love Krishna.[11] The many references to redness display the rather courtly poetic trait of showing off a concept's lexical variety with little repetition. The dawn reddened with love comes straight out of the Sanskritic tradition, and reminds the reader of the many Braj verses also on this trope of dawn as a woman after a tryst. What might be identified as unusual here is the "blood-red" of the *lohita*—although Urdu poetry did use this trope—and perhaps the absence of more overarching conceits in service of a description. Rather, these verses shift the poetic cadence slightly from the world of verbal ornament, *alaṃkāra*, toward the prosaic account of a scene. The verses continue in a pastoral vein, with the flute of Krishna and cows of Braj:

> Making the mountain-cave, the play-arbor
> And the beautiful grove, full of echoes,
> A flute sounded right then
> In the shining bower, on the bank of the sun-born Yamuna river.
> Many lovely music-pipes sounded
> Along with many sounding horns;
> Then in the peaceful outskirts of town
> Was heard the sound of cows running home.[12]

The length of this description, and its inceptive position in the canto and the work as a whole, its meter and diction, remind us of classical Sanskrit *mahākāvya*. The content of these verses, dwelling on the particular beauties of the Braj landscape, might remind us of bhakti poetry on the holy ground of Krishna's lila. However, the nature description of this work is much less in service of a deity, or the practice of verbal ornament, than either of these predecessors. Rather spare in terms of *alaṃkāra*, and so far lacking any reference to Krishna per se, these beginning verses present a scene without the usual poetic motivations for such.

Looking at the inceptive verses of *Absence of the Beloved* in the work's historical context, recognizing their iconic status as "nature poetry," we can see that these verses *describe* what was formerly *assumed*. These verses describe discursively what formerly made the stuff of epithets or descriptions of ideal beauty with *upamā*s (metaphor) or *uddīpanas* (incitants) to *śṛṅgāra rasa*. The very foregrounding of this natural description, and its segregation from a description of Krishna per se, parallels what we will learn is Krishna's message: to make the earth equal to lila, the "real world" equal to heaven. The terms of engagement with the "real world" here mean that Braj becomes a more a place to be described, than a place always already referring to Krishna and his sports.

Beside the first verses of the work, critics have also focused on the atmospheric "nature description" of night in canto two as a concomitant to the plot, i.e., the departure of Krishna, and as an expression of the devastated mental state of the Brajvāsīs. Yaśoda's long lament at the end of this canto has been described (in English) by a 1939 critic as "motherly impulses . . . artistically thrown against the background of Nature which answers to the pensive mood of the Lord's mother," "painted in equally grey colours."[13] This sympathetic Nature of Yaśoda's lament (another oft-anthologized section of the work, originally published separately in *Sarasvatī*) consists of a familiar Sanskritic enumeration of natural objects, flora, and fauna in her line of vision and physical experience. Here, as in *The Half-Bloomed Flower*, nature takes on features of characters' affect, i.e., "answers . . . the pensive mood," and mirrors plot somewhat, i.e., darkness follows when Krishna departs. What seems key for the effectiveness of this nature description is its connection with the mother's grief, a sentiment rooted in *karuṇa*, the pathetic, and its relation of aspects of nature less common because of their lack of happy, *śṛṅgārik* associations.[14]

Ultimately, the piece de resistance of this work of rather discrete scenes and lengthy intertextual allusions, is one which I term Rādhā's "epiphany," and in this passage nature dominates her philosophizing about perception in the world, and the objects of Sanskritic metaphor provide a logical link in her argument that love for Krishna means doing good works in the world. Nature, and by extension, the *lok* (people, world) is identified with the body of Krishna as the "supreme soul" (*paramātma*), and Rādhā is a servant of this very husband/lord. This theoretical maneuver, explicated with transposed Sanskrit metaphoric objects in nature, in effect transfers the conventional affective quality of the sexual relationship of Rādhā and Krishna to a vague patriotism via a vision of nature. Rādhā's monologue concludes with the argument that lila is this world, and therefore one should perform good works and acts of social service in this world.[15]

In Rādhā's vision of nature, we can see a leitmotif of Sanskrit metaphoric objects emerge in a garland of comparisons; but here the base reality consists of the natural objects Rādhā sees, not the ideally beautiful limbs they would normally describe.

> Whenever I look at the sky inlaid with stars,
> Or when lines of happy cranes appear in the clouds,
> Then I become elated, I have such a constant thought,
> As if the chest of Śyām appears, shining [with his] pearl necklace.
> The blooming twilight appears like the loveliness of the supreme Beloved.
> I find in the body of the night the reflection of Śyām's color.
> Dawn comes every day colored with love.
> A luster like his face is found in the sun.
> I find the exquisiteness of his locks in a garland of bees,
> The beauty of his eyes in wagtails and deer.
> Both his arms I remember when I see a young elephant's trunk.

I found the radiance of his nose in the beak of a pretty
parrot.
The glimmer of his teeth appears to me in pomegranates.
In red *bimba* fruits gleams a redness like his lips.
I see the beauty of his two thighs in banana-tree trunks.
A graceful exquisiteness like his ankles appears in roses.[16]
Intoxicating the eyes, a very joyful blueness like his body's
Shines in the lap of the rare blue vault of the sky.
Beauty in the earth, beauty [*rasa*] in water, the divine light
in fire,
Often appear like my darling dear boy.[17]

Her visionary state includes aural and physical elements as well, as she finds "in the calling of the birds / The sweet strains of the . . . flute of the most beloved," and "when the soft wind . . . touches" her body, she is conscious of "the touch of Śyām's lovely hands" and the fragrance of his face.[18] Overall, this passage enumerates objects familiar precisely as the metaphorical pool from which Sanskrit and *bhāṣā* poetry drew.

How should we approach this systematic use of familiar metaphoric objects, given together, and largely outside of the metaphoric framework they emerge from? Krishna's arms are not as if elephants' trunks, rather, when Rādhā sees the elephant trunks, she sees Krishna's arms. We could interpret this kind of talk as merely the madness of *viraha*, but altogether, these identifications and their semantic direction toward physical nature seem intentional. The twilight and the sun, the elephant, the parrot, the swarm of bees, the pomegranate, and other plant and animal life all show themselves to her and affect her as if they are parts of her beloved; they do not serve as directly descriptive comparisons for Krishna's body. Hariaudh's Rādhā does not compare Krishna's body to natural objects, as the semiotics would expect, but rather the direction of the comparison is reversed, and the objects of the metaphors become identified with their subject. Rather than offering a description of an embodied desirable Krishna, the passage disembodies Krishna, identifying his body parts with the concrete objects with which they might be compared. We could analyze this passage in purely Sanskritic poetic terms, as a garland, mala, of metaphors and similes, used in a reversed manner; the *tattvapahvana rūpaka* in which the real subject is denied and the object affirmed in its place might be relevant here, or the *tattvākhyāna rūpaka*, the "literal description," "in which the similitude is assumed to lend itself to a confusion, so that one is obliged to identify the subject and object. . . ."[19] Or perhaps we could look to the "inverse simile," *pratīp upameya*, as defined by the seventeenth-century Bhūṣaṇ, e.g., "to say lotuses became like eyes, the moon like the face."[20] However, these earlier theorizations do not quite match. Here there is a positive and verging on literal identification of Krishna's body with elements of the landscape, in a concrete discernment of an abstract divine in nature.

Rādhā shifts again into philosophical gear, noting that the religious texts (namely, the *Bhagavad Gita*) describe Krishna as being comprised of all the beings of the world: "the heads and eyes of the lord/are countless . . . / . . . without a face, eyes, nose, . . . / he touches, eats, hears, sees, smells," she says, in approximation of verses 13.13–14 of the *Bhagavad Gita*. Then using the term made popular by Vivekananda, she proclaims that this *viśvātma*, universal soul, possesses the senses of all living beings, and "all living beings of the world are divine images (*mūrti*s) of him."[21]

Following the shift of Krishna's image to the living world, the practice of bhakti is also transformed into serving the world. A universal moral code is attached to Krishna bhakti proper and then explicitly defined as good works, turning on the concept of service, *sevā*, a concept already common in reformist Hinduism and literary texts, and which would quickly become part of the vocabulary of citizenship. The nine types of bhakti she then reinterprets as acts of personal compassion and social service, following the logic that the living world and Krishna are interchangeable: "the world pervades the beloved, in the world is the beloved. / In this way I saw the lord of the world in Śyām."[22]

> Forms are those of the universal soul (*viśvātma*), which is the supreme lord.
> All of the creatures, rivers, mountains, creepers, vines, and various trees—
> Protection and worship of them, proper effort (*yatna*) on their behalf, reverence, and service
> Are the heartfelt devotion for the supreme lord that is best of all.

Using the contemporary Vedantin term *viśvātma*, and another term from reformist Bengal, *yatna* (industry, effort), Rādhā lists off the natural objects in our charge, from large and powerful—mountains, rivers—to small and merely beautiful—creepers, vines, and trees, poetic greenery. Immediately afterward, Rādhā launches into her exposition of *navadhā* bhakti, with clear social and political innuendoes.

> To listen with your heart to all the words of the afflicted and oppressed,
> Of sick people, distressed people, and the reformers of the people (*loka-unnāyaka*),

To listen to the recitation of the pure Shastras, to listen to
the words of the virtuous
Is considered the devotion named *śravaṇa* (hearing) among
good folk (*sajjan*).[23]

The following verses continue in the same vein. In the most political of them, she states that *vandanā* (prayer) is "to bow down before scholars, one's own elders, and patriots (*des ke premī*), / wise men, charitable men, the virtuous, brave leaders (*tejasvī*), / holy images of God." Here "brave leaders" is indicated with a term based upon the concept of *tejas*, power or energy, which by then had emerged as a quality imbuing activism, especially nationalist strivings. *Dāsatā* (servitude) becomes to "lift up the base fallen castes"; *smaraṇa* (remembrance) "remembering the troubles of the poor, the helpless widows, / And orphans . . ."; *arcanā* (worship) to give medicine to the afflicted and food to the hungry; *pada-sevana* (serving the feet) to zealously give shelter and dignity to low castes, who are "as if the feet of society's body."[24]

How might we interpret the aesthetic and theological choices Hariaudh made in *The Absence of the Beloved*, in an integrative fashion? While clearly this text exemplifies one of the characteristics of Dvivedī era literature, i.e., didacticism, how we can interpret the placement of this didacticism, embedded within Rādhā, in a climactic vision, after a particularly poetic rendition of the disembodied body of Krishna? The logic of this poetic sleight of hand seems clear: because the natural objects of metaphor—aggregated as Nature—are identified with the real subject, which is Krishna, therefore we should love this "real" world, natural and social. But the motivation for the poetic reversal also seems determined by the didactic message. We might look at this pairing of newfangled poetics and newfangled religion as cut from the same cloth. The theological terms transforming into this-worldly, politicized diktats might mirror, and maybe encourage, the poetics-in-reverse, where metaphorical objects become subjects—become things in themselves, more or less.

In the Nature of modern Hindi poetry from 1900, we observe several aesthetic patterns, of retaining the *śṛṅgāra* imbued in natural objects by the *kāvya* tradition; of putting these objects center stage as objects of *yathārth*, that new literary value; of linking objects of nature in passages redolent of classical descriptive scenes, but with an enumerative, aggregative implication; and of linking this landscape of real things (whether the idealized *upamāna*s of the past, or realist bushes and crags) with political realities. All of these occur while authors self-consciously integrate certain poetic precepts from outside, as Dvivedī incorporated Milton via Urdu, paraphrased Goldsmith, and spoke of independence in reference to the empirical gaze, and the originality of poets. Nature and natural science became a field from which to draw political lessons, but in its descriptions uncertainty remains about the balance between realism and artfulness. The epitome of this quandary can be found in Pāṭhak's "Beauty of Kashmir," examined in the previous chapter, in which his allegedly "Romantic nature poetry" is much like verse on the Braj *nāyikā*. Even so, the link of landscape to political undertones can be seen in his Lady Nature, consort of Dogra king. Ultimately, however, Nature becomes devotionalized, as if the object of worship has shifted from the king, or god of the mountains, to the land itself, a goddess. In Hariaudh we see emotive development in natural scenes, and in his seminal *The Absence of the Beloved*, the real world, *yathārth*, becomes the metaphorical objects of poetics, and poetics serves a social imperative.

In the subsequent section the natural poetics of these authors from the Dvivedī generation will be complemented by an examination of the earliest writings of Jayaśaṅkar Prasād, the young man publishing outside of *Sarasvatī*, whose experiments would be a bellwether of the nature poetry that would later define his Chāyāvād generation.

The New Generation, Nature, and Natural Politics

Jayaśaṅkar Prasād (1889–1937) has the distinction of being the most translated and analyzed modern Hindi poet.[25] His allegorical epic in verse, *Kāmāyanī* (1936), has become a symbol of Chāyāvād and indeed of the modern Hindi literary perspective, using classical motifs in elaboration of the paradoxes of being: sentience and insentience, destruction and rebirth. At the opening scene of *Kāmāyanī* we see a destructive nature, in a scene of the aftermath of a great flood, and hear the musings of Man (the primeval man, Manu of Vedic mythology) on the matter of consciousness (*cetan*) in an unconscious (*jaṛ*) world. This latter theme would in fact provide a springboard for later, psychoanalytically inclined Hindi authors of the following decades. But decades before the massive printings and emotive readings from *Kāmāyanī*, which have made it the icon it remains today, Prasād began his career in the midst of our more pastoral and embodied nature poetry described in the previous chapters, and in the critical context of Dvivedī's linkage of nature with realism and usefulness. The psychology of his early poetry entailed traditional affects, but verged toward something new in its presentation of nature, which we will examine below.

Prasād's biography has been detailed in English several times, and will not be rehearsed here in detail.[26] Suffice it to say that Prasād was born into a tobacco merchant's family in Banaras, where he imbibed the popular and high arts the city is known for, namely music, dancing, and generally the traditional pleasures of the Banarsi aesthete. The social context of these pleasures transformed during his lifetime; as Rubin notes, "he was known to visit houses of dubious reputation, where one might hear the best classical singing."[27] While brought up among the courtesans' arts, Prasād would achieve his fame with works quite distant from this atmosphere, in an irony merely reflecting his times.

His formal education ended at fourteen, but clearly he possessed a vast knowledge of languages and literatures. His return again and again to watery images—the poetic works *Āṁsu* (Tears) of 1925 and 1933, *Jharanā* (Cascade) of 1918, *Lahar* (Wave) of 1933, and the seminal *Kāmāyanī*, described above, of 1935—may indicate his reading of Tagore. Prasād spent his life along the Ganges in Banaras, traveling little, and composing not just poetry, but dramas, stories, and novels. In this chapter we will examine Prasād's early poetry and a prose essay from his breakaway journal, *Indu* (*The Moon*), on topics relevant to nature in particular. These are materials usually overshadowed in literary history by his works of the later twenties onward, especially the epic *Kāmāyanī*. The resemblance of his poetry to some of that of Tagore and the English Romantics, and his discussion in his writings of the influence of Bengali and English poetry upon his generation of Hindi poets, have contributed to the general assignation of "Romantic" to Chāyāvād poetry. Certainly this assertion is largely correct. However, if we closely examine the early Prasād publications, we find a more complex picture of this early "Hindi Romanticism," whose characteristics had a particular cast of *śṛṅgāra* and older poetic forms generally, unexplained by Bengali or English influence.

The distinction between the Dvivedī generation and the Chāyāvād generation is a real one, evident in the publishing politics of the time. Prasād's literary projects differed enough from Dvivedī's vision of modern Hindi literature that he was refused publication in *Sarasvatī*. Prasād turned instead to self-publication in his own journal, *Indu*, founded in 1909. In this chapter we will examine several of Prasād's earliest works from this magazine, but first we will turn to an essay cum prose-poem from the very first issue of *Indu*, indicating the centrality of the abstract notion of Nature to Prasād's poetic enterprise, the article "Prakṛti-saundarya," ("The Beauty of Nature").

Nature signifies many things in this essay. This Nature is a goddess and force of the material world; Prasād's indebtedness to Bengali Shakta traditions is palpable here, as the Tagorean poetics of a terrible sublime in the universe. However, we can see that this Nature also relates to the content of poetry, as a Nature of universal truth and a Nature that comprises the stuff of classical beauty and love. The first line of the essay positions the beauty of nature as an aggregate (*samūh*) of divine creation on the one hand, and as a single example of the creation of god, "a small example of the work of that Great Craftsman," on the other. Prasād then links nature's beauty with the wondrous (*adbhut*) *rasa*, and its ineffability with that of the divine. "To describe it fully is like examining the virtues of God."[28] Mention of this wondrous *rasa* frames the essay, at beginning and end, and in between we see both a *śṛṅgārik* vision of nature, and a terrible, fierce nature that is nevertheless beautiful—again, resembling the tropes of Shaktism. A description of seasons, although not a complete *ṣad-ṛtu varṇan*, appears as well, alluding to classicism along with the *adbhut rasa* itself.

Most notably, Prasād describes this nature in a manner evocative of Pāthak's earlier Lady Nature. As Pāṭhak's Nature "moment by moment changes her appearance" as if a lady adorning herself (*pala pala parivartita prakṛti vesa*), so Prasād's Nature changes in ways that evoke the śṛṅgāra *rasa* atmosphere of love, filled with bees and bloomed lotuses:

> Your periodic changes [*parivartan*] also are so beautiful. According to the division of seasons, in the spring, making the trees beautiful, bearing soft pretty leaves, you give rise to the sweet blossoms. Ah! At that time it is possible to see your wondrous glory! Somewhere . . . on the lotuses bloomed among the flowing water-weeds, a line of honey-devotees are buzzing around with pleasure, taking *rasa*. Somewhere a cuckoo drowned in *rasa* calling out his "*kuhuk*" on the half-bloomed red soft leaved young trees is making the tender branches sway! The beautiful forest, arbor, creeper, grove, mountain, riverbank, and on and on—wherever you look, flowered branches appear there![29]

But here Prasād shifts to description of the harshness of the summer landscape—this in itself is not so unusual, as a scene described by many a lovelorn woman in the *ṣad-ṛtu* or *bārah-māsā* genres, but here the point of the essay is Nature itself, and Prasād's exposition of its fiercer aspects reminds one somewhat of an English style Romantic sublime:

> The suns untiring burning rays, the silence-bursting gusts of the loo wind, the dawn heat full of *tej*, the wilting of trees full of flowers, the slow flow of rivers drying up; the constant emptiness upon the surface of the earth, gives rise to various/strange influences!

> But Nature! In summer also you illuminate at once in the night your almost destroyed spring beauty! Those very reduced and slow flowing rivers, those very cities surrounded with high palaces and beautiful mountain river banks, which are difficult to look at in the blazing sun's day, being cleansed white by the rays drowned in nectar of the lotus-hero, the moon—what a beautiful and enchanting scene they are changing into! And that very poisonous fierce dawn wind, that used to burn up the body, is cooled somewhat by the touch of the moon rays. What is all of this? It is only your illimitable form [*svarūp*].[30]

The *svarūp*, form or incarnation, of nature progresses then to the rainy season, typically *śṛṅgārik* but also presented with a bit of fearsomeness, all of which affect the emotions:

> In the rainy season also what a beautiful and handsome scene of nature! In the vault of the sky spotted with clouds, like sparks glittering from Indra's sword on the dark body of a demon in the form of a cloud, the constant flashing of lightning, and the green line of mountains covered with dense trees, the flowing of a pure full river hidden in the greenery, its rapid visible flow from various places, takes the rippling stream of the heart flowing along with it! The call of the peacock sitting at the top of the high *kadamba* tree, the sound of the group of *kokil* birds, does the shaking line of trees, buzzing with the movement of wind and with the sound of crickets shake its head and call the mind [*citt*] over to it? After that, the relentless stream of heavy drops; greenery encompassing the horizon, the white glow of stopping rain; what a beautiful picture this presents to the eyes. Your form cannot come into the imagination of men. In the pure night your fearsome vision [*dṛśya*] makes the heart tremble. The world surrounded in deep darkness, the sound of the thunderbolt with the flash of lightning from the sky spread with clouds, the deep sound of rain, the glittering of the fireflies along with the resounding of crickets, unsettle the heart.[31]

Like *rasa*'s theory of the emotional effects of observing particular dramatic scenes between hero and heroine in particular settings, here Prasād enacts the emotional effects of observing this setting by itself. This reminds him ultimately of the divine, and here is where we might find a gothic idea of nature, a "fearsome vision" that is intended to unsettle and make tremble the heart. This too, however, can be read through the aesthetics of the terrible sublime of the Goddess.

Next, a particular phrase catches our attention, after an emotive exposition of the beauties of autumn:

> Look at that—outside the city limit and on the riverbank is a growth of grass and the slow flow of pure watery rivers, the full light of the autumn moon, some cool wind, the blooming of lotuses in lakes, green trees, high mansions, rivers, mountains, cut fields of the sprinkled moonlight, and the silver pure light on mother earth! Ah! What a theatrical stage—like a dancing woman—is this, this changing!

This latter phrase, "What a theatrical stage—like a dancing woman—is this, this changing!" [*yah kaisā naṭī kī tarah yavanikā, parivartan!*], is a remarkable poetic maneuver which takes some unpacking to fully understand. The phrase points us to Pāṭhak's "Beauty of Kashmir" yet again, and takes Pāṭhak's conceit further to epitomize what modern Hindi poetry envisioned for nature. The root concept is change, *parivartan*, as in Pāṭhak's Lady Nature, ever-changing in appearance (*pala pala parivartita prakṛti veśa*). Here in Prasād's essay, this *parivartan*—"turning round" or "exchange," at root—is more immediately identified with the change of appearance with the seasons. This change for Prasād is furthermore a *yavanikā*, a stage or stage-curtain in Sanskrit drama, and this stage/-curtain further is as if a *naṭī*, a female dancer, as in Pāṭhak's ornament-of-doubt passage: "Did it [Kashmir] appear as a curtainless stage for the dancer [*naṭī*] Nature?" In Pāṭhak's "Beauty of Kashmir"—which may or may not have been on Prasād's mind here—Kashmir is a stage for the ever-changing heroine Nature, a stage which is a real world nevertheless beautiful as art. Prasād's Nature—as change itself—is both the stage and the heroine. Here Prasād thus articulates the transition to modernity that nature was supposed to embody: the setting is now the main character, the former background is now writ large as Nature.

The essay ends with a short passage describing winter, a scene which both gives pleasure and fear, and is identified with the wondrous play, *adbhut* lila, of the Goddess:

> The current of cold making the heart tremble, the silence of the snowy wind, the dew drops like pearls in the green field,

> the casting of dawn's sunrays upon them! What pleasure this scene gives. Then in the winter of the dark fortnight, the fierce current of deep cold wind, thick darkness, in which the heart shakes with fear at seeing some known thing before it.
>
> What is all this? O Goddess! All this is your surprising lila, so seeing your endlessly colored handsome form, who is not astounded with surprise![32]

Here the usual lila of Krishna belongs to Prakṛti Devī; the vagaries of nature, beautiful and harsh, are her play, which creates *adhbhut rasa*. In this passage, as the others, long descriptive lists, often Sanskritic in their lexicon and familiar scenery, punctuated with emotive exclamations, characterize what has become the normative way to write about nature in prose. In this Prasād's essay is not unlike Hariaudh's nature scenes in *The Half-Bloomed Flower*, evoking "ah"s from the author and presumably the spectator/reader as well. This sweeping vision of seasons, both particular and all together the ever-changing play of the divine, constitutes the natural scene, which in turn ignites the emotion. The effect of the incitant, *uddīpana,* here occurs in a different mode. The late Romantic view could reside in this type of writing, in the emotive import of scenes, but the content of the scene, that is, the content of the description of the scene, suggests Romanticism less than it does English nature writing generically, fitted into a Kalidasa-esque scape of seasons and their objects. And ultimately, the sublimity here resembling that of the English poet, and a Kantian understanding of the beauty of nature's danger, is finally less harsh. Nature is change itself, and comprised of the apparatus of *śṛṅgāra* along with some harsh aspects, all of them resolved with prettiness again in the end—"your endlessly colored handsome form."

The short poems from *Indu* take a different approach from this sweeping scale of this prose essay. In these we see objects as themselves, especially objects formerly infused with *śṛṅgāra,* now independent actors. On the other hand, the poems continue the theme of divinity in nature that Prasād elaborated with his "Beauty of Nature" above, with poems that still feature a *śṛṅgārik* semiotic background, but speak of spiritual overtones. Below we will examine four of Prasād's many poems from *Indu,* 1909–1918, which exemplify these traits.

Objects as themselves appear infused with *śṛṅgāra,* yet detached from human lovers per se. In this Braj Bhāṣā poem "The Mango Blossom" ("Rasāl-mañjarī") from the first year of *Indu,* Prasād develops this trope of personified *upamāna* and even anticipates some of the sentiments of Rādhā in Hariaudh's 1914 *Priyapravās,* discussed in the previous chapter, in her exhortations to her wind-girlfriend. Nirālā's 1923 "Jasmine Bud" would take up virtually the same theme, but in a radically modern verse form. Here Prasād gives us a version of the blossom's "story" in a traditional *mātrik* meter, in Braj Bhāṣā, but still exemplifying a modern value of these images as natural objects. We should note that personification was not new, especially in portrayals of the bee, a reminder of Krishna and men's fickle desires, but here the scene is a small scale landscape of natural objects standing in for actors in a story of *śṛṅgāra*.

> From the kind glance of the hero of the season [*ṛtunāyak*], this very pretty
> New 'mango blossom' he put in place, just right and beautiful.
> Just now some sweet pollen moistens inside it,
> But until now no bee has taken the nectar.[33]
> Oh pure southern wind! Come nicely and calmly.
> Don't run quickly from the beautiful banks of the Kaveri.
> Don't make the lady's *āñcal* fly up forcefully;
> It's a new bloomed flower; come here slowly.
> Oh they listen to the *kokil* bird, sitting nicely at a distance on a branch.
> Then when they hear the *pañcam* raga, they sway and bloom.
> She cannot bear the crimson of your eyes[34]
> Speaking tones very sweetly nearby, what noisy chatter he makes.
> Why do you come here moving so flirtatiously
> A good person doesn't think of their own benefit
> The bloomed flower in the forest should be dallied with—
> O southern wind!—as long as this new blossom blooms.
> See the yellow sash at his waist, see his dark color,
> In every way just like the son of Nanda.
> Constantly drinking honey and flitting amongst the flowers skillfully.
> Oh bee! This blossom seems gladdened and new!
> You should humbly hear this with sweet sympathy,
> Understanding this advice well, give it place in the mind:
> Leaving off your playfulness, thinking of [the effect of] your body
> Obtain the beautiful blossom and give your burden carefully.[35]

The perspective is not unlike that of a Braj Bhāṣā poet writing on the spring season. The famous *dohā* of Bihari on the bee caught by the new bud comes to mind. However, here the *śṛṅgārik* conceit of the wind, the bee, and the blossom is played out more lengthily, and with more interest in both emotion ("She cannot bear the crimson of your eyes," and "This blossom seems gladdened and new!") and in admonitions ("it's a new bloomed flower, come here slowly," and "give your burden carefully").

Considering "The Mango Blossom" with other poems on particular natural objects, we can see the isolation of these objects as objects, agents out of whom the allusions of *śṛṅgāra* emerge, but not in relation to human love per se, just within the world of flowers, bees, and breezes. Furthermore, these object-poems are not always as typically coded with *śṛṅgāra* as the former "The Mango Blossom." Take for instance, "Kokil" (The Cuckoo) (1912),[36] on one of the stock avian creatures of classical Sanskrit, and a term attributed to talented poets and singers. Prasād's Khaṛī Bolī "The Cuckoo" would remind the audience of scenes of love in springtime, on one hand, and the performative voice of the poet as well. Besides this, Prasād's *kokil* bird speaks of newness, of his song, of his era, and at base the new growth of a spring:

> It's a new heart, a new time, a new arbor
> In the midst of the new lotuses is a new group of tendrils
> New is your raga, your enchanting tones pleasing
> New is this desirable veena-like voice.

In its Khaṛī Bolī Hindi, in Prasād's independent magazine *Indu*, such sentiments must have seemed as much those of the new generation of Khaṛī Bolī poets as of the *kokil* bird.[37] Ostensibly though, it is only addressed to the *kokil*, who like the bird of Sanskrit poetry, reflects a human inner state:

> Although it is a joyful simple sound of yours, oh *kokil*!
> Still the heart hears it and is soothed, calmed, delighted
> The new bloomed mango blossom, with drunken bees
> Handsome, full of the most exquisite drops of nectar
> The sweet gust of southern wind shakes the branch
> Which calls the gardener for its sweet fruit.
> Seated in the mass of shoots, with his very passion
> Are you singing, oh *kokil*, in such a beautiful ragas?

The simple, natural *kokil*'s song soothes the heart, sings of passion, and instigates new hearings—new readings, perhaps—of his own song:

> Our friend the moon, friend of the night lotus, with joy
> came into the sky

It came running from a long time ago, and now has got its
chance
Now he has stopped in the middle of the sky with this
desire
Taking some meaning from your new language
Sing with your new gladness, don't stop for a moment
Kokil, for your tones filling the southern wind!

This *kokil* imparts its tones through language, *bhāṣā,* and a new language at that—new at least in the spring season, for that creature hearing it for the first time, and possibly in the poetic analogy, new for the audience of Hindi poetry accustomed to another grammar for poetic speech. Whereas in "The Mango Blossom" emotion pertains to the natural objects themselves, here in "The Cuckoo" Prasād gestures toward the fact that the *kokil* bird's song refracts into the consciousness of its auditors, who derive meaning from it (*le nikāla kucha artha*). The poem ends with merely a happy exhortation to this *kokil,* still the center of gravity for the poem and its suggestion of the timelessness of the simple, passionate voice.

A third poem on a particular object was "Dalit Kumudinī" ("The Crushed Little Lotus Blossom").[38] This poem imagines in long lines of dependent clauses describing the blossom, redolent of Sanskrit *kāvya,* depicting the previous life of a water-lily now broken on the ground:

Oh, in the midst of this man-made pleasure pond the
crushed little lotus opened
Who had been cooled in the shade of the green creeper
bower
Whose pollen the flower-stick[39] of moon rays had made fall
Whom the rays of the fierce sun too didn't find

The poem continues in this vein, including her usual suitors of bees and wind. However, her world was one of more than worldly love, as she who "would tremblingly listen to the new song of Rādhā."

On whom would rest the watchful eyes of tiny golden fish
On whom set the profound color of the feeling of love,
pure and internal
Whose stream of sweet pollen was found bobbing in water
Her fragrance spread in the pure beautiful lake
Her innocence was enchanted, but now she is a casualty of
the world:

By some careless drunk elephant, yes! She was crushed
underfoot
This very lotus, mixed with the hot dust of summer heat
Leaves broken, bereft of pollen, without her lovely beauty
At the side of the thorny path; the way of the cycle of time
is indeed strange.

The flat endnote of philosophizing aside, Prasād leaves us with an image of the object of beauty destroyed. The elephant, known in Sanskrit poetry especially for its rutting, and here drunk and careless, or even selfish (*svārthi*), seems to stand in for the male enjoyer of beauty, whose force can destroy that which he desires. Instead of an image of the "happy heterosexuality" of flower and bee or breeze, here Prasād gives us a story within that framework of *śṛṅgāra*, but ultimately a story about loss. This possibility of the individual object—flower, bird, or what have you—to tell an abject story that speaks to the presence of ruin and death represented something new in the otherwise flowery pastoral landscape of short poems in both Braj and Khaṛī Bolī.

As we turn to two poems from *Jharanā*, Prasād's use of the "stuff" of *śṛṅgāra* becomes more experimental and even cryptic. This is most apparent in the rhyming but apparently meter-less poem "Paricay" ("Acquaintance"), a riddling type of poem in which three of the four stanzas contain a different version of the line, "a lotus bloomed in a lake," and ask the connection of such with another phrase describing a scene of dawn, the bee, or the southern wind. The poem resolves with a cryptic statement alluding to poetic meter as much as to love.

The glow of the dawn in the east
The blooming of the lotus in the lake
What did they know?[40] What was their connection?[41]
In the vault of the sky the play of the sun.
Where does the bee remain in the night?
The lotus bloomed in the lake
What did they know? What was their connection?
The sweet, honeyed, enchanting pollen.
A lotus bloomed in the middle of a lake
From [Mount] Malay[42] the search, the driving of the wind
What did they know? What was their connection?
That fragrance you find everyday.
Pollen melted in the sun with love[43]
Got from the fragrance, joyfully[44]

> This very knowledge, it was that connection
> "The scheme[45] of love of yours and mine."[46]

The first verse seems straightforward enough; the last line seems to answer the question of the connection between dawn and the lotus blooming. The second stanza follows roughly the same pattern, although bees-in-the-night is not an image commonly met with. The third stanza surprises us with its depiction of the southern wind as a search by means of driving wind (*malay se anil calā kar khoj*), and the quotidian and here rhyming word for the sense of "everyday," *roj*. Here both are connected through their fragrant nature. In the final verse, we are surprised by the absence of the lake-lotus. Rather, we get its pollen only, baking in the sunlight. Finally, our riddling questions disappear: the certain connection, the definite knowledge, is given within quotation marks, " 'the scheme of love of yours and mine' " (*prem kā merā terā chand*). The line resists any one definitive reading, with its term *chand*—does it signify the schema of a poetic meter, or a shackling bond, or a prank? All are possible. Seemingly, the bond between lotuses in pools and other natural "characters" of poetry—the wind, the bees, etc.—can be made apparent; but the result of pollen meeting fragrance—perhaps mixing with the southern wind—resolves into a profound abstraction of connection—a poetic meter, a bond, or perhaps the playful trickery of love. While we see Prasād's poetic tone transformed here from his earlier *Indu* poems, still he writes of blooms, bees, and breezes, only appropriate subjects for a poem alluding to the mainstays of poetry: meter and love.

We can interpret these, what I call "object-poems," in light of one of Prasād's statements from the first issue of his *Indu*, on the creation of literature itself: "Literature is the result of the coming-to-light of independent nature (*svatantra prakṛti*) and brilliance (*pratibhā*, talent or light, i.e., genius). It cannot stand anything's being subject (*paratantratā*) to something else. That which is true and beautiful in the universe is the subject of literature."[47] Here "independent nature" we can take as "nature in itself," as in the term *svatantra* (free, independent, self-determined) already established for the concept of empiricism (see Chapter 3 for discussion of Nature "*svatantra rūp se*"). The language of liberty is then further expanded with *paratantratā*, being subject. Prasād seems to state here that literature should not be beholden to any convention, any bond of inequality that hinders the truth of thing-in-itself being described, and the working of individual genius. Freeing nature from bonds of convention—as the literary historiographical narratives have repeated—would define the Chāyāvād generation and its *svacchandatavad* precursors, and provides a logic for Prasād's many object-poems, which atomize objects of nature in exploration of their being in and of themselves, the hero or heroine of their own story. While the semiotics of *śṛṅgāra* informs these poems, still their independence, as singularly described objects, defines them. These poems are stories of singular entities, rather than sets of conventional objects arrayed for allegorical effect in the romantic *śṛṅgārik* mode.

Further, Prasād's invocation of *paratantratā* cries out for a political reading: like the Indian colonial subject, subject to a suppressing power, that which is true and beautiful, Nature in itself, nature's objects—both empirical reality and affective possibilities—and the poet's genius, have been suppressed by convention. Prasād may have alluded here mostly to his perceived oppression by the conventions upheld by Dvivedī, who denied him publication in *Sarasvatī*. However, the language of liberation links significantly, multivalently to the discourses of empiricism, anti-colonialism, and of course Romanticism, and gives a political analogue of shedding subjection to the format of the natural object-poem itself.

Conclusions

Hariaudh's *The Absence of the Beloved* presented a new vision of Sanskritic poetics in an extremely precise, subtle way that is difficult to perceive for many readers, understandably overwhelmed by the saccharine tones of the pining residents of Braj, the earnestness of the social message, and of course, the Sanskrit meters. However, the epiphany of the penultimate canto signals also a paradigm shift in metaphor. Here the "disfiguring ornaments of Oriental verse" (in paraphrase of colonial reviews) become natural subjects in themselves, and writing of nature circumlocuted the erotics of older verse, while still remaining within the domain of familiarity and Sanskritic literary tropes.

This tendency emerged more clearly in Prasād's early object-poems, known for their personifying fancy, the badge of modern poetic subjectivity. This is all very well, but in these poems we see something more than mere Romantic subjectivism, but rather an adherence to natural objects qua objects. Unlike Tagore's nature, these examples of Prasād's early poetry cleave to the world of *upamāna*, Sanskritic metaphoric objects, much more consistently and profoundly. This early Prasād also retains more of the Sanskrit pleasure of the voyeur, and less of the "I" of subjective consciousness already a staple of Tagore and Bengali poetry of the teens. The setting of beautiful, seemingly miniature, scenes comprised of beautiful objects—in a sense still the *uddīpanas*, inspiring the sweet *rasa* of *śṛṅgāra*—distinguished Prasād at this point from Tagore's more typically modernist, and often darker, poetry.

In considering the import of these metaphors-become-subjects, or perhaps *uddipanas* put centerstage, we might look to other expressions of tropic dissatisfaction. It has after all been a poetic trope in itself to deny the efficacy of tropes in description of real beauty. A sixteenth-century song of Sūr Dās plays upon this theme in a way meaningful for our context, segregating *upamāna* from *upameya*:

> Seeing Hari's body, the similes were ashamed.
> Some stayed hid in the water, some in the woods, some others went into the sky.
> Seeing his face, the sun went into the sky, the lightening too, when it saw the brightness of his teeth.
> The fish and the lotus, fearing his hands, feet, and eyes, made their abode in water.
> Seeing his arms, the great serpents were ashamed, and fled into their holes.
> Seeing his waist, the lion felt afraid and stayed hidden in forests.
> The poets' descriptions give abuse, giving comparisons to his sacred body.
> The animals say to Sur Das: you shame us, taking our name.[48]

In the modern Hindi poetic world, the similes have become ashamed again, and have gone to hide, like Krishna's body parts in Hariaudh's Brindavan landscape. But here their "shame" is driven by epistemological and ideological shifts away from the body and towards nature. They also, like Sur's *upamānas*, retreat to the "real" world, denied their identity as *upamānas*, even as they are used as such. The objects of the metaphors and similes have truly become only objects now and the subjects of their own stories, this time not out of shame at their incommensurability, but in a turn to the ideology of realism located for our authors in nature.

Chapter 6

Embodying the World

Look how the Enchanter (Mohan) keeps changing his appearance
Taking off the blue garment, he comes wearing the yellow robe of
Krishna
the jeweled ornament of stars has slowly descended.
Whose bed of union is this arranged here? As if he has just
Got up and left! These drops of sweat mixed with pollen are
scattered about.
Whose splendor of exertion and lassitude was just here right now,
taking the world along? (26.38–48)
. . .
Come, let us meet not limb-to-limb but heart-with-heart
. . .
Come, let's meet in the ocean of love that is beauty . . .
where there is eternal peace—there we might live forever free
(*svacchand*)!"
. . . they began to see—dawn.

—Jayaśaṅkar Prasād, *Pilgrim of Love* (*Prem-pathik*) (1914)[1]

This chapter will pair a rather unlikely combination of poems, dating between 1912–1920, which implemented nature for two often intertwined ends: the spiritualism that was to be a defining feature of Indian arts of the early twentieth century generally, and the nationalism that swept the subcontinent with Gandhi's Non-Cooperation movement. Indeed, nature was integral to the expression in poetry of both of these movements. Freedom as a spiritual vision merged with political vision, and the figure of the Pilgrim or ascetic wayfarer, *pathik*, a term found plentifully in nationalist discourse, and clearly fused with the persona of Gandhi, often delivered this poetical/political theme. The abstractions of spirit, nation, and freedom were in fact evoked materially through nature, the body of God and the body of Bhārat (India).

By the teens, new conceptions of the poet had merged with the political atmosphere, and the concept of *svacchandatā* (freedom, literally "having one's own meter"), representing disregard for convention and the poet's subjective prerogative, emerged as a defining feature of so-called Hindi Romanticism. While Marxist critics linked this freedom with the rise of individualism and the freeing of sexual mores, I would argue that this concept, by the 1910s, already had a poetical valence through nature poetry that happened also to translate to a political theme. The language of empiricism, which had brought nature as a subject "in itself" to the fore, and freed natural objects from their former metaphorical moors, here evolves into a spiritualization of nature and the nation, both representing freedom through union.

We will turn first to Prasād's early poems again, which take themes of Nature in a macrocosmic direction, springing off from the sentiments of his Nature essay that keynoted his entry into the literary publishing world. Then we will address at length his *Prem-pathik* (Pilgrim of Love), which complexly situates social freedoms in a nature-bound spiritualism. Next, we will turn to Rāmanareś Tripāṭhī, a man on the fringes of literary fame, whose popular *Pathik* (The Pilgrim) would integrate an enumerative description of nature with a blatantly Gandhian message. Finally, in closing, we will consider also the many quotidian ways in which, by 1920, "nature poetry"—as nature-description, as object-poems, and as spiritual or political medium—had become the standard of modern Hindi poetics for authors at all levels of fame or talent, representing precisely what was modern in modern Hindi poetics.

The Play of Natural Forms

The leap was not far from the independent subjects of poetry, the natural objects in-and-of-themselves, found in Hariaudh's *The Absence of the Beloved*, and many of Jayaśaṅkar Prasād's early poems, to theological and philosophical musings. This comes as no surprise, considering Prasād's statements in his naturalistic and spiritual "Prākṛtik-saundarya" essay of 1909, examined previously. His indebtedness to Tagore, and less palpably, the English Romantics indubitably played a part in forming the spiritualized nature of his poetry.

Here we will turn to two more poems from *Indu*, "Mahākrīṛā" ("The Great Play") and "Pratham Prabhāt" ("The First Dawn"), and then to a poem from the 1918 edition of Prasād's collection *Jharanā* (*Cascade*), "Paricay" ("Acquaintance"). In all of these Khaṛī Bolī poems we see nature as a site of *śṛṅgāra* that surpasses the objects themselves and integrates with universal, ontological powers and/or the soul of the poet.

In "Mahākrīṛā" of 1912 we are presented with what appears at first to be straightforward nature description through personifications, in rather prosaic yet rhymed Khaṛī Bolī verses:

> Beautiful East is about to wash her face with pure dawn
> The full moon of night is about to set
> The host of stars is about to lose its splendor
> Dawn's redness also is about to wash the surface of the sky
> with golden liquid
> Of whose coming are the birds are singing?
> The southern wind also comes, to remove distress
> The moonlight could not recede, and the good dawn has come
> The soft buds of the grove seem about to bloom[2]

The verses continue in this vein, with some indication of a *śṛṅgārik* theme for this dawn: "What light-filled rising is god Dinakar [the sun] about to make / How joyful the pairs of *cakra* birds are about to become!"[3] Subsequently, Prasād presents us with a verse proclaiming his poetic fancy: "The Imagination says, this [sun] is the ball of the Great Child / Whose play is the union of this entire universe."[4] His "Imagination" may signal a modern literary value gleaned from Romanticism, but the image conjured here is one direct from Krishna poetry—the great child clearly Bāl-Krishna, and his *kṛīṛā* his play as a child, and his love-play as a man. The following verses carry out this vision of love-in-union between ever-morphing proxies for Krishna and Rādhā, who ultimately embody Nature herself:

> Become the southern wind, you play with the buds too
> Become the bee you catch the sweet cascade of pollen
> Singing in the voice of Rādhā in beautiful [*rasile*] ragas
> You look at the adornment of Nature with love
> Giving [her] the veil of dawn, you make Nature your companion
> You placed a true bindi on her brow of the dawn-red-kumkum
> You give shape to her ever-new beauty and gaze at her
> She gazes at you, and as a couple you play together.[5]

Here Nature poetry takes a Vaishnava cast, but still remains the play of natural forms themselves. By extension, the poet himself presents us with his play of forms, in this rearrangement of objects and events of nature well-known from poetry past, into modern nature poetry, about Nature as such. In this 1912 poem we can see poetic trends that would solidify in later Chāyāvād, and which likely affected the poetics of older poets like Hariaudh, whose 1914 *Priyapravās*, and other later poems, evoked similar images of Krishnaite union through the many objects of Nature. Thus while Prasād was spurned by Dvivedī for publication in *Sarasvatī*, his independently published poems were key to poetic shifts for both older and younger Hindi poets of the time, looking for a new, modern way to express the sublimity of Braj Bhāṣā's Krishna lila.

Further, the theme of dawn was obviously in fashion, in politics as well as poetics: in the teens become a byword of claims for future Self-Rule, we can also recall Dvivedī's own poetic prose on a politicized nature at the dawn of a new era in his "Prākṛtik Dṛśya" (Natural Scene) of 1913, as we consider the previous 1912 poem, with its unusual conceit of the sun as the child Krishna's ball. Another dawn poem by Prasād appeared in 1913 as well, "Pratham Prabhāt" ("First Dawn"). Here Prasād presents a somewhat Tagorean merging of the human psychological experience—namely, of love—with nature in its typical characters of flowers, bees, and breezes. In this Khaṛī Bolī poem of five quatrains, roughly 21 *mātrās* to the line, inner and outer nature (*āntarik* and *bāhya prakṛti*) appear in sync:

> Thoughts [*manovṛttiyaṁ*] were sleeping like a flock of birds,
> In the handsome new nest of the mind
> The heart also was peaceful like the blue sky,
> Outer and inner nature, all, were sleeping
> Movelessly, the new bud of the heart was content
> With its own covering of pure pollen[6]

Thus, at first we have a scene in which the thoughts or emotions, mind, and heart correspond with birds sleeping in nests and buds wrapped up in their own pollen: the inner nature of the heart like the outer nature at rest. But like all buds must be jostled into blooming, so the heart needs to be accosted in order to love and to know:

> Ah! Then which southern wind was that, who suddenly,
> (All laden with the fragrance of flowers)—
> Came and touched and tickled us,
> Showed the vision of joy [*ānand*] to our opened eyes?
> Then an emotion [*manoveg*] like a bee buzzing
> Begins to sing a sweet sweet heavenly song.[7]

Then an awakening occurs of more metaphysical proportions within the figures of these erstwhile *uddīpanas*. The *prāṇ* (life, being) of the poet becomes the *prāṇ-papīhā, papīhā* bird of his being, calling out in joy. Again, the sun is a young man, *bāl aruṇ*, Young Sun, who colors—and thereby delights—an empty heart with new love.[8] The poem resolves with only the second explicit "I" of the poem, in the last line—"This was the first dawn of my life." This transformative dawn takes on grand epiphanic proportions: his heart is now "bathed evermore in the holy waters of love," the universe "a house of pure joy." The linkage of the inner mind to the outer natural world certainly made sense in the logic of *śṛṅgāra*, theory of stimulus and response that it was; here natural objects in fact describe response, with emotion "like a bee," the heart-bud, and so forth. However, the inspirational southern wind remains an anonymous force—"which southern wind was that . . . ?"

More immediately than classical poetics, the Bengali poetry of recent decades had also presented such pretty *śṛṅgārik* objects in subjective outpourings on mystical themes, and thus the question of imitation arises perforce in examining this strand of Prasād's poetry. Here, however, is an opportunity to elucidate what "Hindi-ness" we can find in this Hindi poetry of a Bengali cast. The answer lies in Hindi's Nature itself, transmitted through previous decades of Hindi poetry. In Prasād, here the equivalences of object and allegorical meaning are laid out more algebraically, and I would argue this trait is one in keeping with the Hindi neoclassicism that had informed its nature poetry up to this point. This adherence to the *objects* of Sanskrit per se, and interest in arraying them together or mining them for new meaning, is precisely what has inspired readers to assign to *Bengali* a greater "modernity" and "Romanticism." The hazier, more affect-driven Bengali poetry of this same period was less laden with the burden of classical poetics and did indeed resemble English poetry—the model of the modern—more closely. "The Great Play," "First Dawn," and "Acquaintance" of Prasād's poetry of the teens exemplify a little-observed experimentalism within classicism, no less modern.

Freedom in the Ascetic's Abode

The liberatory possibilities of nature find further expression in the last early Prasād poem we will examine, in the particular arcadia of the 1913 Khaṛī Bolī poem, *Prem-pathik*[9] *(The Pilgrim of Love)*, a 270-line narrative poem published in booklet form, as well as in the pages of *Indu*.[10] It took on a metrical scheme unusual for its day, namely thirty *mātrā*s to the line, no consistent rhyme scheme, and frequent enjambment. In its content, however, it was somewhat less renegade. The story is one of love lost, and a man's resultant decision to take to an ascetic life in the woods. There he comes upon a female ascetic, to whom he tells his story; they recognize each other as their lost loves, yet the Pilgrim exhorts her to remain on the path of spiritual love in nature. In features of the narrative itself we cannot help but see shades of Goldsmith's *Hermit*, translated by Sridhar Pāṭhak years before (described here in Chapter 3). The plot motive of the arranged marriage and subsequent early widowhood reflected a concern of literature at large in Hindi and Bengali in recent decades, as prose and poetic works explored the affecting subject of women's social powerlessness. Further, in the Pilgrim's monologue, we find definite strains of Rādhā's epiphany in Hariaudh's *Priyapravās*, albeit with no concrete exhortation to social work. Overall, however, the poem idealizes their human love into a "world-love" or universal love (*viśva-prem*, now a common term of contemporary Hinduism), and leaves the reader with grand and macrocosmic images of union—the ocean and dawn.

Prasād begins the poem much like one of his object-poems, describing a *cameli* flower, and the heroine Cameli herself, concretizing the flower/female equivalence implied in so many poems of this era. Indeed, the first verses might stand alone, as companion to the object-poems described in the previous chapter, and foreshadow the style and content of the classic Chāyāvād poem by Nirālā, "The Jasmine Bud," described in the following chapter. Portions of verse two follow below:

> [The *cameli* (jasmine) flower] blooms with the pure sweet
> southern breeze,
> She who hides her limbs in the green leaves, new shoots,
> Who expands in the pleasing swing of the green branch
> And shows full-grown feeling [*vikasita bhāva*], she so
> delights,
> Whose internal love is bloomed in her simple look
> She smiles, eyes wide, as if she's lost herself completely,
> What can be said of this beauty, natural and fragrant,
> With which nature, the gardener-woman, adorns her hand?

Then the tone shifts to rueful questioning, and intimations of a sad story to follow: "Aha, this very *cameli*—tell me how will she find happiness? / Plucked from her branch, from her constant companions, the buds— / Separated from her loved ones, will the flower adorn a basket? Whose?" Like the object-poems described in the previous chapter, the flower contains her own story—she is set by the bed of an uncaring man, bought for a few cents and cast aside, and ultimately, "A breeze roaming the empty road . . . will touch her. / The pollen of desire will dry up, she will wilt, / On the earth from which she arose, she will fall." This personified flower, given the subjective persona of a powerless young woman, waiting for love, begins this narrative allegorically—Cameli, we will see, is the name of the heroine of this work.

The poem proceeds to a description of a hut in the wood, surrounded by creepers, and a jasmine-bower verandah, in which sit two ascetics, male and female. The female ascetic, *tapasvī*, has invited the male sadhu passing by to stop on his journey and tell his tale. Soon a simile appears, with obvious import for the nature of their real relationship: "The fragrant peaceful breeze with sweet pollen / Moves along like the Pilgrim towards the hut . . . / . . . the Pilgrim set himself down . . . / But the wind began to pick up, . . . / Where he found buds, he shook and jostled them."[11] This Pilgrim, the wind that will jostle the buds into blooming, then proceeds to tell the tale of his idyllic youth in the "town of joy," Ānand Nagar, full of cows and folk songs. He tells of young love, and then her subsequent arranged marriage, and his life-altering decision: "I abandoned [my home,] the place of happiness, all peace, become a Pilgrim on the path of love / The world became my place of exile (*pravās*), all towns were to me foreign places."[12] Here *pravās*, the sojourn abroad away from the beloved of Krishna, Kalidasa's *yakṣa* in *The Cloud Messenger* and Hariaudh's *Priyapravās*, first serialized this very year of 1913, suggests somewhat the alienation of the tormented Romantic poet, but the Pilgrim makes the world his sojourn, more as a wandering sage than as cosmopolite.

A description follows of a beautiful natural scene, and of the Pilgrim sitting on an outcropping of rock under the full moon, reminded of his Cameli. Suddenly a vision comes to him out of the moonlight: "Like a divine messenger from the moon's reflections, a man emerged, glowing," who informs him, "Pilgrim! You have to wanderingly travel the road of love // You have to offer up your self-interest and desire in the sacrificial fire of love / Then you will receive the boon of heavenly sporting with the beloved."[13] Lest the traveler—and the reader—mistake this "sporting" for the actual physical union of the lovers, the man explains, "The meaning of this path is . . . / . . . to arrive at that limit beyond which there is no road / That is, in that land of pleasure which has no limit."

Soon the divine voice's conversation begins to sound much like Rādhā's philosophical discourse in *Priyapravās*, concerning the enchantment of forms versus real love, and importantly, how nature embodies the beloved:

"Love is the impeller [*cālak*] of the world, drawn into its attraction
Dust and waterdrops, everything, spins around day and night
The heat [*garamī*] of love, the desert, the earth, the mountains, the ocean, all hold
Within [themselves] joyfully [*ānand-sahit*], it has a vast eternal effect.
. . .
Look at this world full of your beloved; and then where is the pain of separation (*viraha*)?"[14]

The moonlight-messenger then disappeared, and the Pilgrim went upon his way, transformed: "Thus he wandered, seeing many countries with his own eyes / And came wandering here, thinking this world is full of his beloved."[15] Shortly their mutual recognition occurs, and Prasād signals that their state of age and decrepitude from the sadhu life precludes any resumption of their love affair. The female ascetic tells her tale of widowhood and eventual settling in the forest grove, in terms reminiscent of Śakuntalā: "The birds and deer became my friends, this very hut became my temple."[16] The Pilgrim again speaks, instructing her, and the reader, on the congruence of love, the divine, and the surrounding natural world. Rivers overflowing from rain torrents are not the real form (*vāstavik svarūp*), but rather embody the surge of love of the youthful couple (*yuvak-yuvatī*)—ambiguously here either the passion of Rādhā-Krishna couple or perhaps the passion of Everyman and Everywoman. Entering an internal heaven, the world and the grand aspects of nature specifically transform in one's perception:

Listen Cameli! Forget things past, scouring your heart
Become pure, frolic in an internal heaven, become without desire
Offer the self [*ātma-samarpaṇ*], thrilling [*pulakita*], mix this soul of the world [*viśvātma*]
With nature; in world-love [*viśvaprem*] the world itself is god.
You said just now—"birds and deer have become my companions"
But do not limit love, make affectionate sympathy [*sauhārd*] world pervading.
Don't thrill at ephemeral beauty, [but] look! Look!! (26.26–32)

Tying together the relation of man to nature, the Pilgrim then cites the stars in the sky, flakes of snow, the fragrant wind, the waterfall, the mountain stream, and inevitably, the opening bloom and the desirous bee. Moving from bee to Krishna, and the motive of sexual desire in the world, he continues:

> Look how the Enchanter [*Mohan*] keeps changing his
> appearance
> Taking off the blue garment, he comes wearing the yellow
> robe of Krishna
> The jeweled ornament of stars has slowly descended.
> The beautiful garden of this earth laden with flowers—
> Appears equal to what pleasure grove [*kṛīṛā-kuñj*] in
> beauty?
> Whose bed of union is this arranged here? As if he has just
> Got up and left! These drops of sweat mixed with pollen
> are scattered about.
> Whose splendor of exertion and lassitude was just here
> right now, taking the world along?[17]

The Pilgrim's images here become more grand oceanic abstractions, and then the poem concludes:

> Merged in one ocean, there will be a beautiful eternal
> confluence
> Then we will never have any more fear of separation again.
> Come, let us meet not limb-to-limb but heart-with-heart
> Become a rivulet on the road of life, let's run to that
> ocean!"
> "Come, let's meet in the ocean of love that is beauty"—
> Chameli said then
> "Where there is eternal peace—there we might live forever
> free [*svacchand*]!"
> Their eyes became fixed and they began to see—dawn.[18]

Thus the concept of freedom, *svacchand*—so elemental to the mid-century critics' interpretations of Chāyāvādī nature—here appears in Prasād's 1913 poem within the imagined spiritual arcadia of love, an eternal confluence, an ocean, a dawn. This freedom, I submit, is not so much the social freedoms that critics have traditionally imputed to the "Romantic" Chāyāvād poets, running to nature to escape the bonds of society, but rather a freedom comprehensible through a material concept of nature.

still *śṛṅgārik* and imagined in terms of love-union, but also comprised of things-in-themselves as subjects. The marital bed of the Enchanter Krishna, where the lovers stand, is a patch of forest, ecstatically recognized, but also merely just that—a patch of forest, not a site for physical love. Nature here had become inextricable from the spiritual, such that the familiar forest scene of the ascetic's abode took on new meaning. In the following section of this chapter another pilgrim takes this aesthetical natural theology into a Gandhian frame.

A Song among Rasiks of the Nation

The poet now at hand, Rāmanareś Tripāṭhī (1889–1962) serves as an appropriate counterpoint to Jayaśaṅkar Prasād in the teens. Born in the same year as Prasād, Tripāṭhī's literary career followed a path much more closely linked to the creation and dissemination of the Hindi canon, and the freedom movement of the day. Like the elder Śrīdhar Pāṭhak before him, Tripāṭhī would be considered a *svacchandatāvādī* poet, a "free" poet, literally "of his own meter," who represented Romanticism in the era before Chāyāvād. Although of the same age as Prasād, one of the four famous poets of Chāyāvād, Tripāṭhī can be seen as a poet more deeply influenced by the didactic tendencies of the Dvivedī generation, demonstrated by his political poem, *The Pilgrim* (*Pathik*), and his famous anthologizing of literature for schools.[19]

Much less well-known in literary history than his famous counterpart Prasād. Tripāṭhī's personal background presents yet another picture of life in the districts of Avadh: he was born in Koirīpur village, Jaunpur district, into a Brahman family. His father was a learned pandit, a captain in the Indian army, landholder, and great devotee of Ram. The poet Rāmanareś began his education in the village vernacular school in Urdu, and then was turned toward Hindi by the School Inspector, Rāmanārāyaṇ Miśra, one of the founders of the Nāgarī Pracāriṇī Sabhā in Banaras. Steeped in Tulsi's *Rāmacaritamānas* and the literary periodicals of the day, Tripāṭhī spent a short time learning English in high school at Jaunpur, but left to return to the village and study Sanskrit with his uncle at the local pathshala. He married and moved to Calcutta, where he worked as a door-to-door salesman, came under the influence of the Ārya Samāj and the works of Bengali novelists Baṅkim and Śaratchandra, and made Marwari connections, which then brought him to Rajasthan, where he founded a library.

Tripāṭhī moved to Allahabad around 1917, where he started a Hindi press with the help of Puruṣottam Dās Ṭaṇḍan, nationalist leader and ardent Hindi supporter. Tripāṭhī was closely involved in nationalist circles there, friendly with the Nehrus and Malaviyas, and one of the original members of Annie Besant's Home Rule League in Allahabad. He first met Gandhi at a Hindi Sahitya Sammelan meeting in 1917, which association influenced his literary work profoundly, such that he became somewhat of a publicist for Gandhi's Non-Cooperation movement. Because of Tripāṭhī's long-standing and formative links to the freedom movement, political messages dominated his best-known literary output, especially his trilogy of narrative poems, *Milan* (*The Meeting*, 1917), *Pathik* (*The Pilgrim*, 1920), and *Svapna* (*The Dream*, 1928). Because of the overriding political message of much of his work, his legacy is usually assigned to the Dvivedī era, the time when literature served social causes, and the nationalist cause of Hindi, as much as aesthetic ones. In fact, he would later join in Hindi propagation efforts in the South, and supported the Hindustani movement of the 1940s.[20] Thus, Tripāṭhī's Hindi publications served the particular national vision of his political work, a vision of a Free India united by some version of the Hindi language.

Beyond the narrative poems, one of which—*The Pilgrim*—we examine below, Rāmanareś Tripāṭhī published many other texts, and very often with an eye to educational use. Early on he published new editions of Braj poets such as Rahīm, Bhūṣaṇ, and Sūr, and *nīti* publications of moral aphorisms. Perhaps his greatest contribution was his series of poetic anthologies, *Kavitā-kaumudī,* six volumes in all (1917–1933), which were praised by the famous public figures of the day in their long testimonial sections at the back, and which also testified to their use in school curricula. Tripāṭhī went on to become the major compiler of folk songs, with his *Grām gīt* (*Village Songs*, 1929) in the *Kavitā-kaumudī* series. He was an author truly ingrained in the political and social world of Congress and Non-Cooperation, whose literary legacy is both as a canonizer as well as poet-instigator.

In 1920, Rāmanareś Tripāṭhī published his Gandhian narrative poem, *Pathik* [*The Pilgrim*]. Ostensibly based on recollections of a pilgrimage Tripāṭhī made to the Srīrāmeśvaram temple in Tamil Nadu, this 67-page poem contained a thinly-veiled allegory of Gandhi's Non-Cooperation movement, begun the year of publication.[21] It tells the story of a young renunciant who eventually becomes apotheosized after his murder in prison, where he was incarcerated by an evil raja who objected to his acts of non-cooperation for the "benefit of the people." As a work clearly referencing Gandhi, with depictions of crowds rushing for *darśan* of the Pilgrim, and clearly meant to promote agitation, with a long prose forward making explicit the political message that verse might obscure, "nature poetry" would not immediately seem relevant.

However, nature scenes figure prominently in *The Pilgrim*, as the object upon which the Pilgrim meditates, Shiva-like, before a sadhu awakens him to his higher purpose of working among the people for political independence, *svarājya*.

This nature is one similar to Pāṭhak's Lady Nature of beautiful forms, infused with *sṛṅgāra*: "One free (*svacchand*) pilgrim, lover of the sea breeze, // was looking in amazement, his eyes fixed / on the stage of the world was the performance of the dancing girl Nature (*prakṛti-naṭī*),"[22] and he finds nature his "house of love." Clearly, the performing woman Nature has by now become a stock character of modern Hindi poetry—we saw this figure in Śrīdhar Pāṭhak's "Beauty of Kashmir" of 1904—and nature as the abode of a poetic, spiritual love had been well elaborated by Hariaudh and Prasād, as described previously. But certain penchants for nature distinguish Tripāṭhī's Pilgrim. For one thing, he loves the ocean. The most famous passage of this text is in fact a lengthy description of the ocean, notably a topic beginning to dominate others of the Chāyāvād generation at this time, and already mined for its sublime and allegorical potential by Tagore in Bengali for several decades. However, more à propos to our study of nature in Hindi, he literally "reads" nature (*paṛh-*) as a text, much like a Wertherian Romantic, minus the dark mortality of crags and crevices. But further, he "studies" nature—also a potentiality of *paṛh-*—as a sort of infatuated botanist: "Read! [*paṛho*!] On the waves, the bank, the grass, the trees, the mountains, the sky, the rays of sun, the clouds / is written this sweet story [of nature] that charms the world."[23] A *mala*, string or garland, of natural objects characterizes these moments of emotional "nature description."

Further, he compares the beauty of nature with that of a woman, and his love for each of them. Normally listed as objects shamed by the beauty of the ideally beautiful subject of a metaphor (e.g., the eyes, lips, loins, etc. of Krishna or Rādhā), here are objects of comparison that are more constant in aggregation as Nature, than the thing they would describe: his wife's all too fleeting beauty. Thus he explains his plan to renounce the householding life:

> Lotus, elephant, lion, pond, creeper, mountain, conch, rosebud
> Moon, coral, pomegranate, cuckoo, parrot, deer, *kewra* flower, shell, flock of bees
> The most insignificant inanimate thing, the insects flying in the air—the subject for which they are comparisons is your body.
> But Nature is always a beauty, and your youth is an unstable treasure. (1.37)

Further, he elaborates on the deceit and sorrow of life in the world, such that "the desolate wood (*nirjana vana*) is most pleasing compared to this unjust world" (1.49.4). His wife objects to his departure, and then the Pilgrim responds with sentiments that remind one of the subjective interaction of the self with the divine in nature, as found in both the English Romantics and Tagore, as well as the natural Krishna of Hariaudh's Rādhā:

> This is my desire, to take on the garments of the river and streams,
> I'll ascend the mountains happily as a song being sung (56.3–4)
> My desire is to live among the fragrant forest flowers,
> Become an arrow of *viraha,* I will fly to the lover's heart and penetrate it.
> I desire to roam from arbor to arbor, made the wind,
> I will deliver life again to the wilted plants. (57)
>
> I will make the rose laugh, make the nightingale cry, tousle the creepers
> Then I will make the cloud surround and bathe them
> Become the breath of the voice of the world, I will tell a tale of love
> Amidst pure *rasik*s I will be a song. (58)

Stock poetic scenarios here are what the Pilgrim will become, or effect: the force that makes the peacock cry, the wind and cloud touching flowers (and as we know, women), and finally, a universal voice, of a pure song for pure aesthetes. These proclamations of a desire to merge with the grand physical universe, its longing of *viraha,* its archetypal love story, or its aesthetic moments, are quite innovative, at least in Hindi, and set a very striking setting for the Pilgrim's political vision; echoes of the nature of Hariaudh's Rādhā are augmented with the emphasized selfhood of this Pilgrim-in-nature, rejecting the householding life for a literal oneness with nature, but a nature quite enmeshed in traditional poetics. This nature contains *śṛṅgāra,* and in fact is counterpart to the bonds of conjugality.

That this is the aesthetic atmosphere for a swadeshi-message tract seems particularly telling; the aesthetics of this nationalism contained a particular nature, both analogous to the love of women, and personalized as the spiritual self of the seeker. While nature retains its exalted status as the subject of verse, it leads the Pilgrim to action rather than reflection. He resolves to visit every region of India, in a sense geographically tracing the outline of the incipient nation. As with Dvivedī's poetic prose, love of nature leads to the political, and the rhetorical features of nature description owe much to Sanskrit's natural vision of *śṛṅgāra*.

For this political *rasik*, however, looking upon nature is not enough. While the inspiration for the Pilgrim's grand tour of the subcontinent, indeed equaling his own wife's beauty, he later laments at length the fact that such beauty means nothing to those who are starving and oppressed: "He saw [in his travels] that natural pleasure was in great abundance everywhere / But in comparison the country was extremely ignorant, weary, and hopeless."[24] Looking upon nature then becomes for him an armchair pastime, irrelevant to the people (*janatā*), and he proceeds for twenty-some-odd rather conventional quatrains on precisely these natural beauties, and their innate divinity, punctuating the verses with a pointed question—why do these not make the people of India happy? He realizes they are under the rule of an unjust king, who is against the progress of the people; from thence the narrative progresses along its nationalist course. Thus, while nature had political valences, and valuable aesthetic valences—which he exploits to effect in *The Pilgrim*—Tripāṭhī's suggests that this aesthetical pleasure is ultimately meaningless without just political conditions. The Pilgrim has thus left his wife for the beauties of nature, but discovers that his true calling is to aright what makes nature's beauty insufficient—political oppression. While the interchangeable quality of conjugality for service to the nation has become a commonplace of nationalist stories of sacrifice,[25] and in Tamil nationalism love for the Tamil language has been construed in conjugal/sexual terms, here nature forms a fourth element in the tryst of nationalism with the male activist and his wife left behind for the greater good. The beauty of Nature, in high Sanskritic style, is identified with the conjugal bond, and with the nation; all three are in turn the objects of desire of the Pilgrim who wanders free, *svacchand*.

Nature Poetry, Nature-Love, in the Everyday

The effect of this trend of nature poetry was so profound as to be difficult to perceive ever since. Numerous publications labeled as "nature poetry" or on topics of nature description began to flood the Hindi publishing world around the early 1920s. The Chāyāvād poets were merely the better poets of this ilk, who linked descriptions of natural beauty and sometimes natural awesomeness with the personal psyche in most subtle ways. Most of this poetry, however, had more mundane, but profound effects, as the stuff of the exploding Hindi literary publishing world of the early twenties.

Poetry in magazines featured natural themes prominently, along with the national themes for which the Dvivedī era is known. A representative example of this craze for the natural, especially a personified and erotic nature, include the following: a 1911 poem in *Sarasvatī* by one Saiyad Amir Ali, on Evening, "come embodied, for the meeting of day and night / yes! Through this go-between [of Evening] the bride and groom meet with affection."[26] The many poems in *Sarasvatī*'s first twenty years with titles referencing natural objects, seasons, etc., and sometimes particular landscapes, further confirm that nature as poetic subject had come into its own.[27] Hariaudh's student Girijādatt Śukla "Girīś" published a poem in the women's magazine *Strī-darpaṇ* (*Women's Mirror*) in 1917 combining tropes of nature at dawn, a flowering arbor, *viraha*, and Mother India.[28] Soon he was to pronounce himself a "nature poet" and then in turn, a "Wordsworth of Hindi."

Magazine essays provide another window into the conceptions of nature circulating. Pandit Kapiladev Mālavīya wrote a fascinating piece of poetic prose for the same magazine in 1920, entitled "The sweet, sweet words of nature" (*prakṛti kī pyārī pyārī bāteṁ*), which combined Vaishnavism with talk of sexual pleasure, social freedom, Goddess Nature, and nationalism. This piece of didactic, yet poetical prose for women, probably authored by a member of the famous Mālavīya family of Allahabad, is too charmingly quirky not to quote here, and further, foreshadows the next chapter's discussion of nature as a spiritual object lesson for the "birds and the bees."

> How enchanting is the sweet voice of the *kokil*, wafting along with the pleasing breeze of dawn? How nice is the pretty sound of the birds, bringing thrills like the sound of the anklet bells of the beloved? . . . How beloved is exertion to the body in the flush of youth? . . . To the thirsty, how pleasing is cool water to the heart?

Then follows a reference to Rām sighting Sītā for the first time in the flower garden, in Tulsi's version, and then, perhaps addressed to young male readers: "Why did the sight of that young girl, fair, big-eyed, with *sindūr-bindu*, wearing clothes in the modern style, joining in English joking, of otherworldly beauty, give you so much new-found joy today?"

It turns out the author will make a progressive argument against restrictive social codes, and for social freedoms, based upon the principle of Nature: ". . . for men and women to meet according to independent/ individual feeling [*svatantra bhāv se*], is such a civilized joy [*sabhya ānand*]!" He then asks, from whence does this happiness [*sukh*] come? "This entire happiness, all of these beautiful and enchanting matters are the sweet sweet words [*bāteṁ*] of nature." Then follows praise of Western civilization for following these "sweet sweet words," and criticism of Hindu customs of arranged marriage, gender segregation, etc., for going against them. Mālavīya repeats the title phrase at every occasion, and connects these nature-given pleasures with propriety and progress: "The sweet sweet words of nature don't just make life happy and sweet, but rather make life full of progress [*unnatiśīl*] and elevated [*ucc*]." Hence, Nature here provides a conjunction of *śṛṅgāra*, Hindu divinity, human love and sexuality, and principles of social freedom and progress.[29] Taking the poetry of these several chapters together with Mālavīya's essay described here, we can see the elasticity of the idea of nature in this period for those seeking to synthesize, encompass, and embody the various elements of their intellectual world: theological, European Enlightenment, poetical, and political.

Conclusions: Modern Nature, Modern Love

The idioms of poetic nature in Hindi in this period had multifarious, intermingled strands of empiricism, atomized classicism, theology, and politics, all of which were infused to some extent with the aesthetic erotics of *śṛṅgāra*. We can trace a genealogy of this Hindi poetic nature from the English translations of the nineteenth century onward. Dvivedī's nature clearly adhered to an aesthetic of the real, like the *yathārth* perceived in English, and this realism contained also a political imperative, while still including classicist Sanskritic natural scenes. Pāṭhak's "Beauty of Kashmir" typifies the interesting collusion of courtly idioms of *śṛṅgāra* and praise with modern idioms of natural description and declarations of national identity, in a poem that refutes the pronouncements on realism and usefulness by his friend Dvivedī. Hariaudh's nature refigured the landscape of Braj as a universalistic Nature, but one "made of parts" in Rādhā's epiphany. Sanskritic verbal ornament had become incommensurable to the modern; "real" empirical nature on the other hand, could represent the divine, as the repository for the transcendental Brahma, and as the material for poetic visions. The birds, bees, flowers, and trees of Sanskritic, and *śṛṅgārik* metaphor did not leave the stage, but rather became the heroes and heroines of poetry in themselves. Likewise, so did Nature herself. Further, Hariaudh's Rādhā and Tripāṭhī's Gandhian Pilgrim articulates a vision of nature that logically leads to work in the world. Several of these examples show us a nature of beautiful objects, piled upon each other in cascades of enumerative descriptions. The early poems of Prasād, both the object-poems and the more Tagorean ponderings on macrocosmic themes, also braid together a nature of individual things, at play in the universe, and a nature of embodied, desirous love. While Pāṭhak's Lady Nature frolicked flirtatiously in her mountain arbor, Prasād asked of his patch of forest: "whose bed of union is arranged here? // Whose splendor of exertion and lassitude was here just now, taking the world along?"

This complex natural poetics might be considered the aesthetic legacy of the Dvivedī era authors, which the Chāyāvād poets took up in their own cadences. The self-conscious poetic practice of "nature description" in the early decades of the century, an ecphrasis with the devotional flavor of Braj poetry and intimate connection with the pleasures of *śṛṅgāra* was crucial to later Chāyāvād developments. The newly "traditional" poetic body, "covered" in ornament (as Pope had critiqued, and Ratnākar had translated), took on modern ornaments with different contours. Thus, in the Hindi Nature of the early twentieth century, we find traces of the originary aesthetic proclivities of modern Hindi poetry, and of the ethical world of its characters who, like Arjuna, can look to "this Krishna, Nature," in its grand form—literary locus of realism and disembodied affects of love.[30]

Chapter 7

Women Problems

Poetics without Śṛṅgāra[1]

> Hariaudh says, looking at the sublimity of nature
> [The Lover of her Country] swings, thrilling, on the swing of love,
> Under sway of the glory of the Sarasvatī of India
> She is a good woman, she doesn't forget her Indianness.
>
> —Hariaudh, "The Lover of her Country"[2]

How did moderns accommodate both *śṛṅgāra*, the classical erotic literary mode, and the precepts of propriety regarding girls and women? We might say, anachronistically, that the *śṛṅgāra* tradition exemplifies a "male gaze," much like other pre-modern poetry. Certainly, *śṛṅgārik* poetry was written largely by and for males, for their pleasure and aesthetic delight, since the traditional audience for Sanskrit included few females, much less girls. But as the uplift of girls and women, and eradication of obscenity, became tantamount to civilizational progress in the colonial era, and literature as well became a symbol of identity, how did the *śṛṅgāra* sit with ideas of the modern proper woman? How would *śṛṅgāra* evolve in concert with colonial literary values? Would colonial Indians turn away from the master Sanskrit poetic texts, such as Kalidasa's *Cloud-messenger* or the drama *The Recognition of Śakuntalā*, both beloved paragons of *śṛṅgāra*? Would the erotic mode of devotion also have to fall away entirely? The idealized human body and the affect of desire have always been integral to the concept of *śṛṅgāra*, emerging as it did from literary depictions of heterosexual, reproductive love (à la goddess Uma's lovemaking with god Shiva, in Kalidasa's Sanskrit classic, *The Birth of the Prince*). Later *śṛṅgāra* merged with modes of *bhakti*, devotion for god, in the hugely influential theology of the sixteenth-century Chaitanyite Vaishnavas. The poetry of other sects, notably in the widespread Hindi dialect of Braj Bhāṣā, further exemplified the devotional possibilities of an erotic mode in their *śṛṅgārik* elaborations on the love of Rādhā and god Krishna. Such pre-colonial poetics emerged from a cultural fabric that had defined sexual pleasure as simply one of the features of the refined life, but by 1900 a sea-change was in process in British India.

However, by the late nineteenth century, the poetic subject of the female—unavoidable in *śṛṅgāra* poetry, be she Rādhā, an anonymous courtly beauty, or an historical figure—was now newly seen to reflect upon the status of Indian civilization. Authors began to think that her image should match the social changes afoot in the nationalist discourse of the time: women in literature should be spared the sexualizing "male gaze" of preceding "tradition" so that women in the real world might experience social progress. As the natural object or Nature-in-poetry became a subject in and of itself, so also the poetic "object" of the female became understood as a *political* subject, who should be treated with some degree of sympathy for her contemporary social, and hence emotional, state, in the nascence of what Orsini would call "the right to feel" displayed in women's prose in the 1920s.[3] The era saw in its literature a political impetus to aright, or at least lament, the wrongs committed against fictional female figures: figures clearly standing in for the many real women experiencing such duress. In the process, the literary dialect of court and temple, Braj Bhāṣā, would fall away, more and more dismissed as a relic of an embarrassingly erotic cultural past. Intellectuals began to ask: Can the genres and motifs of *śṛṅgāra* be reinvented for a "modern public" including "proper women"? How can this aesthetic mode and its long history be interpreted as something other than "cultural decadence"?

First, this chapter will consider how women in the Hindi sphere were positioned as bearers of authentic Indian morality in the larger contexts of the "culture wars" of colonial India. Then we will explore two connected aspects of *śṛṅgāra* in modern Hindi poetry: the perception of a political problem with *śṛṅgāra* for the new audience for Hindi poetry, and how "nature in poetry" began to function as a reincarnation of *śṛṅgāra* in poetry. The chapter will end with a look at scientized interpretations of *śṛṅgāra* that transformed the problem of this literary legacy into usable signs of modernity via nature. The famous critic Nāmavar Siṁh's discussion of the changing face of women in poetry and by association, *śṛṅgāra*, will introduce this chapter's exposition of the "problem" of *śṛṅgāra* in this era, and the linkage of poets' new interest in both women's subjectivity and nature. This poetical-cum-political problem of *śṛṅgāra* was in fact corollary to any new poetic "nature," since the "nature poetry" known and loved by these authors—the *cātaka* bird, the night-blooming lotus, the flowering arbor—comprised the field of signifiers for this very *śṛṅgāra*. Where did *śṛṅgāra* end and "nature poetry" begin, and vice versa?

The reframing of the erotic occurred concurrently with the transition from one, older kind of Hindi poetry to another: the shift from the Hindi literary dialect of Braj Bhāṣā—the dialect of the Braj region, and the courtly yet earthy language of devotion to Krishna, in which poet saints composed religious songs and court poets across the land had composed lavish illustrated tomes after classical Sanskrit models—to spoken style Khaṛī Bolī Hindi, the register of speech identical to Urdu, but infused with a Sanskritized lexicon. It was, to paraphrase Wordsworth, the "language near to men" of the lingua franca Hindustani, which authors for the nascent Hindi movement, in their rejection of Urdu, had only recently begun to use for literary purposes. Between 1885–1920 the shift in poetry from Braj Bhāṣā to Khaṛī Bolī Hindi would take full effect, and, I will argue, the disfavor of Braj would have as much to do with its association with the erotic as with any language standardization project.

The Literary Historiography of Śṛṅgāra in Modernity

In his 1955 *Chāyāvād*, on the new generation of poets of the 1920s, Nāmavar Siṁh associates nature-in-poetry with women-in-poetry, and points to this conjunction as a dominant feature of the Chāyāvād generation. He wrote in his chapter devoted to things female, entitled "Goddess, Mother, Companion, Life Itself,"[4] that "like nature, women appear prominently in Chāyāvād poetry, such that for a time those opposed to Chāyāvād called it 'women-poetry.' " Predictably, he located the association of nature and women in Dvivedī era "free" (*svacchand*) poetry, which he believes had escaped the era's moralism, insipidity, and prohibitions: "from the beginning, it was considered appropriate in Free Poetry to compare nature to a woman."[5] Certainly, Siṁh is correct that Chāyāvād's forebears equated nature and women—the *nāyikā* of Pāṭhak's "Beauty of Kashmir" exemplifies this. However, Siṁh here gives as evidence of the nature/woman equation the householder's renunciation to retreat into nature, a theme of poetry in the early decades of the century (and addressed here in previous chapters). While certainly Indic renunciation has been epitomized by austerities in the jungle, Siṁh's reading is a peculiarly Western Romantic one, with his Thoreaux-like "return" or "retreat" to nature, away from the social world. In this 1955 work Siṁh will in fact try to evince the British Romantic line, that social alienation drove poets to the free space of nature. Further, he explains, this "love of nature . . . prepared the background for the love of women" in poetry.[6] This latter proposition especially concerns us in this chapter. How does Siṁh arrive at this association of nature and women, which hints at the philosophical underpinnings of *prakriti* and *śṛṅgāra*, but clearly also derives from his belief in the English Romantic story of the poet-in-nature, emancipated and spiritually attuned?

Siṁh continues in a somewhat more materialist vein, with discussion of the expanding political rights of women in the 1920s, along with "individualism,"[7] developments from which women-in-poetry also transformed. The individualistic self attributed to Romanticism overlaps for him with progressive, desexualized attitudes toward women: "Portraying woman as a life companion, full of respect, compassion, good intentions, artfulness, and love, the Chāyāvād poets have watered society and literature with the *rasa* of new life."[8] Importantly, Siṁh also reads the Dvivedī generation preceding Chāyāvād as one of unsuccessful transcendence of the erotic: "the Dvivedī era poets did not write about love, for fear of being called *rītikālin*; in fact, their perspective was similar to that of the *rītikāl* poets." The Dvivedī era poets kept their lurid thoughts under wraps, he implies, but could not really transcend the *śṛṅgārik* framework; whereas the Chāyāvād poets were able to make love "dominant" without the trappings—ornamental and moral—of *śṛṅgāra*.[9]

This chapter will explore the Chāyāvād poets' immediate forebears of the Dvivedī generation, writing before and during the early Chāyāvād era. From examining these slightly earlier sources, we can see what happened to gender—specifically femaleness and sexuality—poetically speaking, in Hindi, before and in the background of Chāyāvād's heyday in the late 1920s. We will see that a particular way of writing about women and nature both preserved and subverted the pleasures of *śṛṅgāra*.

The Politics of Poetic Change

Calls for women's uplift, and the concomitant criticism of sexuality in literary, religious, and folk mediums created a serious problem for Hindi poets: Should *śṛṅgāra* be dispensed with entirely? How can this aesthetic mode and its long history be salvaged, if at all? In this chapter, I will address how some Hindi poets and critics responded to these questions, by politicizing *śṛṅgāra* itself and by invoking a body of Indic poetics along with English nature writing. I argue that a particular vision of "nature" informed new renditions of poetic love, representing a complex aesthetic effect of the epistemological shifts occurring in colonial India in this period.

Public anxiety over *śṛṅgāra* and its Vaishnava religious adaptations already had an extensive history by the late nineteenth century. The movements of social reform and female education that created the female reading public, in turn caused a redefinition of literary norms in light of the "social risks" posed by sexuality, especially those posed to women in the reading audience. Obscenity laws for publishing, which put literary texts under scrutiny for immorality, had been introduced in India by 1856,[10] and the general atmosphere of English disapproval of *śṛṅgārik* literature—indeed Indian literature generally—changed *śṛṅgāra* into something to be debated and justified in terms of foreign literary standards. If there would be widespread access to literature, including the highly valued Sanskrit, then there would need to be a kind of historicist stance on the one hand, to distance the present from past "decadence," and a forward-looking self-conscious modernity on the other that would abhor those signs of decadence. In short, the problem of *śṛṅgāra* was an object lesson in the larger problem of reframing non-Western "tradition" in terms of an authenticating glorious past and a prescient modernity that would match that of the world's other poetic theories.

In practice, this made for a telling censoriousness, mostly in the contexts of educational texts and texts aspiring to the status of "high literature," in distinction from the allegedly obscene popular press texts, both novels and Braj poetry. As a case in point, we might look to a volume on prosody from the late nineteenth century, written for use in schools. The author Jagannāth Prasād noted in the English introduction that

> Each stanza or verse . . . composed by me [exemplifying each meter] is so written as to be of the fullest use . . . no love matter or love stories are introduced . . . each stanza or verse inculcates some moral principle or relates some harmless idyllic anecdote from ancient lore.[11]

With this replacement of "love matter" with idylls, and the pains Prasād took to present the material simply, clearly, and "scientifically," he had "adapted for the use of both the sexes at all ages of life." In the Hindi introduction, he asks rhetorically, and again with telling reference to females, "of what use are those [metrical] rule-books that a teacher cannot teach with a sense of decency (*lajjā*) to the student, or the father to his son or daughter, the brother to his sister, the mother to her children?"[12] Prasād had his finger on the pulse of the times: even the Varanasi Poets' Society (Kāśī Kavi Samāj), a relative bastion of *śṛṅgārik* poetry, gave the seal of approval to his chaste metrics-book.[13] By 1915, the Hindī Sāhitya Sammelan would select the work for its popular examination curriculum. Prasād's project of the circumlocution or excision of "love matter" suited the modern canon project well.

Taking a different stance, another critic found the standard of English literature useful in *defense* of Braj Bhāṣā. In 1915, in an article referencing a new commentary on seventeenth-century Bhūṣaṇ's *Śivabāvanī*, Kṛṣṇabihārī Miśra defended *nāyikā-bhed* Braj Bhāṣā poetry with the claim that it provided lifelike character development as found in English novels. Like English novels, this poetry provided "instruction" about distinguishing between women of virtue and vice, as in the genre's distinction between the *svakīyā* (one's own woman) and *parakīyā* (another's woman). As for the "obscenity" of *nāyikā-bhed,* he thought fleshier versions should be stopped, to keep the genre "within proper limits." "*Śṛṅgāra* itself," he believed, "when saved from obscenity, isn't harmful," but rather "useful to society" and "of highest thoughts."[14]

Other authors chose to ignore the dictates of these critics. Some concerned themselves with locating and publishing old manuscripts purely for their historical value: for instance, Ratnākar published the *śṛṅgārik* poetry of Kṛpārām in an effort to show the historicity of Hindi poetry on classical *śṛṅgārik* themes, and made no comment whatsoever on the erotic content of the text.[15] Others continued to publish *śṛṅgārik* texts unabated, both for religious audiences and for the pleasure-seeking public, as Charu Gupta has ably demonstrated for the 1920s.[16] Women's folk genres, also amply criticized, persisted despite being diminished. Popular theatre continued to elaborate sexuality with enormous cultural complexities of its own, regardless of the consternation about the social meaning of *śṛṅgāra*. The concern about *śṛṅgāra* was simply not relevant to all classes and groups all the time, but certainly dominated discussion of literature, canon, and women among the literate, and overwhelmingly upper caste males publishing on such in this period.

However, consternation over erotica and "decadence" in general was in fact a pan-Indian concern, hardly limited to the Hindi-reading public. Rather, the very urge to purify erotic literature was one that went hand-in-hand with the desire for national and regional commonweal, across the subcontinent. Urdu critics, well known to the Hindi critics, had written extensively of Urdu poetic decadence from the 1870s.[17]

Amplifying the importance of gender and sexuality in the Hindi literary context, Hindi supporters commonly wrote poetry on "Urdu" as a sexualized "public woman," in contrast to the simple Hindi of the home. This prostitute Urdu often appeared in poems and plays written in support of Nagari/Hindi, which would become an administrative script/language in the United Provinces in 1900.[18] In one example from 1900, Bālamukund Gupta exhorted the "*bibi*" Urdu to abandon her *bazārī* appearance, dressed up in finery, and conduct herself properly in the "court" of the English. "Don't jangle your bells, don't tease us with your dupatta, / Don't show us now the blooming of the buds, / Don't shake your full chest either."[19] Rather Urdu should act respectably, with *adab*, and thank the government for teaching her modesty.[20] This communal aspect of gender politics, this assertion that Hindi represents a better kind of woman, will concern us now in looking at interregional cultural politics of the era.

Women and Morality as a Hindi Literary Problem

The Hindi canon-builders present a particular vision of changing gender norms, because of their pervading sense of difference from the "modernizing vanguard" in Calcutta, the perceived source of social change in India, for good or ill. While Urdu represented the sexual decadence of the past to Hindi promoters, Bengali represented the social freedoms of modernity, which endangered the Hindi-reading public almost as much.

Calcutta was where "progress" happened first, as the seat of the East India Company, and then colonial government until 1911, but it was also the urban den of sin of Hindi fiction. Hindi authors wrote of the place intimating that its inhabitants had sophistication, but also fewer of the older, now "traditional," social norms of the Hindi belt. Whether part of the Brahmo Samaj following minority or not, Calcutta-ites in their view were more cosmopolitan, and—negatively—more like the British colonizers. Many people circulated between Varanasi, Patna, and Calcutta for trade, publishing, pilgrimage, etc., but familiarity did not breed a homogenization of social norms between the Hindi and Bengali-speaking areas; rather, Hindi authors imply a further mounting sense of difference. The presence of "Bengali babus" in the other provinces presented a well-known cultural clash; there was indeed something different about the Bengalis, deriving mainly from their close relationship with the British colonizers. Hindi supporters of the United Provinces clung to an idea of Hindi that represented the authentic, un-deracinated Hindu Indian, and especially the virtuous Indian woman, again an index of her people. The ambivalent relationship to Calcutta culture and the Bengali *bhadralok* can be found in discourse around translations of Bankimchandra Chatterjee's novels into Hindi, found in abundance into the 1920s. As a case in point, we will look in detail at the remarkable epilogue of a Hindi translation of such a novel published in 1898, *Kṛṣṇakānt kā dānapatra* (Kṛṣṇakānt's Will), and translated by Hariaudh at the behest of the Director of Public Instruction of Bengal, for use in the districts of Bihar. His reading of the moral problem of the novel's plot may in fact have been idiosyncratic; while his words may not reflect the reading of the Hindi public at large, at least we reasonably surmise that his anxieties represent those of the Hindi-belt social context.

Bankim's novels had taken the Bengali public by storm in the previous two decades, and in the Hindi market were touted not just as good novels, but useful for developing personal judgment and morality. In an advertisement from 1899 for the Hindi translation by Hariaudh of *Kṛṣṇakānt's Will*, the publisher guaranteed the reader will find out: "1) what is the result of pleasure-seeking (*viṣayalīn hone [aiyāśī] se*); 2) what happens if a wife is not of humble nature; 3) how evil (*kucālī*) women operate; 4) how the life of a pleasure-seeking man is full of sorrow; and 5) how a woman's nature should be, etc."[21] We can find elaboration of numbers 2 and 4 in Hariaudh's epilogue, and surmise from this what he perceived to be at stake in the liberalization of gender norms, and how his vocabulary for discussing the "problem" with literary women invokes an authenticity claim linked to the Hindi public sphere.

The preliminary details of the novel's plot will set the background for examination of Hariaudh's comments in the epilogue: The female character Bhramar is a petulant housewife, literate and privileged, but also childish. While Govindalāl, her husband, inspects a country estate, Bhramar becomes jealous and suspects he harbors feeling for the beautiful Rohinī, a young widow. Bhramar then writes a letter to Govindalāl claiming him unworthy of her love, and leaves for her parents' home. These actions are clearly meant to demonstrate the "bad behavior" of a wife, but not without some sympathy for her point of view, despite her childishness. These precipitous events destroy her and her husband, however, as we shall see below.

At this point, we should look at Hariaudh's perspective on the function of this female character in the novel. In his epilogue, Hariaudh criticized the willful heroine of the story and positioned himself in opposition to the westernization he found in her. The trait to which he objected was an excess of *tejasvita*, "energy" or perhaps "willfulness."

> . . . the more willfulness (*tejasvitā*) is attributed to Bhramar, the more intolerable she is. The author of this novel . . . was

> a man of refined intellect. He passed his B.A. in English. He had much knowledge about Western ways. . . . it is possible to say that . . . this [*tejasvitā* of Bhramar] was very important for this novel.[22]

Hariaudh seems to make an explicit connection here between the trait of *tejasvitā* in the female character, and the author's Western knowledge, to which he somewhat ruefully alludes. Strangely absent from Hariaudh's discussion is any reading of Bhramar's anger as the classical *mān*, the angry pride of the jealous heroine refusing her lover, or at least *mān* gone awry.[23]

At this point Hariaudh denies that the character Bhramar is truly Indian, and invokes an ideal Aryan womanhood, a common rhetorical tactic of the era. He links Bhramar's actions with the *tejasvitā* of Western, white women, as Hariaudh lodges an allegation of literary deracination.

> Dear Reader! Tell me the truth, how do these words strike you? Is not the reflection of the life of Western women, with their fearsome personalities, found in the life of the pure Aryan lady, Bhramar? Actually, our honorable author, infatuated with Western ways and customs, in the process of taking a photo of the character of an Aryan woman, made use of the *tejasvitā* of the European tribe of beauties (*kulakāminiyaṁ*). Otherwise, Bhramar's personality would not be described as so willful (*tejasvī*).[24]

However, Hariaudh did in fact believe he shared many literary values with Bankim; he considered himself reasonably liberal and educated about "the other," i.e., the Europeans. Ultimately though, Hariaudh only selectively bought into the idea that the West represented progress and refinement; he rejected changes in women's behavior such as Bengalis would tolerate, even if only in fiction.

> Your honorable author's opinion was high, perhaps "progressive" (*unnat*), independent (*svatantra*), and refined (*parimārjit*), because he had much knowledge of Western civilization. . . . For this reason, it seemed proper and fitting to portray Bhramar with so much *tejasvitā*. But I am a man of normal intellect. I want to see Aryan women in that appearance and form that is old-fashioned and proper. And this is the reason that it seems unacceptable to me to give Bhramar so much *tejasvitā*.

> In such a state, I have become unable to stop the venting of the feelings of my heart. . . . [which] I have put before the readers and lady-readers.[25]

Hariaudh goes on to exhort his female readers (using the informal pronoun *tum*) to ignore the childishness of Bhramar and remain as they are, famous throughout the world for their forbearance and faithfulness to their husbands, as the famed goddess Sita, the ideal wife of the king Rama. He further connects these qualities with the glory of India and the Aryan race. Hariaudh thus leaves us with yet another beatific picture of Indian womanhood, so common in this era.

Remarkably, Hariaudh does not comment upon the subsequent actions of Bhramar's husband, Govindalāl, who commits much more grievous sins. Govindalāl does in fact take up with the widow Rohinī, lives a life of sensual pleasure with her and then murders her with a bullet to the head in a fit of jealousy and out of regret over Bhramar. In Hariaudh's view, it seems the main ethical problem of the novel is its effect in the world: Bhramar does not fit into her ordained literary role, and therefore refutes her political role as a textual female sign in a canon of Indian self-improvement. Hariaudh's reaction to Bankim's Bhramar illustrates the profound truth of the contention that women especially bore the burden of representing positive moral identity in the realm of the Hindi novel, and by extension, the nascent Indian nation-state.[26] The subjectivity of Rohinī, the widow, furthermore, seems entirely lost on Hariaudh; this innovation in Bankim's novel of realistically imagining the perspective of a "fallen woman" simply did not register.

Hariaudh's reaction demonstrates a strong belief on the part of Hindi authors in the *social effect* of literature: this Bengali "problem woman," like the erotic heroine of classical literature, had to be distanced from the "real Indian women" of Hindi literature and Hindi-region life. Hariaudh's epilogue represents, on the one hand, more fodder for the accepted understanding of gender and nationalism in India; Hariaudh's thoughts merely approach this through a literary venue, at the expense of Westernized Bengalis.[27] The ideal woman of Hindi literature thus, as subject and subjective reader, is a figure we can view as constructed in dialogue, an entity defined as *not* an overeducated Bengali wife, *not* an overly franchised European female, and *not* possessing very much *tejas*.[28]

Here we can recall Hariaudh's Rādhā, whom we could read as his solution to the problem of *tejas* and the modern woman. She forebears Krishna's absence by turning pain into action, and engages in the public sphere only to some extent. While Krishna does political work in the metropolis, Rādhā interprets the meaning of Krishna to the residents of Braj, dispensing a peculiarly female cosmopolitanism, in which she institutes a sort of Gesellschaft for the polity, as wife, daughter, sister, and mother. Further, she comes to this utilitarian bhakti not through Bentham and Mill but through an indigenous logic of dislocated metaphoric objects, without being progressive or cosmopolitan herself. The literary mode then supplies a way of thinking about nationalism, a mode that, like women themselves, represented the home, the self, the a-colonial. While this Rādhā subverts some norms for her character, she ultimately represents a mode of authenticity built out of the literary elements of *śṛṅgāra*, thus evading the problem of women in the public sphere. Her public actions are ultimately out of love for Krishna, just as the world of action is his body. While the Bengali/British woman was willful, the Hindi-belt woman could be modern by serving a conjugal ideal.

Śṛṅgāra in Public Discourse

The entrance of the female subject and citizen, to be educated and consuming texts along with the male public, resulted in new aesthetic choices for the Hindi poetic canon and interpretation. Charu Gupta's *Sexuality, Obscenity, Community* addresses the topic of sexuality in print in some detail, from the helpful perspective of the many popular tracts on sexual topics, both *śṛṅgārik* and scientific in the early twentieth century. Speaking primarily of texts from the twenties and thirties, she notes the distinction in the debates between sex for pleasure and sex for procreation. "Thus Kalidasa's *Kumarasambhava* was considered 'legitimate' in spite of its detailed erotic descriptions because the activities ultimately led to the birth of a male child." On the other hand, medical discourse emerged to ameliorate obscenity concerns in some works, walking a fine line between instructive medical manuals along the lines of the highly moralistic sexological books in English, and books for and about pleasure. But as she points out, conventional Braj Bhāṣā chapbooks continued to be published apace, not merely for devotional uses, but for the erotic enjoyment they had always proffered as well. The erotic *Koka-śāstra* Sanskrit sexological texts consistently numbered among government records of printed texts through the early decades of the century. While a steady stream of sexually oriented publications, both *śṛṅgāra*-oriented and scientific, high- and low-brow, continued throughout this period, the high literary authors crafting the Hindi canon grappled with how to distance themselves from this aspect of "tradition." Although inhabiting a limited, often pedagogical sphere of student's editions, still the many critics of *śṛṅgāra* and/or obscenity in the Hindi press nevertheless successfully affected notions of "modern literature," while making erotic poetry more and more a genre of the past, of the uncouth "folk," or the merely pornographic.

In the rest of this chapter, I will examine some specific texts on *śṛṅgāra* and comprising *śṛṅgārik* themes. I will consider the criticism of *śṛṅgāra* by prominent authors in the early twentieth century, and then turn to the work of two lesser-known critics who attempted to renovate *śṛṅgāra*'s bad reputation. In so doing, I intend to flesh out the particulars of the *śṛṅgāra* of the nationalist Hindi culture of the 1920s and 30s described by Gupta. I suggest that a key identification was made between Braj Bhāṣā and the "obscenity" of *śṛṅgāra,* which would ultimately marginalize new Braj Bhāṣā poetry in the canon, as well as the form and content of some of its common genres, i.e., the verse forms of *ghanākṣarī* and *savaiyyā,* and the themes of the cowherd Krishna and Rādhā/gopis. These changes toward Khaṛī Bolī Hindi and away from the literary dialect of Braj Bhāṣā were, I submit, as much motivated by the perceived "obscenity problem" as by the perceived diktat of European poetic modernity to write in the language of educated speech. Thus, the reexamination of *śṛṅgāra* involved literary changes that altered the face of Hindi poetry dramatically. Nevertheless, *śṛṅgāra* as a way of poetic perceiving survives these attacks, resulting in a quite changed but familiar poetic world through the waning of Chāyāvād in the 1930s. The Chāyāvād poets, influenced clearly by Tagore and the English Romantics, built upon the "nature" in Hindi poetry of the preceding decades in their construction of a modernized poetic *śṛṅgāra,* which has formed, along with some oft-denied Persian motifs, a cultural poetics for late twentieth-century North India, and beyond.

The desire to remove *śṛṅgāra* from modern poetics received its most famous articulation much later, from Sumitranandan Pant's famous introduction to his *Pallav* (Leaves) in 1926, in which he decried the "three-foot world" of the *nakha-śikha* (toe to head) descriptions of heroines, and the lecherous perspective of conventional poets, which he aligned specifically with Braj rather than Sanskrit. He likened Hindi poetry—whether in Braj or Khaṛī Bolī—to a woman, on the one hand, and a landscape, on the other. He wrote that the *nāyikā,* that is, the heroine of old—a courtesan fettered with the heavy ankle bells of traditional meters—was being liberated; the landscape was being rescued from unreality—rather than the idealized arbors, mountains, rivers, the poet should take up the minute description of forgotten, wild, and barren spaces, and thereby a universalistic nature that would bring real experience into poetry. This exposition of modern Hindi nature poetry for which Pant is famed is based upon rejections of *śṛṅgāra* that began twenty years earlier, as I will show below.

I would argue that the *nāyikā* of old, in fact, reappears within a sanctified Nature, and this happened not merely by chance or by the primordial link of the female with Nature herself as *prakṛti* in Indian philosophy, but through the subsumption of *śṛṅgāra* into nature poetry and an ideology of "natural description." Here, I will present the setting for this by examining statements of consternation about *śṛṅgāra* that preceded Pant's famous enunciations by decades.

As stated earlier, by the end of the nineteenth century, Braj Bhāṣā, a major medium for Krishnaite poetry and *śṛṅgārik* poetry generally, was suffering a precipitous fall in status among the English-educated elite. This new disapproval of the literary-religious world of *śṛṅgāra* seems to have far outstripped previous debates over Rādhā's status over whether she belonged to Krishna or another man (either a *svakīyā* or a *parakīyā*). The courtly heroine as a type—Rādhā often identified with her—and Vaishnava religiosity generally came under attack from both the English and Indians. Erotic literature became a metonym for the social evils that progressive organizations combated in the name of national viability,[29] and gender had a potent role in this discourse. These problems were linked, sometimes quite explicitly, to the social problems of women. Further, as Kenneth Jones has noted, Swami Vivekananda blamed India's subjugated state on the gendered and eroticized devotion to Rādhā, through which Indian men had supposedly become effeminate and passive.[30] Partha Chatterjee's analysis of gendered nationalism clearly applies here as well: men seeking to assert their masculinity in the home also sought control of the sexuality of their females. This phenomenon included the literary selections of girls' curricula, and the literary representations of females, encouraging the Sītā ideal, while rejecting certain other aspects of tradition like *śṛṅgāra*. These attitudes of social outrage, commonly attributed to so-called "Victorian" morality imported from England, had profound effects that persisted through mid-twentieth-century literary criticism, and can be seen today surviving most evidently among the non-English speaking public, educated with the critical apparatus now attached to the Hindi canon.[31]

All of this being the case, it is clear that publications using the *nāyikā-bhed* continued to be published: some as republications of older manuscripts, some as original compositions, some clearly for a religious market, others not so clearly. Bhārat Jīvan Press in Banaras, a major publisher of modern Hindi literature, published an original work on the body parts of Rādhā and Krishna in 1893 (*Aṅgādarśa*). Presses in Lucknow and Muzaffarpur published *nakha-śikha* volumes specifically on Rādhā in the same year. By 1901, Bhārat Jīvan published a five-volume series comprised chiefly of poetry on Rādhā and Krishna. Poets such as Ratnākar, who would later edit the Braj Bhāṣā canon, wrote lovingly of Rādhā and Krishna in Braj, as a devotee and *rasik*. More broadly, *śṛṅgāra* never ceased to fascinate the literary public, as Charu Gupta's work on publishing and obscenity in the 1920s shows us. But circa 1900, the climate changed: without attacking Krishnaite religiosity, per se, a new trend emerged in poetic criticism that would target the *nāyikā* and *śṛṅgāra* generally as non-modern.

The authors examined below exhibit a viewpoint predicated on an idea of the profound influence literature can have upon the social world. While, certainly, instruction had always informed thinking about literature in India to some extent, the content of "use" and "virtue" had changed. Where the *Kama Sutra* had once instructed the elite in refined pleasures, now in 1909, the young Rāmacandra Śukla (later to become the preeminent Hindi literary historian) would state with disapproval, "various Hindi poets have filled literature up with so many impassioning phrases of *śṛṅgāra rasa* that poetry too is beginning to be thought the stuff of sensuous pleasure (*vilās kī sāmagrī*)."[32] Literary pleasure itself had changed. Below we will examine the words of critics and poets somewhat preceding Gupta's and Orsini's studies from the 1920s on, authors from the first three decades of the century, who would become the pillars of the Hindi literary canon, and whose diatribes against decadence, obscenity, *śṛṅgāra*, and the Braj Bhāṣā dialect associated with these, ironically emerged in a publishing context replete with such "impassioning stuff."[33] Literary passion became a matter of public debate, intrinsically connected to political questions about the status of women.

An Initial Attack, 1901

Mahavīraprasād Dvivedī, namesake of what is known as a stern and didactic generation of poets, came to his anti-*śṛṅgāra* stance only around the turn of the century. His early work "Sneha-mālā" ("Garland of verses of affection") of 1890 was a Braj rendering based on Sanskrit poet Bhartṛhāri's "Śṛṅgāra-śataka," in the style of *rīti* poet Bihārī Lāl's *dohās*, which in fact embraced bodily description: "The beloved is understood to be a river, of water unfathomably deep / Her breasts are *cakavā* birds, her face a lotus, her navel a bee, and man the bank."[34] However, by 1902, with the publication of his *Kumārasambhava-sār* (*The Essence of the* Kumārasambhava), Dvivedī noted in his introduction the presence of "obscenity" in certain of Kalidasa's later cantos of this work, of which he translated only the first five.[35] How had his perspective changed in the intervening years?

The previous year, 1901, he had just published a famous initial lobby against *śṛṅgāra*: the article "Nāyikā-bhed" ("The Taxonomy of Heroines"), in one of the early issues of *Sarasvatī*, the most famed Hindi literary journal of its time, which Dvivedī would soon take over as editor. In this article, Dvivedī interprets the *nāyikā-bhed* genre, and the *nakha-śikha* as one of its corollary features, as the especial scourge of Hindi/Braj poetry, more than for any other vernacular poetry, or even Sanskrit itself. Dvivedī based his argument against *śṛṅgāra* on the fact that this genre "belongs to the past," a time when *nāyikā-bhed* was not obscene and described only the "regular types" of heroines. He describes with disgust that it has proliferated in a degraded form in the nineteenth century, in the Braj Bhāṣā poetic gatherings, and even in villages, among old men:

> Because someone liked the *navoṛhā* ("newly grown" girl)[36] best among heroines, for the last few years, a book called *Navoṛhādarśa* (*Exemplary* Navoṛhās) has been published just on the greatness of the *navoṛhā* alone, from beginning to end. *Nāyikā bhed* is the end all and be all to the verse-spinning (*samasyāpūrti*-making) poetic societies and gatherings. . . . intoxicated youth . . . become engrossed in sensualism.
>
> . . . [The Sanskrit description of heroines] is not as impassioning and harmful as that of our Hindi poets, fixed on "the beginning of love-making," "after love-making," and "the inverted position." . . . Leave aside cities, even in the littlest villages, with my own eyes I've seen old geezers in their sixties discussing *nāyikā-bhed* and giving lectures on the differentiation of the distinctions between the *jñāta-yauvanā* (self-conscious young woman) and the *ajñāta-yauvanā* (unknowing young woman)."[37]

Dvivedī discounts the role of Krishna devotion in *nāyikā-bhed* as a corruption, and finds the description of types of women harmful—and here he tellingly switches from the term "heroine" to "women" per se (*striyoṁ ke bhed varṇan*).[38] Asserting a direct connection between the taxonomical descriptions of women with social realities, he claims the women described in the *nāyikā-bhed* genre are those of ill-repute, adulteresses and prostitutes, who exert a bad influence on young men. Moreover, they exhibit a certain gender-inversion, as promiscuous women who possess "the exclusively male mind of a husband" (*puruṣamātrā meṁ patibuddhi rakhnevālī kulaṭā*), seemingly a euphemism for sexual desire and/or dominance. Dvivedī thus found this pornography-in-verse to have social ramifications, but he saw this more in terms of the deleterious effects upon men, rather than women.

In counterpoint to Dvivedī's attack, we should note the continued presence of *nāyikā-bhed* texts in the Hindi publishing market. In just the following year, Bhārat Jīvan Press reissued *Jagadvinod* (*Worldly Pleasure*) by nineteenth-century author Padmākar, which included the *navoṛhā* herself: "The woman who doesn't want sex (*rati*), because of too much fear, or shame (*lāj*) / The poets give this *mughdā* (artless girl, the youngest class of heroine) the designation of '*navoṛhā*.' "[39] In this latter-day *nāyikā-bhed* taxonomy we find ample reference to Rādhā and Krishna, and the term *pati* (husband, lord) appears often enough. However, although the sanction of religion and marriage may still have bestowed some social legitimacy to the *nāyikā-bhed* genre, the reformist zeitgeist was against it, and possibly the Age of Consent Bill controversies of the 1890s around just such barely pubescent girls perhaps had turned upper-class readers such as Dvivedī away from such genres, with their description of the young *mugdhā* heroines.[40] Dvivedī's position was that of the new vanguard of Hindi litterateurs, and his ideal of a chastened Hindi would dominate Hindi poetic production only later.

Śṛṅgāra as a National Problem

Roughly a decade after Dvivedī's attack on the *nāyikā-bhed*, his protégé, Maithilīśaraṇ Gupta (1866–1964), would take up the topic again in his hugely popular *Bhārat bhāratī* (*Voice of India*) of 1912–14, which would shortly become an essential verse text of Indian nationalism. Gupta had by then become a well-known young protégé of Dvivedī, whose poems had dotted the pages of *Sarasvati* since 1905.[41] Born in a village in Jhansi district, son of a Vaishnava Brahman pandit, Gupta fit the mold of many Hindi poets of his generation. However, he differed from most in his dominating interest in bringing both the Hindu epics and nationalism (however guarded), into Khaṛī Bolī poetry. Indeed, with the sensation that *Voice of India* caused, Gupta had effected the turn to Khaṛī Bolī that Dvivedī had been promoting in the pages of *Sarasvati* for the previous decade. Along with the nationalist turn and the Khaṛī Bolī turn, we find also a turn against eroticism, a detriment to India's ancient glory and connected to the allegedly low moral state of women in the present day.

In this work, undeniably a political tract more than poetry, "Woman" figured prominently, as the "helpless woman" (*abalā*, "she without strength"), mirroring the now downtrodden Mother India, an image saturating national rhetoric of the era. However, actual Indian women, past and present, formed another subject. In the "Past" section, under the heading of "women" (after "hospitality" and "children," in accounting of all things that were better in the glorious past[42]), Gupta imagines women dedicated to their husbands with *rati* (absorption, enjoyment, passion), a term for pleasure that modern authors had begun to avoid. On the other hand, ancient women had achieved already what modern men desired for their daughters: they were educated (*śikṣitā*), and yet also tirelessly performed the familiar gendered tasks, such as embroidery. Moreover, they were "not like the wives of today."[43]

In the "Contemporary" section, we find the foil for the past ideal. Gupta turns his critique to literature, and sure enough, the *nāyikā-bhed* appears, again as a symbol of Indian decadence. Here in a battle of texts, the *nāyikā-bhed* genre has supplanted all religious texts in this *kali-yuga* of ours: "Cast aside the *śruti*, *śāstras*, *sūtras*, *Purāṇas*, *Ramayana*, *Mahabharata*, / The *nāyikābhed* and the like have come in their place, to stay!!"[44] Gupta finds *śṛṅgāra* harmful even in the religious sphere: "Hiding behind Krishna, we harm the people."[45] Furthermore, contemporary women betray their sexuality in their own gendered world: "Women have this virtue, that they know how to sing dirty songs."[46] The section on the "Future" India continues in the same vein, although augmented with poetic directives this time: "How much longer will the poets keep on rehashing, / The hair, the breasts, the sidelong glances!. . . . // The true *kāminī* (desirable woman) of poetry is a pleasing teacher."[47] Gupta exhorts, "Poets! Arise now . . . / Remove all the base emotions and fill yourselves with high emotions."[48]

It is easy to dismiss Dvivedī's and Gupta's remarks on women and *śṛṅgāra* as mere Victorian moralism, or examples of the now commonplace notions about women and nationalism in India.[49] However, we should notice here the grave import of the aesthetic in Gupta's cultural vision, and take seriously the fact that the *śṛṅgāra* mode could inspire such a degree of shame that shedding it implied a cultural transformation corollary to political Independence and attaining modernity in general. A change in poetics meant a possible change in politics.

But yet again, we must contextualize Gupta's sentiments even within the elite sphere of Hindi literary culture of the time, as Gupta's stridence came from a context of mixed messages on the value of *śṛṅgāra*. The early years of the famous journal *Sarasvatī* are a case in point: poems, articles, and art, took up *śṛṅgārik* subjects and Sanskritic heroines with little consternation. The virtuous heroine Śakuntalā of Kalidasa's *śṛṅgāra*-dominant play had consistent pride of place, a phenomenon directly connected to Tagore's praise for the drama several years earlier.[50] Favor for Kalidasa's *Meghadūtam* (Cloud-Messenger), replete with sensuous metaphors and based on love-in-longing, was reflected in the spare and delicate modernist art print of the "pining *yakṣa*'s wife" in July 1911.[51] But importantly, this issue of the magazine practically thematized the dutiful wife, with a print of Pārvatī worshipping Shiva, photos of King George and his Queen Mary, and a narration on the virtues of Sukanyā, the sage's wife. Articles on *śṛṅgāra*, especially in its Braj Bhāṣā exponents, seemed to merely exposit the features of its poetics.[52] The magazine's poetry would sometimes feature traditionally *śṛṅgārik* themes, but without obtuse sexual reference; the book review column would mention new works on *śṛṅgāra* poetics with no reproval. A selective *śṛṅgāra*, academic *śṛṅgāra*, and safe, subtle *śṛṅgāra* survived in the pages of *Sarasvatī*. This domestication of *śṛṅgāra* to current progressive Edwardian and Indian social codes—through which Goddess Pārvatī and Queen Mary are united as ideal wife-consorts—made *śṛṅgāra* acceptable for the self-consciously modern readership. By extension, in the rhetorical logic of the time, this was the contained eroticism of a people deserving Self-Rule.

Sublimating Śṛṅgāra

Concurrently, "Nature" had begun to appear as a solution for *śṛṅgāra*, and—using Freud's concept loosely—a mode of sublimation of the beloved Sanskritic aesthetic world of erotic pleasure. In the next critical lobby, younger poet Jayaśaṅkar Prasād criticized *śṛṅgārik* Braj poetry in his article "Kavi aur kavitā" (Poet and Poetry) of 1910 in his *Indu*. His criticism of *śṛṅgārik* poetry involved once again a conflation of Braj with *śṛṅgāra*. Furthermore, he proposes that the realist description of nature and of emotion (*bhāva*) is the modern alternative to *śṛṅgāra*. Like a true modern, he found his ideal in the sanctified classical past, in Valmiki who "researched" nature, (*anveṣaṇ karate the*), and to whom "nature's each and every particle, even the tiny veins on the leaves of the braches of huge trees, spoke. . . ."[53] Perhaps with this botanical frame of mind, Prasād evokes the conventional idea that the pleasure of verse is as that of a garden.[54] Nature analyzed and nature cultivated provides for him the basis of literary pleasure, beyond any theoretical precept of *śṛṅgāra*. For Prasād, *śṛṅgāra* was merely a symptom of a poetic myopia toward nature, a perceptual trap preventing realism, and a stifling set of conventions embodied in Braj Bhāṣā.[55]

Prasād finally turns to the current social problem *śṛṅgāra* posed, carefully noting it as acceptable for the devotee in its classical forms (the "pure" *śṛṅgāra* of Kalidasa's *Śakuntalā* is a case in point). While "*śṛṅgāra* is not corrupt, its style of description which is prevalent in Hindi is corrupt," and because of this "Hindi literature lovers are angered at the mention of *śṛṅgāra*. And because of this, people often have distaste for reading works in verse."[56] Western education appears as another source of the rejection of *śṛṅgārik* poetry in particular: "following the current western education, the feelings (*bhāva*) of society are changing. Poetry doesn't match with (these *bhāvas*) and reading old poetry seems like a terrible sin, because that type of poetry has been done to excess."[57] But Prasād has not disowned *śṛṅgāra* completely; he still believes that one can "from an archaeological point of view," get the same pleasure from old *śṛṅgāra* poetry, and at root he claims that modern poetry should give otherworldly, *alaukik,* pleasure, precisely the term for the pleasure of Krishna's *lila,* his desire-filled play beyond social codes of the world.[58]

Prasād supports overturning of the aesthetic precepts of *śṛṅgāra* in favor of nature and emotion, but cleaves to a poetic ideal that resonates with both something like an English natural sublime and the psychological transport of *rasa*. He closes his essay with a transformation—indeed sublimation—of the eroticism of *śṛṅgāra* into aesthetic idioms of nationalism. Here, *śṛṅgāra* per se is the inverse of hope for the future, a destructive intoxicant, whereas the true aesthetic experience beyond the self is one of national proportions: "Drinking the sweetness of "*śṛṅgāra-rasa*," the temperaments have become lax and disturbed." Hence, he prescribes a different kind of poetry: "emotional, stirring poetry that makes you forget yourself. . . . that is full of the people's songs, energizing of the temperaments, conquering lassitude, raining delight. . . ." Thus, replacing the intoxicating emotion of *śṛṅgāra* with energizing songs of the people will bring back the goddess of all arts, and speech itself: "She-with-the-veena (Sarasvatī) will take up her instrument and challenge us with the clarion call, [and the] the voice [or goddess Sarasvatī] of India (*Bhārat kī bhāratī*) will be India's alone once again.[59] The voice of India thus replaces the intoxicating emotion of *śṛṅgāra* with that of incitement to action. His essay ends fittingly with the goddess Sarasvatī, *Bhārat ki Bhāratī* (Sarasvatī, or voice, of India), anticipating the title of Gupta's *Bhārat-Bhārati* of 1912. Uplifted and drowning out *śṛṅgāra,* this voice would be commensurate to the Indian identity he envisions, replete with transcendent emotion.

The Nāyikā Modernized

Although *śṛṅgāra* had suffered attacks on the basis of the harm it manifests in society, and especially in the description of women, many of these same critics produced poems based, perhaps unwittingly, upon the *śṛṅgārik* model of *nāyikā-bhed*. Dvivedī and Gupta, who had criticized *śṛṅgāra* so vociferously, co-edited a volume of poems in Khaṛī Bolī and Braj consisting largely of descriptions of women! Written by Dvivedī, Gupta, and several less-well-known authors, these poems described portraits painted by Raja Ravi Varmā, or in the realist European style of the famed Raja Ravi Varmā, and published in the pages of *Sarasvatī*. Although the paintings were not "on women" per se, functionally the art featured in *Sarasvatī* did feature women quite heavily, whether mythological, literary, or real. On reader demand, Dvivedī republished the paintings with their poems in *Kavitā-kalāp* (*A Collection of Poetry*) in 1909.[60] By all accounts a luxury item "coffee-table book," a substantial part of *Kavitā-kalāp* seems to have constituted a modern version of the classificatory *nāyikā-bhed* genre in the trappings of realist art, visual and poetic.

Dvivedī notably did not mention the shadows of *śṛṅgāra* in the text, nor dwell on the volume's Braj Bhāṣā linguistic content either.[61] He seemed to expect some criticism, however, as he states that the reader must have a mixture of the classical qualities of a connoisseur along with an appreciation for the natural: "He alone can truly assess poetry (*kavitā ka yathārth jāñc*) who is a poet himself, who is a gentleman (*sahṛday*), who is a *rasik*, who has the highest knowledge of human nature and natural laws (*prākṛtik niyam*)." The text's poems on different types of women would presumably demonstrate the congruency of the *rasik*'s expertise and the realistic laws of nature. That is, the *rasik*'s expertise no longer meant merely traditional poetics and an ineffable sympathy; rather, he possessed a sensibility for the naturalistic as well—with this last phrase Dvivedī suggests that knowledge of nature, human and otherwise, stands for precisely what was modern about these paintings in the European mode, and their poems.

So what characterized the modern, "natural" female subject of poetry, as conceived by these anti-*śṛṅgāra* authors? The women portrayed included mythological figures and some from Kalidasa (predictably including Śakuntalā, the ingénue of choice in this era), whose stories are summarized in verse. One, Rambhā (here the famously beautiful dancing nymph [*apsarā*] in paradise), Dvivedī treats in verse in a more blatantly sexual manner, although less systematically than in a proper *nakha-śikha*. Rambha's "expansive breasts and buttocks, / Are truly unsurpassable," and from her "mind-boggling gait" and mannerisms, "Even the ascetic priests (*muṇis*) are enchanted, / They get plenty of *tapa* (heat) in their bodies."[62] Indeed, this description recounts accurately her successful temptation of a *muṇi*, and the plantain-trunk-like loins that her name suggests. This despite the fact that the Rambhā lithograph in question shows her quite covered, compared to other Ravi Varmā paintings and women depicted in Indian art generally. Perhaps the heroines of Sanskrit tradition held a special place for Dvivedī in his moral universe; they perhaps demanded and received a more "pure" *śṛṅgāra* from ancient times, as Dvivedī would have it.

However, "real women" dominated the portraits, their appearance described with imaginative elaborations that drew from *śṛṅgārik* ideals of beauty and female behavior, as well as new moral and social images of the modern woman. Some of the women in the simpler, photograph-like "head-shot" portraits were identified according to their region of origin or religion, in an almost anthropological collation. If the scientific study of nature informed realism in nature poetry, then British anthropology likely colored this taxonomy of women (though such collations of women of various regions resembles other genres, modern and pre-modern).[63] *Kavitā-kalāp* adheres to the practice of the typing of women, if not by age, appearance, and mood, as in the classical mode, then here in a modern realist mode, enumerating various species of that Indian womanhood held up so iconically in political rhetoric.

This mode of modern quasi-ethnographic taxonomy did not preclude the language of desire, however. Several of Dvivedī's own poems show a surprising consistency with idioms of *śṛṅgāra*. While their descriptions often resembled what Sudipta Kaviraj has found in Tagore's fiction, that women were described in terms of their "internal, emotional attractiveness" in terms "deliberately inattentive to eroticism,"[64] still, all of the women are idealized, and often physically so. While these descriptions forego the familiar *nāyikā-bhed* descriptions of love and the toe-to-head descriptions of bodies, and illustrate instead middle- and upper-class housewives, still these women are desirable, and therefore conventionally fit subjects for verse. What remains of *śṛṅgāra* here may indicate what constituted acceptable *śṛṅgāra* in 1909, even for the harsh critics of eroticism. Two examples follow:

Dvivedī's poem on Varmā's painting *Indirā* states that she is a lady from Pune, "the best woman of the south / beloved by her educated husband." He imagines her traits as those of the new woman, but not the Westernized woman. Indirā goes to see the new plays, "always bringing her husband." She doesn't cover her face and can stay out late; she prays for her husband's welfare, and is an ardent devotee. "She goes to functions and society meeting / Listens to speeches . . . / . . . [then] she comes home and animatedly / Talks with her husband, enchanting his mind (*pati-citta curātī*)" Notably, the vocabulary of love remains, as in *citta curana*, a phrase often used for the more ineffable and physical captivation of sexual love. Here, however, intellectual conversation suffices.

Another poem written on *Indirā* by another author exemplifies the *nāyikā* of *śṛṅgāra* reinterpreted with modern poetic tropes of nature and spirit within it. In the experimental mode of the day, the poem appears in Khaṛī Bolī, but in a Sanskrit meter.

> Listen, all who revel in the vast entirety of Brahma!
> Residents in the great country where all is sacrificed!
> Come here a moment, desirous (*ātura*) ones
> And you will see the beauty of nature (*prakṛti*)
>
> A *kamalinī*, beautiful and charming to look at
> A beautiful *(rasīlī)* young woman with deer-like eyes
> Attractive, a beauty among a *kula* of attractive women
> The picture of the pleasing Indirā is beautiful.

The term *kamalinī* comes straight from the *nāyikā-bhed* typology, a fact noted in a footnote in the text itself, that it is "a special class of women." On the other hand, the latter verses turn more philosophical, to the meaning of beauty in the world. At end, "the loveliness in nature is all Brahma." A note informs, "although this is a *śṛṅgāra* poem, the poet is a follower of Vedanta, so the beginning and the end are written in this way."[65] Thus, the poem merges several themes at once: evocations of Sanskrit through the *drutavilambita* meter, a nominally Vedantin reference to Brahma in Nature; a nationalist reference to the striving men of the country; the *śṛṅgāra* mode; and an apposition of verses that identifies this Indirā with nature. Here we find a contained, circumscribed sort of *śṛṅgāra*, suitable for modern pleasure-seekers who would value the varied references to national "sacrifice" and Brahma, and the realism of Varmā's painting, but also savor the beauty of the subject herself in the terminology of *śṛṅgāra*. All of this for a really quite stark portrait, blandly archetypal as much as naturalist. Thus the familiar *nāyikā* remains, in the garb of realism and philsophy, despite the canonizers' condemnations of her forebears.

Dvivedī's other women-poems in *Kavitā-kalāp* maintain their plodding pedestrian tone, and effectively reduce any shadow of *śṛṅgāra* to mere clichés. In a poem illustrating a Ravi Varmā portrait of a Gujarati woman named "Kumudasundarī," we are reminded of Gupta's "Aryan lady" who was also both educated and expert in household handicrafts: Kumudasundarī reads and writes, decorates the house, sews, keeps the attention of her husband, and speaks politely with her friends. She is progressive too: "She always goes out / with her husband in the evening / She doesn't like jewelry / She has no concern with purdah." But she is also familiarly desirable, having a moon-like face and creeper-like limbs, which steal the heart of her husband. Despite the mixed depiction of social progressivism and standard body-description, however, the poem falls much flatter than even a boilerplate *śṛṅgāra* poem: "This is an educated Gujarati woman. / She likes her blue sari. / Her picture delights the eyes. / Ravi Varmā reproduced it well."[66] The admiration here is for the photographic quality of Varma's "reproduction" of the real—the idiom of "taking a photo" itself a trope representing literary realism in this era.

But what of the pleasure of *śṛṅgāra*? Compared to other imaginings of love current in India at the time, this volume—representing Hindi poetry generally—displays a more conservative stance through its resistance to eliminating erotic literary pleasures, especially in the "safe" atmosphere of mythical nymphs. But there is also a definite impetus toward a new literary female figure, somewhat ideal, but photographically realistic, and perhaps fodder for philosophizing on the nature of the world. Thus, poetry in Hindi took a complex stance toward the aesthetics of love and the new woman; *Kavitā-kalāp* ultimately was meant to provide pleasure, however modern its technologies or traditional its tropes.

While these modernized *nāyikā*s of this 1909 book of verse exhibit the authors' intent for a realist, albeit ideal or typed female figures, the classical *nāyikā*s also received extended treatment by some of the famed authors of the teens. Two works, both published in book form in 1914, demonstrate the revision of the classical *nāyikā* as an ideally beautiful woman with ethical as much as physical traits. Maithilīśaraṇ Gupta's Śakuntalā serves as our first example. Gupta described her jungle childhood at the hermit's ashram in typical style: Śakuntalā frolics with the deer, etc. While Kalidasa's Śakuntalā also possesses moral qualities, these became more pronounced in Gupta's initial description, to the detriment of the sensuous bodily description of the Sanskrit original. She not only frolics with the jungle fauna, but learns from it: in terms of her attractiveness, "She learned her slow gait from the cool and fragrant wind," and in her moral character, "From the leaping ritual fire, she learned to spread goodwill (*sadbhāv*) . . . / . . . [and] help others."[67]

> Like the free expanse of the sky, her life was resolutely free of sin;
> Like the light of dawn, her untiring body was pure.
> Like the high shining peaks of the Himalayas her heart was very lofty (*unnat*);
> She was like the supreme principle made evident, her grove of austerities was blessed.

Like Hariaudh's Rādhā, she "would attend and listen to her elders" and "was always engaged in some new effort."[68] But this was all to say that she was ideally nubile, as

Her friends would laugh and loosen her blouse of bark
Always tightening around her limbs, from the expansion of
her breasts.
Wearing flower ornaments the beautiful girl of the wood
Seemed as if a lady from the heavens on earth.[69]

Encompassing these various qualities, the omniscient narrative perspective here subverts the voyeuristic quality of the original drama's scene, when the King spies her among her friends and expresses his desire and love, thus lessening the "*śṛṅgāra* factor." Now Śakuntalā's ethical qualities rival those of her physical beauty.

A similar description of Rādhā appears in Hariaudh's *Priyapravās* in the same year. Here, the pastoral ingénue of courtly Krishna poetry emerges as a Samaritan as much as courtly artiste:

Skilled in the many mannerisms of emotion and its causes,
filled with amusement,
Skilled in casting glances with the flirtatious rolling of her
eyes, a scholar (*paṇḍitā*) of eyebrow gestures,
Excelling in playing instruments, with pleasure, adorned
with adornments,
Rādhā was a beauty, big-eyed, swinging with joy.

She used to redden her lotus-feet, ornamenting the surface
of the earth.
The redness of her lips made the *bimba* and the coral tree
seem less lovely
The excellence of her lotus-face, blooming with joy, was the
foundation of beauty
Rādhā's desirable and lovely beauty was the entrancer of
Kāma's wife Rati.

Well-dressed and well-ornamented, full of virtues and
everywhere respected
Engrossed in helping sick and elderly people, dedicated in
thought to the pure Shastras,
Steeped in goodwill, of incomparable heart, nurturer of pure
love
Was Rādhā, of good soul, with a happy face, as if a jewel of
the race of women.[70]

The first two verses here clearly evoke the *nāyikā* of Sanskrit and Braj poetry. Hariaudh did not shrink from a conventional and somewhat sexualized description of Rādhā, using terms such as *kamaṇīya* (desirable), and attributing to her skills such as *hāva-vibhāva* (flirtatious gestures). These verses do not deny the standard, sexual Rādhā, but neither do they display the thorough and explicit description of body parts found in the *nakha-śikha*. Rādhā's talents are those associated with the highest classes of heroines. Suddenly, however, the view shifts. She remains loving and emotional, but her description becomes punctuated with the prefix *sat-*, literally "pure": *sadvastrā-sadalaṅkṛtā . . . saccastrā cintāparā . . . sadbhāvatiratā . . . satprema-samposikā* (Of pure dress and pure ornament . . . devoted in thought to the pure Shastras . . . steeped in pure feelings [i.e., goodwill], nurturer of pure love). This perhaps dissociated Rādhā from her licentious past, or elevated her to the ingénue status seen in recent renditions of Śakuntalā. Clearly, this Rādhā shared the image of the desirable "proper wife" of epic like the ever-popular Sītā, and the Urmilā who would appear in M. Gupta's 1916 first canto of *Saket*. Become like the epic heroines who populated the poetic world at this time, this pure and august Rādhā might counter objections to her sexualization.

Carrying this theme of purity further, Hariaudh inserts an episode recalling Kalidasa's masterwork of *śṛṅgāra*, the *Cloud-messenger*, in a passage of *Priyapravās* in the same *mandākrāntā* meter, in which Rādhā gives a message to the wind and narrates her journey. Here, her admonition to the wind to do good deeds along her path foreshadows her ultimate decision to work for the good of the world. Further, Rādhā's words refer not only to modesty, but to the sanctioned *rati* of nature:

> If a woman traveler, full of modesty, should come into view,
> Then don't let the beautiful woman's clothes become disheveled.
> . . .
>
> If there are seated together happily, finding the sweet juice of the flowers,
> A male and female bee, be gentle with them.
> May the flower not shake even a little and they not be disturbed.
> May their play not be unsuccessful, may there be no obstacle in their dalliance.

If a sick traveler has fallen somewhere on the path, then
Eagerly, having forgotten about my whole sad state,
Take away all of his sadness. . . .

If a wearied farmer-woman appears in a field,
Slowly touch her and erase her suffering.
If a rain-cloud may come along in the sky, then bring it
over.
Soothe with shade the woman burning with heat.[71]

Rādhā echoes here the sentiments of Kalidasa's *yakṣa*, and she even incorporates the cloud itself ("if a rain-cloud may come along . . ."), but here Rādhā worries mostly about women. Even her messenger is female—the wind-messenger here likely alluding to the female wind-confidante of Persian poetic traditions. While the *viraha* of the original remains, the allusion to pleasure only comes with the bees and flowers here, in a "natural scene" not to be disturbed, rather than the *yakṣa*'s description of pleasure to be taken. Thus Hariaudh's new Rādhā embodied social sympathy and propriety, while still incorporating the pleasure of previous texts.

In another of the myriad instances of the merging of classical heroines and modern ideals, the ethical and desirable heroine is identified with Indianness. In the 1920s, Hariaudh chose to compose some new *nāyikā* poems in Braj meters that would explicitly avoid the troublesome *śṛṅgāra*. He would later publish these together, under the category of "New, best heroines," in his 1931 *Rasakalas* (*A pot of rasa*), as part of a lengthy exposition on *rasa* theory, *śṛṅgāra*, and rationales for them. In describing the heroine "Lover of her Country" ("Deś-premikā"), we see a merging of *śṛṅgārik* pleasures of old with new pleasures of ancient glory, patriotism, and significantly, of nature. This "Nature" seems to signify both a grand modern Nature linked to the state, and the otherworldly natural space of Krishna's *śṛṅgāra*-filled lila. In the lilting *ghanākṣarī* verse form typical of Braj poetry, Hariaudh illustrated the "Lover of her Country" thus:

Glorious forever from past glories
 She proclaims her allegiance to the wisdom of her
 elders.
Delighted, spreading over the earth
 Seeing the artful creeper of praise for God (*kirtan*)
 blooming

Hariaudh says, looking at the sublimity of nature
She swings, thrilling, on the swing of love,
Under sway of the glory of the Sarasvatī of India
She is a good woman, she doesn't forget her Indianness.[72]

In a panoply of multiple identifications of the erotic heroine, India's ancient glory, Sarasvatī, India, and nature, this creeper-like delicate beauty represents the endangered Indianness that others are forgetting. This authentic Indianness comes on "the swing of love," familiar as a place for beautiful girls and lovers in courtly portrayals of springtime, the love-play of Rādhā and Krishna, and even in popular illustrations in the realist Ravi Varma mode, of a girl on a swing, against a vast naturalistic landscape.[73]

As a whole, the eight verses of "Lover of her Country" conjoin bodily love with nationalism, and the heroine herself with India. She is identified with an afflicted India, and yet also with classic descriptions of a young woman in love: "looking upon all existence she becomes full of grandeur / [she is] besieged by the terrible sorrow of misfortune. / the lost memory of the body of India is forgotten / all blooming, all abloom, the woman wanders to a fro."[74] Here the third line on the "lost memory of the body" appears a negative result of the misfortune befallen India's body politic; however, at the same time, such a loss of body-consciousness is typical of the lovelorn, leaving the audience uncertain of the emotional state of this woman "all abloom." At any rate, this heroine's body is emblematic of both India, and love: "in each limb is the love and passion (*anurāga-rāga*) of a woman / the greatness of India pervades her entire body (*roma-roma maiṁ*)."[75] In sum, through these poetic works we see the courtly, sexual, bodily *nāyikā* had indeed become materially and ethically modernized into an identitarian domestic commodity in a world of lithographs, realism, and "the woman question."[76]

The Natural Science of Śṛṅgāra: Nature-Study and Literary Study

Hariaudh's *Pot of Rasa* also provides a window onto a scientific reading of *śṛṅgāra* that began in the early twentieth century. In this publication of 1931, Hariaudh wrote in his lengthy introduction of the integration of nature, realism, morality, and *śṛṅgāra*, avidly trying to resuscitate and revise *śṛṅgāra* for modern use. The work was half prose treatise, half Braj poetry, all on the subject of *rasa* per se, much of it on the meaning of *śṛṅgāra*. The section of poetry contained illustrations of all of the *rasas*, and under *śṛṅgāra* included a *nāyikā-bhed* with considerably altered personae. In his introduction he quoted liberally from a 1925 publication by another author, Kṛṣṇabihārī Miśra, editor of the *Collected Works of Matirām* (*Matirām-granthāvalī*) to which we will now turn.[77]

The seventeenth-century poet Matirām, famed as the author of a taxonomy of heroes and heroines, the *Rasarāj* (*The King of Rasa*), had been in print several times before the 1920s, testifying to his popularity among connoisseurs. The edition at hand from 1925 seems to have had a more pedagogical or canonical purpose than those previously published, because of its quite lengthy introduction explaining principles of *rasa* and *śṛṅgāra* and how to read this *śṛṅgāra* through a modern lens of the "usefulness" of literature. The editor Miśra's comments are especially interesting because of his relative obscurity; his comments represent those of a more anonymous "worker for the cause" of Hindi literature.[78] Through his interpretation of Matirām's poetry, we might elucidate how the problem of the erotic was broached and incorporated into the world-view of a practical critic.[79] As Mahaviraprasād Dvivedī noted in his favorable review of Miśra's Introduction, "considering the special refined taste of these days, very many of Matirām's verses are either obscene or at least 'exciting' (*udvegajanak*); but in the time in which Matirām was born, they were not understood as such. This is something we should not forget."[80] Historicizing aside, Miśra did indeed provide a reading of *śṛṅgāra* that created sympathy with the newly "obscene" subject of *śṛṅgāra*, and he did so by proving *śṛṅgāra* to be a poetic version of biological reason.

From the first page, terms for "love" (*prem*, *prīti*, *praṇay*) dominate. Miśra states that "*rasa* poetry" is pure or true poetry (*satkāvya*), and that the assigned *sthāyī bhāva* of *śṛṅgāra* is properly understood as love; here he simply does not mention the traditional *sthāyī bhāva* of sexual and/or engrossing pleasure (*rati*). Strikingly, Miśra explains the import of this love with lengthy quotations from an American sex educator, whose emotive phrasing on "the birds and the bees" must have struck a chord with the Hindi reader versed in the garlands of phrases of poetry past. The following appears in this introduction to the Matirām volume, quoted from Sylvainus Stall's *What a Young Husband Ought to Know* of 1897:

> It is under the awakening of reproductive life that the fields put on their verdure, the flowers unfold their beauty and fragrance, the birds put on their brightest plumage and sing their sweetest song while the chirp of the cricket, the note of the katydid, is but the call to its mate, for the many tongued voices, which break the stillness of field and forest, are but the myriad notes of love.[81]

This and other extensive quotations from Stall appear transliterated and then translated into Hindi, with certain slight changes (for instance, Stall's chirping cricket above becomes in translation the calling *koyal* bird, a stock feature of *śṛṅgāra* poetry). This "awakening of reproductive life" in nature thus integrated well with the natural poetic world of *śṛṅgāra*.

Stall's words then turn toward God, in phrases that evoke not only *śṛṅgāra*, but the contemporary theology of *viśva-prem*, universal love: the common drive within plants and animals is a "universal god-given passion," which Miśra translates more ambiguously—and chastely—as *viśva-prema*, literally "love for the world," or "love pervasive in the world." This "god-given passion" creates in turn the perception of beauty and love of beauty, both in art and in everyday life. All of this must have sounded strikingly familiar to aesthetic theories of *rasa* and *śṛṅgāra* in particular, and however Miśra meant his translation of "god-given passion" as "world-love," it must have sounded like the elite theologies of the time. Then, in rhetoric even more familiar to the Indian audience, Stall cites the use of happy marital union and reproduction "for the good of the race," and the centrality of the married couple, children, and "home and country" and "the center of all that makes life dear," or in Hindi translation, what makes life full of love or passion, *anurāgamayī*.

The language of love in the translation from Stall is already layered with religious, literary, and philosophical echoes that link heterosexual love and poetics semiotically, if not explicitly. The "most blessed earthly condition" of marriage, as Stall describes, is in Hindi "giving of joy/enjoyment/delight" *(ānandadāyinī)*, and it is this very *ānand* that Miśra identifies as the core of the poetics of both English and ancient Sanskrit scholars, as he proves with ample quotation from the likes of Mammaṭa, Tagore, and Wordsworth. The *ānand* Miśra then identifies as *rasa*, and also as the English "taste." In contrast to the scientized yet still titillating manuals of Charu Gupta's study of popular literature, this scientization is a moralized, theologized, and aesthetic one. The English genre of "birds and bees" nature-writing fit quite happily with the educative intent of Miśra. Hence, incorporating the social into poetics, Miśra merges literary enjoyment with the enjoyment of sanctioned procreation. Such was the potentiality that *śṛṅgāra* could still embody for the colonial critic.

Most importantly, a distinction between mere obscenity and the *śṛṅgāra* of proper enjoyment had to be made. This Miśra takes care to elaborate, identifying the *sthāyī bhāva* of *śṛṅgāra* as love (*prem*), and specifically married love; other kinds of love between a man and a woman are corrupted and the mere illusion of *rasa*.[82] Miśra goes on to resuscitate *śṛṅgāra* by linking "real" married love with the larger concept of the dyad *prakṛti* and *puruṣa*, the condition that makes the world go round.[83] The troubling genre of *nāyikā bhed* here submits to the same logic of part and whole which would later define the shift to modernity for later critics: Miśra writes that when Matirām describes the beauty of any particular part of a woman, he is describing beauty generally, for the stimulation of *bhāva* per se. There was safety in the abstraction of beauty, of Nature, and moral danger in the particularities of bodily description and sexual desire.

When Miśra addresses obscenity in poetry, suddenly English literature appears prominently as the standard against which Hindi is measured. Under the heading of *nāyikā bhed* distinctions of "another's woman" and "the prostitute/dancing girl," Miśra levies charges of obscenity against English poets themselves (namely Byron, with reference to Cardinal Newman's likeminded criticisms), and pleads for a reprieve for poets like Matirām, who only wanted "to gather beauty in all places."[84] Hypocrisy seems to be specific to those Indians invested the English language, and presumably the English themselves. In a comparison of Matirām's verses to lines of Shakespeare, Miśra pointedly comments, "Critics of Braj Bhāṣā poetry . . . who read these very *bhāva*s with great relish in Shakespeare, scorn them in the *śṛṇgārī* poets of their home, calling them 'abhorrent thoughts.'" Astutely, Miśra notes the similarity between Juliet's and the gopi's pain of separation, and the analogous longing of Romeo ("that I were a glove upon that hand, that I might touch that cheek!") to the common sentiment in Braj poetry to wish for reincarnation as Krishna's flute or the garland on his chest.[85]

English literature, and all it represented, clearly inspired defensiveness about the Braj poetic tradition, which for Miśra meant finding commonalities between the two, negative and positive. Ultimately, however, English dominated the terms of engagement. The problem of *śṛṅgāra* was one fed by the colonial situation and the particular sort of universalistic rhetoric promoted by colonialism. Seldom would anyone in this literary sphere fault Shakespeare on the basis of a lack of *rasa*, improper use of *vibhāva*, or the deficiency of erotic pleasure. The grounds for play were against *śṛṅgārik* poetry, and only an aestheticized biologism like that of popular nature writing could redeem it.

But colonial critique and "modern" literary mores did not stamp out this poetry so easily, since Miśra and many other connoisseurs still loved the old poetry. Miśra cites Tagore's poetry of longing for the divine: "I see him everywhere / he is in the pupils of my eyes." In comparison, Miśra asserts that Matirām's beautiful picture of a scene in Brindavan exceeds that of Tagore, explaining that when the gopis find the absent Krishna still embodied on the bank of the Jamuna, playing his flute, Matirām still provides—and here he quotes Matirām's verse—"the pleasure of love, of the body, of the delightful touch" (*sukha prema gāta ko parasa abhirāma ko*).[86] Thus, while Hindi critics criticized their *śṛṅgārik* heritage, in basic ways they could still embrace the directness and tangibility of bodily love, especially in the devotional mode.

This movement to read nature into *śṛṅgāra* would persist in Hindi letters. In his 1931 *Rasakalas*, Hariaudh would continue to elaborate on Miśra's point, enumerating natural objects in poetic prose passages, and asking rhetorically, as did his own Rādhā in *Priyapravās*, "whom do these not enchant, . . . whose heart do they not please?"[87] Later he asks "why does the flower spread its fragrance? . . . why is the *koyal* bird frenzied, and crying all night? . . . is this not the spectacle of *śṛṅgāra*?"[88] Citing Miśra's citations of Stall and poetic sources in English and Hindi, using natural objects of poetic comparison as scientific examples of love in nature, he establishes *śṛṅgāra* as part of a biological phenomenon and thereby proves its merit. Nature redeems the troubling erotic aspect of *śṛṅgāra*, which is then ultimately reinterpreted as the desire that propels biological growth. The bee drinking *rasa*, the common metaphor for the *rasik* connoisseur and the philandering Krishna, are here now a proof and a validation of sorts of the realism of *śṛṅgāra rasa*.

Conclusions

In assessing the period of poetry spanning from 1885–1925, we can surmise that the "women's question" pertaining to nationalist discourse of the time influenced the world of poetics as well. Women readers and women as the subjects of poetry—the *nāyikā* heroine especially—became "problems" for classically trained litterateurs, who also had to answer to questions regarding obscenity. In an atmosphere of cultural critique regarding child marriage and its attendant social woes, and the exaltation of women as index or representative of modern polity, the genre of *nāyikā bhed* especially drew opprobrium. The colonial context must have only intensified this opprobrium. *Śṛṅgāra* itself became an extremely problematic feature of the Hindi literary tradition, and *śṛṅgāra*'s strong association with Braj Bhāṣā effectively turned writers and readers away from Braj Bhāṣā poetry, likely as much as the oft-cited Wordsworthian imperative to write "near to the language of men." The turn away from Braj Bhāṣā was as much about obscenity concerns as about a modernist move toward "linguistic realism" in poetry through the use of the language of speech.

The transformations that occurred because of these "women problems" took place with a revaluation of the poetic ornament of old in the interest of the "real." Women in poetry took the form of either realistic portraits, or idealized according to current social mores, with shadows of their sexual desirability appearing mostly in their wifely or national contexts. *Śṛṅgāra*, the literary mode descriptive of and conducive to erotic desire, was re-envisioned as a theory deriving from biological Nature, and ultimately descriptive of it. This image of nature, as received by Hindi litterateurs, connected vitally with a precept of universal love that resonated with the cosmopolitan religious movements of the day. These Hindi authors implemented what they saw as popular English genres—of sex education texts, nature writing, realist lithographs, and the coffee-table book—in complex and deeply *śṛṅgārik* ways, but for a universalistic rhetorical goal.

This identification of *śṛṅgāra* with nature and a universal principle of love arose out of a nationalist vision of India and engendered further a national image that retained elements of a sanctified *śṛṅgārik* desire. This sanctified *śṛṅgāra* is found in poetry about the natural objects that exemplify *śṛṅgāra*'s "science," and in poetry linking the good, desirable, woman with ideal Indianness. Despite this era's forced new ethicizing of poetic settings, some bodily descriptions and expressions of desire coexisted comfortably with it. We find this most clearly in some of the "new *nāyikā*s" of the teens, and will find this coexistence further developed in the twenties in Chāyāvād poetry on natural objects, many of them the very metaphorical objects of *śṛṅgāra*. In Nandadulāre Vājapeyī's words, "Those people took such an aversion to the just the name of *śṛṅgāra*, that they couldn't even imagine its deep impression (*saṃskār*)," cultural and psychological.[89] Remembering the previous chapters, we recall that in Pāṭhak's "Beauty of Kashmir," nature and its objects sometimes *became* the *nāyikā*. As seen most clearly in Hariaudh's *Priyapravās*, poetic "base reality" began to transfer to the metaphorical of old, rather than the bodies, human or divine, to which the creepers and *koyal* birds alluded. Thus *śṛṅgāra* no longer emerges allegorically, in the manner of classical poetics, but rather its metaphoric objects become "personified." This shift toward personified nature in the place of allusions to human/divine love will characterize Chāyāvād developments detailed in Chapter 9.

We can speculate on the effect of this new *śṛṅgāra* of the early twentieth century consumed by girls and women at home, and in the public space of modern educational institutions. It was precisely in the public sphere of debate over women's status, and society's moral responsibilities to them, that rhetoric against *śṛṅgārik* eroticism was forged. New versions of desire—in nature, and in love of the world—emerged as acceptable modern poetic idioms. If we are to consider the cultural atmosphere of the "inner" world of home and the specificities of its engineered authentic Indianness, then this rhetoric of *śṛṅgāra*-as-realism and *śṛṅgāra*-as-Nature appears as an important development, demonstrating changing epistemologies for persisting sexual poetic tropes. Considering the continuing force of this naturalized, realist *śṛṅgāra*, we might look to national allusions of post-Independence India, where the nation of India figures as a new bride, or read the nationalist affect for land through a more *śṛṅgārik* lens.

In conclusion, to demonstrate the new poetic world forged, I will cite a randomly-found poem on the front page of the famous *Cānd* magazine for women, December 1925, under a title-banner illustrated with etchings of well-covered women reading in front of bookcases, and under a notice in English, "Highly appreciated and recommended for use in Schools and Libraries by Directors of Public Instruction. . . ." The poet "Hṛdayeś," leaves us with an epitome of the convergence of women readers and naturalized *śṛṅgāra* through nature poetry. Here in images of the bees, breezes, and flowers that have made up the allegorical world of *śṛṅgāra*, yet also images that are compatible with scientized nature-writing and the "birds and the bees," the poet speaks of love for the world rather than love for a beloved, describing a proper love for proper ladies that is nevertheless full of the nectarous *rasa* of desire:

> The bumblebee of emotion has again set the sweet bloom abuzz;
> The breeze of pleasure with beautiful feeling has spread a new joy;
> In such a good, auspicious day—let there be no misfortune, let it be;
> In the river of *rasa* of love for the world (*viśva-prema*), oh world!
> Let me be carried away.[90]

Thus was the poetic result of the discourse on women, where gendered ideals were met with transfigured themes of love. We find emotion embodied as a bumblebee, long a symbol of pleasure-seeking men, yet here an image implemented for love-of-the-world, incited by a nature of bud, bloom, and breeze, that is allegorical and yet typically, Sanskritically beautiful. This "world-love" or "universal love"—now a keyword of modern Hinduism, and indeed the poetics contemporary to this poem—suggests to us also the role of public concerns, the gaze of the world, in the aesthetic changes of this era. Along with the individual voice of the poem, and presumably its female reader, great questions of literature's relation to the public world impinged upon the aesthetics being crafted for the Hindi audience and its expanding number of females. The ideal of the humble Aryan bride merged with the sentiment of Christian sex education; the universal love which explains *śṛṅgāra* links up with love-for-the-world, a theme suitable for poetry for the young educated woman, along with ethicized heroines, and the birds and the bees of Nature.

Chapter 8

A Critical Interlude

Rāmacandra Śukla and "Natural Scenes in Poetry" (1923)

> If someone truly loves their country, then he will love the men, animals, birds, creepers, thickets, trees, leaves, forests, mountains, rivers, waterfalls, everything, . . . he will look at everything with an affectionate vision, remembering all of it he will weep in foreign lands . . . How can you have this love without knowing these forms?
>
> —Rāmacandra Śukla[1]

It is difficult to overestimate the importance of Rāmacandra Śukla (1884–1941) to Hindi literary history. His name is mentioned in every college Hindi literature course, and his programmatic history of Hindi and its literature has endured until the present day. His *History of Hindi Literature* (*Hindī sāhitya kā itihās*) looms large in the Hindi literary consciousness, and his critical writings also remain some of the most brilliant and brilliantly difficult texts in Hindi literary criticism, the subject of many Hindi scholarly volumes. Of these critical writings, his essay "What is Poetry?" in its version anthologized in 1930 has probably been most read and assigned; his "Mysticism in poetry" of 1929 earned him the reputation of a conservative opposed to the new Chāyāvād poetry, and his comments in his *History* have cemented that notion for decades. The rest of his critical works, collected into book form in subsequent volumes of *Jewels of Thought* (*Cintāmaṇi*, 3 vols.) and *Analysis of Rasa*

(*Rasa mīmāṁsā*), circulated first in literary journals and formed the vanguard of his influence in the world of Hindi letters.[2] Śukla was also a poet; his poems, some of them of nationalist sentiment, were published in many magazines for the general reading public and those especially for women.

He was also a great proponent of Hindi. As he wrote in the 1917 poem "Our Hindi" ("Hamārī Hindī"), he found Hindi to be "the sound in which we heard the first melody of Nature," as opposed to the stilted speech of those who put on (presumably English) airs, who carry themselves with arrogance.[3] Hindi literature represented for him a bastion of Indianness that was threatened by English. As he wrote at the conclusion of his 1929 History,

> Dancing to the drum of [the fashions of European poetics] is against the glory of our civilization. The Europeans can consider Europe to be the whole world; we will consider it just a corner of the world. We ought to stand on our own feet in the world, with an independent, mature form (*svatantra vikasit rūp*) of our literature.[4]

As Hindi and India merge here, so do literature and civilization, signaling the great import Hindi literature continued to hold for Śukla and the Hindi public sphere generally.

This chapter addresses several of Śukla's early essays whose original publication dates are known, and concentrates primarily on one most apropos to the topic at hand: "Natural Scenes in Poetry" ("Kāvya meṁ prākṛtik-dṛśya"), probably the first original essay in Hindi explicitly on the subject of nature in literature. I will show that not only does this essay, first published in 1923, enunciate a new perspective on the meaning of nature for the Hindi poet, but it also can be seen as a gauge of the mixed and hybrid effects of the selective incorporation of certain themes of empiricism, Romanticism, and landscape nationalism from Europe. Śukla's mixing of these various rationales and modes for literary nature was not a mere pastiche but rather a complex and charged identitarian argument for perceiving the Indian natural world through a modified, realist *rasa* theory—a *rasa* in service of the nation.

The Life and Writings of the Young Śukla

Born in 1884 in the Basti district north of Faizabad, United Provinces, schooled in English and Urdu at the Anglo-Jubilee School of Mirzapur and the Kayastha Pathshala of Allahabad, and a young employee of the Nāgarī Pracāriṇī Sabhā, Śukla emerged from circumstances that epitomized the Hindi literary audience of the era. His father had connections with Varanasi, as a former student of Queen's College, and he served as district *qānūn-go* (i.e., registrar of village accounts), as was Hariaudh in nearby Azamgarh. The young Rāmacandra Śukla appeared as a brilliant literary thinker from an early age. As a young man, he published a translation of Cardinal Newman's section on literature from *The Idea of a University* in *Sarasvatī* (May 1904).[5] Subsequently, in the following year he published the lengthy translation of Joseph Addison's "Pleasures of the Imagination," in the Nāgarī Pracāriṇī Sabhā magazine, which had a profound effect on his critical writings to come. He was employed by the NPS for their massive *Ocean of Hindi Words* (*Hindī Śabd Sāgar*) dictionary project (headed by Śyāmasundar Dās and including Ratnākar, among other major litterateurs) and other endeavors. Several years later, in 1920, his introduction to a translation of Ernst Haeckel's *Riddle of the Universe*[6] broached subjects of popular science (already much in print thanks to M. Dvivedī). According to Nāmavar Siṁh, this trajectory demonstrated his fundamentally Addisonian trend of thought:

> by means of Addison's writings on imagination, Shukla ushered in the scientific materialist/empiricist (*bhautikavād*) perspective, of which the next step was the translation of Haeckel's *Riddle of the Universe*, and which translations introduced a "realist (*yathārthavādī*)" precept of experiencing *rasa* that was revolutionary not only for poetics but aesthetics.[7]

Over the subsequent years, he published essays on psychological topics. In 1921 he began teaching at Banaras Hindu University, and in 1922 he published a Braj Bhāṣā translation of Edwin Arnold's *Light of Asia*. Although he was a full twenty years younger than many other famous Braj poets of the time—Hariaudh, Pāṭhak, Ratnākar—he did not represent a generational break from Braj.[8] Later in the 1920s he would, in fact, come to represent "old guard" thinking about the proper form of verse, even though so much closer in age to the Chāyāvād poets. Here, to the point of this study of the theme of nature in Hindi poetry and criticism, we examine the content of the essay "Natural Scenes in Poetry" of 1923, but first we consider certain relevant features of Śukla's earlier work, namely his 1905 translation of Addison, his 1909 essay "Kavitā kyā hai?" ("What is Poetry?"), and his introduction to his 1920 translation of Haeckel.

Early Writings

Addison was a perfectly natural choice for the young Śukla, as Addison essays had appeared in earlier Hindi, Urdu, and doubtlessly Bengali periodicals for some time. Addison's commentary on Milton also likely endeared him to the Indian audience, Milton being a mainstay of Indian interest in English literature. Although Śukla's course syllabi in Mirzapur and Allahabad are not known, he very likely read a bit of Addison at school as well. Addison's "Pleasures of the Imagination" (the original serial essay of nos. 411–21 in *The Spectator*) suggested vocabulary for Śukla that would merge with that of Sanskritic poetics in fruitful ways, and inform his later "Natural Scenes in Poetry," and his subsequent, more famous articles on mysticism and expressionism in poetry. Going beyond the Paul Hacker's formulation of inclusivism—that is, the argument that Śukla would incorporate Addison's aesthetics into an encompassing and superior Vedantic or other Indic philosophical system like *rasa*—I would argue that Śukla's implementation of such empiricism-driven aesthetics was not merely an incorporation, but a reformulation that had a profound impact in the larger belletristic developments of modern Hindi poetry and criticism thenceforward. Śukla's incorporating maneuvers have effects similar to that of the "poetic landscape = national sentiment" equation of England, but for different reasons and in different manners, with different material altogether. This "material" itself, the material world of India and its poetry, colored deeply what Nāmavar Siṁh has called Śukla's linkage of *pratyakṣānubhūti*, "the perception/experience of what is evident," with *rasa*.[9] Thusly Śukla brought together a kind of materialism with classical aesthetics that would speak to the significance of nature in Hindi poetry in the preceding decades, and in the decades to come.

The critic Siṁh has discussed Śukla's early translation of Addison, "Kalpanā meṁ ānand" ("Pleasure in imagination"), as providing a revolutionary "realist (*yathārthavādī*) precept for the experience of *rasa*."[10] Śukla certainly did Indian-ize Addison's "Pleasures," from which we can infer his opinion of the relevance and a priori universality of Addison's thoughts. Addison wrote of unartificial music, which can transport its auditors to "pleasing dreams of groves and deliriums"; Śukla's "groves" were those of Indra's garden paradise in heaven (*nandan kānan*). The "ghost in every village" applied equally in India as in England. However, Addison's references to "our" English poets as superior, Śukla translated as such: "Among the poets of Europe the English are generally most talented (in stories of ghosts, fairies, spirits) . . . because English people by nature favor imagination (*svabhāv se . . . kalpanāpriya*)."[11] Here, Śukla excised part of the original sentence attributing the good poetry of the British to their "melancholy and gloominess of temper" which gives them "wild notions and visions," and replaced the sense of this with descriptive terms for vaguely gothic, but also folk and folk-romance figures: ghosts, fairies, spirits.[12] Melancholy and gloom per se he had removed, for unclear reasons. It seems that with these emendations to Addison's "Pleasures of the Imagination," Śukla strove to cast poetry as the reserve of beautiful pleasures alone.

The constant example of Nature in Addison indubitably affected Śukla's thinking much more profoundly than any Romantic anti-industrial glorification of nature, and this eighteenth-century Nature can be found in Śukla's later work as well.[13] But what constituted this perceived Nature in Addison? At root, Śukla took from Addison an interest in a poetic visuality that had both empiricist and affective political ramifications. But Śukla was interested in universals that were not owned by Western empiricism alone. His 1920 essay introducing Ernst Haeckel's *Riddle of the Universe* exemplifies this, in numerous comparative references between Vaiśeṣika, Nyāya, and Advaita philosophies with the thought of Kant, Hegel, Darwin, and sciences such as chemistry and biophysics.[14] Śukla in essence extends Haeckel's concern with the "law of substance" and theological monism into the Indian philosophical context, and thereby participated in the contemporary efforts both in Europe and India to connect science and religion.[15] Here Śukla's interest in Haeckel's "substance," in Hindi the Vaiśeṣika term *dravya*, and glossed concretely as "the wind, water, rock, earch, sun, moon, etc.,"[16] might foreshadow the persistent materialist bent in the arguments of "Natural Scenes in Poetry," examined in the following section.

A Reading of "Natural Scenes in Poetry"

Here we will read this remarkable essay with a view toward the poetic ramifications of the turn to nature and anxiety about *śṛṅgāra*, taking one small step in the much larger scholarly project of unpacking Śukla's critical prose. The essay demands to be approached as an integrated whole, rather than a linear argument, a fact that reflects the structure of the essay itself, in which the reader is presented with several interlocking themes and a range of authorial intensities, from rather mundane comments on contemporary culture, to complex and knotted technical topics of poetics, to rhetorically intense repetitions and proclamations.

"Natural Scenes in Poetry" first appeared in one of the early issues of *Mādhurī*, a large-format magazine, luxurious for its day, with many color plates and well-known authors, considered heir in prominence to that of *Sarasvatī*, a journal whose fortunes had diminished with the departure of Dvivedī.[17] The present-day relative obscurity of this essay may reflect its status as the kernel of Śukla's "Kāvya meṁ rahasyavād" ("Mysticism in Poetry") (1929), which took on some similar themes and English Nature poets directly,[18] and as an offshoot of his earlier essay "What is Poetry?" which in its 1909 version, discussed in similar terms the trend of "description of the beauty of Creation (*sṛṣṭi-saundarya*)."[19] Its themes were revisited as well in Śukla's seminal *History of Hindi Literature* of 1929.[20] However Śukla's "Natural Scenes in Poetry" is one of—if not the—first essay by a major Hindi critic addressed explicitly to the topic of "nature" in poetry, its relation to beauty, and to the workings of poetics; and the essay's connection of poetic theory to literary values of realism and nationalism reflects and theorizes on the potency that nature had already taken on in Hindi in the preceding decades.[21] As we shall see, although European modes of literary realism, Romanticism, and landscape nationalism can be detected, Śukla actually implements these as tropes for his argument for a national reading of *rasa* theory.

The essay begins almost exactly as does Addison's first essay on "Pleasures of the Imagination": with discussion of the sense of sight as "the most perfect and most delightful of all our senses," through which every "Image in the Fancy" must first enter.[22] For Śukla as well, the objects of the sense (*viṣay*) of vision dominate those of all other senses. But here the idea of the *dṛśya* (scene), identified in the very title of the essay, "Natural Scenes in Poetry," concerns him more. He begins thus with an invocation of a classical Indic pastoral setting:

> "On the branch of the mango tree laden with fragrant blossoms and swaying with gusts of wind, a black *koyal* (cuckoo) sat singing sweet calls." Although this sentence reports on form, sound, and smell, still we will call it a "scene." . . . All apparent objects of sense can be reflected in the form of a picture (*citra*) in the consciousness (*antaḥakaraṇ*). We call this reflection a "scene" (*dṛśya*).[23]

Śukla then ordains "grasping the image" (*bimbagrahaṇ*) of a scene, in as much detail and vitality as possible, as the goal of poetry; this is accomplished through portrayal with the faculty of imagination. The faculty of imagination then effects the concrete "image-ination" of *bimbagrahaṇ*; the better the *bimbagrahaṇ*, the better the portrayal of the material, yet internalized, scene. Here then, we see first of all a conception of the visual nature of the poetic enterprise, a theme in Urdu critic Āzād's

1880 *Water of Life*, and buttressed with the words of many English authors as well, as Pritchett has shown.[24] But Śukla here departs slightly from the emphasis on the "picture" of his Urdu forebear, foregrounding the concept of "scene," an aggregating vision that is grasped as a unified image in the creation and reception of poetry.

Śukla's thinking in this essay seems to combine various concepts from Addison and possibly a generically Romantic theory of emotion with the dominating theory of *rasa*. The *vibhāvas* of classical poetics—the "causes of emotion (*bhāva*)," consisting of the characters, which are the primary locus of the emotion (*ālambana*[25]), and also the surrounding objects that incite the emotion in these *ālambana* "characters" (*uddīpana*)—here take on a new significance as the subject-matter of a portrayal. These *vibhāvas*, formerly in service to *rasa*, are in Śukla's reckoning now "foremost," and implementing them with imagination, "to completely or exactly represent (*yathātathya pratyakṣīkaraṇ*) is the poet's first and most important task."[26] But he adds that the poet's ultimate purpose is to "set up such dreams" by which the auditor or reader will experience emotion. It is through a description of perception (*anubhūti*) and a "mode of love/pleasure" (*rāgātmikā vṛtti*), that forms are successfully conjured:

> That activity of distinguishing (or "dividing," "categorizing," *vibhājan*) that forms the basis of *rasa*—that alone is the greatest foremost field of activity of the imagination. But . . . it has to proceed at the order of the manner of perception/experience (*anubhūti*) and the loving mode (*rāgātmikā vṛtti*). It has to set up such dreams by which, because of experiencing himself [the *bhāvas* of *rasa* theory:] *rati, hāsa, śoka, krodha*, etc., the poet knows that the listener or reader also will experience such. Only those who keep in their hearts only the perception (*anubhūti*) of man, because of the universality of man's perception and his objects-of-sense (*viṣay*), can bring such forms (*svarūp*) into men's minds, and can be called a poet.[27]

The poet presents his own experience, or perceptions, in order to produce emotion in the audience, and this is both an exercise in empiricism—appealing to universal perception-of-things—and subjectivism—rooting the aesthetic experience in the poet's individual emotion, and his communication of this experience with love.

Further, he strongly states that forms are not successfully conjured by the overuse of poetic ornament (*alaṃkāra*). Śukla associates classical ornament with spectacle, excess, and the unreality of myth. Their unusualness detracts rather than augments the subject at hand. Here

Śukla elaborates on concepts earlier developed in his "What is Poetry?" in which ornament took the role of a kind of material technology with which to work upon the thing-in-itself; for him ornaments are "types of description," which may or may not describe the subject-at-hand. The closest approximation of "natural description" in Sanskrit poetics, *svabhāvokti*, naturally interests him here. *Svabhāvokti* is usually defined generically as an ornament, as the "telling the nature (*svabhāva*) of a thing," including the behavior, attributes, genus, and material form of the thing in question.[28] Here Śukla rejected the classification of *svabhāvokti* as an ornament,[29] and defined it as the object of sense itself, the very subject of the utterance, outside of the category of ornament altogether. Having dismissed the idea of *svabhāvokti* as ornament, Śukla then displays an urge to segregate ornamentation from the core attributes of poetry. In his view, ornament should not be disallowed, but poetry's beauty precedes ornament.[30] Ornament should be present only inasmuch as it contributes clearly to the grasping of image, and the image should have a visual quality accessible to all, not just the cognoscenti, as in the "reflective" sense of *bimba*. Ornament should not "block the attention" of the reader to the thing-at-hand. If the objects of "outer nature" are described well, in his formulation, then "the experience of the beauty, fearsomeness, greatness, etc., will happen somewhat on its own." [31] These were not terribly radical thoughts, in India or elsewhere, but the crucial nature of establishing "real" things as against the extraneous "ornament" or even as against the positively-valued "imagination" suggests that Śukla found the binary of real/imagined, or as he notes, the "Western" objective/subjective binary (*jñātṛpakṣ* (*sabjekṭiv*)/*jñeyapakṣ* (*ābjekṭiv*)) a necessary epistemological point for the rest of his theses.[32]

In this regard, Śukla echoes some very old thoughts on aesthetics in the English context. But clearly, some of his comments had immediate sources in his own reading: his comments on gardens in this essay must have been inspired by the discussion of nature versus artifice found in Addison's comparison of gardens of the world in *The Spectator*, Essay 414. While Addison finds English gardens, with "each shrub" having "marks of scissors," to be quite artificial in comparison to those of China, France, and Italy, Śukla takes the allegations of artificiality into a new set of intercultural politics, finding such unnaturalness only in Persian gardens, i.e., the Mughal-style gardens common in India. However, he finds the English-style park more acceptable: "In today's parks (*pārk*)," he writes, "we find the shadow of the Indian ideal." The idea of the garden-style as moral barometer, while clearly inspired by Addison, Śukla takes into insinuations against Islamicate and indeed courtly culture, in his argument for a "free" nature: one should not enjoy "the circle-square cut-design of a Persian-fashion garden, straight rows of flowerbeds, clumsy elephants and horses of henna bushes, the lines of trees . . . clipped and cut into form, roses blooming in a line, and so forth." In fact, "The man who is pleased only seeing trees made into men marching in step (*kavāyad karate*)" and other unnatural arrangements, is an egoist who makes nature into a reflection of himself, and "does not desire to see the nature outside of himself."[33] The ideal of Hindu ancients, he claims, was in the *upavan*, the grove, and that ideal "has appeared only a little in China and Europe." The *upavan* (grove) he interprets etymologically as a sort of "sub-forest," the forest being a place where one can see "the pure form of nature and her free (*svacchand*) play."[34] Here the imprint of Pathak's Lady Nature is evident, who also frolicked "*svatantratā se*" in the wood.

Further, poetic nature should reflect its local conditions. The ethnic nature of Śukla's claims then becomes even clearer:

> It's a shame that the bad instincts (*kusaṃskār*) of Persia's assembly-poetry (*mahafilī śāyarī*) has settled here for some time in the hearts of Indians, in which only the descriptions of the flower (*caman*), rose, nightingale, tulip, narcissus, and so on, exist only in the form of objects for pleasure (*vilās kī sāmagrī*)—we only find the mountain, the wilderness, etc., . . . in connection with some great obstacle or misfortune. Are there no other trees or plants in Persia? . . .[35]

In contrast, Śukla holds up the ancient poet Vālmīki, whose descriptions he finds practically botanical. (And here we can recall Jayaśaṅkar Prasād's 1910 characterization of Valmiki, to whom "nature's each and every particle spoke."[36]) He submits that beyond the ideal images of poetry, Vālmīki's exactness is found also in the humble non-*uddīpana* flora and fauna. He notes that such botanical realism has inspired poetic emotion in English literature also—a comment he makes in passing, but in a validating gesture toward this thesis:

> But look here at Vālmīki: In describing natural scenes he did not only describe the mango trees covered with blossoms, the jasmine creepers laden with fragrant flowers, the lotuses filled with nectar and pollen, he also described with full absorption the jungle trees of almond (*iṅgudī*), walnut (*aṅkoṭ*), ebony (*tendū*), acacia (*babūl*), gum (*baheṛe*), etc.[37] In this way, the poets of Europe have also made mention of the bushes and grass growing on the banks of the streams flowing near their villages,

> with their eyes filled with tears. [A footnote here directs the reader to Wordsworth's "Admonition to a Traveler."] From this it is clear that the power to bring man out of the gutter of his own affairs and into the great and expansive field of nature is not within the limited poetic tradition of Persia—in the tradition of India and Europe it is.[38]

While clearly culturally partisan—staking India and Europe against "decadent" Persia—Śukla's comments here broach again the central conflict over pleasure: while nature can be "objects for pleasure" in the more lascivious, mundane sense of *vilās kī sāmagrī*, nature in fact is the source of an elevated *ānand* like that of the heavenly groves; nature is also an "expansive field" (*kṣetra*), as in the field of perception cited in the *Bhagavad Gita*. Breaking off one's "loving" (*rāgātmak*) connection with nature decreases one's pleasure in it.[39] Naturalness is likewise an index of emotional value: the humble plants of the homeland give correct pleasure, the topiaries of the garden a solipsistic one. Here Śukla does indeed recall the generic English Romantic stance toward nature as place for the poet's innate bonds, apart from society. Śukla also concurs with Addison, as in the essays he translated in 1905, that the man "of polite imagination" "makes the most rude uncultivated parts of nature administer to his pleasures." We will see below that Śukla follows Addison also in deriving a proprietor's pleasure—"a kind of property in everything he sees"—but with several epistemological twists.[40]

Following precisely the pattern emerging in Hindi poetry of the 1910s, Śukla proposes to collapse the two conventional categories of *vibhāvas*, the *ālambana* (the things upon which *rasa* "depends," i.e., the hero and heroine in *śṛṅgāra*) and the *uddīpana* (incitant to *rasa*, i.e., the objects that incite the emotion of love in the hero and heroine), such that the conventional objects of the latter are included among the former. In fact, "any thing in creation" can be an *ālambana*, "from man to insect, moth, tree, river, mountain, and so on." This is a strident point; however Śukla clearly confines his discussion mostly to the natural objects conventionally found in poetry as incitants of *śṛṅgāra*: "in the view of scholars of literature, the forest, grove, seasons, etc., are only the *uddīpana*s of *śṛṅgāra*; they are only for making the hero or heroine laugh or cry. . . ." He continues rhetorically—then did Kalidasa write his description of the Himalayas in the *Kumārasambhava* with only *uddīpana*s in mind? Rather, Śukla suggests, these descriptions "mark the circumstances (*paristhiti*) of the *ālambana*s," and further, "circumstance is the *ālambana* of our lives, therefore . . . the *ālambana* of our emotions (*bhāva*s)."[41] Here the term "circumstance" can be taken most materially:

the "surrounding condition" that literally translates *paristhiti*.[42] For Śukla then, *bhāva* occurs in a realist mode, not through any poetic theory, and accordingly the poet should describe thoroughly the real thing that is an *ālambana*, as Vālmīki "carefully outlined the forms" of the rainy season, with "nothing left out."[43] *Bhāva* actually requires that the "form of things" be established.[44] Rather than mere signals (*saṅket*) of *rasa* by means of their presence, these natural entities as *ālambana* require detail in full flush of vitality (*sphuraṇ*), to allow for image-grasping (the *bimba-grahaṇ* mentioned above), the *bhāva* of enjoyment/pleasure (*rati*), and engrossment (*tallīnatā*) for the auditor or reader.[45]

Beyond giving "local color," nature descriptions themselves, in independent form (*svatantra rūp se*), can be *ālambana*. So not only will the category of *ālambana* include human characters, but the objects of sense, and "natural scenes" that inspire them—and us—to emotion: "The effect that a scene creates in the form of *uddīpana* is in connection with another—the *ālambana*—, not in an independent form (*svatantra rup se*). But, as was made clear above, natural scenes are also independent (*svatantra*) *ālambanas* of the *bhāvas* of men."[46] Examples of such description—nature-description-as-*ālambana*—include the description of the Himalaya mountains from the beginning of the *Kumārasambhava*, and the description of the jungle dwelling Pañcavatī by Lakṣmaṇ in Vālmīki's *Rāmāyaṇa*.[47]

Śukla clearly seeks to extricate natural objects, singly and aggregatively, from the realm of *uddīpanas* of *śṛṅgāra*, such that they are no longer subjugated to being incitants of erotic love in some hero or heroine, but instead represent dominant, coherent subjects, in and of themselves. No longer merely listed-off natural objects that signal *śṛṅgāra* by their mere mention, these "real objects" (*vastu*) will accomplish the "setting out of things" (*vastu-vinyās*), and effect emotion. They become the subject-matter (or even plot, in the earlier sense of *vastu* from Sanskrit drama), instead of the stuff of poetic ornament, or the incitants to a character's *bhāva* of *śṛṅgāra rasa*. This is a project of recovery; Śukla claims that since the *rīti* era, the "linking objects-of-sense" (*saṁyojak viṣay*) of *rasa* of old had been classified either as mere inciting *uddīpanas* or had been "removed from the field of *bhāva*" to be classified as ornament. What was left of "description of natural (*svabhāv*) forms and actions" became what he considers the false "ornament" of "natural speech," *svabhāvokti*.[48]

Śukla more or less abolishes the category of incitants per se; the *uddīpana* is now an *ālambana*. But this collapsing of categories leaves him without a term for the recipient of *bhāva*, the *āśray*, "resting place," of incited *bhāvas*. In response to this problem, it seems, he redefines the *vibhāva* category. While traditionally the category of *vibhāva* was comprised of *ālambana* and *uddīpana*, here Śukla proposes that *vibhāva* is comprised of *ālambana* (encompassing the erstwhile *uddīpanas*) and the *āśray*, the "resting place, exponent," i.e., "feeler" of a *bhāva*, a subcategory of the former *ālambanas* of hero and heroine.[49] However, now this receptor-*āśray* can and should be the reader. The reader receives *bhāva* directly from the *ālambana*-objects—i.e., the poetic subject-matter—of nature. Here the refiguration of categories is doubly confusing: *ālambanas*, which were heroes and heroines of old, are now the former inciting objects, *uddīpanas*, of the *bhāva* which the hero and heroines felt; and a human perceiver, the reader,[50] is an *āśray* just as were the hero and heroines feeling *bhāva*. What is missing most are the embodied human characters of the heroes and heroines. They have become plants or animals or other "matter," and the job of experiencing *bhāva* is usurped by the perceiver of nature, and the reader of the poetry itself. The origin of *bhāva* is no longer the vision of the human *ālambana* of heroes and heroines.[51] *Bhāva* is accessed by the reader as if himself the seeing, feeling hero or heroine. Natural objects of sense are then no longer *uddīpanas*, but while being *ālambanas*, function as *uddīpanas* for the feeling reader.

> There is hardly a need to explain that the forest, mountain, river, waterfall, etc. of natural scenes are the independent *ālambanas* of our love/enjoyment (*rāg*) and *rati bhāva*, and in them there is a natural (*sahaj*) attraction for the connoisseur. Within these scenes are such objects and actions that are the reflection of the root forms and conditions of life . . .[52]

The *bhāva* of pleasure (*rati*) that characterizes *śṛṅgāra* thus emerges out of the individuated "forest, mountain, river," in aggregate, as natural scenes; nature leads to *śṛṅgāra*, and its *bhāva* of *rati* arrives without the help of any intermediary human *ālambana*. As Śukla pushed a material *ālambana* to the fore, he also pushed forward an experiential *bhāva* that surpasses the strictures of *rasa*.[53] He believed this solved the poetic problem that "nature poetry" presented: when natural scenes, as poetic subject-matter create *bhāva* within the readers, then there is no need to concern oneself with "which *rasa* applies here?" because what is happening is *bhāva*, over and above *rasa*.[54] The *bhāva* itself suffices, whether the *ālambanas* are recognizably of *rasa* theory or not. As conventionally *rasa* is created with the *rati bhāva* in the *ālambanā* of the couple, so here a *bhāva* is available to experience through the presentation of images of natural scenes (as in a tree reminding a man of his childhood days, an example Śukla gives obviously referencing Wordsworth); this new modern *bhāva* thus equals or even surpasses *rasa*.[55]

Therefore, writing poetry that is full-of-*bhāva* is linked to the paramount task of imparting the image (*bimba-grahaṇ*), which is the matter that creates *bhāva*.[56] This is not merely "realism," but a familiar sort of *advaita* implementation of the external "real" and internal "spirit," bringing both together in the image. Śukla's thinking also involves the precept that the ultimate trait of poetry is to create an experience in which everything that exists (*sarvabhūt*, all beings) becomes internalized (*ātmabhūt*, become of the soul/self), in a kind of inverse of Krishna's statement that "I am the spirit within all things"[57]; the goal is not to see things as "real" things, as much as to effect a sense of the whole of empirical things—the *sarvabhūt*—which in turn corresponds to the internal self, in classic *advaita* style. This internal turn, through the poetic vision of the reality of worldly things, requires the renunciation of ego.[58] Ironically, Śukla is directing his audience toward a realism that is a subjectivism so complete as to be spiritualized.

But what does all this mean in concrete terms? How does Śukla describe the contents of such nature-images? With masses of objects ranging a transhistorical landscape. The very types of objects which are no longer "listed-off" as incitants in Śukla's vision of modern poetics, are the contents of Śukla's poetic-prose passages in this essay, passages of both rhetorical weight and heightened emotion, in which the very same "listing" occurs. Rather than cite "nature" per se, Śukla causes us to think of its particular objects en masse:

> . . . this is clear, that our love for the forest, mountain, river, waterfall, animal, birds, fields, water, and so on, is natural (*svābhāvik*), or at least is contained in the consciousness as an impression/desire (*vāsanā*).[59]

> . . . the life of both the wild and the village are ancient, both are spent among the trees and plants, animals and birds, rivers and streams, and mountains and fields, therefore they retain greater relationship with nature. . . .[60]

This of course resonates strongly with the generic Romantic sentiment that both rural life and wild nature had a salubrious timelessness, and that they represent a disappearing past world in the industrialized present. Here we should note the apparent rhetorical intent of such listing-of-things in nature—Śukla implements it to reinforce the psychological and historical significance of Nature, implying a crucial link between place and identity.

Śukla praises the subtle "observation" (*nirīkṣaṇ*) in the portrayal of a scene (*dṛśyacitraṇ*) from Vālmīki's *Rāmāyaṇa*, which itself is comprised of a litany of natural objects and their actions (*vyāpārī*):

> the flowing of the stream of the river, red from the mixing with the minerals of the mountain in the rainy season; the splashing of the wide stream of water falling on the black rocks, the dripping of drops of rain water from the tips of the leaves and the birds drinking them; the lotuses being only stems in the winter and the scattering of the pollen beside them, such actions (*vyāpārī*) he brings before us.[61]

Śukla's term *nirīkṣaṇ*, "observation," or "inspection, examination," rooted in a Sanskrit verb for seeing, seems to invite a scene-making, by collecting parts—each "inspected" individually in the telling—into a whole. Śukla later does his own scene-making with an enumerative exhortation in support of his belief that emotion can arise from ordinary objects:

> Go outside and open your eyes, and see how the field [of crops] is waving, how among the bushes the stream is flowing, how the forest grove has become red with the *ṭesu* flowers, how in the lowland the animals are grazing, the herdsmen are calling, how a village peeps out from among the mango groves . . .[62]

These familiar natural items are indeed "listed-off," but generally with more detail, reference to action—the old *utprekṣās*—and including objects less common in poetry, equivalent in import to the "meanest flower" of Wordsworth's intimations: particular, humble, evoking the real along with ideal.

Śukla presents a link between nature and emotion that is ontological and organic. The process of cognizing natural objects is not only mental and emotional, but physical. Our urge to dance along with the happy peacocks at the coming of the rains is only proof that *sañcārī bhāva* (the "emotion of the hero/ine that inspires the same emotion in the audience") and the permanent emotion (*sthāyī bhāva*) of enjoyment (*rati*) exist, and inhere in such natural scenes. The connective factor—the generalizing of love—between nature and humans is likewise part of an organic force, larger than the world of *śṛṅgārik* incitants alone.

> Sparrows barge into our houses; for the cat's part, it begs with its meowing or steals; dogs guard the house. . . . In the

> days of rain, when . . . the green grass creeps up onto the old terrace, then I feel love for it. It comes as if searching for me, and says, why are you running away from me?[63]

The material of ordinary life itself—both animal and vegetable—exists in a kind of social contract—the grass and the birds inspire love in us, and we in turn love them.This materiality of the permanent emotions (*sthāyī bhāva*)—the ubiquity and inexorability of living enactions of emotions of *rati, hāsa,* etc.—proves for him the universality of *rasa*.

In one of many ennumerative garland-like passages, Śukla moves our vision of nature beyond the classical ideals, and into items that might qualify as "sublime" in the European mode. However, he does this not to link these with sublimic awe or pleasure in the "fearsome" (*bhayānaka*) *rasa*, but rather in order to instruct us in the moral hierarchy of perception. All material of nature, however ordinary, is fit for poetry; to see only classical ideals is the habit of the unrestrained and acquisitive:

> The attraction we have for forests, mountains, rivers and streams, wetlands, barren lands, field-streams, creeks cutting through the grass, plow and ox, huts, and farmers set at their labor, etc.—that is because of an impression (*vāsanā*[64]) in our consciousness, not an unusual astonishing thing or unprecedented beauty. He who can only be pleased looking at the forests and fields at the time of rainy season greenery or at the merriment of the spring flowers; who finds dear only the sight of the mango tree covered with flowers, blossoming *kadamba* trees, or dense arbors of jasmine; he whose heart is untouched by the open barren fields and plains of summer, the naked leafless trees of winter, and shrubs and acacia . . . has a tendency that should be understood as "passionate" (*rājasī*). He only searches in nature for things of pleasure or happiness. He has a deficiency of "goodness/truth" (*satva*).[65]

In this passage we see the rhetorical flourishes that distinguish so much "nature-talk" in literature and its criticism: the garland of images, and the linkage of nature and love. But we also perceive an intimation of the political and aesthetic possibilities of seeing the humble acacia instead of the jasmine vine, the barren field rather than the flowering grove, the farmer in distress rather than the farmer being cooled by rainclouds.

Like Hariaudh's Radha, Śukla foregrounds a moralized way of seeing, that of the *satva* quality of Sāṅkhya, which sees the object of love but with an ascetic detachment that is somewhat a-*śṛṅgārik*, though "enchanted" nonetheless. Hariaudh's Radha in fact invoked this very same concept of the *sātvik guṇa* in correct perception to explicate her view of nature-as-Krishna.

> Those who consider natural scenes to be only the stuff of *uddīpanas* of erotic enjoyment (*kāma*), their taste has become corrupted . . . I have seen . . . many sadhus who see the swaying green and lush jungles, waterfalls pouring onto bare rocks like silver, the singing birds, and become enchanted (*mugdh*).[66]

As did Prasad and Tripathi's recent sadhus-in-nature, Śukla's vision of nature poetry is critically inflected by the idea of *vanāśram* (the forest-stage) as the material circumstance of spiritual quest. Nature is the atmosphere for ascetic transcendence as much as the setting of love, it is "not just incitants for *kāma*." Sukla thus attempts to reframe nature poetry within a version of the sublime that the Romantics never really knew. Sadhus being putatively celibate, their enchantment with nature itself forms part of their meditative or devotional practice; this proves Śukla's point here, but also references the ascetic/erotic pilgrims of recent Hindi literary fame, not to mention Shiva, the king of erotic ascetics himself.[67] For Śukla, thus, nature poetry clearly holds deep resonances with Indic traditions of accessing the divine and and divine truths, and these resonances would have strongly colored any Wordsworthian visionary models also present in this exposition on nature poetry.

And poetry is not just aesthetic: "both philosophy (*darśan*) and poetry, taking refuge in different modes, take the consciousness to the same purpose." In a remarkable and complex passage, Śukla explains that their shared goal of truth/purity (*sattva*) is reached through knowing and experiencing, and that the person with right, *sātvik*, perception of the phenomenal world has access to that truth, which is identified with the charged term *sattā* (existence and reality, or power and sovereignty),[68] which in turn is linked with an equally ambiguous *bhāva*, regularly "emotion," as in the *rati bhāva* referenced previously, but possibly signifying "existence, reality" as well.

> . . . [In the *rājasik* (acquisitive/lustful) person,] there is a deficiency of that truth (*satva*), [a deficiency] that, mixed with the feeling of uniting with existence/power/sovereignty (*sattā*) alone, gives the [mere] appearance of the all-pervasiveness of one's personal existence (*ātmasattā*). Complete *sattā*, whether material or spiritual, is within only one supreme *sattā* or supreme *bhāva*, therefore that *advaita bhāva*[69] we arrive at by

> means of knowledge or logic *(tarkabuddhi)*, is also arrived at through our loving mode (*rāgātmik vṛtti*), on the strength of this quality of "*satva.*" In this way, both modes come together. If by means of knowledge we are able to know that everything is of-us (*ātmavat,* within us, ours), then by means of the loving mode we can experience this. Defeated by logic, the greatest scholars take refuge in this "personal experience" (*svānubhūti*). Therefore, from the view of a highest aim, both philosophy and poetry, taking refuge in different modes, take the consciousness to the same goal. From this pervading/universal (*vyāpak*) view, the parochialism in the discussion of poetry that is presented us in works of *rīti* criticism (*lakṣaṇagranth*) irritates here and there. One is not happy merely understanding the forest, grove, moonlight, etc., as only incitants (*uddīpanas*) to the couple's lovemaking (*dāmpatya rati*).

So beyond the conventional "romance" of forest, grove, moonlight, and so on, which Śukla suggests have become mere stock-in-trade of versifying, there is alternatively, the loving mode. This loving mode, and the "personal experience" it entails, ultimately reigns when scholars become "defeated by logic." While the logical mode produces philosophy for the purpose of this singular supreme Existence of *sattā*, the loving mode produces poetry for this same end. However, the loving mode of experience achieves *sattā* in poetry only on the strength of its own virtue, its *sātvik* qualities; otherwise, it is presumably less good, more *rājasik,* more banal. In summary, the Existence toward which both logical discourse and good poetry lead is one that is a universal, and all-encompassing monism, the *advaita bhāva*. Good poetry is produced from the loving mode (*rāgātmik vṛtti*), which is the mode of personal experience, beyond logic per se, and is importantly, colored by *sattva* (truth/purity), and best embodied in poetry with graspable images of nature.

Witness to a Common Circumstance

As alluded to above, nature functions as it does for the philospher-poet because of our inherent integrality with it. Śukla analogized this to love (the grass growing on the terrace "comes as if in search of me"), and this human-nature relationship has a true similarity to that of love, having physical and philosophical pleasures, as in the components and theory of *śṛṅgāra* itself. However, the import of nature takes on another crucial strain of thought for Śukla: it is a connection to the ancients. This conduit for imbibing the ancients' divine brilliance clearly draws upon the familiar Herderian-style ethnic nationalism—Śukla references the Aryans (by then a de rigueur practice for decades), and lauds the naturalness of Vālmīki and Kalidasa's language as a European might Homer's. A European (and perhaps somewhat Persian) sense of the glories of the golden past pervades Śukla's essay. History gives access to *bhāv* through description: "educated people read histories and the places described therein become like pilgrimage places. An affecting (*bhāvuk*) description stays in your heart." Śukla himself waxes lyrically on the pleasure and poignancy of suddenly seeing the activities along his lane as those in the "ancient Ujjaini" of Kalidasa, but then "the street lanterns of the municipality (*myunisipailiṭī*) came into view. That was all; the whole imagining/feeling (*bhāvanā*) disappeared in the air."[70] The past inspires *bhāvanā* but its effect is fleeting.

The use of the figures of the ancient past takes on an urgent tone for Śukla. The ancients were "in tune" with nature in a way we are not, and recovery of their vision seems to imply much more than a Romantic rapture, like Goethe's Werther felt over the pages of Osian. Rather, nature provides a timeless unity of past and present, where we see the objects (*vastu*) that our forebears saw, and therefore perhaps feel the same *bhāv*:

> Finding ourselves confronted with those objects and actions (*vastu aur vyāpār*) toward which our ancestors expressed their "*bhāv*," it is as if we have come close to those earlier men, and experiencing *bhāvs* of that type, mixing our hearts with theirs, we become their kin.
>
> Where contemporary society has not entered, in those forests, mountains, villages, and fields, we can imagine ourselves standing in the time of Vālmīki, Kalidasa or Bhavabhuti . . . In the valleys and caves of the mountains, in the blooming net of flowers of dawn, in scattered moonlight, in bloomed lotuses, our eyes merge with those of Kalidasa, Bhavabhuti, et al. We are standing now too in the forests of flame-of-the-forest trees, almond trees, and Alangium plants; now too the lotuses are blooming in the tanks; even now the lotuses are laughing with the moonlight in the lakes, now too the fig tree branches bend down and kiss the water on the bank, but our eyes actively avoid them, it is as if our hearts have no affection in them. We are not able to see Agnimitra, Vikramaditya, and the rest, now . . . but we are still able to see such things that they too must have seen.[71]

Here "objects and actions" are natural objects, many conventional to poetic descriptions, nature's movements and nature's laws, that link this world with the classical golden era.[72] This real world then appears as that of Kalidasa, as Śukla continues, in his own voice, describing scenes from the *Meghadūtam,* and envisioning Kalidasa himself standing in the present-day landscape:

> Stand at sunset on the mounds of ancient Ujjaini spread out along the bank of the Sipra, the mountains surrounding are saying that Kalidasa, on his way to do *darśan* of Mahākāl (Shiva) is gazing at us; at that time "the Siprā wind" ruffled his shawl. On the banks of the pure streams of the Vetravatī flowing over black rocks, those bricks and stones in the ruins of Vidiśā are still laying there, that would have been touched by the hands of beautiful women, their full hair perfumed and bodies covered in sandal.[73]

The historical scene mingles with the present natural scene, imbued with desire as in Kalidasa's verse itself. The sensual memory of women haunts the atmosphere; the Vidiśā of the *Meghadūtam,* where the messenger-cloud obtains the "fruit of lover's desire"[74] by drinking of the Vetravatī river, exists here only as intertext among artifacts: river, rocks, ruins. Then suddenly the tone changes, and the urgency of recovering this landscape becomes clear:

> In the new English style of cities, glittering with electric lights, facing the smoke-spitting mills and Whiteaway Laidlaw stores,[75] we find Kalidasa, et al, very far away from us. But in the vast field of nature our feeling of difference is erased, by witness of a common circumstance we experience the eternally pervasive pure "humanity" (*manuṣyatva*). . . .[76]

This is perhaps the only anti-industrialization statement per se in the essay, but it is in service of a "back to nature" argument that is much more philosophically focused than Romantically-inclined in the manner of European poets. This epistemology of "witnessing" the "circumstance" of the "field" (in the abstract sense of *kṣetra*) of nature leads to an emotional cum political conclusion, with a very different sort of nostalgia than that of the European mode. Sharing a material nature, its forms, its sensations, leads to shared perceptions, and these are social, racial markers that exist in worldwide hierarchy and competition.

> . . . while it's true that there is no humanity specific to any era, is it certain that there is a humanity connected to country (*deś*)? Yes, it is. From the experience of this humanity that is tied to a country (*deśabaddh*) comes the establishment of true devotion or love-of-country. The heart which is not able to experience the independent power/existence (*svatantra sattā*) of his race (*jāti*) among the races of the world cannot claim love of country. By this "independent power" is meant the independent power of Form (*svarūp*); not only the independence of amassing wealth and means and enjoying rights. If Indians obtain all wealth and happiness in the world, while forgetting their Form, then so what? Because they have ripped away their connection to the continuous tradition that excites the elevated/sublime (*udātt*) ways, and have written their name among the history-less savage races newly sprung up. Their honor (*māryādā*) is not much more than that of the Philippine islanders.[77]

The humanity of a people is thus tied to its geographic locale, and this love is dependent on the experience of an independent *sattā*—the term for non-dual "existence" and "power." This *svatantra sattā* is a necessary experience for love-of-country, but Śukla elaborates that he does not merely speak here of political independence from Britain. Rather, this is an "independent power of Form (*svarūp*)," which surpasses or perhaps completes political and economic self-rule.[78] It is such an exalted or distinguished "form" that Śukla identifies as crucial to the "independent power/existence" of *svatantra sattā*, of capital, means of production and rights. *Svatantra*, "independent" (as in the "independent form" of *svatantra rūp* in the modern turn of Hindi literary nature), was only now gaining ground as a term for India's political independence.[79] At this moment, as much as it signified self-determination, freedom from other's control, etc. (from Sanskrit onward), it was also grounded in merely descriptive language, as a term for "separate." Now the very forms of nature that were newly described *svatantra rūp se*—both as "independent objects," and "in an independent form"—the form tied inextricably to homeland, to *svatantra sattā*, and to the people of that land—are the forms required for a political independence, in a sort of aesthetic logic for nationalism.

Immediately following comes—what else?—a mala, garland, of objects, spilling over in result of Śukla's algebraic connection of love, country, feeling subjects and poetic objects:

> What is love of country? It is love itself. What is the *ālambana* of this love? The entire country, that is, the entire land, with its men, animals, birds, rivers, streams, forests, and mountains. What kind of love is it? It is the love from association (*sāha-caryagat*[80]). With those among whom we live, which always remains before our eyes, whose words we always hear, who remain with us every hour, in sum, those whose proximity we are accustomed to, for which we have greed (*lobh*) or passion (*rāg*).

The familiar objects and people of everyday life are thus the heroes and heroines that inspire the *bhāv* of love-of-country, he proclaims. Another couple of malas of the objects and reminders of desire follow in a climactic rhetorical flourish:

> If someone truly loves his country, then he will love the men, animals, birds, creepers, thickets, trees, leaves, forests, mountains, rivers, waterfalls, everything, of his country, he will look at everything with an affectionate[81] vision, remembering all of it he will weep in foreign lands.

And this love is importantly one that references classical *uddīpanas*, qua real objects in the world. Not knowing these objects of Indian reality and Indian poetry is to not be truly Indian.

> They who do not even know what bird is the *koyal*, who do not even hear where the *cātak* shrieks, who do not drink in the sight of the mango tree so laden with blooms full of the fragrance of love, who do not even glimpse what happens within the farmers' huts, if they, in their clique of well-dressed friends, reporting on the buying-power of the average income of each Indian, claim to love of country, then you should ask them: "Brothers! How can you have this love without knowing the form/beauty (*rūp*)?" Those whose sorrow you've never been partner to, you [claim to] want to see happy—how can this be? [Living your whole life] miles away from them, you repeat "economics" ("*arthaśāstra*") in foreign speech; but don't drag the name of love into it. Love is not account books. You can rent out an accountant, but not people who love (*prem karanevāle*).[82]

In this remarkable passage, Śukla enunciates a "structure of feeling," so to speak, in which the "things" of nature, "forms" identified as the objects of poetry, mold their native viewer/lover into an authentic Indian, as these *uddīpana*s of nature-objects inspire *bhāva* in the citizen-*ālambana*. This process happens through love, not the ways and means of politics; while this love creates a political subject, it has little to do with the elite politicoes to whom Śukla alludes. The subsequent paragraph then fittingly cites from sixteenth-century poet Rasakhān, courtly poet and devotee of Krishna: "When Rasakhān's eyes gaze upon the forests, gardens, ponds, of Braj / the arbors of thorny bushes seem better than hundreds of those houses of gold." This sentiment he contrasts with the wealthy men who claim to patriotism, yet "restraining themselves from joking about the ragged old clothes of their exhausted brother, they keep their hearts clean but let the floor get dirty."[83] This represents a nationalism vividly informed by Sanskritic poetics and ways of seeing as much as by the wide prospects of landscape nationalism of the English. The history of the aesthetics of the ideas of "nation" and "Indian" would necessarily need to account for such vernacular epistemologies.

At this point we can view Śukla's love for the *koyal* and *cātak* birds, and the cultural allegiance that represents to him, as a corollary to his pairing of right representation and the loving mode of *rāgātmikā vṛtti*. Loving one's country is loving its nature, and representing scenes of that nature accurately. We might analogize here to a correlation made by the Victorian critic John Ruskin, whose writings on economics influenced Gandhi, and whose writings on the truths of nature in art Śukla may have read. For Ruskin the perception of facts of nature was a capacity that was cultivated by an infinite love, the "higher sensibility" of the good nature-poet or painter. For him, intellectual observation of physical nature is linked physiologically and spiritually to moral character, an "acuteness of bodily sense . . . associated with love":

> . . . bodily sensibility to color and form is intimately connected that higher sensibility which we revere as one of the chief atributes of all noble minds, and as the chief spring of real poetry. This kind of sensibility may be entirely resolved into the acuteness of bodily sense . . . associated with love, love I mean in its infinite and holy functions, as it embraces divine and human and brutal intelligences, and hallows the physical perception of external objects by association, gratitude, veneration, and other pure feelings of our moral nature.[84]

Śukla's loving mode, *rāgātmikā vṛtti*, fits well with Ruskin's conception of truth as something perceived with love, beyond the intellectual perception of facts. However, Śukla's love is notably one of attachment to the natural objects of the homeland, a statement of allegiance more strictly political than Ruskin's sense of love "in its infinite and holy functions" but in spirit very similar to Ruskin's idea that the moral, loving person sees the physical world more fully: "perception is so quickened by love, and judgment so tempered by veneration, that, practically, a man of deadened moral sensation is always dull in his perception of truth."[85] Indeed, Śukla's men of "deadened moral sensation" are precisely those unable to value the objects of Indian nature in poetry, and the life of their "exhausted brother" in rags. Natural scenes in poetry are, as for Ruskin, linked with poet's scientifically objective—as realist—yet morally-illuminated—as loving—perspective.[86]

Conclusions

There is something of a liberation narrative at work here in Śukla's account of the subject-matter of poetry: natural objects as "real things," should not be merely cogs in the wheel of poetics, but things-in-themselves. Śukla reads the *rasa* of old as disempowering, even as this *rasa* theory informs his own thinking profoundly. It is probably too far-fetched to analogize Śukla's transversal of *ālambanas* into real things and people with a political transversal of colonized subjects into determining subjects; however, the polemic of this essay does lead the reader to the conclusion that a change to realist subject-matter for poetry, the world as *vastu*, unrestrained by any poetic convention, will create possibilities for knowing oneself as an Indian. The question of political import aside, we see here overlapping vocabularies for political liberation and empiricized aesthetics in *svatantra*; we have seen in the preceding chapters that from Śrīdhar Pāṭhak, at least, these subjects merged in nature, and Śukla continues this theme in this essay. On the other hand, Śukla also taps into a longer history of attention to form: the gopis, who love Krishna because they know his *saguṇa svarūp*, his bodily, material form, might themselves ask "how can you love without knowing the form?" They too perceive the material world of form—and the materiality of Krishna's body—with love. The essay thus might be read as expressing a sort of *saguṇa* patriotism.

Nature clearly functions as a trigger of affect especially when it opens an avenue to the perceptions of classical forebears. Śukla cites an *aitihāsik sahṛdayatā* (historical sympathy or "connoisseurship" in the poetic sense),[87] through which one perceives the harmony of natural forms with one's individual heart. The material *vastu* of the natural world forms a constant, and recovering the ancients' gaze perhaps effects more literally what Addison called gaining "a kind of property in everything he sees." But what kind of "property" is this for Śukla? Seemingly one of Indian authenticity versus the technology and irremovable foreignness of others, and one that depends vitally on ideal correspondence of inner and outer worlds, itself a precept that pervaded Hindu religious thought.

At the level of the epistemological work of this essay, several possibilities about the import and "work" of poetic nature emerge: Does this call to recognize "sva"-*rūp*, one's *own* forms, and in the generalized sense of *svarūp*, as the form of a whole, the shape of an incarnation, amount to an arument that *seeing* is affected by colonialism? To what extent is Śukla in fact advocating for a return of determinative sovereignty to Indian "forms" as signs, poetically and otherwise? Whether or not this is so, Śukla's essay gives us crucial insight into the particular, self-consciously semi-classical, and self-consciously only semi-"westernized" way-of-seeing he inhabited. He presents us with a conjugal poetics of nature, which is not marital conjugality, but the conjunction of human with nature within the syntagmatical world of *śṛṅgāra* in its "highest form." The pleasure of the receptor, the *rati bhāva*, if you will, is abstracted here into a relationship between a subjective, seeing, Indian person and natural, material, surroundings of the Indian natural and poetic landscape.

Chapter 9

The Prospect of Chāyāvād, 1920–25

Developing Perspectives on Natural Poetics

> That little bud of unknowing youth (*ajñāt yauvan kalikā*) has bloomed (*vikasit*); the morning sun kisses her shining face, giving her infinite blessings; bees come from all around and begin telling her new messages; the wind has begun spreading her fragrance here and there; the world's mother, Nature, has applied with her own hand the auspicious mark (*suhāg ṭīkā*) of pollen to her brow; her breaths are filled with eternal honey.
>
> —Sumitrānandan Pant[1]

In the passage above, Pant describes the transition Hindi poetry had made, from being a child as Braj Bhāṣā to a full-blown, pollinated flower as Khaṛī Bolī, in his generation-defining introduction to his *Pallav* of 1926. The auspicious imagery of nubile desirability and connubiality of this passage—Nature herself has applied the blessing-mark of pollen to the flower's brow, as if a saffron-colored *ṭīkā* mark painted on the forehead of a new bride—is augmented not only by the familiar images of flower, bee, and honey, but also the extended meaning of *vikasit* in colonial India: "developed" or "progressed," as well as "bloomed." This early passage in the essay appears within a longer account of the emergence of Khaṛī Bolī poetry as a natural process of maturation, and clearly marks Braj Bhāṣā and Khaṛī Bolī as not merely dialects but world views. Pant here creates an homology between Hindi poetry in the world, as the flower and bees—both natural and *śṛṅgārik*—and the march of progress. In conjoining these two discourses, Pant spoke in the critical language of *rasiks* who perused flowers of verse, and also the language of natural science, that index of progress along with literature itself.

Considering the many poets and critics, and the poetry and prose explored in previous chapters, we very well know how to read this image of Hindi as flower. In this book I argue for a similar sort of organicism, but in regard to the recent past of Chāyāvād poetry and the homegrown readings of modernity, rather than the idea that English poetry and specifically the Romantics, created a salvific blooming effect upon verse, as mid-century critics would have it, including Pant himself in his later Marxist phase. In this chapter I aim to show that along with their clear innovations, Chāyāvādīs wrote in clear consonance with their Dvivedī era forebears in regard to nature. *Śṛṅgāra* appeared naturalized and philosophized; the term "personification" came to the fore as natural objects appear as hero and heroine. Nature was not reinvented along Romantic lines, I argue, but rather emerged in the Chāyāvād poetry of the early twenties along an already established path treading the ground in between the world of *śṛṅgāra* and the world of scientific and political *yathārth*, "commensurate reality," as defined in decades previous. The Chāyāvād prospect upon nature grew organically out of the perspectives evident in Hindi poetry of the immediately preceding decades as much as any new Romantic influence. I should be clear that Chāyāvād poetry contains many things; my portrait here of Chāyāvād illustrates only a few crucial aspects of Chāyāvād era poetry, which era has left a deep impression on the saṃskāra of modern Hindi literature.

The origin of the term Chāyāvād has been disputed by scholars and poets over the decades. Etymologically speaking, it means "of the movement of *chaya*," *chāyā* having the following range of meanings: shade (i.e., from cloud cover, a tree, etc.), reflection (i.e., in a mirror, etc.), and shadow (of an object). As Rubin has pointed out, the term *chāyā* had currency in the *Upanishads* as a term for the universe as a phenomenal reflection of transcendental reality; this connotation is quite plausible, as theologians and poets of the day (e.g., Vivekananda, Tagore) were indeed reexamining the *Upanishads*, and in effect popularizing modernist readings of them.[2] Some proposed that it came from Bengali, as a term for the type of poetry exemplified by Tagore's *Gitāñjalī*, and connected in turn to English trends of phantasm and symbolism; others considered it a homegrown Hindi term. Clearly Chāyāvād came into widest popular use first as a disparaging term for the newfangled poetic style, which was criticized for being overly vague and thereby "full of shadows." As critic Brajaratnadās put it pithily in 1932, "this poetry is too much bent toward the illimitable, imperceptible, invisible, endless, etc., and is full of "world-love" (*viśva-prem*) [and] "unknown sorrow" (*ajñāt vedanā*)."[3] Others implied that the poets were merely shadowing or reflecting Bengali poetry, and in turn English poetry. As it happened, there was also a preponderance of the term *chāyā* in poetry throughout the twenties, most often denoting a literal shade from clouds or trees, and only sometimes reflection, in early poems. Whatever the origin of the term, and despite the poets' eventual popularity, the aspersions cast had an effect, and Chāyāvād became the name for a generation of new Khaṛī Bolī poets.

The allegations of vagueness were in a basic way true: clearly these poets consciously broke conventions of scene and poetic diction, creating a sort of semiotic "no-man's land," even while they reiterated these conventions in changed form. The Chāyāvād poets sought out a certain obliquity in their poetry, in pursuit of the very persona of the Romantic poet as misunderstood visionary. Indeed, it is this very intentional practice of disregarding literal, grammatical sense, the use of unusual abstractions, and the resistance of prose diction norms that made Chāyāvād poetry more recognizable as modern poetry worldwide. Unlike their immediate predecessors, the Chāyāvādīs largely dispensed with traditional meters, and while they supported conceptions of modernity already established in the late nineteenth century—namely, that poetry should reflect demotic speech and should demonstrate a "realism" in description that Braj Bhāṣā lacked—they exercised a new kind of obliquity in their poetry that was revolutionary in its time, and undeniably part of the global understanding of modern poetry. As representatives of a youth movement in comparison to that first Dvivedī-led vanguard of Hindi literature, and members of the youth movement of the Gandhian campaigns, nationalist and progressive feeling is palpable and blatant at times.

The mid-century critics used a panoply of terms to describe Chāyāvādi innovations: *navīn* (new) and *svacchand* (unbound, independent) especially, and sometimes just *ādhunik* (modern). They also saw some continuity from the previous twenty years, that is, Dvivedī era poets who laid the groundwork for Chāyāvād. In the words of Hazārīprasād Dvivedī in 1955, the poets of 1900–20

> . . . did important work preparing the environment of love of nature (*prakṛti-prem*), the independent stream-of-love (*svacchand premadhārā*), and personal freedom. Śrīdhar Pāṭhak's poetry gave nourishment to nature-love and independent love (*svacchand premadhārā*) and Rāmanareś Tripāṭhī's *Milan*, *Pathik*, etc., [also] developed the inclination of freedom. . . . Today we have forgotten the importance of these poems. They are

> called prosaic (*itivṛttātmak*) and forgotten. But in fact they laid the groundwork for Chāyāvād, now considered the glory of Hindi poetry.[4]

These keywords of freedom (*svatantratā*), independent love (*svacchand prem*), and love of nature (*prakṛti prem*), although not new to Hindi in the 1920s, thus came to distinguish the Chāyāvād generation's poetic iconoclasm.

Chāyāvād represents the most well-canonized, and even loved, poetry of the modern Hindi poetic canon. Its innovations would come to define those of quotidian poetry in Hindi, poetry submitted by readers to middle-brow magazines, poetry composed and recited by the amateur in public events even today. These features are both formal and thematic. Chāyāvād generation poets gradually abandoned Braj composition for Khaṛī Bolī, and often flouted current metrical conventions in their Khaṛī Bolī poetry; the meters they did use were sometimes *mātrik* and sometimes, in the pace of the *gīt* form, alluding to folk songs. Ever since, Hindi poetry has simply never returned in any meaningful way to the traditional reckoning of meter, *mātrik* or *varṇavṛtta*, of Braj and early Khaṛī Bolī Hindi. The Chāyāvādī poets ushered in an era of Whitmanesque cascades of imagistic short lines and visual poetry, experimenting in truly radical ways for their time.

Thematically, the Chāyāvād poets began a perspectival revolution in Hindi. While the arcadia of bees and flowers remained in abundance, Chāyāvād poetry foregrounded voice, and a voice that spoke in abstractions and symbols; in contrast, in Braj poetry the voice of Sūr, or Rādhā, etc., though no less poignant or "real," would nevertheless recede against the determining *bhāva* that ordained such a voice and its circumstances. This *bhāva*, as we have seen earlier, would become the term for the emotional content of modern poetry. And this new poetry contained not only bees, flowers, and breezes, but much oceanic imagery, taken from *nirguṇa* thought on the illusion of the world, only to be crossed over, and suggestive of the kind of awesome sublimity of the English Romantics. Further, the description of these scenes takes on a much more onomatopoeic character, as the sound of waterfalls, rainstorms, thunder fill its lines. More renegade personification of natural objects, shifting between the micro- and macrocosmic scenes, and a Vivekananda-Tagore-influenced vision of the divine all characterize the Chāyāvād innovations, which are now the given features of Hindi poetry. Later Hindi poetry would fundamentally spring from their new vision.

Of all of the modern Hindi poets, the academy has examined the four major Chāyāvād poets most extensively. Karine Schomer's and David Rubin's works represent a substantial offering from American academics on these poets; many works in English from India address these authors, and many, many more academic works in Hindi testify to the great interest and admiration for these poets. Nāmavar Siṁh's *Chāyāvād* has already been mentioned many times in this work. Prasād's *Kāmāyanī*, the post-diluvium allegorical epic, a work outside the scope of this study, is probably the most translated modern Hindi poetic work, and one which has inspired a flood of analyses in India. Pant's 1926 introduction to *Pallav* remains the standard statement of the Chāyāvādi perspective on modern Hindi poetics. Nirālā is widely considered the best Hindi poet of the entire twentieth century. Mahādevī, the youngest of them, still looms large as the first female poet in modern Hindi to gain wide public success and recognition. To write of Chāyāvād is to take on a cast of poetic legends, with a vast and complex textual archive that cannot possibly be summarized and analyzed fully here.

Although representatives of cultural sea-change in the Hindi public sphere, as in India generally, this new generation of poets did not completely dispense with the semiotic world and formal poetics of their elders. Rather, they wrote through its lens in many respects. Their free verse was truly shocking to the older literati, but often they retained a modicum of metricality. Their playful alliterative bent was from one perspective just a freewheeling version of the metrically bound word games of Braj poets. As we will consider below, many of their personified natural objects and scale-shifting scenes of nature could be read as of a piece with early developments of the twentieth century.

Here we will look only at an early part of the Chāyāvād era, from 1921 up to Pant's landmark *Pallav* of 1926, which so stridently argued for a new poetic order. What we will find is that the Introduction to *Pallav*, itself a work of nature poetry, in many ways emerged organically from the Hindi poetry and poetics of 1885 onward. The mid-twentieth-century critics, finding in Chāyāvād a revolution inspired by European Romanticism, have de-emphasized the many immediate predecessors of Pant's adamant statements, and preexistent aesthetic trends within Hindi poetry in the Dvivedī era. While certainly Chāyāvād represented a generation more well-read in English Romantic literature than ever before, the Chāyāvād poetic stance evolved from decades of their elders' thinking on poetic ornament, the import of nature, and the social problem of the erotic for the new public sphere. While Hindi critics acknowledge the Romantic or *svacchandatāvād* influence of the Dvivedī era, mostly of Śrīdhar Pāṭhak, even this underplays the organic evolution of thought on nature, love, and the concept of *svacchand* in poetry. In this chapter we will consider how exactly the poetry of the early years of Chāyāvād embodied these values that would take on new life under their youthful mantle. With reference to Pant's seminal Introduction and the mid-century critical precepts on Chāyāvād, I will examine certain poems only from 1921–25 by two giants of Chāyāvād, Pant and Nirālā, outlining continuities with Hindi poetry's past, as well as more politically charged uses of those same natural, *śṛṅgārik* tropes.[5]

Pant, His "Sighs," and Fanciful Nature

Sumitrānandan Pant (1900–77) came from the foothills of the Himalayas in Almora to the Hindi literary centers of Banaras and Allahabad in the Gaṅgetic valley, thus beginning in 1918 a literary career forged in the atmosphere of Queen's and Muir Colleges, and popular English poets of the day, Sarojini Naidu, Tagore, and the English Romantics.[6] Pant was an icon of the college literary scene of poetry readings held in dormitories and attended by elders as well as the youth, newly invigorated with Gandhi's Non-Cooperation movement. Pant's *Pallav* (*Leaves*) of 1926 brought his first burst of fame, as much for its nature-oriented poetry as its introduction, already discussed above. Pant typifies the "nature poet" persona associated with Chāyāvād, and indeed later in life he wrote that he was "raised in the lap of nature. . . . My first poems were influenced by the vision of natural beauty"[7]; and

> the inspiration of natural beauty alone was the root power, in my view, that drew my mind which favored solitude toward the creation of poetry. And even today, the sweet rustling sound of the mirror of the soul that is natural beauty bursts forth from the bowers of my words.[8]

It may in fact seem odd to many to discuss nature in Hindi poetry without studying Pant's *Leaves*—such was the profound effect of the work. However, this is precisely what we will do here, in an attempt to recreate the poetic world as the Hindi reading public would perceive it, in the years preceding Chāyāvād's glory days. Hence, this chapter presents a sort of anticipative reading in that Pant and Nirālā, like Prasād as previously discussed, will go on to become "nature poets" of Hindi, but here we will limit ourselves to their poetry published in their earliest years, before 1925. English language studies of Chāyāvād have been exactly that—studies of the Chāyāvād generation as a whole; here my purpose is to isolate the earliest known published documents by Chāyāvād poets for a clearer picture of the cultural shift taking place as the Dvivedī generation recedes and the Chāyāvādīs emerge to greater prominence. So with some reference to Pant's Introduction to *Pallav*, we will proceed to examine only his first known published poem.

Pant's poem "Sighs" ("Ucchvās") was published in 1921 from an obscure publisher in Ajmer, then a British province within Rajputana, and yet still reached the Hindi audience further afield in the United Provinces. Critics called Pant a number of things, including a eunuch, effeminate, and a *sakhī-panthī*, and *sajanī-panthī*, i.e., a follower of the persona of the female mistress characters of *śṛṅgāra* literature, and possibly a follower of Krishnaite devotional transvestism. Harshly, his poem was called "shallow breathing" (*laghu laghu prāṇ*) rather than "Sighs." Nirālā, on the other hand, said it was the first real Chāyāvād poem.[9] What did this poem do to incite such reactions?

In basic ways, Pant's "Sighs" simply expands upon the innovative features of Śrīdhar Pāṭhak's poetry. Firstly, the tendency toward free verse seen earlier in Śrīdhar Pāṭhak's "Beauty of Kashmir" here was full-blown.[10] What ictus or song-like quality of the poem appeared, did so in constantly changing form, as also did the printed appearance of the poetry itself, arranged in stanzas of multifarious shape and rhyme. This *svacchandatā* of verse was not the only similarity to Pāṭhak; one famous line of Pant's poem strongly reminds us of Pāṭhak's "Beauty of Kashmir." Pant wrote, "Moment by moment nature transforms her garb!" (*pala pala parivartita prakṛti veś!*), in uncanny resemblance to Pāṭhak's Lady Nature of his 1904 "Beauty of Kashmir," who "moment by moment changes her garb, moment by moment, takes on new splendors" (*pala pala palaṭati bhesa chanika chavi china china dhārati*).[11] The importance of this couplet to understanding Pant's "nature poetry" is buttressed by the fact that Pant recycled this couplet and several verses following in his later work *Raśmi-badh*, with the "moment by moment" couplet at the beginning.[12] Nature, and in particular, the *nāyikā*-like vision of nature inherited from Pāṭhak, was thus basic to Pant's thematic poetics.

However, Pant's ever-changing beauty of nature appears in the poem as part of a larger schema of shifting between the minute and grand scales of nature, both impregnated with personal desire. The following passages excerpt about a third of the poem, in medias res, presented here in the same, then-renegade format of irregular verse length and visual effects through indentation.

We begin with a slight twisting of the trope of the spring season with the placement of the first-person voice, and self-hood within the context of a "vast garden of the universe":

O honey-season springtime of sweetness!
My life like a bee's:
Hard work, soft heart;
Scented by abundant gentle flowers,
The vast garden of the universe is in bloom!

These are my body, heart, life,
These are my thoughts, my pride;
Unknown in a pile of dust
Are hidden my honeyed songs!

With this anonymous pile of dust, we begin to see more in this springtime than merely pretty greenery. The singer is searching for his own songs amidst some difficult terrain of "harsh crooked thorns," and "nets of tangled trees," constantly "picking flowers"—perhaps flowers of verse, as commonly understood. This he does to "find that unknown shore," an allusion to death and salvation, but intentionally odd here in apposition to flower-picking, and without mention of water. Immediately following, we are led to think he found his salvation: "—it was a new flower bud! / With that simplicity of hers / I adorned my heart." And this bud is sympathetic to him: "From the constant sweet song / Her heart was aroused!" He moves on to the mythological wishing-tree, where he tells of his "imaginings." "I found pollen there / Of many new desires [or perceptions (*bhavanā*)]!" Taking this pollen is characteristically *śr̥ṅgārik*: "I, like a slow smile, / Hovered about her sweet lips; / And by her pleasing fragrance / Was everyday drawn near."

Then suddenly the frame shifts, in something of a panning shot of the larger landscape, as Pant writes his famous lines on Nature:

It was the rainy season, the mountain region,
Moment by moment nature transforms her garb!
The band of impassable mountains
Rend open their thousand eyes of flowers
And examine again and again
Below in the water, their own great creation;
—which lake nurtured at their feet
Is spread out like a mirror vast!!

Here we cannot deny the *mahākāvya*-like scope of this passage, with echoes of Kalidasa's description of the Himalaya mountains, and in the "thousand eyes of flowers" looking into the mirror-lake, an echo of Kalidasa's very description of Indra's thousand eyes, "beautiful as a sheet of lotuses / rippling in a slow wind."[13]

Singing of the mountains' greatness with their rushing
Exciting the veins with liquid of passion (*mada*)

Lovely like strings of pearls
The frothy waterfalls cascade!
Rising up from the heart of the mountains
Trees like lofty ideals
Are staring into the silent sky
Unblinking, unwavering, as if in thought!
—suddenly, look, the earth-holding mountain took flight
Making its wings of distant clouds flutter
The waterfall still yet sounds
The sky burst open upon on the earth!
The *śāl* trees sunk into the earth fearfully
Vapor rising, water burned!
Roaming in a ship of clouds
Was Indra playing his sorcery!
(That sweet simple girl used to call that mountain a cloud
home!)
In this way my painter heart's
Astonishing picture appeared, become outer nature;
Like the recollection of simple childhood that
Girl was my delightful friend!

Here we see several features that would in fact characterize Chāyāvād generally: waterfalls joining the more conventionally Sanskritic mountains and clouds; a free-wheeling, almost psychedelic vision of natural objects in action; the voice of the poet embedded in the object itself; a shifting of scale from the smallest of scenes (bee on flower) to largest (the line of mountains); a general interest in paradox (water burned); the idea of a linked outer and inner nature, as a subject in itself (my painter heart's/ outer nature) and as an understood element of the personification of the bee, flower, and so on. It is quite safe to say that this poetry resembles that of Tagore, and somewhat even European poetry. Its intentional obliquity, use of the subjective "I," images of beauty in succession—here with some allusion to a fearsome sublime nature—, and its emotive apostrophe to a beloved, are relatively at home in English translation, and one imagines this would be more so in Bengali translation. In fact, apart from the stormy oceanic scenes, found so much in Tagore, that would appear more and more often in Chāyāvād poetry, the enchanted garden of bees, buds, and breezes evoked British fairy paintings as much as any Indic garden scene. Here flower-bud fairies; bees, clouds, mountains—the familiar objects—take on a certain impish charm, though pointing to grand sublime truths all the while.

Sex and the Singular Flower: "The Jasmine Bud" and "To a Flower on the Road"

Personification becomes a trademark of Chāyāvād. We will recall Prasād's object-poems of the teens, which first signaled the rising popularity of personification in Hindi poetry. This trend would continue apace, but often in a more opaque vein in the full-fledged Chāyāvād era of the 1920s. An iconic example of such personification, in a manner that directly addresses *śṛṅgāra*, is Nirālā's famous "Jasmine Bud" ("Juhī kī kalī").

Nirālā's "The Jasmine Bud," one of his first poems, presents English Romantic fancy much less than simply a *śṛṅgārik* version of the object poem, already begun in Prasād (see Chapter 5), in which the apparatus of *śṛṅgāra* has merged with the *uddīpana*s cum *upamāna*s themselves. "The Jasmine Bud" of 1922 will illustrate how nature-poetry could accommodate the world of *śṛṅgāra* in modern Hindi poetry. Let us turn briefly to Nirālā himself.

Nirālā is considered by many to be the best of this generation of poets. He was probably born in 1899 in a district of Bengal to a family of Kanyākubja Brahmins of Kannauj in the United Provinces, an Avadhi speaking region to the west of Lucknow. He had a strong and deep connection to the Bengali language and Bengali literature, by virtue of his childhood location in Bengal, and his eventual employment in Calcutta at the Ramakrishna Mission Press, and subsequently other literary presses. During the early 1920s he lived in and published from Calcutta. The question of Hindi's literary distinction from Bengali was one of his great concerns, as his early essay on the insufficiency and effeminacy of Bengali grammar shows.[14] After later living in Lucknow and Allahabad, he died in penury in 1961. He was the most colorful personality of the Chāyāvād poets, a sort of "loose cannon," who allegedly suffered from mental illness. His pen name "Nirālā" means "strange," or "unusual," reflecting this persona. Marxist critic Rambilas Sharma's biography of Nirālā stands as a monumental work depicting this complex author whose predilections changed over the decades. One might say that through Nirālā we can trace the history of twentieth-century Hindi poetic movements, from Chāyāvād to progressivism to experimentalism. For our purposes, his very beginning years as a Hindi poet deserve our attention; from 1922 to 1924 Nirālā published some audacious poems that later became icons of Chāyāvād and the aesthetic atmosphere of modern Hindi poetry.

The Chāyāvād era generally affected a poetic aura of Sanskrit within a modernist agenda, and Nirālā accomplished this very clearly in his early poem, "Juhī kī kalī" ("The Jasmine Bud"). It contains a simple conceit, and an admittedly saccharine tone; but its success lies in its quirky, playful use of Sanskritic vocabulary, in a free verse that contrasted sharply with the pre-modern meter-bound verses it evokes. This poem was in fact rejected by editor Dvivedī, because of its free verse, but later the poem became famous for this very fact, as a representative poem of the Chāyāvād movement, first published in 1922.

> On a vine in a deserted forest
> was sleeping, full of *suhāg*, immersed in affectionate dream
> a young woman, pure soft slender—a jasmine bud
> she closed her eyes, languorous—in the lap of surrounding
> leaves,

Into this spring vignette enters the male Malay breeze, longing for her in separation:

> he remembered the moonlight's washed midnight,
> he remembered his beloved's trembling desirable body,
> and then? The wind
> crossed the lakes and rivers of the grove, the dense mountain
> forest
> . . .
> she slept,
> how could she know of the coming of her lover?
> The *nāyak* kissed her cheeks,
> the garland of the vine swayed like a swing.
> . . .
> Brazenly that *nāyak*
> suddenly was cruel
> from the downpours of blows
> her entire beautiful delicate body shook violently,
> he crushed her pale round cheeks;
> the young woman woke up startled—
> . . .
> with a shy lowered face she smiled—opened,
> enjoyed, united with her lover.[15]

So Nirālā has dislocated the *nāyak* and *nāyikā* into a natural scene; it is a seemingly precious poetic maneuver. Nirālā's female flower has taken on the familiar auspiciously beautiful and erotic qualities of the classical poetic *nāyikā*.[16] The poem begins in an especially Sanskritized manner, with compounds interspersed with Hindi markers: *vijana-vana-*

vallarī par / sotī thī suhāg-bharī—sneha-svapna-magna— / amala-komala-tanu tarunī—juhī kī kalī. This Sanskritized quality pervades the poem linguistically, and substantially also in terms of content: like a Sanskrit or Braj poem, a vignette depicting an interaction of lovers is presented, almost voyeuristically, to the reader. A similar scenario of the *nāyak* rudely awakening a flower-like youthful *nāyikā* can be found in the Braj *rīti* poet Keśav Dās, for instance: "and you have forced her / The soft lotus-like girl, [is] like a garland of jasmine, crushed. . . ." The wind is specifically a *nāyak,* explicitly recalling the human examples of earlier texts on poetics. This poem is undeniably precious, but this preciousness, if it were perceived by Nirālā's original reader, would have been overlooked by virtue of the interesting twisting of the natural settings and epithets of Sanskrit and Braj poetry into poetry about nature. However, Nirālā's jasmine bud *is,* ultimately, a flower, cajoled into opening by these somewhat violent gusts of the wind, again evoking the sexual scenario of the *mugdhā,* innocent, artless girl.

I would argue, on the basis of the previous chapter presented here, that Nirālā here followed a poetic transformation that had started years earlier in Hindi poetry, of converting the natural trappings of Sanskritic poetry, and items used as conventional objects of comparison, to poetic subjects in and of themselves, transposing the previously immanent allegory of and the western idea of "personification," as the natural objects in these poems function less as metaphoric objects than as actors in an independent poetic world. While the practice of "personification" in the modern western context carries a connotation of fanciful-ness, for the Hindi poet, such images as wind and flower were still truly referential to the *śṛṅgāra* context. However, ultimately the sexual content of *śṛṅgāra* is defused by its new, concretely allegorical context. The interaction of bud and wind here is merely nature-poetry, and rather light poetry at that. We might read this poem as a poetic corollary of the apologetics for the concept of *śṛṅgāra* then entering the world of Hindi letters, which explained the emergence of *śṛṅgāra* as a natural expression of biology, pertaining to indigenous knowledge of the birds and the bees, so to speak. This poem was known to have offended some because of its supposed sensuousness, but unlike the Braj Bhāṣā poetry that was under attack, this poem was ultimately *about nature,* however un-naturalistic and erotically suggestive it may have been.

Buttressing the argument that "The Jasmine Bud" continues in the vein of object-poems such as Prasād's in the teens, detailed in Chapter 5, another poem displays a clear relationship to Prasād's poetics. Nirālā's 1924 "To a Flower on the Road" ("Rāste ke phūl se"), evokes strongly both conceit of Prasād's "Crushed Little Lotus Blossom" ("Dalit kumudinī") and in its conclusion, Prasād's cryptic lotus-on-lake poem, "Acquaintance" ("Paricay"). There are differences from Prasād however: the flower in question here is male, as we can see in the Hindi grammar, and the flower's various possible stories are presented as possibilities within the poet's consciousness.

Nirālā sets the premise at the beginning, with a pathetic, insignificant object, the crushed or downtrodden (*dalit*) flower on the ground, used and then forgotten:

> A cloth spread out for catching begged pity,
> O downtrodden (*dalit*) flower! Tell me why,
> Are you scattered about staring downwards into the dust?
> With the mute emotion of your dirty gaze—
> . . .
> What do you say?—"in the blow
> Of a gust of wind the tree bent over,
> Although spared, alas, I couldn't stay to the end."
> . . .
> Not that? Then tell me—then what!—
> At this point Nirālā mixes voices—the flower speaks and yet Nirālā speaks to it:
> greed hidden in the heart, [but] applying the auspicious sandal-paste
> . . .
> Somebody offered you up sometime to the goddess' altar,
> . . .
> But this story also, of being thrown out after wilting on the altar, is not quite right. Instead,
> The sweet gaze of attainment's
> Love-filled concurrence on the pair's meeting,
> When there were two seekers, intent on the practice of love,
> They made a beautiful love-offering of me,
> The rituals were carried out with me—
> I alone was their teacher,—
> When one soft hand met the lotus hand
> Their act was accomplished by me alone;
> Of their bond of love I alone was the link—
> Of "graceful imagination"—"soft feet"
> I was beautiful bond of meter!"[17]

Here the soft feet (*komal pad*), allude to the metrical feet of verse, *komalakānt padāvalī*, implying homologies between this rite of love and the practice of writing poetry. The poem itself mirrors this, "using" the offering-flower—a bond of love, and bond of meter—for this poem. Meanwhile, this verse itself is idiosyncratic in content, syntax, and meter, especially for its day. Nirālā has here effected the identification of *yugal-milan*, the meeting of the couple, with the meeting of a poem with its meter, all through the figure of the ritual flower.

Natural Love versus Society? The Natural Romance Reconsidered

The characterization of Chāyāvādī nature as a place of personal freedom, where the imagination, and the social persona of the poet, could shed the bonds of society and roam freely, *svachand, svatantra*, is a familiar theme of the Hindi literary critical narrative. Certainly this new generation of poets evoked this, and must have looked to the sentiments of British Romantic poets exclaiming over a landscape or a scene and its relation to god, the self, and mortality. However, many of these early Chāyāvād poems evoke a nature that is "free," socially and otherwise, through a very Indic lens. Most clearly, the landscape of Krishna's lila—itself full of private spaces and freedom from the normal social world—figures prominently. In this matter we can to some extent read in the influence of recent poets of the Dvivedī generation, who wrote of nature as a vast site of divine traces of Krishna. Likewise, the ascetic's abode of the hut, or the Himalayan mountain grove, the ashram in the wood, reemerged as a place that correlates to romantic love, as Hariaudh's Rādhā sees nature anew in her ascetic vow of virginity, as Prasād's Pilgrim of Love took to the wood when Camelī married, and as Tripāṭhī's Pilgrim left his wife for the immutably beautiful Nature. Objects from the settings of classical poetry become "freed," and the Chāyāvād poets play with these redolent signs; the "free space" of the ascetic's grove implies a certain eroticism—as does the ascetic Shiva himself, and a separation from the social world, which Chāyāvād poets may have interpreted with a dose of British Romanticism.

In contrast to the argument that such poetic traits signal a bona fide Romanticism, I would argue that these poems represent a modernism that is not dependent upon an idea of nature as not-culture, a space renewing a diminished connection to the divine, or a place representing the past. Rather, the bonds broken in these Chāyāvādī nature poems are those of the interrelation of signs; nature remains represented (largely) by familiar objects, and scenes as ideal as any Braj pastoral setting. The individuality attributed to the Chāyāvād Romanticism is also not so much a symptom of the social distance of the privileged poet, but rather the emotion of an individual writ large. The following poem can illustrate both the quality of semiotic play of the new Chāyāvādī nature, with a concomitant trait of expanding the personal emotion to universal proportions, a trait which may come equally from Romanticism as from Hindu philosophizing.

"Right Here" ("Yahīṁ") of 1924 begins with yet another reference to the southern breeze, but takes a different direction than is typical:

> Right here in the sweet southern breeze
> . . .
> . . . in eyes' pupils
> black, soft, as if undefeated,
> the sound of anklet bells
> spreads among the peaks and its gait
> has performed the beat and melody.

Lines run together such that it is difficult to assign memory's light of the early lines to any one entity—clouds, eyes, heart—and difficult to contain its movement, as dancer and sound itself. Then Nirālā turns to another familiar set of tropes, defamiliarized in his free verse and unusual diction. "Crooking the neck (*baṅkim kara grīva*) / Extending creeper arms (*bāhu-vallariyoṁ ko baṛhākara*) / Those so many prayers for the kiss full of union" rise to a desirous face. Implying a vision of the divine and also the humility of the human lover before his unattainable beloved, Nirālā's "right here" seems part temple tableau of Krishna's lila with the gopis, part palace hall of courtesans:

> With insatiable desire.
> So many of those eyes
> Thrilling with love
> Bestowed gifts (*dān*) here
> Freed from pride!
> In black dense locks
> How many ecstasies of lovers are enclosed here!

Indeed, here this verse speaks of illicit union outside the bonds of society, but this is an abstracted union dripping with Krishnaite, and generic Sanskritic images, beautifully dislocated, and mixed with new ones.

Finally, the resolution places us on the Yamuna bank, in an atmosphere of abstracted *suhāg*, the auspicious coupled state, and overpowering love.

The beautiful sound of the Yamuna
Even today tells the bygone ballad of *suhāg*.
Bathing the bank she
Tells of the power
Of love's flood.[18]

Nirālā's nature, as much as he innovated in the telling of it, still shows an overwhelming concern to portray the power of the particular space of an Indic *suhāg*, the auspiciousness of couplehood, perhaps of Rādhā and Krishna, and always ultimately of humans with their god.

Encompassing the Arbor: Macrocosmic Nature, Śṛṅgāra and the Female Divine

Pant in his 1926 *Leaves* essay would give another enunciation to the idea, already apparent in Sukla's 1923 essay on natural scenes, that poetry should contain the world. Beyond Sukla, though, Pant linked the problem of encompassing the world with the use of Braj Bhāṣā.

> In the foothills of Braj Bhāṣā, in the shade of its affectionate *āñcal*,[19] a Kashmir of beauty can certainly be established, where waterfalls of moonlight rain down loads and loads of pearls, the calls of birds are braided with . . . stars of sound, the rainbow of imagination can lay half asleep on a thousand-colored flower bed, where she sees dreams of Indra's spring-time heaven of beauty—but her breast is not big enough that on it the eastern and western hemispheres; water and land, fire and sky, light and darkness, forest and mountain, river and valley, canal and bay, island and colony, natural beauty from the northern to southern pole star, the botanical features of hot and cold countries, flowers and plants, animals and birds, the water and wind of various regions, behavior and comportment—in whose words the pleasant wind and the turmoil, fire and flood, meteors and earthquakes, everything is contained, can be included; on whose pages the rise and fall of the civilization of man, old age and death, recurrence and change, new and old, everything can be portrayed; in whose cabinets philosophy and science, history and geography, politics and sociology, art and craft, tales and stories, poetry and drama, everything can be arranged before you.[20]

The language of all genres, of all fields of knowledge, of the grand swath of experience that Pant understands to be the purview of poetry, could never be Braj Bhāṣā. His statement reminds us of the long enumerative lists of Hindi essays and poetry noted previously (e.g., Śukla and the sexological nature writing described in Chapter 6), but here the emphasis is encompassing complementary pairs of geographic, geologic, historic forms, along with terms for academic disciplines and literary genres, high and low.

This prospect of wholeness justified for Pant the turn to Khaṛī Bolī Hindi, but this gathering of parts on a grand scale characterized much of Chāyāvād poetry already by this time. A macrocosmic Nature, which elaborated Nature as the Upanishadic principle by conjoining the complementary but unlinked phenomenon, etc., in paradoxical resolution of contradiction, *virodhābhās*, mixed with a Vedantin *nāyikā* evocative of the *śṛṅgārik nāyikā* generally, and the Bengali goddess, both fierce mother and desirable woman. This of course had to do with the burgeoning popularity of Bengali religious movements, the very presence of some Chāyāvād poets in Bengal, and the poetry of Tagore on this very sort of universalized female presence, evocative of the Goddess abstracted into natural scenes.

Pant's "Sighs" above illustrates the characteristic shifts between micro- and macrocosmic vignettes in Chāyāvād, which comprised a feature of the new poetic nature this generation put forward. In contrast to his "Jasmine Bud" above, many of Nirālā's poems concern nature in an explicitly metaphysical framework, reflecting his *advaita* beliefs no doubt garnered from his close association with the Ramakrishna Mission during his early years in Calcutta. An idea of nature as the manifestation of the Absolute was de rigueur among the young Chāyāvād poets, who read Vivekananda, Aurobindo, and Tagore; but Nirālā embodied the macrocosmic natural world of *prakṛti*, not only as a female, but as a fundamentally erotic entity. "Sandhyā sundarī" ("Evening, a Beautiful Woman"), from 1923, is a cogent example, which suggests again the figure of the *nāyikā*. Nirālā describes the coming night, descending from the sky, a star entangled in her hair, as a universal female entity—a powerful, somber *nāyikā*—"there is no laughing flirtation in her"—who pervades the universe. She is linked with all-pervading primeval sound, an *omkār* that is, surprisingly, the sound of an ankle-bracelet communicating a barely perceptible meditative word, and a sound that "buzzes" (*gūñj-*) like the bee:

> . . . only one imperceptible word, "still, still, still"
> buzzes everywhere—
> in the realm of the sky—on the surface of the earth—
> in the pure lotuses sleeping on the peaceful lake—
> in the ample breast of the river beautiful and proud—

> in the snowy-peaked steadfast mountain on whose peak are steadfast profound sages
> in the power of the ocean's heavy roaring of towering wave-blows of destruction—
> in the earth—in water—in the sky—in fire and wind—
> . . .
> what else is there? nothing

Her sound resounds through nature, and as Nirālā writes of these natural elements, it is as if he code-switches to a Sanskritic diction recalling the landscapes of Sanskrit poetry, again listing items in the now-familiar pacing rhythm of this trait in modern poetic Hindi: "*sotī śānta sarovara para usa amara kamalinī-dala meṁ— / saundarya-garvitā-saritā ke ati vistṛta vakṣaḥsthala meṁ— // uttāla-taraṅgāghāta-pralaya-ghana-garjana-jaladhi-prabala meṁ / kṣiti meṁ—jala meṁ—nabha meṁ—anila-anala meṁ—*"

Furthermore, she is linked to the poet, and poetic creation itself, as we read in the last verse that at midnight the poet's "passion increases" in a fervor of *śṛṅgāra*: "from a throat of desire, disturbed with *viraha* / spontaneously, then, a raga of separation bursts forth."[21] This suggests a sort of inspiration from nature that is superficially similar to that of the British Romantic "nature poets," but filtered a framework of *prakṛti* and desire that had little to do with Wordsworth. The female body and longing for it pervade Nirālā's poetics—and indeed Chāyāvād poetics—whether in light poetry of fancied personification, or in contemplation of nature as principle.

On the other hand, we find in Nirālā another tendency to identify nature with the binary monism generically, and in turn to identify this interplay with the creation of poetry, much as in "Evening, a Beautiful Woman" above. Nirālā's famous "You and Me" ("Tum aur maiṁ," 1923) of the Ramakrishna magazine *Samanvay* presents a set of natural scenes and poetic commonplaces, in which "you" and "me," god and devotee, are integrally connected. Here the statements of equivalence, and the sometimes unconventional pairs of entities make for a modern poem. Selected verses are given below, with a view toward showing how nature functions multifariously in this philosophical love poem:

> You are the high Himalaya peaks
> And I a holy river of restless gait.
> You are the pure heart's sigh (*ucchvās*)
> And I the poem of the beloved's desired one
> . . .
> You are the separation of years,

I am the last recognition.
. . .
You are the forest, dense as Indra's paradise
And I am a branch with cool happiness underneath.

Many of these pairings are typically gendered: "you" is identified with life-breath (*prāṇa*), brahma, Man, Shiva, Ram, and Madan, while "I" represents body, maya, "nature, chain of love," shakti, Sita, and "the innocent girl (*mugdhā*) unaware," respectively. However, several pairings defy such conventions, altogether envisioning novel ways of oneness, often in the natural landscape.

You are the young moon of autumn
I am midnight sweetness.
You are the soft pollen of fragrant flowers,
I am the soft-gaited southern wind,
. . .
You are the springtime honey-season of hope,
And I am the song of the pretty calling of the cuckoo,
. . .
You are the artist, dark with a covering of clouds,
I lightning, creation of the brush.
. . .
You are the whiteness of the jasmine and lotus
So I am pure ubiquity.[22]

Images of utter unity—blueness with sky, the flute with Krishna's lip, etc., mix with those of inevitable desire—Kama as Madan with the *mugdhā*, the desirable young girl of *nāyikā-bhed*, and the honey-season and the cuckoo's call. The "I" of this poem generally evokes the female gender, but these pairs join together variously as "heterosexual" pairs or intermingled abstractions, and not always in their gender-normative ways either (e.g., "you" as pollen in flower and "I" as the wind). Ultimately the poem invokes the creative power implicit in the ontological pairing of *puruṣa* and *prakṛti*, with analogues in Shiva/Shakti, and Rām/Sītā. In the end, a fittingly *sātvik* image of natural whiteness pairs with an equally philosophically redolent ubiquity, the *vyāpti* of logic, the principle of invariable concomitance that brings together the "I" and "you."

Rambilas Sharma names these thoughts as Vedantic; surely Nirālā's mind did dwell in Vedantic themes during these years in Calcutta at the Ramakrishna Mission. But as Sharma rightly points out, Nirālā expressed this sentiment in a unique manner, "braiding metaphorical objects of various emotions (*bhāv*) of *śṛṅgāra* and delight (*ullās*) into poetry." Indeed Sharma sees in this poem similarities also to Shelley's "Skylark" and contemporary Bangla poet Nazrul Islam's "Vidrohī" in the great abundance (*bharmār*) of metaphorical objects (*upamāna*).[23] This is an astute observation: the metaphorical objects dominate the poem with their sheer abundance, such that the metaphor itself no longer seems so suppositional. The objects—most of them direct or oblique allusions to commonly known metaphorical objects—demonstrate in their abundance a vast world *identified* with the always concomitant nature/spirit, female/male, *māyā/brahma*. As in other poems we have examined, the metaphorical object has come into its own, but here functions together in demonstration of a universal principle. Perhaps the new poetics of independent, aggregated, natural objects was particularly suited to the modernist theology of Vedanta.

Śṛṅgāra Distanced

As we saw above, Chāyāvād poets did not eschew the erotic per se, and in fact received some criticism for writing poetry sometimes thought more sexual than *rīti* poetry itself.[24] However, classical *śṛṅgāra*, of Braj and Sanskrit, still represented the unmodern past to be disdained or poignantly, regretfully reframed. As in the essays on "problem women" examined in Chapter 7, the *nāyikā* in Chāyāvād sometimes functioned metonymically for traditional poetry. In Nirālā's poems on the subject of poetry in his early years, we find some ambiguity toward *śṛṅgāra rasa*. One very light Braj Bhāṣā poem, "Satire on the *virahinī* (lady separated from her lover)" (1922), toes the party line, mocking the archetypal lamenting heroine, whose nose flows as much as do tears from her eyes. However, another early poem, entitled simply "Poetry" ("Kavitā") enigmatically suggests hope for the poetic world of the *nāyikā* and *śṛṅgāra*, even as the author clearly distances himself from it. In this scene, a woman sits on a rock in the wind and rain, her hair and sari erotically fluttering and sticking to her body. Then with the third stanza, Nirālā announces:

> *This* was poetry and its decoration
> just her *śṛṅgāra*,—
> if those strings of the sitar didn't sound,
> that was simply the failure of the poet,
> from whence arises the poet's pathetic call,—
> "I devised a means of description
> but the traditional usages failed!"

. . .
she was guileless, perfect,
sounds arose from her limbs
they reached the poet, and said—
"you go, she's called you, quick,
to the other side."[25]

The register of the language of the poetry augments the literary points made therein. The last two lines of the second stanza are comprised of long pseudo-Sanskrit compounds, including the hackneyed *alaṃkāra* of alliteration and pun (*yamaka*). "This was poetry and its decoration just her *śṛṅgāra*"—the term itself meaning both the erotic sentiment and the decoration of the body. Nirālā here paints a picture of a poet who is bound by traditional usages, a poet whose true purpose is to strike a chord of resonance, the sympathetic strings of the sitar. The poet is a pathetic figure, well-meaning, as is the *nāyikā* Poetry herself. Her perfect body emanates the sounds that call him, perhaps allure him, to an undefined "other side," *pār*, a term used in bhakti poetry for the goal of moksha. Like the "Evening, a Beautiful Woman," this *nāyikā* is a source of inspiration, but ambiguously so; her value, and that of poetry and its traditional usages, is in question.

This questioning, and ultimately public sphere rejection of Braj as a language of obscenity was to be most famously voiced by Pant in *Leaves*, of course, where he coined the phrase "the three foot world of the toe-to-head description," in which the poets' pens were as if "licking each limb of the *nāyikā*." But as we see from previous chapters and the poetry above, the linkage of Braj with limitation and lack of progressive gender politics had already been established. We can see in Nirālā, at least, serious poetic grappling with the import of rejecting *śṛṅgāra* for a modern love in a modern poetry.

The Aesthetics of a Colonial Circumstance: Nature/Nation/Love and Longing

Notwithstanding all of the talk of the poetics and theology of nature above, it is possible to discern a particular orientation toward anti-colonialism in Nirālā's early "nature poetry." One example might be "Anutāp" ("Burning," 1924), which describes in long Sanskrit compounds a fairy-land sort of space as described earlier, and then proclaims, "Today a deep darkness is spread over this forest of life." But this is not the relieving rainy season which has come; rather, a cloud of smoke: "Alas!

From the fire of repression (*daman-dāh*) that forest grove is withered!" While Krishna's swallowing of the forest fire might come to mind as well, the *daman-dāh* of some kind of punitive repression suggests a more political reading.

Fascinatingly, when Nirālā wrote on independence per se, as *svādhīnatā*, he wrote of the force of nature. Two poems, "On Independence" 1 and 2, were published within a week of each other in *Matavālā*, August 1924. We cannot help but think of the overlap of the language of empiricism and liberty, found in nature poetry discussion from the nineteenth century, as described in Chapter 3. Here nature appears as an argument from principle in poem 1, and makes explicit reference to oppression. He begins the poem with the question: Is the world independent (*svādhīn*) or dependent, subjugated (*parādhīn*)? He points to the Shastras, which say that leaves on a tree sprout and fall independently, free of desire. Here Nirālā then gives a Shastraic interpretation of free action as unmotivated action. Nirālā seems to see more in the falling leaves, however:

> Free independent! (*mukt svadhīn*!)
> In the rustling then who is crying?—
> If they are independent
> Then why do they keep sounding their song of sorrow?
> Nirālā's responds to this question by linking independence with the universe-pervading sound or word known as *śabd*.
> I only know just the independent word (*ek bas svādhīn śabd*)
> The wind flows,
> In the empty heart of the flower it takes an independent breath,
> The earth finds an independent motion . . .
> In the joyous-praise-of-the-dance-of-turning-and-change,—
> In each moment of the abundant rapturous world,—
> In the world's each particle great and small
> A vast happiness of independence buzzes.[26]

Here we are reminded of the buzzing sound of the divine presence of "Evening, a Beautiful Woman," with its ". . . only one imperceptible word, 'still, still, still' / buzzes everywhere—." Nirālā may also have meant that this "*svādhīn*" itself is a *śabd*, a word that resounds like the universal *śabd*—"this one word [of] independent (*ek bas svādhīn śabd*)." This *svādhīnatā* is also a sentiment, ambiguously both message and description. Ultimately, like maya, this *svādhīnatā* pervades and defines "the world's each particle great and small," a sort of spritual truth hidden within the world.

The second poem takes another angle, picking up where the last one left off, with the buzz (*gūñj*). Here Nirālā begins methodically identifying independent actions, which are also all natural actions: bees buzzing, rising and setting of the sun, etc. However:

My companions my thoughts—
My people—
My downtrodden—
Are silent—asleep—
Defeated even in their dreams!
What great weakness!

Nirālā counters again with nature's principles—unlike weak humans and the downtrodden, he asks: Who can stop the thunder? What kind of measure (*vyavasthā*) can be taken to hold back a storm? The poem then ends:

Fear alone is the father of measures,
The fearless to themselves
And the weak to society
Have something to prove—
Another meaning of this very
"independence" is "fearless."[27]

Here Nirālā's nature is nothing like the pastoral landscape familiar to us in poetry; principles of nature come with a fearsome quality. It is precisely this terrible aspect of nature—the earthquake, storm, and hail—that will inexorably prevail, he suggests. The *vyavasthā*—a term of public policy, of measures taken and statutes drawn up—is an ineffectual thing born of fear. Independence, he suggests, is something obtained as if by force of nature, and implicitly, deserved by all in principle. While these two poems are thematically at a distance from the others outlined in this chapter, still we can see the continuance of the Hindi literary connection of nature with the language of nationalism such as *svādhīn* and *svatantra*.

The "Cloud Songs" of 1924 are some of Nirālā's more famous verses, and in no little part because of their rather muscular exposition of a storm that has clear nationalist implications. As Heidi Pauwels has noted, through these poems Nirālā "forge[d] romanticism into a vehicle of nationalist expression,"[28] and more precisely, he forged the cloud, the main natural accoutrement of love scenes both classical and folk, into a vehicle of nationalist longing. The end of "Cloud Song 3" depicts the hope for a union under the clouds of the rainy season, as a martial India comes home from battle to regenerate:

Victory! Filling the world with new life,
Come down from your chariot, India!
In that forest is sitting the beloved distressed,
So many days worshipped have seemed worthless up to now,
The silent hut.
Today will be the reunion—
Yes, it will happen surely,
Today the cool shade of eternal joy will be the forest home
Today the unending exhausting separation *(pravās)* will be done,
Today the thirst on sad Rādhā's lips will disappear.[29]

Saṃyog, union, remains the ultimate aspiration. The scene of union with the beloved, contained within the forest scene, here joins with nationalist aspiration in a modern message to a cloud.

Concluding Remarks

> In the east, as the sun strikes up the wedding pipes of its rays,
> Sindoor glimmered on the flowers, redness spread to the west;
> The bride set off . . . in her tri-color blouse. . . .
>
> —lyrics from the film *Pūrab aur paścim*[1]

I began this work by articulating the several complicating and, as I have shown, determining cultural-historical factors for modern Hindi poetry, in the under-analyzed period of 1885–1925. Sociocultural linguistic matters dominated the very idea of Hindi, and these matters defined in turn the qualities of Hindi poetry. Modern Hindi poetry was at first launched as a counterpart of Urdu, as in the words of Pratāpanārāyaṇ Miśra, with aspirations to "say with pride to those arrogant people of Urdu poetry that our poetry is no less."[2] In matters of high poetry, Hindi was to imbibe the *rasa* of the bhakti tradition and its cosmopolitan renditions, but not emulate these overmuch and thereby fall into the trap of "courtly decadence" consisting of mere mannerism and erotica. Hindi poets also saw themselves as at a distance from the Indian version of modernity exemplified in the colonial center of Calcutta, socially and literarily. English literary values, delivered through educational texts and anthologies, impinged upon the style, content, and even linguistics, of Hindi poetic production. Such were the circumstances for Hindi, as a language being primed for large-scale nationalism.

Out of this context, within the space of fifty years, grew a body of modern Hindi poetry which, by the time of its consolidation in the anthologies of the early twenties, had settled upon a theme that was the sine qua non of literary modernity: the description of nature, ostensibly divorced from any schema of poetics, and presenting instead realistic landscapes, or depictions of natural objects and phenomenon with reference to their empirical observation, even though colored by poetic fancy.

The interest in identifying nature-in-poetry has come to define standard practice in Hindi literary criticism. Furthermore, mid-century Hindi literary critics assigned a narrative of English Romanticism to Hindi literary history, and thereby linked "modern nature" in Hindi poetry to scientific progress and social emancipation. This narrative holds serious problems for the understanding of why Hindi poetic nature, and its putative Romantic poets, the Chāyāvādīs, have peculiarities quite distinct from English poetic nature and its Romantics. It is crucial to recognize the panoply of significations poetic nature had for the Hindi poet from the nineteenth century, and that in addition to its predictable alliance with philosophical precepts, Indic and Western, and colonial inculcations of science, Hindi poetic nature was centrally linked to poetic love, often derived from the erotic mode of Sanskrit, and linked to the devotional idioms of both medieval pastoral and contemporary Bengali modernism. In other words, nature-in-poetry represented much more than the English Romantic "modern nature" that critics emphasize.

To assess the complexity of this situation, I first examined some evidence of the adoption of English poetry, through translation, into Braj Bhāṣā. These two translations were notably eighteenth-century works of Goldsmith and Pope, and were prominently situated in the new, self-conscious public sphere of Hindi publishing. In both original works, Goldsmith's *The Deserted Village* and Pope's *Essay on Criticism*, the social good is imbricated in the natural, whether a pastoral ideal as in Goldsmith, or a theoretical precept as in Pope. The translation of pastoral nostalgia and its political implications comes through almost more clearly in Hindi than the original. In the latter, we see the emergence of a vocabulary for poetic description, that of describing *yathārth*, that which is "commensurate" with reality, doing which sometimes overlaps with the political vocabulary of nationalism: *unnati* (progress) and—what would only later become a prevalent political term—*svatantratā* (independence). The English Nature inculcated in Hindi might thus be characterized as a proto-Romantic, classically-inclined one, and one that was read by its Hindi audience as having both political and epistemological underpinnings that encouraged empirical perception, on one hand, and liberalism on the other. In other words, English poetic influence in late nineteenth-century Hindi consisted of an empiricized poetics merged with the language of liberty, often dressed in the garb of Nature poetry. Nature in translation in these seminal works before 1900 exemplified not only an ontological truth, but an innovative way of seeing things both "in independent form" and "as a whole"; these rhetorics of Nature clearly held political valences for their Hindi translators.

Examining nature in literary criticism and poetry of the period 1900–1920, several themes come to light. Dvivedī continues the theme of *yathārth,* reality, via "nature description," in contradistinction to "blind tradition" epitomized for him in *śṛṅgārik* poetry descriptive of women. The realistic description of nature represents the expressive freedom of the poet. Poetic nature description represents a corollary of political revolution: as a man oppressed, the "traditional poet" is shackled by convention. However, *śṛṅgāra* persists as a mode of comprehension of the natural world, and it in fact infuses the national sentiments of the poetry. This fact is embodied most readily by Pāṭhak's Braj Bhāṣā "Beauty of Kashmir," which despite its relative metrical freedom, uses highly conventional classical idioms and ornament to lionize Kashmir as the prize of the subcontinent and its nature as a classical heroine. The shift from the particular pastoral world of Braj to modern nature-poetry was felt keenly by Hariaudh, as his own commentary and oeuvre attest. A crucial moment in the poetics of nature and nationalism comes with Hariaudh's *The Absence of the Beloved* in 1914, in which Sanskritic metaphorical objects become freed from their normative bodily referents in *śṛṅgāra* and becomes things in themselves, objects in nature that still remind Rādhā of her beloved, but also have logical force in Hariaudh's argument for a bhakti-like dedication to the social polity.

As the second decade progresses, certain authors write of nature as a truly political landscape, often with clear Sanskritic allusions, especially Dvivedī and Tripāṭhī. These use the multivalent poetics of a Sanskritic cum empiricist "nature description" that leads the audience to nationalist sentiment. In the meantime, several young poets write of the Sanskritic erotic arcadia as a place of refuge from social restriction, but often with reference to ascetic figures and with a microcosmic eye for the single flower, or other object of the landscape. In sum, the transformations of "nature-in-poetry" in Hindi of the early twentieth century demonstrate the critical necessity of the Braj Bhāṣā poetic tradition and/or *śṛṅgāra* for the "modern" poetic nature-description, demonstrative of modernity and liberal politics.

While *śṛṅgāra* deeply colored the poetic traditions out of which Hindi poets wrote, it always presented a problem for the colonial poet. Obscenity and age-of-consent debates, the women's question, the expansion of female education, and generally political discourse on women as citizen-subjects, all functioned to politicize poetry about women. The very medium of Braj Bhāṣā was linked inextricably to the genre of the taxonomy of women [*nāyikā-bhed*], and the description of body parts, the *nakha-śikha*, and thence exemplified for many a backwardness or moral dissolution in regard to women. The shift away from Braj Bhāṣā to Kharī Bolī Hindi, already a desideratum on generic grounds that modern poetry should not be in a specialized dialect, here took on a further dimension. Evidence suggests that Braj Bhāṣā lost favor as a poetic medium just as much because of its association with obscenity, as because of a linguistic modernization argument. Hindi poets, who obviously implemented the world of signs of Sanskritic *śṛṅgāra* (those of Persian landscapes were often abjured, after all), dealt with its new obscenity creatively. To this effect, they created descriptions of women in a manner allusive to but distanced from the bodily and carnal descriptions of previous eras. This was effected by transferring reality to the metaphorical objects, rather than the bodily subjects, of classical poetry. The Dvivedī-era impetus to prosaic "natural description" of women necessarily had to proceed with contemporary propriety, and thus women-in-poetry became the naturalistic yet still-idealized and well-covered figures of Raja Ravi Varmā paintings. As canon consolidated, apologies for *śṛṅgāra* emerged, which provided a solution of sorts for the obscenity of *śṛṅgāra* with the integration of erotics with the rhetorics of biological "nature-study" and a conjugal nationalism of auspicious and socially beneficial union. Aesthetically, the tone of critical resuscitations of *śṛṅgāra* and that of English nature writing merged somewhat. All of these factors of obscenity and realism converged to create a poetic situation where the characters and the affect of *śṛṅgāra* morphed into poetry about natural objects, while women-in-poetry became typed in categories of political identity. Here we can consider "the nation as a field for the play of erotic desire," in Sumathi Ramaswamy's words on Tamil language nationalism, but in place of the triangle of desire she formulates, between nation, man, and woman, here the idea of national character provides the "regime for regulating pleasure," through tropes of nature.[3] A reformation of national character in poetry meant presenting an only vaguely erotic literary nature, allusive to both disavowed erotic poetics and a spiritualized realism. The erotics of embodied male and female, be they gods or humans, seeps through natural images obliquely, or is refigured, as it was most baldly in Hariaudh's *Priyapravās*, as a chaste sexuality of usefulness to the social polity.

As the younger generation of Chāyāvād poets began to publish widely and become the new poetic vanguard, critic Rāmacandra Śukla, allied with the older generation, began to achieve substantial influence, and in this capacity his early essay "Natural scenes in poetry" of 1923 gave a critical reiteration of what nature in Hindi poetry had become, and importantly, what it promised for the future. In a familiar rhetorical style inherited from the Hindi authors of the previous twenty years,

Śukla enumerated the landscape in such a way to evoke the compendium-like nature of Sanskrit texts, and discursive nature-description of objects beyond the scope of the Sanskrit poetic stock. Here the *upamānas* (objects of comparison) and realistic botany become congruent, and both comprise the "natural scene," a literary mode linked for him inextricably with swadesh. As we have already seen in the poetry of the decade preceding Śukla's essay, literary objects, once used for comparisons in service of another description, here become the subject themselves, and further, here aggregate as a scene. Seemingly parallel to an idea of representational politics, Śukla voices a narrative of liberation for poetic objects that exalts the specificity of India, and defines the true Indian poet, one who aligns himself with the natural objects of India, both poetic and realist. Although these sentiments clearly echo those of the English Romantics, the logic of this argument, and the style of its enunciation palpably derives from the poetic world of Sanskritic metaphor.

All of these events and evolutions defined the ground from which Chāyāvād grew. In many ways Chāyāvād poetry enunciated the poetic ideals of its forebears, albeit in a more radical and more recognizably "modern" style. *Śṛṅgāra* remains infused, but also substantially philosophized. This is achieved through its "naturalization" a step beyond those of the previous poets: the objects of metaphor become actors in the drama, the hero and heroine, themselves, such that a poem is ultimately "about nature." The terms of engagement had changed: nature is the referential object that is thought to be "personified" in a *śṛṅgārik* mode, with the "imagination" of the poet. English poetic terms thus express the result of previous decades of thinking and writing on poetic nature. The Chāyāvādīs broke formal conventions more substantially than any previous generation, but still wrote out of a comprehensible world of Sanskritic poetics, playing with or speaking against ornaments, more than embodying a new slate of tropes. The revolutionary aspect of the generation is indisputable, but their innovations had an organic history within Hindi poetics. Nature here was not simply reinvented along Romantic lines, but rather repositioned in-between the affective world of *śṛṅgāra* and the world of *yathārth*, the real, which is composed of the material things of old metaphor and present materialist politics.

In conclusion, I would submit that the Chāyāvād poets, contrary to their exaltation in literary criticism, actually accomplished their poetic revolution in concert with the concerns and poetic practices of the Dvivedī era generation, at least in terms of their self-conscious use of "tradition" for "modern" poetic purposes. Natural subjects in poetry—that is, natural objects as subjects of poetry—could not only be swadeshi, as Śukla advocated, but could shelter the—now only furtively beloved—poetics of *śṛṅgāra*. Nature-in-poetry was read from the late nineteenth century with an English-inflected epistemology with political dimensions. A poetics of nature, both *śṛṅgārik* and social, would ultimately point to "the real," the domain of progress, science, and the subjects of colonial India.

Does the poetic world of 1885–1925 have any relevance to later poetry or cultural formations? I would argue that it most certainly does. The way in which poetics incorporated a scientific and political nature affected later media images profoundly. Poetry turned to progressive political subjects and experimental forms; in film media the images of a Sanskritic erotic arcadia abound, often mixed with that of the Persian garden. Particular associations of women with state, of specifically *śṛṅgārik* images with natural beauty, make sense most through the lens of the early twentieth-century Hindi episteme. When a landscape is filmed, with the obligatory swelling violins in the background, with numerous microcosmic shots interspersed of natural objects in isolation, or of villagers in the field, it is not merely pastoral but an expression of a poetics that exalts not only these particular images, but also their successive presentation, as if one of the poetic descriptions of a season of Sanskrit, or a prose "garland" of Śukla, both alluding ultimately to love. The convergence of a poetics of nature with modern, national love, has created something we might call a natural state of *śṛṅgāra* in the Indian media, epitomized by things like the lyrics of a film song written about India's freedom itself as if a bride, set in the late 1960s, in the context of a growing transnational diaspora.

> In the east, as the sun strikes up the wedding pipes of its rays,
> Sindoor glimmered on the flowers, redness spread to the west;
> The bride set off . . . in her tri-color blouse. . . .
> She'll become more beautiful, more adorned
> She's growing up and glowing more
> Our freedom-bride has passed twenty
> The bride set off . . . in her tri-color blouse
> Love of country is the bride's groom
> The sindoor of married auspiciousness of this beautiful bride is immortal
> . . .
> The bride set off . . . in her tri-color blouse[4]

This bride of freedom, wearing the colors of the Indian flag, emerging from within a macrocosmic marriage party of dawn, is not too different from Pāṭhak's nature of Kashmir as a sporting heroine, or Hariaudh's new *nāyikā*, thrilling at nature on her springtime swing. Here the nation—represented visually with a female dancer before India's map icon, and images of temples, mosques, dams, and mustard fields—encompasses nature, and sets forth an image of the modern state as auspiciously heterosexual, with the marriage of free India with patriotism for it. The vexed association of nature, *śṛṅgāra*, and the social/political world in the enactment of modernity in Hindi literature between 1885 and 1925, while linked with English poetical values, opened up a later world of signs for speaking of a distinctly Indian nation and a distinctly Indian love. The flowers that were once Kāma's arrows, the poetics of the past and its pleasures, transformed into flowers of the empirical world and experience, which in turn have aestheticized the social and political concerns of modern India since.

Notes

Foreword

1. Quoted from *Vāmana Purāṇa* 6.94–107 in Wendy Doniger, *Śiva: the Erotic Ascetic* (New York: Oxford University Press, 1981), 159.

2. This has been explored in depth, and in reference to narrative, by Sudhir Kakar in his *Intimate Relations: Exploring Indian Sexuality* (Chicago: University of Chicago Press, 1989). Here it is important to note that there is an inherent problem in using the term "erotic" in reference to *śṛṅgāra*, and the broader category of *kāma*, which is a problem deriving from the connotations and structural relations of this term in English. The problem is complicated by the various categories of texts that would fall under this "erotic" rubric. For instance, Kenneth Zysk has recently emphasized the marriage-centered and socially practical aspects of texts on *rati*, love-making, distinguishing this concept from a classical erotics per se in the category of *kāma*, and the literary erotics of *śṛṅgāra* (Preface, *Conjugal Love in India:* Ratiśāstra *and* Ratiramaṇa (Sir Henry Wellcome Asian Series, vol. 1; Leiden: Brill, 2002; ix.) As of the late nineteenth century, however, the distinctly negative category of "the erotic," in the English sense, had begun to hold sway among the literati and other elites in regard to all of these terms.

3. As a columnist remarked recently on Indian prudery, in Hindi films babies are born from "nodding flowers" (See Mousumi Sengupta, "Nekkid? What's That?" (*Hindustan Times*, May 20, 2007. See http://www.hindustantimes.com, Accessed Jan. 4, 2008.

4. Now the West is often the target of obscenity debates, e.g., the annual protests by right-wing Hindu groups against the celebration of St. Valentine's Day. See, most recently, Duncan Bartlett, "Valentine's Day wins Indian hearts" in *BBC News*, Feb. 14, 2007 (http://news.bbc.co.uk/2/hi/business/6358531.stm).

5. On South Asian love and Williams's structures of feeling, see Francesca Orsini, Introduction to *Love in South Asia: A Cultural History*, ed. F. Orsini (University of Cambridge Oriental Publications; Cambridge: Cambridge University Press, 2006), 1–42.

6. Jacques Lacan, *Le Séminaire VII: L'Ethique de la psychanalyse (1959–60,)* ed. Jacques-Alain Miller (Paris: Seuil 1986), 178.

7. *Reconfiguring Modernity: Concepts of Nature in Japanese Political Ideology*, Twentieth Century Japan: The Emergence of a World Power Series (Berkeley: University of California Press, 2001).

8. *The Lure of the Modern: Writing Modernism in Semicolonial China, 1917–1937* (Berkeley: University of California Press, 2001), 57.

9. Ibid., 196, 206.

10. Ibid., 53.

11. In the colorful words of prominent essayist Pratāpanārāyaṇ Miśra on this term, in 1893,

> These days wherever you go you hear this very word. In newspapers is this great to-do about progress (*unnati kī dhūm*), in speeches this to-do about progress, in the societies this to-do about progress. Besides the innocent babes and the elderly who are counting the seconds until their death, whomever you see has this obsession, that the state of the country is being ruined day by day, and because of this there ought to be social progress, ought to be political progress, ought to be religious progress, ought to be intellectual progress, ought to be economic progress, ought to be progress in power.

From "Unnati kī dhūm" ("The Great To-do about Progress") (*Brāhmaṇ* 8:6 [Jan. 1893]; reprinted in *Pratāpanārāyaṇ-granthāvalī* [*The Collected Works of Pratāpanārāyaṇ*], V. Mall, ed.; Varanasi: NPS, 1992; 334–37), 334.

12. (London: Penguin Books, 2005), 56.

13. Michel Foucault, *The History of Sexuality*, vol. 1. *An Introduction*, R. Hurley, trans., 1978 (New York: Vintage Books, 1990), 24, 18, 35.

14. Jayaśaṅkar Prasād, "Prastāvanā" ("Foreword"), (*Indu* [*The Moon*] 1:1 [1909], reprinted in *Prasād granthāvalī* [*The Collected Works of Prasād*] [6 vols. (New Delhi: Bhāratīya Granth Niketan, 1997 6: 144–45], 144).

15. Thomas B. Macaulay, "Minute on Indian Education," Feb. 1835.

Note on Translations

1. Michael Riffaterre, "Transposing Presuppositions on the Semiotics of Literary Translation" (*Texte: Revue de Critique et de Théorie Littéraire* 4 [1985], 99–110, excerpted in Rainier Schulte and J. Biguenet, eds., *Theories of Translation: An Anthology of Essays from Dryden to Derrida* [Chicago: University of Chicago Press, 1992, 204–17]), 205.

Chapter 1

1. For a full treatment of Hindi literary and linguistic history up to this period, I direct the reader to R. S. McGregor's works, which do much fuller justice to these topics than I can accomplish in this space. *Hindi Literature from*

its Beginnings to the Nineteenth Century. A History of Indian Literature, vol. 8, fasc. 6; ed. J. Gonda (Wiesbaden: Otto Harrassowitz, 1984); *Hindi Literature of the Nineteenth and Early Twentieth Centuries.* A History of Indian Literature, vol. VIII, fasc. 2; ed. J. Gonda (Wiesbaden: Otto Harrassowitz, 1974). For the nineteenth century preceding 1885 especially, see Vasudha Dalmia, *The Nationalization of Hindu Traditions: Bharatendu Harischandra and Nineteenth-century Banaras* (Delhi: Oxford University Press, 1997) and Sagaree Sengupta, "The Nineteenth-century Brajbhāṣā Poetry of 'Bhāratendu' Hariścandra: To the Limits of Tradition and Beyond" (Dissertation, University of Pennsylvania, 1992).

2. New York: Columbia University Press, 1989.

3. For example, from after the turn of the century, we find several books published as helps to students in English classes, most as keys to textbooks such as the *Royal Reader* or Macmillan *Reader*, but many as keys to particular anthologies of English poetry. Taking the year 1904 of the *Statement* of registered books in the United Provinces as an example, we find three guides for Cookson's *Poetry for Schools* (London: Macmillan, 1899) and four for J. G. Jennings' *English Poems* (London: Macmillan, 1903), among several other keys for readers. (See *Statement of Particulars regarding Books and Periodicals published in the United Provinces* [United Provinces of Agra and Oudh (India); Allahabad; 1904–1907], especially 1904, part 3, p. 3.) Both Cookson and Jennings were educationists of the empire: Cookson compiled his volume for his school in Cairo, and Jennings was a professor at Muir College, Allahabad.

4. For instance, the *Calendars* and other curricula publications of the various educational institutions. The English literature curricula indicated in the Allahabad University Calendars, from entrance to MA exams, between 1889–1908 regularly included anthologies such as: the *Senior Reader* (n.a.; London: T. Nelson, 1862), F. J. Rowe and W. T. Webb's *Selections from Tennyson* (London: Macmillan, 1888) (both editors were of Presidency College, Calcutta); T. H. Ward's *English Poets* (Macmillan, 1880); and again, Cookson and Houghton's *Poetry*. Of the independent works assigned for these English curricula were (among many more) Addison, Arnold, the Brownings, Byron, Chaucer, Dickens, Eliot, Goldsmith, Gray, Irving, Keats, Longfellow, Milton, Cardinal Newman, Ruskin, Scott, Shakespeare, Shelley, Tennyson, Thackeray, and Wordsworth, and included history (Macaulay) and philosophy (Locke, Bacon, Mill) as well. (Data culled from publications of *Calendar for the Year* [Allahabad: Allahabad University, 1889–1908].)

5. Priya Joshi, *In Another Country: Colonialism, Culture, and the English Novel in India* (New York: Columbia, 2002).

6. *Nets of Awareness: Urdu Poetry and Its Critics* (Berkeley: University of California Press, 1994).

7. Cited in Sudhir Chandra, *The Oppressive Present: Literature and Social Consciousness in Colonial India* (Delhi: Oxford University Press, 1994), 18.

8. To use Urdu poet Āzād's—and Pritchett's—phrase.

9. See Chapter 7 of Sisir Kumar Das, *A History of Indian Literature*, vol. 8, *1800–1910* (New Delhi: Sahitya Akademi, 1991); the individual literary histories of Bengali and Marathi published by the Sahitya Akademi, and Pritchett, *Nets*.

10. Sushil Kumar De, *Sanskrit Poetics as a Study of Aesthetic* (Berkeley: University of California Press, 1963); Gerow, *Indian Poetics* (Wiesbaden: Harrassowitz, 1977); and a canonical Hindi exposition, Nagendra, *Rasa-siddhānt* (*The Principle of Rasa*) (Delhi: National Publishing House, 1964).

11. Gerow, *Poetics*, 247–48.

12. Gerow, "Indian Poetics" (idem, *The New Princeton Encyclopedia of Poetry and Poetics* [New York: MJF Books, 1993]), 584.

13. As every summary of Sanskrit poetics details, these are *śṛṅgāra* (erotic), *karuṇa* (pitiful), *vīra* (heroic), *hāsya* (comedic), *raudra* (angry), *bhayānak* (terrible), *bibhatsa* (disgusting), *adbhuta* (amazing). Some renditions include also śā*nta* and *vātsalya rasas*, the peaceful sentiment and that of parental love, respectively.

14. For instance, the common instance in *śṛṅgāra* of *karuṇa*, the pitiful sentiment, and *vīra*, the heroic sentiment.

15. Gerow, "Indian Poetics," 584.

16. Martha Ann Selby, *Grow Long Blessed Night: Love Poems from Classical India* (New York: Oxford University Press, 2000), 43.

17. Gerow, *Poetics*, 257.

18. In the words of Kṛṣṇalāl Śarmā, "One might suppose that the full influence of *dhvani* would have fallen upon Hindi . . . But the opposite has occurred. In Hindi this tradition has come down in a very corrupt and diminished form, and until the full development of Khari Boli, has remained in this state." Part Two of this latter-day study analyzes Chāyāvād and later poetry in terms of *dhvani*. (*Ādhunik Hindī kavitā meṁ dhvani* [Dhvani *in Modern Hindi Poetry*]; Kanpur: Grantham, 1964], 75.) The reappearance of *dhvani* in the late twenties seems to have roughly coincided with Rāmacandra Śukla's *Rasa-mīmāṁsa* from circa 1930, which broached this subject. See below and Chapter 8 for information on Śukla.

19. Gerow, *Poetics*, 284–85.

20. A complete account of the theological schools of Krishna-centered Vaishnavism is found in Entwistle, *Braj: centre of Krishna pilgrimage* (Groningen: Egbert Forsten, 1987).

21. McGregor, *Beginnings*, 125.

22. Entwistle, *Braj*, 11.

23. Here I am thinking primarily of the Vallabha sect, whose rituals are described and illustrated in detail in Amit Ambalal's *Krishna as Shrinathji: Rajasthani Paintings from Nathdvara* (Ahmedabad: Mapin, 1987).

24. *Rīti* was a term in Sanskrit poetics for "style," and was particularly concerned with *alaṃkāra*; the term was reconceived as dialectically opposed to the category of bhakti by 1929, when foundational critic Rāmacandra Śukla used these categories in his *Hindī sāhitya kā itihās* (*The History of Hindi Literature*) (1929, 1942). The courtly poetry to which Śukla referred with this appellation was indeed often replete with *alaṃkāra*s in the Sanskrit style. Today *rīti* poetry functionally refers to "courtly poetry" in Braj Bhāṣā, and connotes its artificiality or moral decadence. More discussion of the literary eras defined by Śukla follows below.

25. See Alan W. Entwistle, "The Cult of Krishna-Gopal as a Version of Pastoral" in *Devotion Divine: Bhakti Traditions from the Regions of India*; edited by D. L. Eck and F. Mallison; Groningen Oriental Series VIII (Groningen: Egbert Forsten, 1991; 73–90).

26. This could be said of the other major literary dialect of Avadhī as well, associated with Ram devotion and Sufi allegorical love narratives, although it remained much less relevant to the tradition of high Hindi poetry in the nineteenth century than was Braj. Major English works on the Avadhī genres are Philip Lutgendorf, *The Life of a Text: Performing the Rāmcaritmānas of Tulsidas* (Berkeley: University of California Press, 1991); Aditya Behl and Simon Weightman, Introduction to Mañjhan, *Madhumalati: An Indian Sufi Romance* (New York: Oxford University Press, 2000); Thomas de Bruijn, "The Ruby Hidden in the Dust: A Study of the Poetics of Malik Muhammad Jayasi's *Padmavat*" (Dissertation, University of Leiden, 1996).

27. The following chapters describe this slow process. Here again we can also note, in regard to Avadhī, by 1926 Avadhī is virtually a non-entity for modern Hindi poets, as Sumitrānandan Pant enfolded Avadhī into the category of Braj Bhāṣā in his castigation of the poetics of the latter in his introduction to *Pallav* (*New Leaves*) published that year (9th ed., New Delhi: Rājakamal Prakāśan, 1993, 15–50), 16.

28. Sūr Dās, *Maiyā morī maiṁ nahiṁ mākhana khāyo: Sūradās ke cune hue padoṁ meṁ se cune hue atyant lokapriya amar pad* (*O Mother of Mine, I Didn't Eat the Butter: A Selection of the Most Beloved Immortal Verses from Selected Verses of Sūr Dās*). Edited by "Kṛṣṇa Prem." (Haridwar: Raṇadhīr Book Sales, 1995), 7. My translation follows Snell's translation of a variant of this verse, but I depart somewhat from it here and there, according to my text and my taste (Rupert Snell, *The Hindi Classical Tradition: A Braj Bhāṣā Reader* [SOAS South Asian Texts 2. New Delhi: Heritage Publishers, 1992], 101).

29. As Kenneth Bryant has demonstrated for other poems in his *Poems to the Child-God: Structures and Strategies in the Poetry of Surdas* (Berkeley: University of California Press, 1978).

30. Or "watery-eyed," according to one commentator, Sūratimiśra, in *Jorāvar Prakāś: Ācārya Keśavadāsakṛta Rasikapriyākī ṭīkā* (1743; edited by Y. Siṁh; Sammelan ākār granthamālā 10; Allahabad: Hindi Sāhitya Sammelan, 1992), 259.

31. Keśav Dās, *Rasikapriyā* (*Beloved of the Connoisseur*) (1591). Reprinted in *Keśav-granthāvalī* [*Collected Works of Keśav*] vol. 1. Edited by V. P. Miśra, 1954; reprint (Allahabad: Hindustānī Academy, 1990, 1–93), 11.4.

32. Translation of D. J. Matthews and C. Shackle, *Classical Urdu Love Lyrics: Text and Translations* (London: Oxford University Press, 1972), 3.1.

33. It should be noted though that the oral nature of poetry has ensured Urdu's continuing poetic popularity, which thrives among those who understand but cannot read Urdu in the present day.

34. Ulrike Stark has also noted this practice of providing Urdu glosses of "difficult" Sanskritic words in Hindi/Nagari versions of Urdu-script texts, and the persistence of Urdu-script texts of Hindu devotional works into the 1880s, in

An Empire of Books: The Naval Kishore Press and the Diffusion of the Printed Word in Colonial India (Ranikhet: Permanent Black, 2007), 439–41, 438.

35. See my brief discussion of this text in "Networks, Patrons, and Genres, for Late Braj Bhāṣā Poets" in *Hindi and Urdu Before the Divide*, ed., F. Orsini (Delhi: Orient Longman, 2009). The visual outline of *śṛṅgāra* given in the work was later reproduced in the first curriculum of Hindi, compiled for Calcutta University in 1924. See Lālā Sītārām, comp., *Ars Poetica, Selections from Hindi Literature*, Book V (Calcutta: University of Calcutta, 1924).

36. Stark, 443–44.

37. Here I refer to Hariścandra's essay "Hindi kavitā" ("Hindi Poetry") of 1872, described in Dalmia, *Nationalization*, 274–78, and the several anthologies dating between 1878–96, outlined in Stark, 425–28.

38. Pratāpanārāyaṇ Miśra, in what appears to be an advance review of *Khaṛī Bolī kā padya* (addressed below) in his magazine *Brāhmaṇ* (4:7–8 [15 Feb. and March, 1888]; reprinted in *Collected Works* (117–18), 117. For Miśra's biography and outline of his political views, see Chandra, 39–43.

39. See Christopher R. King, *One Language, Two Scripts: The Hindi Movement in Nineteenth Century North India* (Bombay: Oxford University Press, 1994) and Paul R. Brass, *Language, religion and politics in North India* (London: Cambridge University Press, 1974).

40. On the movement for Hindi as a language of education, see Vasudha Dalmia, *Nationalization*, 212 ff.; for the alignment of Hindi and Hindus, see ibid., Chapter 4, and King, *One Language*.

41. King, *One Language*, 77.

42. In this they had picked up the movement started by Bālakṛṣṇa Bhaṭṭ, whose Hindī Vardhinī Sabhā (Society for the Increase of Hindi) began in 1877, and by Hariścandra, who argued for Hindi's institutionalization in his statements before W. W. Hunter's Education Commission in 1882, in an unsuccessful bid that nevertheless inspired several public associations to support Hindi. See Dalmia, *Nationalization*, and King, *One Language*.

43. King, *One Language*, 147.

44. Francesca Orsini, *The Hindi Public Sphere, 1920–1940: Language and Literature in the Age of Nationalism* (New Delhi: Oxford University Press, 2002), 137.

45. See Orsini, *Hindi Public Sphere*, and Karine Schomer, *Mahadevi Varma and the Chhayavad Era of Modern Hindi Poetry* (Berkeley: University of California Press, 1983), for extended treatment of the significance of the HSS.

46. Orsini, *Hindi Public Sphere*, 135.

47. It is important, however, to remember the complexity of this moment for the authors themselves. Pamela Lothspeich addresses this, and also how Hindu literary themes supported the linguistic aims of the Hindi movement, in "The Khari Boli Campaign and a Renaissance of Hindu Myth," Chapter 5 of *Epic Nation: Reimagining the Mahabharata in the Age of the Empire* (New Delhi: Oxford University Press, 2009; 96–105).

48. I refer the reader to Dalmia, *Nationalization*, Chapter 4; King, *One Language*, Glossary; Colin Masica, *The Indo-Aryan Languages* (1991; Cambridge

Language Surveys; Cambridge: Cambridge University Press, 1993), 27–30; McGregor, *Beginnings* and *Nineteenth;* and Francesca Orsini, ed., *Hindi and Urdu Before the Divide* (Delhi: Orient Longman, 2009). The interpretations of Amrit Rai in *A House Divided* (Delhi: Oxford University Press, 1984) and Alok Rai, *Hindi Nationalism* (Delhi: Orient Longman, 2001) are also important contributions.

49. In my comments here I draw somewhat upon my article, "Networks," op. cit.

50. Masica, 27.

51. Both terms denoting the "language of the region of the river Sind and beyond," a Persian term used by early Muslims in the subcontinent, and found in the writings of Amīr Khusraw (13th–14th c.) in reference to the speech of Delhi.

52. Scholars have written much on the colonial hand in defining the various terms of Hindi and Urdu, originating with the projects of John Gilchrist (1759–1842) at Fort William College in the early nineteenth century (see Dalmia, *Nationalization*, 161 ff., S. K. Das, *Sāhibs and Munshis: An Account of the College of Fort William* (New Delhi: Orion Publications, 1978). This is not to mention the work of Rev. S. H. Kellogg, Sir George Abraham Grierson, and Pincott (which latter is discussed below). Among Hindi-language formulations, Hariścandra's list of twelve types of Hindi is most famous (see Dalmia, *Nationalization*, 215); Hariaudh [Ayodhyāsiṁh Upādhyāy] wrote another précis of the types of Hindi in his volume *Bolacāl* (*The Way of Speech*) (Bankipore: Khaḍgavilās Press, 1927; reprint, Varanasi: Hindī-Sāhitya-Kuṭīr, n.d.).

53. See Orsini, *Hindi Public Sphere*, 3.

54. The questions of dating, and of the perceived distinctions between "Urdu" and other terms for the various (or identical) registers of language, are extremely vexed. See Shamsur Rahman Faruqi, "History, Faith, Politics: Origin Myths of Urdu and Hindi" for a recent account of the known history of the term "Urdu" and its relation to the designations "Hindavī," "Dehlavī," "Hindustani," and "Rekhtah" (Ch. 1 of *Early Urdu Literary Culture and History*; New Delhi: Oxford, 2001; 21–42).

55. As Orsini has noted, the result was that supporters of a more "pure" Hindi cemented ties with politicians sharing a belief in Hindi as a conservative cultural symbol, despite Gandhi's concurrent support for a Hindustani that was a bipartisan spoken register of Hindi/Urdu. For detailed accounts, see Orsini, *Hindi Public Sphere*, 357–65, and David Lelyveld, "The Fate of Hindustani: Colonial Knowledge and the Project of a National Language" in C. A. Breckenridge and P. van der Veer, eds., *Orientalism and Postcolonial Predicament* (Philadelphia: University of Pennsylvania Press, 1993).

56. This is not to ignore the presence of Muslim authors in Hindi, although there were relatively few.

57. Frederic Pincott (1836–96) was a well-known scholar of Indian languages in England. He supported the inclusion of Hindi for the civil service exam in England, and the movement for Hindi as a government language generally. He edited several literary texts, wrote a grammar (*The Hindi Manual* [London: W. H. Allen, 1882]) and educational texts such as the *Bāladīpak: A New Series of Hindi*

Readers for the Use of Schools and Pāṭhaśālās (Bankipore: Khaḍgavilās Press, 1886). He was a regular contributor to *The Indian Magazine*, published in London. He was a friend of several famous Hindi litterateurs, and wrote in Sanskritized Hindi himself.

58. Miśrabandhu [The Miśra Brothers, Śyāmabihārī, Śukadevabihārī, and Gaṇeṣabihārī Miśra], *Miśrabandhu vinod* (vol. 3–4; 1913, 1933; new revised and enlarged ed., Hyderabad: Gaṅgā-Granthāgār, 1972), 152. (Rāmacandra Śukla, *Hindī sāhitya kā itihāsa* [*The History of Hindi literature*] [1929, Varanasi: NPS; revised and enlarged 1942, 1991; 32nd ed., Nāgarīpracāriṇī granthamālā 53; Varanasi: NPS, 1997], 324).

59. In the recollection of Rāmacandra Śukla:

> He approached [a pandit] and said, "people say that good poetry cannot be written in Khaṛī Bolī. Do you agree? If not, then assist me." This pandit then wrote some verse and gave it to him, which he then attached in the notebook. In this way, those he met who agreed with the party of Khaṛī Bolī were entered into the notebook. Soon it became a large folder which he would tuck under his arm and take to wherever there was a meeting connected to Hindi. If he didn't get a chance to speak he would leave angrily.

(Śukla, *History*, 325).

60. I.e., what he terms "the Persianized form of Hindi," which became a language of practical and secular literature in its "extraordinary development" as the official language of the English government. Pincott presented a particular point of view here, likely influenced by his Indian friends and associates.

61. Frederic Pincott, "Preface by the editor," in Ayodhyā Prasād Khatrī, comp., *Khaṛī Bolī ka padya: Poetical Reader of Khaṛī Bolī* (London: W. H. Allen, 1889), 4–5.

62. Which interestingly, includes a long excerpt from the Urdu poet Alṭāf Ḥusain Ḥālī's recent "Munājāt-e-bevā," except of course in Nagari, and titled "Beve [sic] kī munājāt." As a "Petition of a Widow," this work in "Urdu" (or "Munshi-style Khaṛī Bolī," as Pincott says) is in the voice of a child-widowed female, hence her speech is not Persianized overmuch.

63. Pincott, v–vi.

64. Ibid., vi–vii.

65. Ibid., i.

66. Ibid., vii–viii.

67. Līke līka gāṛī cale līke cale kapūta / binā līka tīnoṁ caleṁ śāyara śūra sapūta. Khatrī, 45.

68. The passage is worth quoting at length for its full force:

> If you can get the taste of the juice (*ras*) from sucking on bamboo, then why did God make sugarcane? . . . without filling it with too many Urdu words, we can enjoy a pleasure (*mazā*) like that of Urdu, and we can say with pride to those arrogant people of Urdu poetry (*uradū* [sic] *kavitābhimāniyoṁ se*) that our poetry is no less. Although

> Urdu is not bad for [Hindi] poetry, it gives the pleasure of the flirtations (*hāvabhāv*) of the prostitute (*bāralalanā*) to the connoisseurs of poetics. . . .
>
> A lot of people say that not everyone can understand Braj Bhāṣā. . . . If the project is only to explain to everyone then go right ahead and write prose . . . those who know poetry will never say it's good to put a rock in the path of the moving cart. Braj Bhāṣā is also the true sister of Nagari Devī; to give over its own birthright [*svatva*] to another sister is to slit the throat of gentlemanliness (*sahṛdayatā*). . . . What has befallen the poets that in order to explain [themselves] to someone they have messed up their own dialect (*bolī*)? (P. Miśra, review of *Khaṛī Bolī kā padya*, op. cit.)

69. Orsini, *Hindi Public Sphere,* 4.

70. Interestingly, the Sanskritization of Bengali in the nineteenth century drew little note or criticism, and if it was referenced in discussion of Hindi, only as a positive model, and reason to Sanskritize Hindi as well.

71. *Fractured Modernity: Making of a Middle Class in Colonial North India* (New Delhi: Oxford University Press, 2001).

72. Indeed, it would be fascinating to examine the many Hindi translations of Gray's "Elegy Written in a Country Churchyard" with John Guillory's dense reading of its significance in the English canon (Chapter 2 of *Cultural Capital: The Problem of Literary Canon Formation* [Chicago: University of Chicago Press, 1993]). And here it would be important to note that the vernacular "middle class" for Hindi was not quite the bourgeoisie of Habermas, as practically realized in Calcutta, but a more "subordinate elite" that used the ideology of "the people" in their self representation. See Orsini, *Hindi Public Sphere,* 14.

73. A few of these many "modernities" publications include: *Multiple Modernities* (*Daedelus: Journal of the American Academy of Arts and Sciences,* 129:1 [Winter 2000]); *Alter/native Modernities* (vol. 1 of the Millenial Quartet, a *Public Culture* miniseries, 11:1 [2000]); and *Divergent Modernities: Critical Perspectives on Orientalism, Islamism, and Nationalism* (Comparative Studies of South Asia, Africa, and the Middle East; special issue 16:1 [1996]). "Colonial modernity" has been taken up primarily by Southeast and East Asia specialists, as well as some scholars of British India, e.g., Tani Barlow, *Colonial Modernity* (Durham: Duke University Press, 1993); Antoinette Burton, ed., *Gender, Sexuality and Colonial Modernities* (London: Routledge, 1999); Dipesh Chakrabarty, "The Difference-Differential of a Colonial Modernity: Public Debates on Domesticity in British India" *Subaltern Studies* VIII, R. Guha, ed.(Delhi: Oxford University Press, 1994); Andrew Jones, *Yellow Music: Media Culture and Colonial Modernity in the Chinese Jazz Age* (Durham, Duke University Press, 2001); Tamara Loos, *Subject Siam: Family, Law, and Colonial Modernity* (Ithaca: Cornell University Press, 2006); and Gi-wook Shin and M. Robinson, *Colonial Modernity in Korea* (Cambridge: Harvard University Press, 2000).

74. See for example, publications by participants in the "Sanskrit knowledge systems on the eve of colonialism" project (http://www.columbia.edu/itc/mealac/pollock/sks/index.html, last accessed July 5, 2009).

75. This is Macaulay's famous phrase from his "Minute on Indian Education" of 1835.

76. This is not to discount the significance of other conceptions of modernity that have located it in certain social formations, e.g., Benedict Anderson's print culture and nationalism, in the background of many scholarly works on British India, and Jürgen Habermas' public sphere, which Orsini has outlined in the Hindi-language context for 1920–40.

77. As noted by Dipesh Chakrabarty, often "narratives of 'modernity' . . . point to a certain 'Europe' as the primary habitus of the modern" (*Provincializing Europe: Postcolonial Thought and Historical Difference*; Princeton: Princeton University Press, 2000), 43.

78. To use Mary Louise Pratt's phrase (*Imperial Eyes: Travel Writing and Transculturation* [London: Routledge, 1992], 6).

79. Gyan Prakash, *Another Reason: Science and the Imagination of Modern India* (Princeton: Princeton University Press, 1999).

80. Vasudha Dalmia, "Sanskrit Scholars and Pandits of the Old School: The Benares Sanskrit College and the Constitution of Authority in the Late Nineteenth Century" (*Journal of Indian Philosophy* 24 [1996]: 321–37), 321.

81. Chandra, 3.

82. 1884–1941. See biography in Chapter 8.

83. In just 2003, Devendra Caube and R. Caudharī, in the article "Itihās aur kavitā" (History and Poetry) in the journal *Tadbhava* lamented that, aside from Hazārīprasād Dvivedī, there have been no great new advances in Hindi literary histories, all of them being based on the foundational texts of Rāmacandra Śukla (no. 9 [April 2003], 223).

84. For discussion of this see Dalmia, *Nationalization*, 277.

85. On Hariścandra and his Urdu poetry, see Sagaree Sengupta, "Kṛṣṇa the Cruel Beloved: Hariścandra and Urdu" (*The Annual of Urdu Studies* 9 (1994), 133–52). On his Braj poetry, see Sengupta, "Nineteenth Century" (op. cit.). As noted by Orsini, *Hindi Public Sphere* (6), Hariścandra used all ranges of Hindi whereas later authors cleaved to a more standardized, singular register.

86. See the biography of M. Dvivedī in Chapter 4.

87. See Valerie Ritter, "The Language of Hariaudh's Priyapravās: Notes toward an Archaeology of Modern Standard Hindi" (*Journal of the American Oriental Society* 124:3 [July–September 2004], 417–38).

88. Rāmasvarūp Caturvedī, *Hindī sāhitya aur saṃvedanā kā vikās* (*Hindi Literature and the Development of Sensibility*). 1986. 8th rev. ed. (Allahabad: Lokabhāratī Prakāśan, 1998), 94.

89. As in the bee taking *svacchandam marandam* (free/loose pollen), in a verse from Mughal-era Sanskrit poet Jagannāth Paṇḍit, *Bhāminī-vilās*, ed. M. Dvivedī, 1891 (Kalyāṇ: Gaṅgāviṣṇu Śrīkṛṣṇadās Prakāśan, 1934), 15.1.

90. This we can surmise from Rāmacandra Śukla's use of the term explicitly for Romanticism in his 1942 edition of *The History of Hindi Literature*, whereas the first edition of 1929 does not seem to contain this term. Cf. the 1929 edition, p. 651, and the expanded 1942 edition, pp. 325–28.

91. See Rambilas Sharma, *Mahāvīraprasād Dvivedī aur Hindī navajāgaraṇ* (*Mahāvīraprasād Dvivedī and the Renaissance of Hindi*) 1977. (New Delhi: Rājakamal Prakāśan, 1989).

92. This phenomenon of a troubling, interstitial, not-quite-modern literary period is seen in other literatures as well. See for example Velcheru Narayana Rao's "Historical After-Essay" in *Hibiscus on the Lake: Twentieth-Century Telugu Poetry from India* (Madison: University of Wisconsin Press, 2002). Beyond India, we find that in Chinese, post-May Fourth literature has dominated scholarship and contributed to a general opinion that late Qing and early Republican literature is "traditional," "conservative," and to be dismissed as such. See David Wang, *Fin de Siecle Splendor: Repressed Modernities of Late Qing Fiction, 1849–1911* (Stanford: Stanford University Press, 1997). See also Shumei Shi on teleology in modern Chinese literary history in *The Lure of the Modern: Writing Modernism in Semi-colonial China, 1917–1937* (Berkeley: University of California Press, 2001), 56 ff.

93. David Rubin, *The Return of Sarasvatī: Four Hindi Poets* (Delhi: Oxford University Press, 1998), 8–9, and Schomer, 69.

94. See Heidi Pauwels, "Diptych in Verse: Gender Hybridity, Language Consciousness, and National Identity in Nirālā's 'Jāgo Phir Ek Bār,' " (*Journal of the American Oriental Society* 121.3 [2001], 449–81), section 3.2, for discussion of the Tagore inspiration in regard to Nirālā in particular, and generally an excellent account of the aesthetic and nationalist concerns of early twentieth-century Hindi.

95. One exception to this has been Anne Daisy Rockwell, "The Drama of Hindi Literary Histories," Chapter Three in "The Novelty of Ashk: Conflict, Originality and Novelization in the Life and Work of Upendranath Ashk (1910–1996)" (Dissertation, University of Chicago, 1998).

96. The term of choice for many an essay and volume on Hindi literary matters (e.g., in the perennial phrase of "*udbhav aur vikās*" [origin and development]).

97. See Chapter 2, note 5.

98. Moreshwar Ramchandra Kale, "Introduction," *The Raghuvaṁśa of Kālidāsa* (1895?; Varanasi: Motilal Banarsidass, 1998), x, among other of Kale's editions of Kalidasa. The quotation is uncited.

99. One critic has announced his view of the death of the progressivist short story by stating "the *rīti-kal* of fiction . . . is now in its prime." Vidyāsāgar Nautiyāl, "Abhī rītikāl pūre sabab par hai" ("Even Now the *Rītikāl* is in Full Force") (*Haṁs*, 239:21:1 [August 2006], 209–10), 210.

100. *Prakṛti*, does function in this sense, but does not closely parallel the hermeneutics of English "nature"'s multiple senses. Additionally, in modern Hindi the "nature of" an animate thing is often expressed with a separate term (*svabhāv*). Because this sense of the term is not the object of "nature description" here, I am leaving aside the question of "nature" as "the inherent or essential quality or constitution of a thing" (*OED*), and other senses relating to innate character.

Although critics and poets have perennially linked the description of nature with the description of human nature, emotion, and psychology from the mid-twenties on, the empiricism of nature description relating directly to interest in subjectivity, the viewer and enunciator of description, this is large and complex subject that is beyond our scope here.

Chapter 2

1. Nāmavar Siṁh, *Chāyāvād* (*Shadow-ism*) 1955. (Reprint. New Delhi: Rājakamal Prakāśan, 2001), 37. This sentence alludes to the god Krishna's revelation of himself to Arjuna as Arjuna goes off to battle against his cousins in war, as described in the *Bhagavad Gita*. Krishna advises not to fear death, nor causing death, assures Arjuna that he, as Krishna, suffuses the world, and instructs him to do his duty (dharma). The *Bhagavad Gita*'s significance surged in nineteenth-century Indian nationalism, and remains popularly viewed as an exemplar of the Hindu ethical world.

2. Pritchett, *Nets*, 167–68.

3. This statement is based upon database searches of titles and subject headings in the OCLC and British Library catalogs, so it is possible that it could be disproved in some fashion as more complete publication records become available; however, I strongly suspect that the catalog records taken as a whole accurately reflect this aspect of the Indian literary critical landscape.

4. Orsini, *Hindi Public Sphere*, 14.

5. Raghuvaṁś's two volumes epitomize this enterprise, at more than 500 pages each: *Prakṛti aur Hindī kāvya (madhya-yuga)* (*Nature and Hindi Poetry [in the Middle Ages]*) of 1948 and *Prakṛti aur kāvya (Saṁskṛt khaṇḍ)* (*Nature and Poetry [Sanskrit volume]*) of 1951, both published in Allahabad by Hindī Sāhitya Bhavan Limited. See also Rameśvaralāl Khaṇḍelavāl "Taruṇ," *Kavitā meṁ prakṛti-citra: siddhānt-samīkṣā evam vivecan* (*The Portrayal of Nature in Poetry: a Study of Criticism and Analysis*) (Delhi: National Publishing House, 1954). A notable example of the nature-oriented critic of the 1950s is Gulāb Rāy, who wrote essays on the portrayal of nature in Senapati (fl. 17th c.), Bhāratendu Hariścandra, and Jayaśaṅkar Prasād, as well as an exposition on plants and animals in poetry, in his *Adhyayan aur āsvād: sāhityik nibandh* (*Study and Taste: Literary Essays*) (Delhi: Ātmarām and Sons, 1957).

6. With S. Saksenā, *Rūpāmbarā: ādhunik hindīke prakṛti-kāvyakā saṅkalan aur vivecan* (*Dressed in Forms/Beauty: An Anthology and Analysis of Modern Hindi Nature-Poetry*), Jñānapīṭh lokoday granthamālā 122, ed. L. Jain (Varanasi: Bhāratīya Jñānapīṭh, 1960).

7. Here my words echo those of Brian A. Hatcher, who has written of eclecticism as an intellectual mode in modern Bengal, in *Eclecticism and Modern Hindu Discourse* (New York: Oxford University Press, 1999).

8. Note that as there is no practice of capitalization in order to signify abstract principles, or another explicit orthographic marker of "nature" versus "Nature" in Hindi, this distinction is difficult to generalize.

9. N. Siṁh, *Chāyāvād*, 41.

10. This view mirrors the evolutionary narrative in English art history regarding landscape painting, as described by W. J. T. Mitchell, an evolution

"from subordination to emancipation, [from] convention to nature, [which] has as its ultimate goal the *unification* of nature in the perception and representation of landscape."As proof of this, Mitchell quotes a line startlingly similar to N. Simh's above, from the *Oxford Companion to Art* [n.d.] "It seems that until fairly recent times men looked at nature as an assemblage of isolated objects, without connecting trees, rivers, mountains, roads, rocks, and forest into a unified scene." W. J. T. Mitchell, "Imperial Landscape" in *Landscape and Power*, ed. W. Mitchell (Chicago: University of Chicago Press, 1994; 5–34), 12–13.

11. Śukla, *History*, 328.

12. In this regard, Śukla compares them to Cowper, Burns, and Scott (*History*, 327).

13. N. Simh, *Chāyāvād*, 31.

14. Ibid.

15. Hazārīprasād Dvivedī, *Hindī sāhitya: unakā udbhav aur vikās* (*Hindi Literature: Its Origin and Development*), 1952? (Delhi: Attaracand Kapūr and sons, 1955), 444.

16. N. Simh, *Chāyāvād*, 32.

17. Ibid., 33.

18. Ibid., 89, 96.

19. Schomer has so far explicated the poetical world of Chāyāvād most thoroughly in English, and David Rubin in the Introduction to *The Return of Sarasvati*, and the Introduction to his recent *Of Love and War: A Chayavad Anthology* (Delhi: Oxford University Press, 2005) has also contributed to critical writing in English on these matters.

20. N. Simh, *Chāyāvād*, 9.

21. Mitchell, 5.

22. Tracy Pintchman's "Prakṛti, Māyā, and Śakti: The Feminine Principle in Philosophical Discourse," (Chapter Two of *The Rise of the Goddess in the Hindu Tradition* [Albany: State University of New York Press, 1994], 61–115), provides a very useful overview and analysis of these related terms in a variety of philosophical contexts.

23. M. Hiriyanna, *Essentials of Indian Philosophy* (London: Diamond Books, 1996), 114. This matter is of course extremely complicated, and this is only the briefest and most general interpretation, which is consonant with commonplace philosophy, as it has appeared in Hindi texts over the last century or so.

24. Monier Monier-Williams, *A Sanskrit-English Dictionary: Etymologically and Philologically Arranged with Special Reference to Cognate Indo-European Languages*, new edition, 1899. Reprint (Delhi: Motilal Banarsidass, 1997), 654.

25. Ibid. This Vedantic analogy of "illusion" (*māyā*) versus "soul" (*brahman*), while already a commonplace of popular Hindu theology for centuries, was particularly relevant to late nineteenth-century intellectual contexts, in which Vedanta philosophy had achieved a new currency as an international religious "product" that appealed to American transcendentalists, British theosophists, and elite Indians.

26. Ibid.

27. Conceptions of an abstract and/or scientific Nature deriving from Persian and Arabic, and indeed Aristotelian, sources undoubtedly were present

within the zeitgeist of the Hindi authors addressed in this book, although study these conceptions' presence and influence remains beyond the scope of my research thus far. Theologically, the Garden of Paradise obviously figured into conceptions of ideal natural spaces. Mughal paintings in the realist vein of scientific drawing may have been known somewhat to these colonial Hindi authors, although probably were not as familiar as botanical drawings produced for the British. Many of the Hindi authors in question here would have been unaware of and indeed uninterested in admitting to any Islamicate branch of their intellectual geneaology.

28. This is verse from the corpus of the Haridāsī sect, named for a sixteenth-century poet-saint. See Ludmila L. Rosenstein, *The Devotional Poetry of* Svāmī Haridās (Groningen: Egbert Forsten, 1997), and the notes on this translation, 298.

29. On the relation to the pre-Romantic European pastoral, see Entwistle's article "The Cult of Krishna-Gopāl."

30. See Allison Busch, "The Courtly Vernacular: The Transformation of Brajbhāṣā Literary Culture, 1590–1690" (Dissertation, University of Chicago, 2003), 127 ff., for discussion of the text's innovations.

31. Keśav Dās, *Kavipriyā* (*Handbook for the Poet*) in *Collected Works,* vol. 1, 7.1.

32. This is merely one of countless examples. Ingall's translation, Vidyākara, *An Anthology of Sanskrit Court Poetry: Vidyākara's "Subhāṣitaratnakoṣa,"* trans. Daniel H. H. Ingalls, Harvard Oriental Series, No. 44. ed. D. H. H. Ingalls (Cambridge: Harvard University Press, 1965), v. 610 by Bhaṭṭa Śrī Śivasvāmin.

33. Hans Heifetz's translation, *The Origin of the Young God: Kalidasa's* Kumārasambhava (Berkeley: University of California Press, 1985), 1.49.

34. Cited in Raghuvaṁś, *Nature and Hindi Poetry*, 466, from Dev's *Bhāva-vilāsa.*

35. This type of phenomenon was not limited to Sanskrit poetics. A. K. Ramanujan located in classical Tamil poetics a different but similar pattern of linkages between seasons and natural locales, and specific moments of the love relationship (Afterword, *The Interior Landscape: Love Poems from a Classical Tamil Anthology* [Delhi: Oxford University Press, 1967]).

36. The bee was a common metaphor for Krishna, pleasure-seeking men, and aesthetes. The bee was also addressed by *gopi*s in "bee songs" on *viraha.* Legend has it that Bihārī wrote this couplet as a warning of sorts for his patron Jayasiṁh of Amber, who neglected matters of state because of his infatuation with a new young mistress (Snell, 135).

37. In Snell, 134–35, with reference to his translation.

38. Cited in Ibid., with reference to his translation, 173, v.1.

39. Cited in Ibid., with reference to his translation, 175, v.12.

40. This is merely a concrete observation of what Ronald Inden observes broadly in his "Transnational Class, Erotic Arcadia and Commercial Utopia in Hindi Films" in *Image Journeys: Audio-Visual Media and Cultural Change in India,* eds. C. Boresius and M. Butcher (New Delhi: Sage Publications, 1999), 41–66.

41. A most accessible exposition of the religious and literary ramifications of the *haqīqī/ majāzī* binary in Sufi allegorical romance is found in the introduction of Behl and Weightman to Mañjhan's *Madhumālatī*.

42. Śukla, *History*, 52.

43. Pritchett, *Nets*, 98.

44. Bābū Pramadādās Mitra (dates unknown) was among the elite Bengalis of Banaras, one of Swami Vivekananda's friends and advisors, and also thanked by Annie Besant in her 1895 translation of the *Bhagavad Gita*. For an account of his 1884 debate with the Principal of Benares College over the merits of European historical criticism in Sanskrit studies, see Dalmia, "Sanskrit Scholars."

45. Pramadā-Dās Mitra, Preface to *The Mirror of Composition, a Treatise on Poetical Criticism, being an English Translation of the Sahitya-Darpana of Viswanatha Kaviraja; the first 128 pages revised from the work of the late Dr. J. R. Ballantyne, and the rest by Pramada-Dasa Mitra* (Calcutta: Baptist Mission Press, 1875), iv–v.

46. The quotation is from Mill's "What Is Poetry?" section of "Thoughts on Poetry and its Varieties," published in *Dissertations and Discussions*, probably available in India through Longman from at least 1870, and perhaps excerpted in anthologies.

47. Saint Nihal Singh, "The Macaulay Maya" (in *Dvivedīabhinandan granth* [*Festschrift for Dvivedī*]; Varanasi: NPS, 1933; 495–514) 504, 507–08.

48. J. N. Muzumdar, "English and Indian Literature" (London, *The Indian Magazine*, vol. XVI, no. 192, new series no. 12 (Dec. 1886), 664–66), 665–66.

49. This has yet to be systematically documented, to my knowledge, but I can vouch for the presence of such translations in periodicals and book publications (often for student use) in Hindi from the 1890s onward. For example, Śivanandan Sahāy, ed., *Kavitā kusum: Shelley tathā Tennyson ādi kaviyoṁ ke kaī ek padyoṁ kā bhāṣānuvād* (*Bloom of Verse: A Translation of a few Verses of Shelley, Tennyson, and other such poets*) (Bankipur: Khaḍgavilās Press, 1906), which contained poems by Southey, Longfellow, Clough, Bryant, Wordsworth, Montgomery, Watts, Cowper, Watton, and Pope in addition to Shelley and Tennyson. Urmila Varma briefly lists some translations in the journal *Sarasvatī* and elsewhere in *Influence of English Poetry on Modern Hindi Poetry, 1900–1940: With Special Reference to Technique, Imagery, Metre, and Diction* (Allahabad: Lokbharti Prakashan, 1980). It is generally known that Gray's "Elegy" was one of the most often translated selections, mostly in anthologies and journals, but also independently, as in the 1897 Hindi/Braj translation in Sanskrit meter of "Vidyārasik" *Grāmasth-śavāgār-likhit-śokokti* (*Words of Grief written in a Village Corpse-ground*) (Bombay: Khemarāj Śrīkṛṣṇadās, Śrīveṅkaṭeśvar Yantrālay, 1897).

50. For instance, Hīrālāl, *A Translation of all the Poetical Pieces of* English Royal Reader *nos. 1–3 into Hindi Poetical Pieces* (Lucknow: Muṁśī Naval Kiśor, 1881). See also my description of poetry in the Allahabad University examinations, 1889–1908, Chapter 1, note 4.

51. Chapter One of Chandra.

52. "Premchand" (1881–1936) the most famous prose author in Hindi, wrote in his reminiscences of the many translated novels of this type on the

market in his youth. See "Merī pahalī racanā" ("My First Composition") in *A Premchand Reader*, ed. N. H. Zide (Honolulu: East-West Center, 1965), 81–89; and Meenakshi Mukherjee, *Realism and Reality: The Novel and Society in India* (Delhi: Oxford University Press, 1994).

53. Marathi criticism also engaged with nature through the terms *prakṛti-rasa* and *udātt rasa*, which pertained to "nature poetry." The latter clearly references the English "sublime," and was first put forth by Cipalūṅkār (1850–82). More work on the status of nature as a poetic subject and critical category in Marathi is needed. (B. G. Deśapāṇḍe, *Marāṭhī kā ādhunik sāhitya: itihās, 1805 se 1960* [*Modern Literature in Marathi: A History, 1805 to 1960*] [Amaravati: Navayug Book Stall, 1963]), passim, 141–161.

54. See especially Part III, Chapter Eleven, "Natural Poetry," 155–168.

55. Quote from 1874. Ibid., 35.

56. Muhammad Sadiq, *A History of Urdu Literature*, 2nd revised and enlarged ed. (Delhi: Oxford University Press, 1995), 341.

57. Ibid., 343.

58. Muḥammad Ḥusain Āzād, *Āb-e-ḥayāt: Shaping the Canon of Urdu Poetry*, trans. F. Pritchett (Delhi: Oxford University Press, 2001), 81.

59. Ibid., 83.

60. Ibid., 98.

61. *Nairaṅg-e khiyāl* (*The Wonder-World of Thought*) (1880), 11, cited in Pritchett, *Nets*, 40.

62. Āzād, 63–64.

63. Ibid., 79.

64. Geeta Kapur, *When was Modernism?: Essays on Contemporary Cultural Practice in India* (New Delhi: Tulika, 2000), 150, my emphasis.

65. It is important to note that "nature description" does not include the European concept of literary "naturalism," which Hazārīprasād Dvivedī has termed *prakṛtivād* and identifies as realist description of non-ideal subjects. As in European languages, this is a style associated mostly with prose. (H. Dvivedī, 428–29).

66. Āzād (Pritchett's translation), 90, all bracketed glosses but the first are my own.

67. Ibid., 91.

68. Ibid., with my references to terms in the original: Muḥammad Ḥusain Āzād, *Āb-e-ḥayāt*; 1880; 2nd ed., 1883, 1907. Reprint (Lucknow: Uttar Pradesh Urdu Academy, 1982), 92.

69. Āzād, 106.

70. Sadiq, 267–68.

71. The *Musaddas* went into many printings, and is best known in its 1886 edition. Its tone and message were the inspiration for the 1912–14 Hindi work, *Bhārat-bhāratī (Voice of India)* by Maithilīśaraṇ Gupta, examined here in Chapter 7.

72. Cited and translated in Pritchett, *Nets*, 165.

73. See Pritchett, *Nets*, 148–51, for full discussion of the relationship of Ḥālī's text to Milton's.

74. Pritchett, *Nets*, 166.

75. Ibid., 148.

76. Mahāvīraprasād Dvivedī, "Kavi aur kavitā" ("The Poet and Poetry") in *Mahāvīraprasād Dvivedī racanāvalī (The Collected Works of Dvivedī)* ed. B. Yāyāvar, 13 vols. (New Delhi: Kitāb Ghar, 1995), 2: 68.

77. Ibid., 70.

78. Ibid., 73–74.

79. Ibid., 76. Incidentally, it is worth noting also the preponderance of realist natural and patriotic themes in the "munshi-style" section of A. Khatrī, comp., *Khaṛī Bolī kā Padya: Poetical Reader of Khaṛī Bolī* (op. cit.), comparatively with other styles of Hindi presented therein.

80. Sadiq, 154 ff.

81. Aditya Behl, "Poet of the Bazaars: Naẓīr Akbarābādī" in *A Wilderness of Possibilities: Urdu Studies in Transnational Perspective*, eds. K. Hansen and D Lelyveld (New Delhi: Oxford University Press, 2005, 192–222), 195–96.

82. Preface to *A New Hindustani-English Dictionary: With Illustrations from Hindustani Literature and Folklore* (Banaras: Medical Hall Press, 1879). Reprint (New Delhi: Asian Educational Services, 1989), ix. Also quoted in Sadiq, 163.

83. Fallon, ix.

84. Sadiq, 161.

85. Ibid.

86. Sadiq, 374.

87. Ibid., 390.

88. Sir Muhammad Iqbal was one of the foremost figures of modern South Asian history, a man closely associated with the Muslim League and the early concept of Pakistan, and a figure of great learning and influence, who was knighted in 1922 and whose philosophical writings, theological thought, and poetry, in both Urdu and Persian, has carried profound cultural import.

89. Sadiq, 451.

90. Reprinted in his first volume of poetry, the *Bāng-e-darā* (*Sound of the Camel-Bell*) of 1924. It was accompanied in the volume with the pan-Islamic anthem "Tarāna-e Millī," composed 1910. Bibliographic information and transliterations from Muhammad Iqbal, *Iqbal: A Selection of the Urdu Verse*, ed. and trans. D. J. Matthews (Heritage Publishers: New Delhi, 1993), 150–54.

91. Ibid. (Matthews' translation), 17.

92. This translation is a combination of that in ibid., 41, and that of Khushwant Singh in Muhammad Iqbal, *Shikwa and Jawab-i-Shikwa: Complaint and Answer: Iqbal's Dialogue with Allah* (Delhi: Oxford University Press, 1981), 56, with some reference to the original Urdu.

93. Iqbal (K. Singh's translation), 86.

94. Shamsur Rahman Faruqi, "Iqbal's Romantic Dilemma" in *The Secret Mirror: Essays on Urdu Poetry* (Delhi: Academic Literature, 1981, 95–106), 100.

95. Ibid., 102.

96. Ibid., 104.

97. C. M. Naim, " 'Pseudo-dramatic' Poems of Iqbal" in *Urdu Texts and Contexts: The Selected Essays of C.M. Naim* (Delhi: Permanent Black, 2004), 96–107.

98. *Aiyyārī* literally signifies wizardry, i.e., novels containing characters with magical powers and fantastical events, etc. *Qissā-goī* here refers literally to "story-telling," a reference to the folk recitation of fantastical *qissā* narratives and their popular literary form in the Urdu script.

99. H. Dvivedī, 420.

100. "Sujalāṁ suphalāṁ/ malayajaśītalāṁ/ śasyaśyāmalāṁ / Mātaram! / śubhra-jyotsnā-pulakita-yāminīm / phullakusumita-drumadalaśobhinīm, / Suhāsiniṁ sumadhurabhaṣiṇīm." As given in Bankim Chandra Chatterjee, *Ānandamaṭh*, Baṅkim-Śatabārṣik edition (Calcutta: Baṅgīya-Sāhitya-Pariṣat, 1938), 21.

101. M. Dvivedī, *Collected Works*, 13:186. This poem was published sometime during 1905–6. Sri Aurobindo's rhyming English translation of 1909 similarly portrays an explicit land/goddess/nationalism connection.

102. See discussion quoted in Introduction to the novel in the edition mentioned in note 100.

103. Although a thorough examination of "nature in Bengali" in the nineteenth century is a huge undertaking not possible here, by me.

104. I am thinking here of the descriptions at the start of Canto 7 (Michael Madhusūdan Datt, *The Slaying of Meghanada: A Ramayana from Colonial Bengal*, trans. C. B. Seely (New York: Oxford University Press, 2004).

105. Rabindranath Tagore, *Selected Poems* (trans. W. Radice (London: Penguin, 1994), 56. Radice notes the similarity of these sentiments to those in his *Reminiscences* (1917) on sailing into Calcutta in 1881.

106. Ibid., 61–62, and 137.

107. Rabindranath Tagore, "Shakuntala" (1902) in *Selected Writings on Literature and Language*, trans. S. Chaudhuri, The Oxford Tagore Translations (New Delhi: Oxford University Press, 2001), 244.

Chapter 3

1. "Samālocanādarś" (*Nāgarīpracāriṇī patrikā* 1:1 [1897]), 55.5–6, translation from Pope's 1711 "Essay on Criticism," "In Wit, as Nature, what affects our hearts / Is not th'exactness of peculiar parts."

2. Viswanathan, 54–55.

3. "Reading English, Writing Hindi: English Literature and Indian Creative Writing" in *Rethinking English: Essays in Literature, Language, History* (Delhi: Oxford University Press, 1994, 181–205), 185.

4. Pritchett's discussion of Urdu critic Ḥālī's use of English sources in his seminal *Muqaddamah* of 1893 suggests that the pre-nineteenth-century English authors may have been less important in the Urdu literary world than, for instance, Thomas Babington Macaulay's words about them. Particularly striking is Ḥālī's only perfunctory interest in Goldsmith's *Deserted Village*, the important Hindi translation of which is discussed herein. See Pritchett, *Nets*, 151–52.

5. In this biography I draw upon my introduction to my chapter on Pāṭhak in S. Nijhawan, ed., *Nationalism in the Vernacular: Hind, Urdu, and the Literature of Indian Freedom,* (Hyderabad: Orient Blackswan, 2010).

6. Śukla, *History,* 328. There are differences between the 1929 and 1941 editions. I refer to the 1941 edition unless noted otherwise. Imre Bangha has noted efforts by critics to identify "free" (*svacchand*) poets in the *rīti* era, in order to establish precursors for Chāyāvād in "Romantic Poetry in the Era of Convention? The Emergence of the Idea of a *Rītimukt* Trend within Hindi Mannerist Literature" (*South Asia Research* 25:1 [2005], 13–30).

7. H. Dvivedī, 444.

8. For example, "The Coming of the Spring," "The Reign of Spring," "Verses to the Bee," "Description of the Summer" (based on Kālidāsa's *Ṛtusaṃhāra* [*Collection of Seasons*])," and "Plea to a Cloud," among many others. See Śrīdhar Pāṭhak, *Śrīdhar Pāṭhak Granthāvalī (The Collected Works of Śrīdhar Pāṭhak)*, ed. P. Pāṭhak, 3 vols. (Jodhpur: Rājasthānī Granthāgār, 1996).

9. In the *Kāśī Patrikā* (*Kāśī Magazine*), and also as a stand-alone publication.

10. From ll. 50–66 of its separate 1916 edition reprinted in his *Collected Works*, 128–29. Attesting to the popular dissemination of such "nature description" passages, the preceding lines, including continuing lines of "nature description," elided here for reasons of space, were excerpted in the widely used school anthology, *Kavitā kaumudī* (*Guide to poetry*), ed. Rāmanareś Tripāṭhī, vol. 2, *Hindī;* 1920, 1923; 3rd rev. ed., (Allahabad: Hindī-Mandir, 1926), 116.

11. Pāṭhak held a prodigious number of appointments within various institutions of the British Raj. During his career he worked for the Governor, Postmaster General, at a Government High School, the Censor Commission, the Railway, the Public Works, as a Divisional Head Clerk, and lastly, as assistant to the Irrigation Commission Superintendent.

12. April 30 and Oct. 20, 1893. Cited in Padmadhar Pāṭhak,"Jīvanī" ("Life"), in S. Pāṭhak's *Collected Works* (1:1–61), 47.

13. For example, Pāṭhak wrote in the introduction to his 1916 edition of *Digest of the Truth of the World* that India had benefited from British rule, as it had understood the material world only mythically, "in the lap of the lady of illusion [*māyā-mānavī*, i.e., physical nature?]. If the ornament-of-good-deeds, Master England [Māsṭar Iṅgalaiṇḍ] had never become connected with this land, then who could say what would have happened?"

14. Śukla, *History*, 329.

15. Raghuvaṁś, *Śrīdhar Pāṭhak* (1985; Bhāratīya sāhitya ke nirmātā; reprint, New Delhi: Sāhitya Academy, 1991), 29.

16. Ibid., 31.

17. Rāmacandra Miśra, *Śrīdhar Pāṭhak tathā Hindī kā pūrv-svacchandatāvādī kāvya* (1875 i. se 1925 ī. tak) (*Śrīdhar Pāṭhak and Hindi's Pre-Romantic Poetry [1875 to 1925 A.D.]*) (Delhi: Raṇajīt Printers and Publishers, 1959), 24.

18. Śukla, *History*, 324, 326.

19. Mukherjee, 13.

20. Arthur Barrett, Introduction to *Oliver Goldsmith,* The Traveller *and* The Deserted Village (1888; ed. A. Barrett; reprint, London: Macmillan, 1931).

21. For proof of this, we can consult the *Calendars* of Allahabad University, which functioned as an examination board for the prestigious colleges of the province until 1922 (Orsini, *Hindi Public Sphere,* 35). Goldsmith was listed on the syllabus for the entrance exam at least as early as 1897, and his *The Deserted Village* as of 1901 (*Calendar for the Year 1895–96* and . . . *1901–02;* Allahabad: Allahabad University, 1895 and 1901, respectively, op. cit.). A later translation of *The Deserted Village* by one Puttanalāla Suśīl of 1899 may also attest to such curricular demand of this text (Dhīrendranāth Siṁh, *Ādhunik Hindī ke vikās meṁ Khaḍgavilās Press kī bhūmikā* [*The Role of the Khaḍgavilās Press in the Development of Modern Hindi*] [Patna: Bihār-Rāṣṭrabhāṣā-Pariṣad, 1986], 291).

22. N.a., *Padyāvalī,* noted by R. T. H. Griffith, Director of Public Instruction, North-Western Provinces and Oudh, in a report on publications registered in the Province in 1881, reprinted in *Selections from the Records of the Government of India, Home Dept.,* no. CXCI (Calcutta, 1883), 125.

23. Anonymous, from *The Indian Magazine,* London, June 1888, quoted in Preface, "Opinions and Reviews," Śrīdhar Pāṭhak, *Ūjaṛ gām: England ke prasiddh kavi Goldsmith ke* Deserted Village *kā anuvād* (*The Desolate Village: A Translation of the Deserted Village of England's Famous Poet Goldsmith*) (Varanasi: Medical Hall Press, 1889), i–iii. An interesting extract from another letter:

> It is not often that we give unmodified praise to Indian verse, for there can be no doubt that what India wants now is sound commonsense prose matters of fact; but, when the inspirations of poetic genius come before us, no anxiety for India's material welfare shall hinder us from extending a hearty welcome to literary genius. . . . This translation of Goldsmith's "Hermit" is a valuable addition to Hindi literature, for it will tend to divert the Indian mind from the extravagances of Oriental imagery and fix it upon the sympathies and affections of the human heart. . . . his translation will give to the people of India an accurate idea of what is deemed beautiful on this side of the world.

(anonymous, from *Homeward Mail,* London, May 1888, quoted in ibid., iii–iv).

24. Miśrabandhu [The Miśra Brothers, Gaṇeṣabihāri, Śyāmabihārī, and Sukhadevabiharī], "Śrīdhar Pāṭhak kī kavitā kī samālocanā" ("A Literary Critique of Śrīdhar Pāṭhak's Poetry") (*Sarasvati,* Nov. 1900; cited in Haraprakāś Gauṛ, *Sarasvatī aur rāṣṭrīya jāgaraṇ* [*Sarasvatī and National Awakening*] [New Delhi: National Publishing House, 1983], 75.

25. "No flocks that range the valley free / To slaughter I condemn; / Taught by that power that pities me, / I learn to pity them; / But from the mountain's grassy side / A guiltless feast I bring."

26. Frederic Pincott (1836–96), Chapter 1, note 57.

27. Extract from a letter from Pincott, London, May 10, 1888, in Preface, "Opinions and Reviews," Pāṭhak, *Desolate Village,* viii.

28. Alfred Lutz, "The Politics of Reception: The Case of Goldsmith's 'The Deserted Village'" (*Studies in Philology* 95, no. 2 [Spring 1998], 174–96), 177.

29. That is, Braj Bhāṣā in grammar, but containing a few lexical items considered shibboleths of "modern standard Hindi," e.g., *maiṁ* as the first person direct pronoun.

30. Cited in Raghuvaṁś, *Śrīdhar Pāṭhak*, 40.

31. Here I use an edition published a year earlier for Indian student use, edited by Arthur Barrett, a professor at Elphinstone College, Bombay (op. cit.).

32. Pyārī pyāri . . . hariyālī kuñjeṁ / sobhā chavi ānanda bharīṁ saba sukha kī puñjeṁ.

33. To paraphrase Walter Benjamin in "The Task of the Translator" in *Illuminations*, ed. H. Arendt, trans. H. Zohn (New York: Schocken, 1968).

34. In the second stanza, the term he uses for church (*girajāghara*) could easily be mistaken for a term for a temple to the goddess Parvati, which would be naturally situated at the top of a mountain foothill, as he terms it. His more explicit and plural rendering of Goldsmith's "bashful virgin's sidelong looks of love" as "the virgins' long lovely sidelong looks, full of desire" (ll. 39–40), *Kvārina . . . cāhabharī deralauṁ cāru citavana* fits neatly into the trope of "sidelong looks" common in Sanskritic poetry, and suggests the many desirous *gopī*s of the Krishna story. The village preacher is a "religious speaker" (*upadeśaka*). Decades later, in 1915, Pāṭhak cited several of his own verses from *Desolate Village* on the "village preacher" in the frontispiece of his poetic eulogy for Gopālakṛṣṇa Gokhale, clearly identifying the reformer and nationalist with the altruistic preacher (frontispiece, *ŚrīGokhale guṇāṣṭak: golokavāsī lokamānya Śrīmān Gopālakṛṣṇa Gokhale kā smārak* [*Eight Verses on Śrī Gokhale: A Remembrance of the Esteemed Late Śrīmān Gopālakṛṣṇa Gokhale*] [Allahabad: Lālā Rāmadayāl Agaravāl]). Goldsmith's village beggar became the familiar "alms-seeker" (*bhikhārī*), the village master a guru, and the "[rural virtue] piety" as "devotion to the feet of Krishna" (*hari caranana cita*). Interestingly, Pāṭhak shies away from Goldsmith's widow, soon a popular object of social reform discourse in Hindi literature, describing her in an odd phrase, *pariyata nārī*, a woman "on the margin," "wandering."

35. Pāṭhak, Postscript to *Desolate Village*, 2.

36. Pāṭhak, *Desolate Village*, ll. 41–42.

37. Ibid., ll. 47–48.

38. Ibid., ll. 76–80.

39. As Goldsmith wrote in the dedication, "I have taken all possible pains, in my country excursions, . . . to be certain of what I allege, . . . that all my views and enquiries have led me to believe those miseries are real, which I here attempt to display." He further explains defensively,

> In regretting the depopulation of our country, I inveigh against the increase of our luxuries and here also I expect the shout of modern politicians against me . . . it has been the fashion to consider luxury as one of the greatest national advantages . . . however, I . . . continue

> to think those luxuries prejudicial to states, by which so many vices are introduced, and so many kingdoms have been undone.

Oliver Goldsmith, *The Deserted Village: A Poem,* 2nd ed. (London: Griffin, 1770).

40. Thomas Babington Macaulay, "Memoir of Oliver Goldsmith," foreword to *The Poetical Works of Oliver Goldsmith, with a Life by Thomas Babington Macaulay* (Boston: Little, Brown, 1857), 108. Macaulay's essays were staples of the Indian English curriculum, and so it is quite possible Pāṭhak was aware of these objections.

41. See Elizabeth Whitcombe, *Agrarian Conditions in Northern India* (Berkeley: University of California Press, 1972), passim, for description of the complex factors, varying by region, that would affect village populations, e.g., the growth of the zamindari presence in villages, occupancy and debt litigation, and Government works.

42. Pāṭhak, *Desolate Village,* ll. 281–82.

43. Ibid., l. 50.

44. Whitcombe, 275.

45. Pāṭhak, *Desolate Village,* ll. 51–52, 65–66.

46. Ibid., l. 55.

47. Ibid., ll. 55–60.

48. Goldsmith, ll. 37–40.

49. Pāṭhak, *Desolate Village,* ll. 471–74.

50. Goldsmith, ll. 387–390.

51. In "Hindī kī unnati par vyākhyān" ("Statements on the progress of Hindi") (1877) in *Bhāratendu samagra (Complete Works of Bhāratendu)* ed. H. Śarmā, 3rd ed. (Varanasi: Pracārak Granthāvalī Pariyojanā, Hindī Pracārak Saṃsthān, 1989), 228.

52. Cited in Foreword, note XXX.

53. Pāṭhak, *Desolate Village,* ll. 491–95.

54. Ibid., ll. 509–10.

55. Goldsmith, ll. 425–26.

56. For the perspective of British/Irish administrators in India, and on the Bengal Tenancy Act of 1885, see S. B. Cook, *Imperial Affinities: Nineteenth-century Analogies and Exchanges between India and Ireland* (New Delhi: Sage Publications, 1993). For an account of the Irish connection with Bengali nationalist thought, see Elleke Boehmer, *Empire, the National, and the Postcolonial, 1890–1920: Resistance in Interaction* (Oxford: Oxford University Press, 2002).

57. Cited in "Ḍāyariyoṁ se liye gae uddhāraṇ" ("Excerpts from the Diaries") in Pāṭhak, *Collected Works,* 3: 204–28, 210.

58. In continuation, "And elements have freest play and pranks. // Where hied from distant deep by Nature's freak // Those misty giants climb and cling and creak." The poem continues to a lonely moment of Romantic sublimity, "Could I find calm and contemplative rest; // ecstasy and sweet celestial sights / Unreached by World's tumult, untouched by pain / In love and life, lone, evermore remain." These lines, written in Simla in a letter to a friend, were

perhaps somewhat facetious ("Herein frail Fancy frisks in raptures free. / And Poetry seems gone on drunken spree"). "The Cloudy Himalayas," composed 1903, published 1916 (Pāṭhak, *Collected Works*, 329).

59. Śukla, *History*, 329.

60. To use Saree Makdisi's term, albeit somewhat differently (*Romantic Imperialism: Universal Empire and the Culture of Modernity*; Cambridge: Cambridge University Press, 1998).

61. For more details on Ratnākar's biography and works, see Valerie Ritter, "Networks."

62. Vasudha Dalmia's "Hariścandra of Banaras and the reassessement of Vaiṣṇava bhakti in the late nineteenth century" most succinctly describes the milieu I evoke here (in *Devotional Literature in South Asia: Current research, 1985–88*; ed. R. S. McGregor; Cambridge: Cambridge University Press, 1992; 281–293). The work of C. A. Bayly's *Rulers, Townsmen, and Bazaars*, is also of note in elucidating nineteenth-century merchant culture in Varanasi.

63. Ātmarām Śarmā "Aruṇ," *Ratnākar dvārā upekṣit kavi maṇḍal: navinatam khoj evam śodh par ādhārit* (*The Poets Ratnākar Neglected: Based on the Newest Research and Investigation*) (Delhi: Bhāgyavantī Prakāśan, 2000), ii–iii. Interestingly, this author believes that Ratnākar has plagiarized his Braj poetry from the old manuscripts he collected in Patiala and other sources, although I have not yet seen compelling direct evidence of this in Aruṇ's publication.

64. A *mātrik* meter of a 24 *mātrā* line, with end rhyme for every couplet, and verses of varying length; loosely following the caesura conventions of the *rolā*, as defined by Snell, 23.

65. Pope was included in the MA syllabus from 1896 of Queen's College's testing institution, Allahabad University, with an excerpt from the *Essay on Criticism* in Thomas Humphrey Ward, ed., *The English Poets: Selections with Critical Introductions by Various Writers and a General Introduction by Matthew Arnold*, vol. III (London: Macmillan, 1880). Other works of Pope dominate in this anthology, and the University *Calendar* generally in the nineteenth century. (See *Calendar for the Year 1895–96* and subsequent years; op. cit.) Clearly, Ratnākar went to some effort to translate the work almost in toto; this was not merely a work for student exam preparation.

66. Thomas B. Shaw, *The Student's Manual of English Literature: A History of English Literature*, ed. W. Smith, 10th ed., 1875 (London: John Murray, 1876), 287. This was an assigned text for Allahabad exams as well.

67. Ward, 57 ff.; quote from 61.

68. Ward, 61.

69. For a description of this complex and lengthy controversy over the merits of Pope, and the conflation of naturalness with Englishness, see James Chandler, "The Pope Controversy: Romantic Poetics and the English Canon" (*Critical Inquiry* 10: 3 [Mar. 1984], 481–509), especially 495 ff.

70. Prakṛti-prabhāva nihāri prathama nija sumati sudhārau, / Take jāñca-jantra sauṁ, jo nita ika-rasa-vārau: (19.1–2).

71. Compare also Gandhi's translation of the related Gujarati term *sudhāro*, literally meaning "improvement" or "reform" as "civilization" in his *Hind Svaraj*

(1908), and the assignment of the name "*sudhārak yug*" to Gujarati literature from 1851–1875 (Sitamshu Yashascandra, "From Hemachandra to *Hind Svaraj*: Region and Power in Gujarati Literary Culture" in *Literary Cultures in History: Reconstructions from South Asia*, ed. S. Pollock; Berkeley: University of California Press, 2003; 567–611), 605. This usage may also derive from John Stuart Mill's articulation of civilization (in the eponymous essay) as "human improvement" generally, or "certain kinds of improvement," especially "that which distinguishes a wealthy and powerful nation from savages." While Mill's elaboration departs from the topic at hand, "improvement" could easily translate as "*sudhār*," and perhaps this accounts for this slippage. Mill's *Dissertations and Discussions* was certainly available in India in a Longman edition, from 1875 or earlier.

72. Yāsauṁ sīkhau niyama purātana ke guṇa gāvana, / Prakṛti-pantha kau hai calibau tina-patha kau dhāvana (33).

73. See Chapter 7 in this volume for a description of the anti-*nakha-śikha* sentiments popularized by Mahāviraprasād Dvivedī from 1901.

74. However, Ratnākar was at this point relatively indifferent to the criticism of this genre of body-description, and of the erotic mode generally. The previous year, 1896, he had published a *nakha-śikha* of Keśav Dās, ostensibly because he thought it to be Keśav's oldest work (Introduction, *Keśodās kṛt nakhaśikha* [*A Nakhaśikha by Keśavadās*] [Varanasi: Bhārat Jīvan Press, 1893]).

75. Kabitā maiṁ jyauṁ prakṛti-dṛśya maiṁ jo mana mohai, / prati aṅgani kau pṛthaka suḍaulapanau nahiṁ. (55.5–6)

76. Jihiṁ sundaratā kahata adhara dṛga so jani jānau, / Pai misrita prabhāva saba kau parināma bakhānau. (56.1–2)

77. Another term for "simile" or "metaphor" with its own technicalities.

78. *Yathārtha*: a Sanskrit term meaning "accordant with reality," "conformable to truth" (Monier-Williams, idem). In keeping with the relative function of its first component, *yathā*, this compound might be glossed as "commensurate." *Vād* here is a suffix denoting a something propounded.

79. Cāla calana prācīnani ko jānau āchī gati; / Tina gāthā aru barnya prayojana prati paṅktini ke. (29.2–3)

80. Until the 1743 edition, this term was "Monarchy" instead of "Liberty." John Churton Collins, ed., in an 1896 edition of the "Essay on Criticism" published by Macmillan for student use "both in England and the colonies" (v), commented: "The meaning is: Nature, like liberty, is restrained only by the laws which she herself ordained—a questionable and somewhat unintelligible remark" (*Pope's Essay on Criticism: Edited, with Introduction and Notes*; London: Macmillan, 1896, 28). Pope scholars have not read overmuch into this emendation, nor the term Liberty itself, which in its original context can safely be considered an abstraction, the "faculty or power to do as one likes," scope, license, franchise, or personal sovereignty (*OED*, idem).

81. The possibility that *svatantratā* approximates political franchise or self-rule is further suggested by a reference in Pratāpanārāyaṇ Miśra's poem on forced labor (*begārī*) from 1883, in which he critiques the persistence of the practice under the British Raj: Everyone has got independence (*svatantratā*) under British rule, / for us [indentured servants] slavery persists, calamity befalls our

fate. ("Begārī bilāp" ["A Lament of Forced Labor"], 15 April 1883; reprinted in *Kavitāvali* [*Collected Poetry*], ed. N. Caturvedī [Allahabad: Hindī Sāhitya Sammelan, 1987, 66–69], 67.)

82. Here *yathāratha* (= *yathārtha*) functions grammatically as an adverbial (which *yathā-*, as a relative particle, allows).

83. Jahaṁ kahuṁ koū niyama hohiṁ na samartha yathāratha, / (kāhe sauṁ kai niyama-kāja sādhana udesa patha,) / tahaṁ abhīṣṭa jo kou svatantratā subhagati sājai, / tau svatantratā hī tā thala kau niyama. (35)

84. In the words of a recent literary historian, "In order to contrive a culturally nationalist taunt against the French, Pope momentarily and oddly associates himself with woad-painted ancient Britons, but his own critical principles are very much in line with Boileau." James Sambrook, "Poetry, 1660–1740," in *The Cambridge History of Literary Criticism*, eds. H. B. Nisbet and C. Rawson (Cambridge: Cambridge University Press, 1997, 7–116), 105.

85. Three faults in logic according to Nyāya logic. Definitions that are overly broad, too narrow, and an impossibility, respectively.

86. *Anuprāsa* denotes both alliteration and assonance.

87. *Translingual Practice: Literature, Culture, and Translated Modernity, China 1900–1937* (Stanford: Stanford University Press, 1995).

Chapter 4

1. S. K. Das calls him a "colossal figure of Hindi, "noted for his inclination toward moral teaching" (9:247). From a Brahman lineage of Rai Bareilly district that had lived and worked across India, he was a railway clerk and telegraph signaler in Bombay. He learned English, Marathi, Gujarati, and Bengali while living in Bombay, and brought these to bear upon his ideas for the future shape of Hindi when he took over as editor of *Sarasvatī* in 1903. Dvivedī's biography has been elaborated in virtually every account of modern Hindi literature. See e.g., Orsini, *Hindi Public Sphere*, 396–97.

2. "Vidyānāth," pseudo. [Mahāvīraprasād Dvivedī], "Kavi-kartavya" ("The Duty of the Poet") (Pt. 1, *Sarasvatī*, July 1901; reprinted in M. Dvivedī, *Collected Works* 2: 44–51), 48.

3. Vidyānāth [M. Dvivedī], "The Duty of the Poet," 49.

4. Yāyāvar, Introduction to M. Dvivedī, *Collected Works*, 13:10.

5. The quotations are uncited, but presumably both of Monier-Williams, the famous philologist and author of the classic Sanskrit-English dictionary. *Meghadūta-Bhāṣā: Mahākavi Kālidāsa ke prasiddh Saṃskṛt granth kā Bhāṣā chandoṁ meṁ anuvād [Sītārām's Hindi* Meghadūta*]* (1883; 2nd ed., 1892; 4th ed. (Prayag: National Press, 1917).

6. Dvivedī's Braj poem, "Meghopalambha" ("Reproach of the cloud") of 1899 takes up the same theme. S. Pāṭhak's poetic oeuvre also contains numerous examples of the "cloud poems" popular in this period, which would continue in more experimental forms in the Chāyāvād poetry of the 1920s and beyond.

7. See discussion in Chapter 2.

8. *The Hindi Scientific Glossary, containing the terms of astronomy, chemistry, geography, mathematics, philosophy, physics and political economy, with their Hindi equivalents* (1904; Banaras: Nāgarī Pracāriṇī Sabhā, 1906).

9. M. Dvivedī, "Kavi aur kavitā" ("Poet and Poetry") (*Sarasvatī*, July 1907; reprinted in M. Dvivedī, *Collected Works* 2: 68–79), 70.

10. Ibid.

11. Ibid., 72.

12. Ibid., 72–73.

13. Ibid., 73.

14. Ibid., 74–76.

15. Ibid., 77–79.

16. M. Dvivedī, "Kavi banane ke lie sāpekṣ sādhan" ("The Necessary Means for Becoming a Poet") (*Sarasvatī*, June 1911, reprinted in M. Dvivedī, *Collected Works* 2: 83–89), 86.

17. Ibid., 88.

18. Editor of Dvivedī's *Collected Works* Bhārat Yāyāvar does not cite the source of this essay. However, an author "Kuñj" published two essays in *Sarasvatī* around this time: "Ek vaijñānik kā sapanā" ("Dream of a scientist") (1912) and "Sūryoday aur sūryāst" ("Sunrise and sunset") (1913). Gauṛ categorized both as "science writing" in his index of the magazine's early years.

19. M. Dvivedī, "Natural scene" ("Prākṛtik dṛśya") (August 1913; reprinted in M. Dvivedī, *Collected Works* 2: 351–54), 351–52.

20. Ibid., 353.

21. Ibid., 354.

22. M. Dvivedī, "Kavitā kā bhaviṣya" ("The Future of Poetry") (*Sarasvatī*, September 1920; reprinted in M. Dvivedī, *Collected Works* 2: 94–98), 97–98.

23. Harish Trivedi, "The Progress of Hindi: Part 2" in *Literary Cultures in History: Reconstructions from South Asia*, ed. S. Pollock (Berkeley: University of California Press, 2003; 958–1022), 986.

24. Ibid., 987.

25. The diction here very much borrows from classical Sanskrit and Braj texts describing ideal women. The latter term is somewhat unusual for its *madana-sadmini*, a term possibly meaning "she who is the seat of god Kama, i.e., Love" designating women, the object of love; or "she of the house of Kama, i.e., Rati" designating sexual pleasure. These interpretations assume *mocana* as essentially "emitting," as in elephants emitting their rut liquid (incidentally a.k.a. *mada*).

26. Heifetz, trans., *The Origin of the Young God*, 6.38.

27. Kashmiri term for "bridge," as P. Pāṭhak's edition explains.

28. These may in fact be electric (*bijalī*) lamps: *bijju-dīpa*.

29. A reference to god Indra as the "fortress-destroyer."

30. Gadādhar is normally a term for Vishnu as club-bearer; the text indicates that this is here an epithet for Krishna.

31. *Prītipatha poṣanahārī*, perhaps indicating Krishna devotion. Prātap Siṁh was not particularly known for his Krishna devotion, however.

32. Emphasizing the idea that everyone, Hindu and Muslim, considers this king their own; *"sovata sukha kī nīnda sabai nija-nṛpahi asīsata."*

33. See Chitralekha Zutshi, *Languages of Belonging: Islam, Regional Identity, and the Making of Kashmir* (New Delhi: Permanent Black, 2003).

34. In the minced words of a London *Times* writer in 1905:

> with the Maharaja's personal followers working against a Council which is naturally repugnant to one who is accustomed to regard himself as the absolute head of the State, and is so regarded by the majority of his people, it has been impossible even for the best of Residents to prevent intrigue and dissensions. Latterly, the influences surrounding the Maharaja have, fortunately, been better than they were a few years ago; and the Government of India has seized the opportunity to abolish the Council. . . . This change . . . is entirely in accord with native sentiment. . . . Unfortunately, recent events have rendered it impossible for Lord Curzon to carry out his intention of personally visiting Kashmir to install the Maharaja in his new position with the ceremony so much appreciated in a native State.

Anonymous, "Indian Affairs: The Future of Kashmir" (*The Times* [London], Sept. 26, 1905, p. 2, col. D).

35. "*Āpahi . . . vārati,*" i.e., averts the evil eye from herself.

36. Or perhaps "nibbles" (*dasati*)?

37. *Taruvara*: also the *kalpa-vṛkṣa*, wishing-tree of god Indra's paradise.

38. "Bāndhī . . . bhārata sira selī." Literally, "necklace tied at the top/head of India."

39. A feature noted in the analysis of R. Miśra, 285.

40. I.e., Vidhi, or Fate.

41. Puruṣa prakṛti kauṁ . . . jobana rasa āyau.

42. Prema-keli rasa-reli karana raṅga mahala sajāyau.

43. Cāṛhyau . . . bhārata ke mastaka.

44. Vibhūti.

45. Tapa-puñja-prasūta viśva-shobhā-śrī mandala.

46. An *ananvaya alaṃkāra*, "comparison of an object with its ideal" (idem, Monier-Williams), as pointed out by R. Miśra, 283.

47. Tripāṭhī, *Guide to Poetry*, 2: 118–19. I have drawn from my translation and introduction to this work in S. Nijhawan, ed., op. cit.

48. Compiled in Pāṭhak's 1918 collection *Bhārat-gīt* (*Songs of India*).

Chapter 5

1. "Prologue," 144.

2. For more information on Sumerasiṁh, see Ritter, "Networks."

3. *Kāvyopavan arthāt nānārasamayī kavitāvalī* (*A Garden of Verse, a Collection of Poems full of Various Rasas*) (Patna: Khaḍgavilās Press, 1909).

4. Or perhaps "natural portraits," as in naturalistically or realistically drawn.

5. Hariaudh, Introduction to *Garden*, 2–3.

6. Ibid., 3. Interestingly, in this phrase Hariaudh lapses from his otherwise Sanskritized diction with the phrase "*maze le lekar*."

7. This trope might come from Persian, and the common *gul-e-caman* of Urdu poetry. Like most learned men of his era, Hariaudh was well-versed in both Urdu and Persian; he had translated a canto of the thirteenth-century Sa'dī's Persian *Rose-Garden* with considerable success a few years earlier (*Upadeś kusum arthāt aṣṭam bāb Gulistāṁ kā bhāṣānuvād* [*Flowers of Instruction, a Translation into Vernacular of the Eight Chapter of* The Rose-Garden], 1901; 7th ed. [Allahabad: Indian Press, 1927]). Translations of Sa'dī in particular remained popular educational texts in the early twentieth century.

8. This is a feature found in many novels of the era, Hindi and Bengali, though not always with the emotion found in Hariaudh's *Half-Bloomed Flower*. These scenes in this included the following: 1: a night in the month of Baisakh; 4: the moon; 6: dawn; 7: twilight; 10: a windstorm; 11: a flower garden and a bee; 13: mountain streams; 15: a nighttime rainstorm; 17: women bathing in a river; 18: a forest before a storm; 19: a dense forest; 20: dawn on a cloudy day; 22: the passage of time and the beauty of nature; 23: life and death in nature; 27: just before dawn. We might also compare this structure to that of the Hindi story "The Worship of Three Deities at Even-Fall" in Hariścandra's *Kavivacanasudhā* of 1873, influenced by the Hindi translation of a Bengali translation of the Sanskrit *Kādambarī*. Dalmia describes the 1873 work as

> . . . remarkable for its alternation of set descriptive passages, which verge on the brink of a new, romantic perception of nature, and a narration of action, which seems psychologically motivated but . . . often remains inexplicable. . . . There are clear signs of a *Kādambarī*-like organization of narrative, of set descriptions of landscape and season, interspersed with a short, almost incidental description of story-line. (Dalmia, *Nationalization*, 294–95)

Hariaudh's *The Half-bloomed Flower* does not lack in plot, but may represent an extension of this *Kādambarī*-influenced prose style, and likely the influence of Bengali novel conventions of the time.

9. For details regarding the various editions of this work, which progressed toward a less Braj Bhāṣā-like and more Sanskritized diction, along with other syntactical changes, see Ritter, "The Language of Hariaudh's *Priyapravās*."

10. Hariaudh, *Priyapravās: Khaṛī-Bolī kā sarvaśreṣṭh mahākāvya* (*The Absence of the Beloved: The Foremost Khaṛī Bolī* Mahākāvya) (1914; rev. 1941; 23rd printing) (Varanasi: Hindī Sāhitya Kuṭīr, 1996), 1.1–5.

11. See Viśvambhar Mānav, *Priya-pravās kī ṭīkā* (*A Commentary on Priya-pravās*) (Allahabad: Lokabhāratī Prakāśan, 1968).

12. Hariaudh, *Absence*, 1.6–7.

13. Indar Nath Madan, *Modern Hindi Literature: A Critical Analysis* (Lahore: Minerva Book Shop, 1939), 36.

14. But the ascription of "nature poetry" to this work was ultimately a selectively applied appellation. This sympathetic nature of Yaśoda's lament, similar to that of classical literature but perhaps more linked to her subjective voice, garnered critical praise; on the other hand, the rendition of the "bee-song" found in canto 15 also enumerated varieties of jasmine flowers in a gopi's mournful entreaties in a garden, but this passage hardly finds mention in critical literature. Somehow the mother's view of nature in her pitiful grief suited the designation of "modern" better than the equally affectively charged bee-song genre of *śṛṅgāra*.

15. I address this epiphany in more detail in my article "Epiphany in Rādhā's Arbor: Nature and the Reform of Bhakti in Hariaudh's *Priyapravās*" in *Alternative Krishnas: Regional and Vernacular Variations on a Hindu Deity*, ed. G. Beck (Albany: State University of New York Press, 2005; 177–208), which I draw from in this section of this chapter. I have also drawn from my translation and introduction to this work in *Nationalism in the Vernacular*, ed. S. Nijhawan, op. cit.

16. The commentator Mānav has remarked on this strange simile, and the Persian term *gul* [rose, flower] within it.

17. Hariaudh, *Absence*, 16.80, 84–87.

18. Ibid., 16.88 and 81.

19. Edwin Gerow, *A Glossary of Indian Figures of Speech* (The Hague: Mouton, 1971), 249 and 156. Gerow illustrates the latter with a line from Daṇḍin, "That is no lotus, that is a face; those are not bees, they are eyes."

20. Loyana se ambuja bane, mukha so canda bakhāna. From the *Bhāṣā-Bhūṣaṇ* of Jasvant Siṁh "Bhūṣaṇ" in Snell, 151.

21. Hariaudh, *Absence*, 16.107–08.

22. Ibid., 16.112.3–4.

23. Ibid., 16.120.

24. Ibid., 16.21–22, 24, 26.

25. Scores of works on him can be found in Western libraries, including probably the most dissertations outside of India on any single Hindi author. There are indubitably many more studies of J. S. Prasād housed in Indian libraries.

26. See Rajendra Singh, *Jaishankar Prasad*, World Authors Series (Boston: Twayne, 1982); Ramesh Chandra Shah, *Jaishankar Prasad*, Makers of Indian Literature (New Delhi: Sahitya Akademi, 1978); Nagendra, *Jayashankar Prasad. His Mind and Art* (Delhi: Prabhat Prakashan, 1989); and the chapters on J. S. Prasād in the works of David Rubin, trans., *The Return of Sarasvati*, and *Of Love and War: A Chayavad Anthology*.

27. Rubin, *Return of Sarasvati*, 28.

28. Jayaśaṅkar Prasād, "Prakṛti-saundarya" ("The Beauty of Nature") (*Indu* [*The Moon*] 1:1 [1909]; reprinted in *Citrādhār (Album)* [1928] and *Collected Works* 6: 136–39), 136. Much of the publication information given here comes from Ūṣā Miśra, *'Prasād' kā pūrvavartī kāvya* (The Early Poetry of 'Prasād') (Allahabad: Sāhitya Bhavan, 1970), passim.

29. J. S. Prasād, "Beauty of Nature," 137.

30. Ibid., 137–38.

31. Ibid., 138.
32. Ibid., 139.
33. Quotation marks and other punctuation as given in Hindi.
34. A reference to the trope of the unfaithful lover returning from his tryst with eyes red from lack of sleep or from the betel juice of the other woman.
35. J. S. Prasād, "The Mango Blossom" ("Rasāl-mañjarī") (*Indu* 1:8 [1909], reprinted in *Album* (1918), and *Collected Works*, 1: 31–32). This poem is in Braj Bhāṣā with some Khaṛī Bolī copulas, and a 24 *mātrā* quatrain meter.
36. *Indu (The Moon)* 3:5 (1912), reprinted in *Kānan Kusum* (*Forest Flowers*) (1917?), and *Collected Works*, 125–26. Rubin has noted that the date of *Forest Flowers* remains unclear. Some scholars maintain a date of 1912 or 1913. The *Collected Works* reprint describes the work as containing poems from 1909–17. See Rubin, *Return of Sarasvati*, 29 and J. S. Prasād's *Collected Works* 1:105.
37. But we should remember that J. S. Prasād had not abandoned Braj poetry yet. In March 1913 (*Indu* [*The Moon*] 4:2) he published a Braj *kavitt* with just a few Khaṛī Bolī forms, entitled "Vasantotsav" ("The Spring Festival"). This poem took up exactly these tropes of the mango blossom, bee, and the cuckoo bird, although with perhaps somewhat more bhakti undertones, as in his signature line at the end, "Offering up the body entire, 'Prasād' is fulfilled [or an offering is completed] / Only from play [lila, and ostensibly the play of Holi] does the desert of the heart bloom like a garden."
38. "Dalit kumudini" ("The Crushed Little Lotus Blossom"), *Indu* (*The Moon*) 4:5 (1913); reprinted in *Forest Flowers* (1917?) and *Collected Works* 1:128–29.
39. OHED: a stick covered with flowers with which bride and groom playfully hit each other.
40. Here I am translating "*kaun paricay*?" as such. Alternatively, one might translate this as "what was their acquaintance [with the other]?," "did they meet?," or "how could they have met?" None of these quite capture the ambiguity of the phrase, which additionally names no subject who might have an acquaintance, etc., of something.
41. The original "*kyā thā sambandh*?" has a strong interrogatory tone from its inverted syntax; this is lost in any translation.
42. The mountain in the southern region of the subcontinent that is considered the source of cool breezes.
43. Other readings are possible. The image here seems to relate to the fragrance of the previous and following lines.
44. Or "met the fragrance, joyfully"; i.e., the fragrance of the wind.
45. *Chand*, a term denoting "meter" and "bond," and "ingenuity," or "trickery" as well; all are applicable to love in Indic poetry.
46. Jayaśaṅkar Prasād, "Paricay" ("Acquaintance"), in *Jharanā* (*Cascade*; 1918 edition), reprinted in *Collected Works*, 161–62.
47. Cited in U. Miśra, 5.
48. My translation, *Sūrasāgar* 2375 (1934; vol. 2; eds. Ratnākar, et al. [Varanasi: NPS, 1961]). I follow Snell but differ from his reading somewhat

(Snell, 101). The trope of this poem is of course not particular to Sur Das; it can be found in earlier Sanskrit poetry as well.

Chapter 6

1. 26.43–48, 59; 27 (reprinted in *Collected Works* 1:57–71).

2. Jayaśaṅkar Prasād, "Mahākṛīrā" ("The Great Play") (*Indu* [*The Moon*] 3:4 [1912]; reprinted in *Kānan Kusum* [*Forest Flowers*] [1917?] and *Collected Works* 1: 108–09), ll.1–8.

3. Ibid., ll. 13–14.

4. Ibid., ll. 17–18.

5. Ibid., ll. 25–32 (end).

6. Jayaśaṅkar Prasād, "Pratham Prabhāt" ("First Dawn") (*Indu* [*The Moon*] 4:5 [1913]; reprinted in *Kānan Kusum* [*Forest Flowers*] [1917?], *Jharanā* [*Cascade*] [2nd ed., 1928], and *Collected Works*, 111–12, ll. 1–6.

7. Ibid., ll. 7–12.

8. Ibid., v. 4.

9. *Pathik*: literally "one on the path"; a term for both traveler and pilgrim, and as noted above, and a term then newly in use for national rhetoric.

10. Jayaśaṅkar Prasād, *Prem-pathik* (*Pilgrim of Love*) was published in *Indu* (*The Moon*) 5:1:1 (1914; partial), as a stand-alone chapbook in the same year (Sāhitya suman mālā 4; Allahabad: Bhāratī Bhaṇḍār, 1914), in a second edition of 1928, and in a third edition (n.d.) which latter is reprinted in *Collected Works*, 1:57–71. The variants are not very substantial between the various editions of this Khaṛī Bolī *Pilgrim of Love*. The seed of this poem can be found in a Braj Bhāṣā poem of some 100 lines published in *Indu*'s first volume of 1909. For a comparison of the Braj and Khaṛī Bolī versions of *Prem-pathik*, see Anūp Kumār, *Prasād kī racanāoṁ meṁ saṃskaraṇāgat parivartanoṁ kā adhyayan* (*A Study of the Changes between Editions of the Works of Prasād*) (Allahabad: Hindī Pariṣad Prakāśan, 1984), 34 ff. Citations here are from the *Collected Works*.

11. J. S. Prasād, *Pilgrim*, v. 5.

12. Ibid., 16.25–26, end of verse.

13. Ibid., vv. 18–19.

14. Ibid., 19.16–22.

15. Ibid., 21.10, last line.

16. Ibid., 24.50.

17. Ibid., 26.38–48.

18. The *Collected Works* edition, following the minor revisions of the later Bhāratī Bhaṇḍār editions, contains a line immediately preceding this one, which does not appear in the 1914 edition: "The yellow splendor of heat (*tapan*) began to make a golden world." Ibid., 26.57–60, 27.

19. For biographical information, consult Orsini, *Hindi Public Sphere*, 439–40, the section on Tripāṭhī in *Nationalism in the Vernacular: Hindi, Urdu, and the Literature of Indian Freedom*, ed. S. Nijhawan (Hyderabad: Orient Blackswan, 2010) and "Adhīr" [Indararāj Baid], Chapter 1 of *Rāmanareś Tripāṭhī* (1987; Bhāratīya

Sāhitya ke Nirmātā; 2nd ed.; New Delhi: Sāhitya Academy, 1993). The information summarized below is given with reference to Adhīr.

20. See Chapter 1, note 55. for references on the Hindustani movement.

21. Gandhi himself praised the text, and it was later spared from proscription by the tweaked translations of Lālā Sītārām of Ayodhya (see earlier chapters, passim), who was at that time a Government reporter. Tripāṭhī would be jailed in the following year as part of a mass arrest of fifty-five Allahabad movement leaders (Adhīr, 42, 16).

22. *Paṭa-parivartana*, literally, "raising of the curtain" (Rāmanareś Tripāṭhī, *Pathik: khaṇḍakāvya* [*The Pilgrim: A Narrative Poem*] [1920; 29th ed., Delhi: Rājapāl and Sons, 1952]), 1.2.1, 3–4.

23. Tripāṭhī, *Pilgrim*, 1.21.3–4.

24. Ibid., 3.8.3–4.

25. See the studies of celibacy in the context of nationalism, such as Joseph S. Alter, "Celibacy, Sexuality, and the Transformation of Gender into Nationalism in North India" (*The Journal of Asian Studies* 53:1 [Feb., 1994], 45–66). And as Purnima Mankekar has noted in regard to contemporary television serials, gender is a prominent subtext of nationalism, such that "in Param Veer Chakra ["Purple Hearts," a serial on war heroes] . . . the male protagonists' relationships with women are *constantly* posed against their devotion to their country" ("National Texts and Gendered Lives: An Ethnography of Television Viewers in a North Indian City," *American Ethnologist* 20:3 [Aug., 1993], 543–563; quotation on 546).

26. Saiyad Amīr Alī, "Sandhyā" ("Evening") (*Sarasvatī* 12:7 [July 1911], 326–27).

27. See the "Poetry" section in the index by genre of the appendix to Gauṛ.

28. Girijādatt Śukla "Girīś," "Merā svapna" ("My Dream") (*Strī-darpaṇ* [*Women's Mirror*] 17:5 [Nov. 1917], 267–69).

29. Kapiladev Mālavīya, "Prakṛti kī pyārī pyārī bāteṁ" ("The Sweet Sweet Words of Nature") (*Strī-darpaṇ* [*Women's Mirror*] 22:1 [Jan. 1920], 41–44).

30. Here I recall the revelatory identification that Nāmavar Siṁh described, examined in Chapter 2.

Chapter 7

1. This chapter is an expanded version of my article, "The Proper Female Subject: Poetics and Erotics in Early Twentieth Century Hindi" (*Journal of Women's History* 22:1 [Spring 2010]).

2. Reprinted in *Rasakalas* (*A Pot of* Rasa) (Varanasi: Hindī Sāhitya Kuṭīr, 1931, 99–102, quotation here v.1, 99); original date in the 1920s.

3. In reference to a "fallen woman" magazine story of the 1920s, "the fact that the [fallen woman's] story was told from [her] point of view and expressed her feelings provoked in the readers a sense of 'alienation' (the *ostranenie* of the Russian formalists) that forced them to feel the enormity of the injustice done to her" (Orsini, *Hindi Public Sphere*, 280).

4. "Devī, māṁ, sahacarī, prāṇ"; the last line of Sumitrānandan Pant's poem "Nārī rūp" ("Forms of woman"), in his *New Leaves* (op. cit.), 112–13.

5. N. Siṁh, *Chāyāvād*, 42. He illustrates the latter with a quote from Pant, uncited.

6. Ibid., 43.

7. Ibid., 46.

8. Ibid., 64.

9. Ibid., 46–47.

10. See Stark, 91 ff.

11. Jagannāth Prasād, English Introduction to the first edition, *Chandaḥ-prabhākar* (*Illuminator of meter*) (1894; 3rd ed., n.p.: 1915), 3. Jagannāth Prasād (1859–1947) (a.k.a. "Bhānu kavi") worked for the Revenue Settlement Department in Wardha, Central Provinces, in which state the book was designated as a library and prize book.

12. Ibid., Hindi Introduction, footnote, 3.

13. Ibid., English Introduction, 4.

14. Kṛṣṇabihārī Miśra, "Brajabhāṣā meṁ kavitā" ("Poetry in Braj Bhāṣā"), *Indu* (*The Moon*) 6:1:1 (Jan. 1915), 2–11, 9 ff.

15. Ratnākar, Introduction, Kṛpārām, *Hitataraṅginī*, 1894.

16. Charu Gupta, *Sexuality, Obscenity, Community: Women, Muslims, and the Hindu Public in Colonial India*, 2001 (New York: Palgrave, 2002).

17. Here I refer the reader to Pritchett, *Nets*, and Āzād, both op. cit.

18. An examination of a few examples of this theme in poetry and drama from 1889 is found in Christopher King, "Images of Vice and Virtue: The Hindi-Urdu controversy in Two Nineteenth Century Hindi Plays" in *Religious Controversy in British India: Dialogues in South Asian Languages*, ed. K. Jones, (Albany: State University of New York Press, 1992) and *One Language*, 135 ff. I have happened upon a few more examples in my research, attesting to the popularity of this personification of Urdu, and often Hindi, as women.

19. This is clearly an erotic motif. Cf. Rasakhān's verse, "Why go to the gardens, beloved—just sitting at home I'll plant a garden to show you / my heels are like flower-buds of pomegranate, my two arms I shall bend over you like *campak* branches" (Snell's translation, with minor adjustments) (from *Sujān-Rasakhān* [sixteenth century] in Snell), 119.

20. Bālamukund Gupta, "Urdū ko uttar" in Tripāṭhī, ed., *Guide to Poetry* 2: 209–14.

21. Advertisement on the back cover of Hariaudh's *Ṭheṭh Hindī kā ṭhāṭ arthāt ṭheṭh Hindī meṁ likhī gaī ek man lubhānevālī kahānī* (*An Exposition in Authentic Hindi, or a Pleasing Story written in Authentic Hindi*) (Bankipur: Khaḍgavilās Press, 1899).

22. Further, Hariaudh connects Bankim's Swadeshi sentiments to the willfulness to Bhramar: "Gracing the post of Deputy Collector for a long time, he also had great feeling on the subject of Independence (*svadeś*)" (Ed. and trans. Hariaudh, Afterword to *Rāy Bahādur Baṅkimacandra Caṭṭopādhyāy C.I.E. kṛt Kṛṣṇakānter uil arthāt Kṛṣṇakānt kā dānapātra* [by the order of A. Croft, Dir. Public Instruction, Bengal; Bankipore: Khaḍgavilās Press, 1898; 261–68], 263). Further research on

the complexities of loyalism/Swadeshi and "traditional"/"progressive" gender politics is needed.

23. It should be noted that Hariaudh did not oppose *tejas* generally, but rather its excess in women. Further, *tejas* appears later as a positive term for the affect of nationalist agitation. From its epic meaning of "fierceness," "power," "energy," or "majesty," and literally "fire" in the Vaiśeṣika theory of natural elements, *tejas* and its associated forms would become bywords for positive action. In Mathilīśaraṇ Gupta's 1910 *Jayadrathavadha*, an epic poem containing a rather guarded national allegory, the *tejasvī* are the Pāṇḍava protagonists of the *Mahabharata*. In Hariaudh's own *Priyapravās* (1914) we find the term *tejas* is attributed positively to presumably male political leaders. Thenceforward, it is not uncommonly found as an attribute of activists for Swadesh. Not coincidentally, the Indian military named a fighter jet "Tejas" in 2003; it is clearly a term with nationalist resonance.

24. Hariaudh, Afterword, 265.

25. Ibid., 266–67.

26. It is notable here that Hariaudh's translation ends a few paragraphs shorter than other editions. In his version, the novel ends with the epitaph on Govindalāl's memorial to Bhramar; in another version, an ascetic Govindalāl returns to visit the statue after twelve years, having found peace in god, and then disappears again. Cf. Bankim Chandra Chatterjee, *The Poison Tree: Three Novellas*, trans. M. Maddern and S. N. Mukherjee (New Delhi: Penguin Books, 1996).

27. This approach was not unusual: Tagore himself would later lament the fact that even in his own Bengal literary criticism had been reduced to the assessment of female characters' propriety. In this regard he mentions Bankim's Bhramar specifically: ". . . critics go to the extreme tenuity of debate as to the excellence of Bankim's heroines in their strict conformity with the canons of Hinduism. Whether the indignation which Bhramar showed against her husband took away from the transcendental preciosity of her Hindu womanhood." He further lamented, "these are the questions seriously discussed in the name of literary criticism [,which] . . . can only be found in our country, among all the countries of the world." This essay responded to criticism of Tagore's novel *Home and the World*, with its own transgressing heroine ("The Object and Subject of a Story," *Modern Review*, September 1918 [reprinted in *The English Writings of Rabindranath Tagore*, ed. S. K. Das (New Delhi: Sahitya Akademi, 1994; 737–41)], 741).

28. Not just the politicized term *tejas*, but also *svatantratā* (independence), was drawn into discussion of the evils of the Westernized woman. In the foreword to his 1899 novel *Independent Ramā and Dependent Lakṣmī* (*Svatantra Ramā aur paratantra Lakṣmī*), the early Hindi journalist Lajjārām Śarmā Mehatā explicates his point that the character Ramā was ill-served by her English education and its new social standards: "Ramā got so much trouble from obtaining independence, and Lakṣmī got so much happiness from remaining dependent." Cited in Ṛturāj, *Lajjārām Mehatā*, Hamāre purodhā-5 (Udaipur: Rājasthān Sāhitya Academy, 1989), 18. Thus the very terms of discourse for political freedom were also negative Westernized attributes for women, and may buttress the widely accepted view of the Indian man's feeling of effeminization as colonial subject, expected unjustly to be *paratantra* and forego *tejas*.

29. On attacks on such religious/courtly tropes, see David L. Haberman, "On Trial: The Love of the Sixteen Thousand Gopees." (*History of Religions* 33:1 [Aug. 1993], 44–70); George A. Grierson, *The Modern Vernacular Literature of Hindustan* (Calcutta: Asiatic Society, 1889); and Bankim Chandra Chatterjee, *Krishna-Charitra* (1892; trans. and ed. P. Bhattacharya (Calcutta: M.P. Birla Foundation, 1991). Scholarly anxiety about religious and literary uses of the erotic and/or *śṛṅgāra* persists into the present day.

30. Kenneth W. Jones, *Socio-Religious Reform Movements in British India*, The New Cambridge History of India, vol. 3, no.1 (Cambridge: Cambridge University Press, 1994 [Indian edition]), 45.

31. Here we may note that while at its inception, Hindi literary criticism was essentially an elite enterprise, as any printed text at the time, the cultural power of this early twentieth-century criticism and its moral politics are now reproduced among vast numbers of literate, college-educated Hindi speakers.

32. "What is poetry?" ("Kavitā kyā hai?"), 1909; reprinted in *Cintāmaṇi*. N. Siṁh, ed. (New Delhi: Rājakamal Prakāśan, 1985, 3:91–101), 93.

33. Additionally, two authors in particular used traditional erotics in complex ways in their oeuvre which otherwise fully engaged with "modern" literary subjects of nation and morality: the essayist and critic of the English Raj Pratāpanārāyaṇ Miśra (1856–1894), and Badarī Nārāyaṇ Upādhyāy "Premaghan" (1855–1922), who published Braj poetry in the erotic mode into the teens.

34. M. Dvivedī, *Collected Works* 13:303.

35. Introduction to *Kumārasambhavasār* (*The Essence of* The Birth of the Prince) (Varanasi: NPS, 1902; reprinted in Ibid., 13:509).

36. "A newly married woman or [in poetics] a woman afraid or embarrassed to keep an assignation" (*OHED*).

37. M. Dvivedī, "Nāyikā-bhed" (1901, reprinted in *Collected Works* 2:55–58), 55–56.

38. Ibid., 56–57.

39. Padmākar, *Jagavinod* (*Worldly pleasure*) (Banaras: Bhārat Jivan Press, 1902), 8.

40. Śrīdhar Pāṭhak was himself the Allahabad respondent for the Age of Consent Committee in the 1920s. See his responses to its questionnaire in his *Collected Works* 3:179–88.

41. For an extensive examination of Gupta's biography and the national sentiments embedded within his earlier *Jayadratha-vadh* of 1910, see Lothspeich, "The Edifying Waves of *Jayadratha-vadh*," (Chapter 6 of *Epic Nation*, 106–37).

42. Alṭāf Ḥusain Ḥālī's *Musaddas* served as the inspiration for the schemata of this work; see the Introduction of Christopher Shackle and J. Majeed's translation of the *Musaddas* for an analysis of this theme of the glorious past and fallen present state in the original Islamicate context of Ḥālī's work (*Ḥālī's* Musaddas: *The Flow and Ebb of Islam* [Delhi: Oxford University Press, 1997]).

43. Maithilīśaraṇ Gupta, *Bhārat-bhāratī* (*The Voice of India*), 1912–14 (Jhansi: Sāhitya Sadan, 1991), "Past," 161–62.

44. "Contemporary," 158.3–4.

45. Ibid., 162.2.

46. Ibid., 232.1. This recalls Sumanta Banerjee's article on female folk singers ("The Marginalization of Women's Popular Culture in Nineteenth Century Bengal," in K. Sangari and S. Vaid, eds., *Recasting Women: Essays in Indian Colonial History* [New Brunswick: Rutgers UP, 1990]).

47. Ibid., 92.1–2, 93.1.

48. Ibid., v. 98.

49. We can of course see these developments in light of the larger developments of gender and nationalism of the time. The exaltation of female figures, mythological, historical, and significantly for us, as the motherland—continued apace in the context of nationalism. Continuing in the vein of "Bande Mātaram" with its goddess-like Mother India described in large-scale natural, almost geographical terms, Maithilīśaraṇ Gupta published a poem in a 1911 issue of *Sarasvatī*, "Matṛbhūmi" ("The Motherland"), on an embodied divine image of nature. Similarly, Śrīdhar Pāṭhak published "Bhārat gagan" ("The Sky of India") along the same thematic lines, later published in his *Bhārat gīt* (*Songs of India*) of 1917, a nationalist volume including marching songs. His "Beauty of Kashmir" of 1904, addressed here in Chapter 4, had already hinted at an embodied geographical India, in the appearance of an ideal beauty, with Kashmir as her crown. These are just a few examples by canonized poets, reflecting a trend seen so widely in periodical literature it would be difficult to document.

50. For Tagore's thoughts, see the essay "Śakuntalā" of 1904 (op. cit.).

51. Facing page one, details p. 352, signed "Seyne," reportedly a Japanese artist, in a style similar to that of Abanīndranāth Tagore and Nandalāl Bose of that period. The following issue would carry a print portraying the pining *yakṣa*.

52. E.g., a "Bihārī kā viraha varṇan" ("Bihārī's description of *viraha*"), 8:12 (Aug. 1911), 382–88.

53. Jayaśaṅkar Prasād, "Kavi aur kavitā" ("The Poet and Poetry") (*Indu* [*The Moon*] 2:1 [1910], reprinted in Prasād's *Collected Works* 6:152–58), 153.

54. Ibid., 152.

55. The Chāyāvād poets are more known for their appeal to a corollary to this nature-realism: a realism of *bhāva*—emotion, feeling, or affect. J. S. Prasād here identifies *bhāva* with the same term from Sanskrit poetics, *sañcārī* and *sthāyī bhāva*, the "suggesting" and "permanent" emotions comprised in, for instance, the setting and portrayal of a *śṛṅgārik* scene. However, he finds these categories incompetent to the variety of mental dispositions, *manovṛttiyaṁ*, both good and bad. And he found *śṛṅgāra*'s *bhāva* limited: "thanks to the *śṛṅgāra* poets, these *bhāva*s found a home only in their *srngārī nāyikās*." Real emotion and real nature here thus align as modern allies against *śṛṅgāra*. Resolving this problem would mean the creation of poetry "showing the emotions of the harsh, generous, evil, cruel, compassionate, and pondering heart, emotional (*bhāvamayī*) poetry of the way of the world," which would then affect "man's character, by which he is uplifted (*sudharatā*)." This familiar "uplift" via naturalistic description of emotion J. S. Prasād locates in Pāṭhak's *Desolate Village* (i.e., Goldsmith's *Deserted Village*, transcreated, as discussed in Chapter 3), and a certain poem of Maithilīśaraṇ Gupta, the woeful "Story of Draupadi's hair" (J. S. Prasād, "Poet and Poetry," 154).

56. Ibid., 157.
57. Ibid., 158.
58. Ibid.
59. Ibid.
60. K. D. Sharma, "Maithilīśaraṇa Gupta: A Literary Biography," in *Maithilīśaraṇa Gupta: An Anthology*, ed. Nagendra (Delhi: Bansal and Co., 1981; 13–29), 20.
61. Incidentally, Dvivedī stated that he published the volume as part of his project to promote the use of Khaṛī Bolī instead of Braj, so that "someday the language of Hindi's prose and poetry will be the same" (Foreword to *Kavitā Kalāp* [*A collection of poetry*] in *Collected Works*, 561).
62. Conventionally, the ascetic practice of abstaining from sex is considered to generate *tapas* (heat) in the body of the (male) ascetic. It is also worth noting another aspect of Rambhā's sexual persona: she was raped by the demon Rāvaṇa in the Rāmāyaṇa. *Collected Works*, 177.
63. Here we might consider travel literature (in its colonial-era incarnation), as well as the regionally marked *nāyikā*s found scattered in Sanskrit *kāvya*, and gathered in regional "competition" in a twelfth-century inscription, and in contemporary ephemera showcasing "Brides of India." See Timothy Lenz, "A New Interpretation of the Rāula-Vela Inscription," in *Studies in Early Modern Indo-Aryan Languages, Literature and Culture*, eds. A.W. Entwistle, et al., (New Delhi: Manohar, 1999). I possess such a "Brides of India" advertisement calendar, gifted to me in Allahabad, 1998, distributed by Cadila Pharmaceuticals, Ltd., Ahmedabad.
64. Sudipta Kaviraj, "Tagore and Transformations in the Ideals of Love" in *Love in South Asia: A Cultural History*, ed. F. Orsini, (Cambridge: Cambridge UP, 2006; 161–82), 171–72.
65. Dvivedī, *Kavitā*, 9.
66. Ibid., 65.
67. M. Gupta, *Śakuntalā* (Jhansi: Sahitya-sadan, 1914), "Janm aur bālyakāl" ("Birth and childhood"), 10.3–4.
68. Ibid., 12.1, 13.1–2.
69. Ibid., 11, 16.
70. Hariaudh, *Absence*, 4:6–8.
71. Ibid., 6.41.1–2, 6.42, 6.45.2–4, 6.46.
72. Cited above, note 2.
73. The Ravi Varma classic is a depiction of Mohini, "the temptress," a seductive nymph of mythology. The image was a popular one, used in advertisements and home decoration, and it inspired many more versions of it by various artists, for journals and popular art, often unlabeled as Mohini per se, and likely transformed into simply a female human beauty.
74. Bipati ke ghere ghora-dukha te ghirati hai / Bhārata ke bhūle gāta-sudhi bhūli bhūli jāti / phūle phūle phūlī phūlī lalanā phirati hai (Hariaudh, "Lover," 3.5–8).
75. Ibid., 5.7–8.
76. Here we might consider the ethical valence of the modern *nāyikā* in terms of the significance of the mother, i.e., the moral mother for the sons of

the nation, or the "virgin mother" model of Tamil. Strikingly, while the sexual purity of these figures is implied by the absence of straightforward erotics, their role as mother—even in this political context of Mother India rhetoric, and even when Bhārat is invoked in a poem, as in Hariaudh's above—is seldom found. Certainly we can assume however that the "self-help" urge to reform Hindi poetry had some basic motivation to provide proper poetry for women as mothers of the nation's progeny. For discussion of the nationalist virgin/ mother see Sumathi Ramaswamy, "Virgin Mother, Beloved Other: The Erotics of Tamil Nationalism in Colonial and Post-Colonial India" in *Signposts: Gender Issues in Post-Independence India* (New Delhi: Kali for Women, 1999), 26 ff. The desirable virgin/mother trope also had resonance in Śākta theology, but these female figures become prominent only with the Chāyāvādīs, for whom the problem of erotics was already somewhat "resolved" by nature poetry (see the subsequent chapters).

77. Matirām, *Matirām-granthāvalī* (*The Collected Works of Matirām*), eds. K. Miśra and B. K. Miśra (Lucknow: Gaṅgā-granthāgār, 1925). Reprint, Ākār Series 6, eds. K. D. P. Gauṛ, et al. (Varanasi: NPS, 1964). K. Miśra advocated the "practical use" of *nāyikā-bhed* in an article in *Sarasvatī* referenced above. See note 14.

78. Kṛṣṇabihārī Miśra should not be mistaken for one of the "Miśrabandhu" (Miśra brothers), Śyāmabihārī, Śukadevabihārī, and Gaṇeṣabihārī Miśra, well-known twentieth-century literary historians. Though now obscure, K. Miśra was in fact well established in the literary journals of the era. His articles appeared in almost every issue of the early years of the journal *Mādhurī* in the early 1920s.

79. A note from the publisher in the third edition of 1939 indicates the book was in high demand, as part of the Hindī Sāhitya Sammelan's highest examination. See Orsini, *Hindi Public Sphere*, 1.4.4 for a description of the cultural reach of this curriculum.

80. M. Dvivedī, review of *Matirām-granthāvalī* (*Mādhurī*, Oct. 1926, reprinted in Dvivedī's *Collected Works* 2: 288–89), 289.

81. This and the following quotations are from Sylvanus Stall, *What a Young Husband Ought to Know*, Self and Sex Series for Men, vol. 3 (Philadelphia: Vir Publishing Company, unknown edition [1897 or 1907]), 26–27, in translation (trans. unknown) and transliterated into English in Kṛṣṇabihārī Miśra, introduction to *Matirām*, 3. Stall's serious of epistolary books appear to have been translated widely, including into several Indian languages, a fact advertised in their frontispieces in a foldout world map overlaid with pages from the Self and Sex books in various languages, and Stall's portrait at top. These publications were also produced as phonograph recordings. K. Miśra's edition may have been published in a London house of Vir Publishing, or it may have been disseminated in India by American missionaries. Incidentally, another Vir publication was transcreated (not translated) by Chabināth Pāṇḍey in 1924 (*Caritra-Cintan: brahmacāryya aur ātma-saṃyamapar vicār aur usake sādhak upāyakoṁkā digdarśan* [*Thinking on Character: Thoughts on the Student Stage of Life and Self-Control and Directions for their Practical Implementation*]; Calcutta: Hindī Pustak Agency); it was based on the 1922 *Out*

for Character: Twenty-six Articles, described as "written by twenty-six thoughtful and eminent persons interested in the vital questions concerning the mental and moral well-being of young men and women."

82. K. Miśra, Introduction, 22.
83. Ibid., 25–28.
84. Ibid., 84.
85. Ibid., 153.
86. Uncited lines, ibid., 156.
87. Hariaudh, *Rasakalas*, 82.
88. Ibid., 85.
89. Nandadulāre Vājapeyī, "Ārambhik kāvya-vikās" ("The Initial Development of Poetry") in *Jayaśaṅkar Prasād*, rev. ed. (Allahabad: Bhāratī-Bhaṇḍār, 1959, 50–64), 52.
90. "Hṛdayeś" (Hṛdayanārāyaṇ Pāṇḍey), "Rasa-dhārā" ("Stream of rasa") (*Cānd* [*The Moon*] 4:1:2:39 [Dec. 1925], 1).

Chapter 8

1. Rāmacandra Śukla, "Kāvya meṁ prākṛtik dṛśya" ("Natural scenes in poetry") in two parts, *Mādhurī*, June 21, 1923, and following issue. Reprinted in Rāmacandra Śukla, *Cintāmaṇi* vol. 2, 1945; ed. V. Miśra; Nāgarīpracāriṇī granthamālā 70; 4th ed. (Varanasi: NPS, 1996; 1–33), 30–31.
2. Hindi critic Nāmavar Siṁh has traced and astutely commented upon many early Śukla essays and their various renditions before publication in anthologies; an in-depth study of the dating of his other anthologized essays is yet to be done.
3. *Akaṛ kar jo tane / bānī bānā badal bahut bigaṛe. Nāgarīpracāriṇī patrikā (The Magazine for the Promotion of Hindi)*, September–December, 1917. Reprinted in *Madhusrot: ācārya Rāmacandra Śukla kī kavitāoṁ kā saṃgraha* [*Spring of Nectar: A Collection of Ācārya Rāmacandra Śukla's poetry*] (Nāgarīpracāriṇī granthamālā 79; Varanasi: NPS, 1971), 79–80.
4. Śukla, *History* (1929 edition), 684.
5. The Irish context and anti-imperialist message of Cardinal Newman's book on education and canon, composed of lectures while rector at the Catholic University in Dublin, probably appealed strongly to colonial-era Indians.
6. *Die Welträtsel*, first published in German in 1899, and translated by Śukla from the English translation of Joseph McCabe, *The Riddle of the Universe at the Close of the Nineteenth Century* (New York: Harper and Bros., 1900).
7. Nāmavar Siṁh, "Ek antaryātrā ke pradeś" ("The Regions of an Inner Journey"), introduction to *Cintāmaṇi*, vol. 3, ed. N. Siṁh (New Delhi: Rājakamal Prakāśan, 1985; 5–21), 10.
8. Most recently in English, Milind Wakankar has written on Śukla in "The Moment of Criticism in Indian Nationalist Thought: Ramchandra Shukla and the Poetics of a Hindi Responsibility" (*South Atlantic Quarterly* 101:4 [Fall

2002], 987–1014). Most of the well-known critics in Hindi have analyzed Śukla's works to some extent, the foremost including Nāmavar Siṁh, Nagendra, and Rambilas Sharma.

9. *Pratyakṣ*, i.e., what is visually evident, or witnessed, before one's eyes (N. Siṁh, "Regions of an Inner Journey," 12).

10. Ibid., 10.

11. Śukla, "Kalpanā meṁ ānand" ("Pleasure of the Imagination") (*Nāgarīpracāriṇī Patrikā [The Magazine for the Promotion of Hindi]*, vol. 9 [1905]; reprinted in *Cintāmaṇi* 3: 34–60), 55.

12. For elaboration of the fantastical characters of the folk-romance, see Frances W. Pritchett, *Marvelous Encounters: Folk Romance in Urdu and Hindi* (Riverdale: Riverdale Co., 1985).

13. Along with the topic of gardens as an index of a culture's proclivity to "follow nature." See below.

14. Passim, Introduction to Ernst Haeckel, *Viśva-prapañc* (*Wonder of the World*) (trans. [from English] R. Śukla, ed. S. Dās; Varanasi: NPS, 1920). Reprinted in Śukla, *Cintāmaṇi* 3: 113–185). He also stated that Vaiśeṣika thought was equivalent to that of modern chemistry (117), mentions his contemporary Jagdish Chandra Basu, Calcutta biophysicist of international repute, and defines the term "science" (*vijñān*) as follows: the object of modern science is *aparā* (of this world, secondary) nature; *parā* (otherworldly) nature the object of "metaphysics" (Engl. *meṭāfiziks*).

15. For an analysis of Haeckel's monism, a "natural religion" "written in nature everywhere," and "philosophy of science," see Niles R. Holt, who has described this view in detail, as "not merely Darwinism, or pantheism, or mechanism, or a 'natural religion,' but a combination of all of these systems" ("Ernst Haeckel's Monistic Religion," *Journal of the History of Ideas* 32:2 (Apr.–June 1971), 265–280, 271). On the controversy surrounding Haeckel's ideas, see Robert J. Richards, "Ernst Haeckel and the Struggles over Evolution and Religion" (*Annals of the History and Philosophy of Biology*, vol. 10 [2005]: 89–115).

16. Śukla, Introduction to *Wonder*, 114.

17. See Orsini, *Hindi Public Sphere*, 55–57.

18. Many similar images, and extensive discussion of "the expression of nature" in poetry can be found in this essay, among many other English sources. This intensely integrative essay includes references to: Robert Browning's "Rabbi Ben Ezra"; I. A. Richards' *Principles of Literary Criticism*; Wordsworth's "A Lesson" and "Ode on Intimations of Immortality"; Lascelles Abercrombie's "The Fool's Adventure," "The Trance," "Sale of St. Thomas," "The Eternal Wedding," and "An Escape"; Shelley's "The Question," "Alastor," "Hymn to Intellectual Beauty," and "The Poet's Dream"; Yeats' "To the Rose upon the Rood of Time" and *Ideas of Good and Evil*; J. E. Spingarn's *The New Criticism*; Clive Bell's *Art*; Gayley and Kurtz's *Methods and Materials of Literary Criticism*; A. Symons' *The Symbolist Movement in Literature*; Blake's *From a Vision of the Last Judgement*; A. B. DeMille's *Literature in the Century*; R. Macaulay's *The Two Blind Countries*; and M. Sturgeon's *Studies of Contemporary Poets*.

19. This essay appeared in varying forms from 1909 to 1930, as N. Siṁh has explained in some detail. I have limited myself to the 1909 version reprinted in *Cintāmaṇi* 3:91–101.

20. Śukla, *History*, 322.

21. It is possible that Śyāmasundar Dās's first 1923 edition of *Sāhityālocanā* (*Literary Criticism*) contained such discussion of nature in poetry because this work is considered to be a Hindi version of the English textbook by William Henry Hudson, *An Introduction to the Study of Literature*, of which the second 1910 edition contains an appendix, "On the Treatment of Nature in Poetry" (London and Calcutta: Harrap, 1922). I have not been able to locate a first edition of the Dās volume, and Dās extensively revised later editions, so whether Śukla's article is the first instance of a literary-critical "Nature" in Hindi remains an open question. However, if Dās' volume in its first edition did contain discussion of nature as per Hudson's appendix, such discussion would still be translation or transcreation at most, whereas Śukla's essay appears wholly original.

22. Joseph Addison, *The Spectator*, vol. 6, no. 411 (1713), 83–84.

23. Śukla, "Natural Scenes," 1.

24. True poets "make pictures stand before us," for Āzād. Pritchett links this stance very convincingly with similar statements from Johnson, Coleridge, and Macaulay (Pritchett, *Nets*, 158–59).

25. The "supporting object" of a sensory experience, here in poetics, e.g., the hero and heroine within the *śṛṅgāra rasa*.

26. Śukla, "Natural Scenes," 1.

27. Ibid., 2.

28. Gerow, *Glossary*, 324–26. See also the discussion in Chapter 1.

29. In this Śukla cites seventh/eighth century rhetorician Daṇḍin, who "distinguishes the figure from the rest of the *alaṃkāras*," in "one of the longest standing disputes of the *alaṃkāraśāstra*" (Ibid., 324). In Śukla's 1909 "What is Poetry?" he makes the same objection, also with the point that the definition of *svabhāvokti* is overly general (*ativyāpt*) and therefore should not be an ornament (100–01).

30. Śukla, "Pleasure," 101.

31. Śukla, "Natural Scenes," 13.

32. The "bad reputation" of ornament as extraneous would survive into contemporary times, as Gerow would point out in reference to Sushil Kumar De's distate for a "formalist poetic" deriving from his "distinctions of inner and outer, of truth and show, of insight and pretense, of genius (art) and scholasticism" (Gerow, *Glossary*, 10). Śukla's thought here represents an earlier, Hindi-medium version of such binarism.

33. Śukla, "Natural Scenes," 5.

34. *Svacchand*: see Chapter Two for this term's usage in modern criticism.

35. Śukla, "Natural Scenes," 5.

36. See the previous chapter, note 53.

37. These are not plants often cited in poetry—Śukla's point is that Vālmīki is not merely conventional in his description, but realistic. The *babūl* (acacia) is associated with worthlessness: to plant acacias is "to do something which can produce no good result" (idem, *OHED*). The *tendū* could be a variety of plants, such as a melon, a tree yielding ebony, or an evergreen (idem, *OHED*).

38. Śukla, "Natural Scenes," 6.

39. Śukla, "Natural Scenes," 5.

40.

> A man of a polite imagination is let into a great many pleasures that the vulgar are not capable of receiving. . . . He meets with secret refreshment in a description, and often feels greater satisfaction in the prospect of fields and meadows, than another does in the possession. It gives him, indeed, a kind of property in everything he sees, and makes the most rude uncultivated parts of nature administer to his pleasures: so that he looks upon the world, as it were, in a different light, and discovers in it a multitude of charms, that conceal themselves from the generality of mankind. (Addison, 86.)

41. Śukla, "Natural Scenes," 2–3.

42. *Paristhiti* is a calque of English "circumstance" in Bengali, then adopted in Hindi (idem, *OHED*).

43. Śukla, "Natural Scenes," 9.

44. Ibid., 16–17.

45. Ibid., 19.

46. Ibid., 18–19.

47. The former consists of what might be called in English a "personification" of the Himalayas as a god, although Śukla does not broach this matter. The latter, being in the voice of Lakṣmaṇ, implies a certain subjectivity framing the presentation of the description—an *ālambana* that is not accounted for in the original *ālambana* category: the would-be *ālambana*, Lakṣmaṇ, here creates *ālambana*s within the literary text.

48. Śukla, "Natural Scenes," 3.

49. Ibid., 2 ff. The object of the emotion (*bhāva*) possessed by the *āśray-ālamban* would be the *viṣāy-ālamban*, the *ālamban* that is the "object of sense." See the use of the term *viṣay* generally, and in Śukla's essay, cited passim. E.g., a hero experiencing the *bhāva* of *rati* (pleasure) would be the *āśrāy*; his lover would be the object toward which this *bhāva* is projected.

50. Śukla, "Natural Scenes," 32. He also cites the genre of *nāyika-bhed* as proof that poetry works without an *āśray* in the text (26). This whole argument seems to be straw dog; perhaps Śukla wrote of the "problem" of no *āśray* in response to traditionalist arguments for the necessity of the hero and heroine as *ālambana*s.

51. By his logic *bhāva* may be possessed by natural objects themselves, as *ālambana*s of poetry's content, although ironically Śukla would disapprove of the younger Chāyāvād generation's use of this sort of personification.

52. Śukla, "Natural Scenes," 25.

53. Siṁh has noted that the idea of poetry as *bhāva yoga* was further elaborated by Śukla in the 1930s (N. Siṁh, "Regions of an Inner Journey," 13).

54. In this theme Śukla's thought resembles that of his contemporary Radhakrishnan as described by Halbfass in *India and Europe*, whose philosophical

writings reflected a turn toward the value of experience. See William Halbfass, *India and Europe: An Essay in Understanding* (Albany: State University of New York Press, 1988), 395 ff. Further, Śukla's *bhāva* suggests the experiential *bhāva* of Vaishnava religiosity, and its dominance over conventions of *rasa* per se hints at the bhakti ethos generally.

55. Śukla, "Natural Scenes," 25.

56. Ibid., 13.

57. "*Ahamātmā . . . sarvambhūtāśayasthitaḥ*," *Bhagavad Gita* 10.20.

58. Śukla, "Natural Scenes," 5.

59. Ibid., 4.

60. Ibid., 7.

61. Ibid., 14.

62. Ibid., 31.

63. Ibid., 8.

64. Also "fancy" or "desire."

65. Śukla, "Natural Scenes," 8. The quotation marks are as given in the original text.

66. Ibid., 3.

67. Here I of course reference the title of Wendy Doniger's *Śiva: The Erotic Ascetic* (New York: Oxford University Press, 1973).

68. The *HŚS* cites a quotation from M. Dvivedī (1864–1938) using *sattā* in reference to political rule over "savage tribes," but does not name a source.

69. "Feeling/condition of oneness/non-duality"; a clear reference to the philosophical monism of *advaita* Vedanta.

70. Śukla, "Natural Scenes," 27–28.

71. Ibid., 29.

72. Here we can see shades of Alṭāf Ḥusain "Ḥālī"'s *Muqaddamah*, in which the power of the poet "frees him from the bonds of time and space, and brings the past and the future into the present age," "[describing] Adam and Heaven, Doomsday and the rising of the dead, as though he has seen all these events with his own eyes." Cited in Pritchett, *Nets*, 165.

73. Śukla, "Natural Scenes," 29–30.

74. *Phalamavikalam kāmukatvasya.* Here I have followed Chandra Rajan's translation (Kalidasa, *Kalidasa: The Loom of Time: A Selection of His Plays and Poems*; trans. C. Rajan; New Delhi: Penguin Books, 1989).

75. A large British department store then in Calcutta and Bombay.

76. Śukla, "Natural Scenes," 30.

77. Ibid.

78. *Svarūp*, a term denoting "own form or shape," and in this distinguishing function, "essential properties, nature" and "appearance, type, identity," connotes a wholeness of form. The term's religious usage denotes various forms taken by a god (e.g., Vishnu as the boar, dwarf, Krishna, etc.), and the physical images of such forms.

79. It was only later in 1926 that Subhadrakumārī Cauhān published her famous "Jhāṁsī kī rānī" which spoke of "*svatantratā kī cinagārī*" (the sparks of

independence) (*The National Bibliography of Indian Literature: 1901–1953* [4 vols.; New Delhi: Sahitya Akademi, 1962–1974]).

80. This also connotes the "love of a companion" mode of Krishnaite devotion.

81. Here Śukla uses the term *cāhabharī*, connoting desire in romantic/sexual love as well.

82. Śukla, "Natural Scenes," 30–31.

83. Ibid., 31.

84. From *Modern Painters*, vol. 1 (1843), Sec. 1, Ch. 2, reprinted in John Ruskin, *The Genius of John Ruskin: Selections from His Writings*, ed. J. D. Rosenberg (Charlottesville: University of Virginia Press, 1998), 25.

85. Ibid.

86. We should note that this conjunction of Ruskin's and Śukla's theories does not indicate a wholesale convergence of the two writers' views. In fact, Hindi literary critics have noted Śukla's opposition to the attribution of "external religious, moral, or political purposes" to literature, as found in Ruskin and Tolstoy (two authors often paired together in Hindi criticism). See Śubhanāth Siṁh, "Samālocanā sāhitya kā vikās"("The Development of Critical Literature"), pt. 4 of Dr. Sampūrṇānand, ed., *Hindī sāhitya kā bṛhat itihās* (*A Comprehensive History of Hindi Literature*), vol. 13, *Samālocanā, nibandh aur patrakāritā (sam. 1975–95)* (Criticism, essays, and journalism [1918–1938]) (Varanasi: NPS, 1981, 147–328), 179.

87. Śukla, "Natural Scenes," 11.

Chapter 9

1. Introduction to *New Leaves*, 16.

2. David Rubin, *Return of Saraswati*, 120.

3. Brajaratnadās, *Hindī sāhitya kā itihās* (*The History of Hindi Literature*) (1932; Śrī kamalamaṇi granthamālā 9; Sāhitya laṛī 6; "Approved for Bhushan Examination of Punjab University"; third reprint, Varanasi: Hindī-Sāhitya-Kuṭīr, 1939), 148. Here Brajaratnadās follows critic Rāmacandra Śukla's critiques of 1929.

4. H. Dvivedī, 444.

5. Here we must take special note of the chronological purview: I have selected poems from the limited scope of those known to be *published* between 1921–25. Therefore, only the very earliest of Pant's first known published poem of 1921, "Ucchvās" ("Sighs"), appears here. Pant clearly possessed a larger body of poetry in the early twenties, which journals likely published during this time, but I have not yet found a secondary source that can name which poems, in which journals. The publication history of Nirālā's poetry has been very assiduously dated by Nandakiśor Naval in his *Nirālā Racanāvalī* (*Collected Works of Nirālā*), vols. 1–2, 1983 (New Delhi: Rājakamal Prakāśan, 2006).

Nirālā figures more prominently here because of the greater evidence of his poetry publication in these years. J. S. Prasād's *Indu* (*The Moon*) was defunct in this period, and evidence of his publication in other journals is scant at present. (See U. Miśra). His 1925 *Āṁsū* (*Tears*) is not addressed here, in the interest of brevity and the cogency of the data presented here; *Tears* presents similar tropes, but does so in a particularly complex subjectivity that deserves separate analysis. For this I refer the reader to the introduction and translation of *Tears* by Rubin in *Of Love and War*. It seems that only a few of the young Mahādevī Varmā's poems were published by 1925, in *Cānd* magazine, and those are not significant; none of these will appear here. For a description of these, see Schomer, 185–87.

6. Rubin, *Return of Sarasvati*, 105.

7. Sumitrānandan Pant, "Merī kavitā kā paricay" ("An Introduction to my Poetry") (in *Art and Philosophy*, 255–57), 255. The essay dates from 1959 or later.

8. Pant, "Maiṁne kavitā likhanā kaise prārambh kiyā" ("How I Began to Write Poetry") (in *Art and Philosophy*, 241–42), 242. The essay dates from 1955 or later.

9. Premalatā Bāphanā, *Pant kā kāvya: Chāyāvādī kāvya kī pṛṣṭabhūmi par Sumitrānandan Pant ke kāvya kā anuśīlan* (*The Poetry of Pant: A Study of Sumitrānandan Pant's Poetry against the Background of Chāyāvādī poetry*) (Dehradun: Sāhitya Sadan, 1969), 154.

10. Here I reference the version of "Sighs" in *New Leaves* of 1926, as given in *Sumitrānandan Pant Granthāvalī* (*The Collected Works of Sumitrānandan Pant*) 7 vols. (New Delhi: Rājakamal Prakāśan, 1979, 1: 178–83), in the hope that it does not differ substantially from the first edition, now unavailable.

11. S. Pāṭhak, "The Beauty of Kashmir," 9.2.

12. See "Rain-time in the Mountain Region," in Rubin, *Return of Sarasvati*, 121–22.

13. Heifetz's translation (op. cit.), 2.29.2–3.

14. See Pauwels, "Diptych in Verse."

15. *Ādarś*, Nov.–Dec. 1922; *Collected Works* 1:31–32.

16. This is very clearly seen in "Śephālikā [flower]," in which a bud has a "tight-shut bodice," yet unlike the set emotions of the *rīti* heroine, this bud has a more complicated experience of desire and fulfillment. See Rubin, *Return of Sarasvati*, 79.

17. *"Manahar chand,"* literally "handsome meter," but also a term for the meter of the Braj *kavitt* or *ghanākṣarī* (*HŚS*). Thus, though Nirālā did not write Braj bhāṣā poetry, he wrote of it. *Matavālā* 26 January 1924, by the title "To a Wilted (*murajhāye*) Flower by the Road"; *Collected Works*, 1:90–91.

18. *Matavālā*, 16 February 1924; *Collected Works*, 1:93–94.

19. The end of a woman's sari, wrapped around a child in the lap, also representing a woman's embrace and maternal bosom.

20. Pant, *New Leaves*, 23.

21. *Matavālā*, 24 November 1923; *Collected Works*, 1: 77–78).

22. *Mādhurī*, 20 July 1923; *Collected Works*, 1:49–50.

23. Rambilas Sharma, *Nirālā kī sāhitya sādhanā* (*Nirālā's Literary Method*), vol. 1: *Jīvan-carit (Biography)* (Delhi: Rājakamal Prakāśan, 1969), 65.

24. Schomer, 97, quoting critical articles from the late twenties.

25. Published with the title "Us pār!" ("The other side!"), *Matavālā*, 10 November 1923; reprinted in *Collected Works*, 1: 75–76. The poem bears some resemblance to Nirālā's slightly later "Śṛṅgāramayī" ("She of *Śṛṅgāra*") of 1924 (*Collected Works*, 1: 87–88), analysis of which space does not permit here.

26. *Matavālā* 23 August 1924; *Collected Works* 1: 131–32.

27. *Matavālā* 30 August 1924; *Collected Works* 1:132–33.
28. Pauwels, "Diptych in Verse," 455.
29. *Matavālā*, 9 Aug. 1924; *Collected Works*, 1: 129–30, 130.

Concluding Remarks

1. Indīvar, initial lines of the first song of the film *Pūrab aur Paścim* (*East and West*), directed by Manoj Kumār, "Dulhana calī" ("The Bride Set Off"), 1970. The song is performed in the film as part of a "cultural program" at a university in the 1960s.
2. See Chapter 1, note 68.
3. Ramaswamy, op. cit. Further comparative study is needed of the nexuses linking erotics and nationalism in South Asia.
4. *"Dulhana calī"* (*"The Bride Set Off"*), op. cit.

Select Bibliography

Notes

1. Hindi authors' names are transliterated as other Indic terms in the text. If the author has published in English, then that spelling is used instead. Certain authors whose names have a particular standardized English form, namely Tagore and Premchand, are spelled as such.

2. Vikramāditya dates are translated by subtracting 57, which will admittedly create an occasional inaccuracy.

3. Multiple works by the same author are listed by original publication date.

Works in Hindi and Other Indic Languages

"Adhīr" [Indararāj Baid]. *Rāmanareś Tripāṭhī*. 1987. Bhāratīya Sāhitya ke Nirmātā, 2nd ed. New Delhi: Sāhitya Academy, 1993.

"Agyeya" [Sachchidanand Vatsyayan], and S. Saksenā, *Rūpāmbarā: ādhunik hindīke prakṛti-kāvyakā saṅkalan aur vivecan (Dressed in forms/beauty: an anthology and analysis of modern Hindi nature-poetry)*. Jñānapīṭh lokoday granthamālā 122. Edited by L. Jain. Varanasi: Bhāratīya Jñānapīṭh, 1960.

Aruṇ [Ātmarām Śarmā]. *Ratnākar dvārā upekṣit kavi maṇḍal: navinatam khoj evam śodh par ādhārit (The Poets Ratnākar Neglected: Based on the Newest Research and Investigation)*. Delhi: Bhagyavantī Prakāśan, 2000.

Āzād, Muhammad Husain. *Āb-e-ḥayāt (The Water of Life)*. 1880. 2nd ed. 1883. Reprint, Lucknow: Uttar Pradesh Urdu Academy, 1982.

Bāphanā, Premalatā. *Pant kā kāvya: Chāyāvādī kāvya kī pṛṣṭabhūmi par Sumitrānandan Pant ke kāvya kā anuśīlan (The Poetry of Pant: A Study of Sumitrānandan Pant's Poetry against the Background of Chāyāvādī Poetry)*. Dehradun: Sāhitya Sadan, 1969.

The Bhagavadgītā or the Song Divine (with Sanskrit Text and English Translation). Introduction and essay by J. Goyandaka. 35th ed. Gorakhpur: Gita Press, 1996.

Bihārī Lāl. *The Satsaiyā of Bihārī, with a commentary entitled the* Lālacandrikā, *by Sri Lallu Lāl Kavi*. Edited with introduction and notes by G. A. Grierson. Calcutta: Office of the Superintendent of Government Printing, 1896.

Caturvedī, Rāmasvarūp. *Hindī sāhitya aur saṃvedanā kā vikās* (*Hindi Literature and the Development of Sensibility*). 1986. 8th rev. ed., Allahabad: Lokabhāratī Prakāśan, 1998.

Caube, Devendra, and R. Caudharī. "Itihās aur kavitā" ("History and Poetry"), *Tadbhava* 9 (April 2003), 217–226.

Chatterjee, Bankimchandra. "Bande mātaram" ("Hail to the Mother") in *Ānandamaṭh* (*Abbey of Bliss*), 1880; reprinted in *Baṅkim-satabārshik-saṃskaraṇ*, vol. 4. Calcutta: Baṅgīya-Sāhitya-Pariṣat, 1938.

Das, Syam Sundar. *The Hindi Scientific Glossary, containing the terms of astronomy, chemistry, geography, mathematics, philosophy, physics and political economy, with their Hindi equivalents*. 1904. Reprint. Banaras: Nāgarī Pracāriṇī Sabha, 1906.

Deśapāṇḍe, B. G. *Marāṭhī kā ādhunik sāhitya: itihās, 1805 se 1960* (*Modern Literature in Marathi: A History, 1805 to 1960*). Amaravati: Navayuga Book Stall, 1963.

Dvivedī, Hazārīprasād. *Hindī sāhitya: unakā udbhav aur vikās* (*Hindi Literature: Its Origin and Development*). 1952?; Delhi: Attaracand Kapūr and sons, 1955.

Dvivedī, Mahāvīraprasād. *Kavitā Kalāp* (*A Collection of Poetry*). Allahabad: Indian Press, 1909.

———. *Mahāvīraprasād Dvivedī racanāvalī* (*The Collected Works of Mahavīraprasād Dvivedī*), 15 vols. Edited and with an introduction by B. Yāyāvar. New Delhi: Kitāb Ghar, 1995.

Gauṛ, Haraprakāś. *Sarasvatī aur rāṣṭrīya jāgaraṇ* (Sarasvatī *and national awakening*). New Delhi: National Publishing House, 1983.

Gautam, Lakṣmaṇadatt. *Priyapravās kī ṭīkā: Kavi Hariaudh racit* Priya pravās *kā sarvāṅgapūrṇ ṭīkā* (*Commentary on* Priyapravās*: A Thorough Commentary on Priya pravās by the Poet Hariaudh*). Delhi: Aśok Prakaśan, n.d.

"Girīś" [Girijādatt Śukla]. *Mahākavi Hariaudh [caritāmūlak samīkṣā]* (*The Poet Hariaudh [A Biographical Study]*), 3rd ed. Allahabad: Rāmanārāyaṇ Lāl, 1959.

Gupta, Maithilīśaraṇ. *Bhārat-bhāratī* (*The Voice of India*). 1912–14. 37th ed. Jhansi: Sāhitya Sadan, 1991.

———. *Śakuntalā*. Jhansi: Sahitya-sadan, 1914.

Hariaudh [Ayodhyāsiṁh Upādhyāy]. *Ṭheṭh Hindī kā ṭhāṭ arthāt ṭheṭh Hindī meṁ likhī gaī ek man lubhānevālī kahānī* (*An Exposition in Authentic Hindi, or a Pleasing Story written in Authentic Hindi*). Bankipur: Khaḍgavilās Press, 1899.

———. *Adhakhilā phul, arthāt ṭheṭh Hindī meṁ likhī gaī ek man lubhānevālī kahānī* (*The Half-bloomed Flower, or a Pleasing Story written in Authentic Hindi*). Khaḍgavilās Press, 1906?; rev. ed. 1943; 4th reprint, Varanasi: Hindī Sāhitya Kuṭīr, 1968.

———. *Kāvyopavan arthāt nānārasamayī kavitāvalī* (*A Garden of Verse, a Collection of Poems full of Various Rasas*). Patna: Khaḍgavilās Press, 1909.

———. *Priyapravās: bhinnatukānt kavitā kā ek Hindī mahākāvya* (*The Absence of the Beloved: A Hindi* Mahākāvya *of Unrhymed Poetry*). Bankipore: Khaḍgavilās Press, 1914; rev. ed., *Priyapravās: Khaṛī-Bolī kā sarvaśreṣṭh mahākāvya* (*The Absence of the Beloved: The Foremost Khaṛī Bolī* Mahākāvya), 1941; 23rd printing, Varanasi: Hindī Sāhitya Kuṭīr, 1996.

———. *Bolacāl (The Way of Speech)*. Baṇkipore: Khaḍgavilās Press, 1927. Reprint, Varanasi: Hindī-Sāhitya-Kuṭīr, n.d.

———. *Rasakalas: rasa-sambandhī anūṭhā kāvya-granth (A Pot of Rasa: A New Work of Poetry on Rasa)*. Patna: Pustak Bhaṇḍār, 1931; 4th printing, Varanasi: Hindī Sāhitya Kuṭīr, 1964.

Hīrālāl. *A Translation of all the Poetical Pieces of English Royal Reader nos. 1–3 into Hindi Poetical Pieces*. Lucknow: Muṁśī Naval Kiśor, 1881.

Hṛdayeś [Hṛdayanārāyaṇ Pāṇḍey]. "Rasa-dhārā" ("Stream of *rasa*"), *Cānd (The Moon)* 4:1:2:39 (Dec. 1925), 1.

Indīvar. "Dulhana calī" ("The Bride Set Off"), song in the film *Pūrab aur Paścim (East and West)*. Directed by Manoj Kumār, 1970.

Kalidasa. *The* Meghaduta *of Kalidasa*. Translated by M. R. Kale. 8th ed. Delhi: Motilal Banarsidass, 1993.

Keśav Dās, *Rasikapriyā (Beloved of the Connoisseur)*. 1591. Reprinted in *Keśav-granthāvalī (The Collected Works of Keśav)*, vol. 1. Edited by V. P. Miśra, 1954. Reprint, Allahabad: Hindustānī Academy, 1990.

———. *Kavipriyā (Handbook for the Poet)*. 1601. Reprinted in *Keśav-granthāvalī (The Collected Works of Keśav)*, vol. 1. Edited by V. P. Miśra, 1954. Reprint, Allahabad: Hindustānī Academy, 1990.

Khatrī, Ayodhyā Prasād, comp. *Khaṛī Bolī ka padya: Poetical Reader of Khaṛī Bolī*. Preface by F. Pincott. London: W. H. Allen, 1889.

Kumār, Anūp. *Prasād kī racanāoṁ meṁ saṃskaraṇāgat parivartanoṁ kā adhyayan (A Study of the Changes between Editions of the Works of Prasād)*. Allahabad: Hindī Pariṣad Prakāśan, 1984.

Mālavīya, Kapiladev. "Prakṛti kī pyārī pyārī bāteṁ" ("The Sweet, Sweet Words of Nature"), *Strī-darpaṇ (Women's Mirror)* 22:1 (Jan. 1920), 41–44.

Miśra, Kṛṣṇabihārī. "Brajabhāṣā meṁ kavitā" ("Poetry in Braj Bhāṣā"), *Indu (The Moon)* 6:1:1 (Jan. 1915), 2–11.

Mānav, Viśvambhar. Priya-pravās *kī ṭīkā (Commentary on* Priya-pravās). Allahabad: Lokabhāratī Prakāśan, 1968.

Miśra, Kṛṣṇabihārī. Introduction to *Matirām-granthāvalī (The Collected Works of Matirām)*. Edited by K. Miśra. Lucknow: Gaṅgā-granthāgār, 1925. Reprint, edited by B. K. Miśra. Ākār Series 6, edited by K. D. P. Gauṛ, et al. Varanasi: Nāgarī Pracārinī Sabhā, 1964.

Miśra, Pratāpanārāyaṇ. *Pratāpanārāyaṇ-granthāvalī (The Collected Works of Pratāpanārāyaṇ)*. Varanasi: Nāgarīpracāriṇī Sabhā, 1992.

———. *Kavitāvali (Collected Poetry)*. N. Caturvedī, ed. Allahabad: Hindī Sāhitya Sammelan, 1987.

Miśra, Rāmacandra. *Śrīdhar Pāṭhak tathā Hindī kā pūrv-svacchandatāvādī kāvya (1875 i. se 1925 ī. tak) (Śrīdhar Pāṭhak and Pre-Romantic Poetry in Hindi, 1875–1925 A.D.)*. Delhi: Raṇajīt Printers and Publishers, 1959.

Miśra, Uṣā *'Prasād' kā pūrvavartī kāvya (Prasād's Early Poetry)*. Allahabad: Sāhitya Bhavan, 1970.

Nagendra. *Rasa-siddhānt (The Principle of Rasa)*. Delhi: National Publishing House, 1964.

Nautiyāl, Vidyāsāgar. "Abhī rītikāl pūre sabab par hai" ("Even Now the *Rītikāl* is in Full Force"). *Haṁs*, 239:21:1 (August 2006), 209–10.

Nirālā [Sūryakānt Tripāṭhī]. *Nirālā racanāvalī (The Collected Works of Nirālā)*. 8 vols. Edited by N. Naval. New Delhi: Rājakamal, 1983.

Padmākar. *Jagadvinod (Worldly Pleasure)*. Banaras: Bhārat Jivan Press, 1902.

Pāṇḍey, Sudhākar, et al. *Hindī sāhitya kā bṛhat itihās (A Comprehensive History of Hindi Literature)*, vol. 9 (*Dwivedī kāl [1893–1918]*). Varanasi: Nāgarī Pracāriṇī Sabhā, 1978.

Pant, Sumitrānandan. *Sumitrānandan Pant Granthāvalī (The Collected Works of Sumitrānandan Pant)*, vol. 1. New Delhi: Rājakamal Prakāśan, 1979.

———. *Pallav (New Leaves)*. 1926; 9th ed. New Delhi: Rājakamal Prakāśan, 1993.

———. *Śilpa aur darśan (Art and Philosophy)*. Allahabad: Rāmanārāyaṇ Lāl Benī Mādhav, 1961.

Pāṭhak, Śrīdhar. *Śrīdhar Pāṭhak granthāvalī (The Collected Works of Śrīdhar Pāṭhak)*, 3 vols. Edited by Padmādhar Pāṭhak. Jodhpur: Rājasthānī Granthāgār, 1996.

Prasād, Jagannāth. *Chandaḥprabhākara (Illuminator of meter)*. 1894. 3rd ed., n.p., 1915.

Prasād, Jayaśaṅkar. *Prasād granthāvalī (The Collected Works of Prasād)*, 6 vols. New Delhi: Bhāratīya Granth Niketan, 1997.

Raghuvaṁś. *Prakṛti aur Hindī kāvya (madhya-yuga) (Nature and Hindi Poetry [Middle Ages])*. Allahabad: Hindī Sāhitya Bhavan Limited, 1948.

———. *Prakṛti aur kāvya (Saṃskṛt khaṇḍ) (Nature and Poetry [Sanskrit volume])* Allahabad: Hindī Sāhitya Bhavan Limited, 1951.

———. *Śrīdhar Pāṭhak*. Bhāratīya sāhitya ke nirmātā. 1985. Reprint, New Delhi: Sāhitya Academy, 1991.

Ratnākar [Jagannāth Dās]. *Ratnākar arthāt golokavāsī Śrī Jagannāthadās Ratnākar ke saṃpūrṇ kāvyoṁ kā saṃgraha (Ratnākar, or a Collection of the Entirety of the Poetry of the late Jagannāth Dās Ratnākar)*. Edited by S. S. Dās, 1933. Vol. 1. 4th ed. Varanasi: Nāgarī Pracāriṇī Sabhā, 1950.

Rāy, Lallan. *Ratnākar aur unakā* Uddhavaśatak: *kavivar Ratnākar ke kāvya kī viśad ālocanā aur* Uddhavaśatak *kī vistṛt vyākhyā (Ratnākar and his Uddhavaśatak: Lucid Criticism of Ratnākar's Poetry and a Detailed Explanation of Uddhavaśatak)*. Varanasi: Nandakiśor and Brothers, 1958.

Śarmā, Mukundadev. *Hariaudh: jīvan aur kṛtitva (Hariaudh: Life and Works)*. Varanasi: Nandkiśor and Sons, 1960.

Sharma, Rambilas. *Nirālā kī sāhitya sādhanā (The Literary Method of Nirālā)*, vol. 1, *Jīvan-carit (Biography)*. Delhi: Rājakamal Prakāśan, 1969.

Siṁh, Dhīrendranāth. *Ādhunik Hindī ke vikās meṁ Khaḍgavilās Press kī bhūmikā (The Role of the Khaḍgavilās Press in the Development of Modern Hindi)*. Patna: Bihār-Rāṣṭrabhāṣā-Pariṣad, 1986.

Siṁh, Nāmavar. *Chāyāvād (Shadow-ism)*. 1955. Reprint, New Delhi: Rājakamal Prakāśan, 2001.

Singh, Pratap Narayan, Maharaja. *Rasakusumākār, or a Book on Rhetoric: Rasakusumākār arthāt sāhitya kā ek anūṭhāgranth*. Allahabad: Indian Press, 1894.

Sītārām, Lālā, comp. *Ars Poetica, Selections from Hindi Literature*, Book V. Calcutta: University of Calcutta, 1924.

———. *Meghadūta-bhāṣā: Mahākavi Kālidāsa ke prasiddh saṁskṛt granth kā bhāṣā chandoṁ meṁ anuvād [Sitaram's Hindi Kalidasa Meghaduta]*. 1883. 2nd ed., 1892; 4th ed., Allahabad: National Press, 1917.

Śukla, Rāmacandra. *Hindī sāhitya kā itihāsa (The History of Hindi Literature)*. 1929. Revised and enlarged 1940, 1991. 32nd ed., Nāgarīpracāriṇī granthamālā 53; Varanasi: Nāgarīpracāriṇī Sabhā, 1997.

———. *Rasa mīmāṃsā (Analysis of Rasa)*. Edited by V. Miśra. Śāstravijñān Granthamālā 4. 1946. Varanasi: Nāgarī Pracāriṇī Sabhā, 1991.

———. *Madhusrot: Ācārya Rāmacandra Śukla kī kavitāoṁ kā saṁgraha (Spring of Nectar: A Collection of Ācārya Rāmacandra Śukla's Poetry)*. Nāgarīpracāriṇī granthamālā 79. Varanasi: Nāgarī Pracāriṇī Sabhā, 1971.

———. *Cintāmaṇi*. Vol. 2, edited by V. Miśra. Nāgarīpracāriṇī granthamālā 70. 1945. 4th ed., Varanasi: NPS, 1996. Vol. 3, edited by N. Siṁh, 1983. New Delhi: Rājakamal Prakāśan, 1985.

Sūr Dās. *Sūrasāgar (The Ocean of Sūr)*, vol. 2. Ratnākar, et al., eds. Varanasi: Nāgarī Pracāriṇī Sabhā, 1976.

Sūratimiśra. *Jorāvar Prakāś: Ācārya Keśavadāsakṛta Rasikapriyākī ṭīkā*. 1743. Edited by Y. Siṁh. Sammelan ākār granthamālā 10. Allahabad: Hindi Sāhitya Sammelan, 1992.

Tripāṭhī, Rāmanareś, ed. *Hindī*, vol. 2 of *Kavitā kaumudī (Guide to Poetry)*. 1920. 3rd rev. ed., Allahabad: Hindī-Mandir, 1926.

———. *Pathik: khaṇḍakāvya (The Pilgrim: a Narrative Poem)*. 1920. 29th ed., Delhi: Rājapāl and Sons, 1952.

Vājapeyī, Nandadulāre. "Ārambhik kāvya-vikās" ("The Initial Development of Poetry") in N. Vājapeyī, *Jayaśaṅkar Prasād*. Rev. ed., Allahabad: Bhāratī-Bhaṇḍār, 1959, 50–64.

Var [Dān Bahādur Pāṭhak]. *Ratnākar kī sāhitya-sādhanā (Ratnākar's Literary Method)*. Agra: Vinod Pustak Mandir, 1965.

Varmā, Vrindāvanalāl. *Jhāṁsī kī Rānī Lakṣmībāī: aitihāsik upanyās (The Queen Lakṣmībāī of Jhansi: A Historical Novel)*. 1946. New Delhi: Diamond Pocket Books, 1996.

Works in English

Addison, Joseph. *The Spectator*, vol. 6 (1713), no. 411.

Ambalal, Amit. *Krishna as Shrinathji: Rajasthani Paintings from Nathdvara*. Ahmedabad: Mapin, 1987.

Āzād, Muhammad Husain. *Āb-e-ḥayāt: Shaping the Canon of Urdu Poetry*. Translated and with an introduction by Frances Pritchett in association with S. R. Faruqi. Delhi: Oxford University Press, 2001.

Banerjee, Sumanta. "Marginalization of Women's Popular Culture in Nineteenth Century Bengal" in *Recasting Women: Essays in Colonial History*, op. cit., 127–79.

Bangha, Imre. "Romantic Poetry in the Era of Convention? The Emergence of the Idea of a *Rītimukt* Trend within Hindi Mannerist Literature," *South Asia Research* 25:1 (2005), 13–30.

Bard, Amy and V. Ritter, "A House Overturned: A Classical Urdu Lament in Braj Bhāṣā," in *Shared Idioms, Sacred Symbols: Process, Power, and the Articulation of Religious Identities in South Asia*. Edited by Kelly Pemberton and M. Nijhawan. Oxford: Routledge, 2008.

Barrett, Arthur, ed. Introduction to *Oliver Goldsmith,* The Traveller *and* The Deserted Village. 1888. Reprint, London: Macmillan, 1931.

Bayly, C. A. *Rulers, Townsmen, and Bazaars: North Indian Society in the Age of British Expansion, 1770–1870*. Cambridge: Cambridge University Press, 1983.

———. "Patrons and Politics in Northern India," in *Locality, Province and Nation: Essays on Indian Politics, 1870–1940*. Edited by J. Gallagher, G. Johnson, and A. Seal. Cambridge: Cambridge University Press, 1983, 29–68.

———, editor. *The Raj: India and the British, 1600–1947*. London: National Portrait Gallery, 1990.

Benjamin, Walter. "The Task of the Translator," in *Illuminations*. Edited by H. Arendt, translated by H. Zohn. New York: Schocken, 1968.

Bhabha, Homi. "Of Mimicry and Man: The ambivalence of colonial discourse," in *The Location of Culture*. London: Routledge, 1994, 85–92.

Brass, Paul R. *Language, Religion and Politics in North India*. London: Cambridge University Press, 1974.

Busch, Allison. "The Anxiety of Innovation: The Practice of Literary Science in the Hindi/Riti Tradition," *Comparative Studies of South Asia, Africa and the Middle East* 24, no. 2 (2004), 45–59.

Bryant, Kenneth. *Poems to the Child-God: Structures and Strategies in the Poetry of Surdas*. Berkeley: University of California Press, 1978.

Chandra, Sudhir. *The Oppressive Present: Literature and Social Consciousness in Colonial India*. Delhi: Oxford University Press, 1994.

Chatterjee, Bankimchandra. *Krishna-Charitra*. 1892. Translated and with an introduction by P. Bhattacharya. Classics of the East. Calcutta: M. P. Birla Foundation, 1991.

———. "Krishnakanta's Will" in *The Poison Tree: Three Novellas*. Translated by M. Maddern and S. N. Mukherjee. New Delhi: Penguin Books, 1996.

Cook, S.B. *Imperial Affinities: Nineteenth-century Analogies and Exchanges between India and Ireland*. New Delhi: Sage Publications, 1993.

Das, Sisir Kumar. *A History of Indian Literature*, vol. 8–9. Delhi: Sahitya Akademi, 1991.

Doniger, Wendy. *Śiva: The Erotic Ascetic*. New York: Oxford University Press, 1973.

Chatterjee, Partha. "The Nationalist Resolution of the Women's Question," in *Recasting Women: Essays in Colonial History*. Edited by Kumkum Sangari and Sudesh Vaid. Delhi: Kali for Women, 1989, 233–253.

Dalmia, Vasudha. "Hariścandra of Banaras and the reassessement of Vaishṇava bhakti in the late nineteenth century" in *Devotional Literature in South*

Asia: Current Research, 1985–88, edited by R. S. McGregor. Cambridge: Cambridge University Press, 1992.

———. "Sanskrit Scholars and Pandits of the Old School: The Benares Sanskrit College and the Constitution of Authority in the Late Nineteenth Century." (*Journal of Indian Philosophy* 24 (1996), 321–37.

———. *The Nationalization of Hindu Traditions: Bharatendu Harischandra and Nineteenth-century Banaras*. Delhi: Oxford University Press, 1997.

Datt, Michael Madhusūdan. *The Slaying of Meghanada: A Ramayana from Colonial Bengal*. Translated and with an introduction by C. B. Seely. New York: Oxford University Press, 2004.

De, Sushil Kumar. *Sanskrit Poetics as a Study of Aesthetic*. Berkeley: University of California Press, 1963.

Entwistle, Alan W. *Braj: Centre of Krishna Pilgrimage*. Groningen: Egbert Forsten, 1987.

———. "The Cult of Krishna-Gopāl as a Version of Pastoral" in *Devotion Divine: Bhakti Traditions from the Regions of India, Studies in Honour of Charlotte Vaudeville*, edited by Diana Eck and F. Mallison. Groningen Oriental Studies Vol. VIII. Groningen: Egbert Forsten, 1991, 73–90.

Gaeffke, Peter. *Hindi Literature in the Twentieth Century*. A History of Indian Literature, vol. 8, fasc. 5. Edited by Jan Gonda. Wiesbaden: Otto Harrassowitz, 1978.

Gerow, Edwin. *A Glossary of Indian Figures of Speech*. The Hague: Mouton, 1971.

———. *Indian Poetics*. Wiesbaden: Harrassowitz, 1977.

———. "Indian Poetics" in *The New Princeton Encyclopedia of Poetry and Poetics*. New York: MJF Books, 1993.

Goldsmith, Oliver. *Oliver Goldsmith*, The Traveller *and* The Deserted Village. 1888. Reprint, London: Macmillan, 1931.

Grierson, George Abraham, Sir. *The Modern Vernacular Literature of Hindustan*. Calcutta: Asiatic Society, 1889.

Guillory, John. *Cutural Capital: The Problem of Literary Canon Formation*. Chicago: University of Chicago Press, 1993.

Gupta, Charu. *Sexuality, Obscenity, Community: Women, Muslims, and the Hindu Public in Colonial India*. 2001. New York: Palgrave, 2002.

Haberman, David L. "On Trial: The Love of the Sixteen Thousand Gopees," *History of Religions* 33:1 (Aug. 1993), 44–70.

Halbfass, William. *India and Europe: An Essay in Understanding*. Albany: State University of New York Press, 1988.

Ḥālī, Alṭāf Ḥusain. *Ḥālī's* Musaddas*: The Flow and Ebb of Islam*. Delhi: Oxford University Press, 1997.

Hatcher, Brian A. *Eclecticism and Modern Hindu Discourse*. New York: Oxford University Press, 1999.

Hawley, John S., and D. Wulff, eds. *The Divine Consort: Rādhā and the Goddesses of India*. Berkeley: Graduate Theological Union, 1983.

The Imperial Gazetteer of India. Vols. VI and XXIV. Oxford: Clarendon Press, 1908.

Inden, Ronald. "Transnational Class, Erotic Arcadia and Commercial Utopia in Hindi Films" in *Image Journeys: Audio-Visual Media and Cultural Change in India*. Edited by C. Boresius and M. Butcher. New Delhi: Sage Publications, 1999, 41–66.

Jayadeva. *Love Song of the Dark Lord: Jayadeva's 'Gitagovinda.'* Translated by Barbara Stoler Miller. New York: Columbia University Press, 1977.

Jones, Kenneth W. *Socio-religious Reform Movements in British India*. The New Cambridge History of India, vol. 3, book 1. Edited by G. Johnson. New Delhi: Foundation Books, 1994.

Joshi, Priya. *In Another Country: Colonialism, Culture, and the English Novel in India*. New York: Columbia, 2002.

Kalidasa. *Kalidasa: The Loom of Time: A Selection of His Plays and Poems*. Translated by C. Rajan. New Delhi: Penguin Books, 1989.

———. *The Origin of the Young God: Kālidāsa's* Kumārasambhava. Translated by H. Heifetz. 1985. Berkeley: University of California Press, 1990.

Kapur, Geeta. *When was Modernism?: Essays on Contemporary Cultural Practice in India*. New Delhi: Tulika, 2000.

King, Christopher R. *One Language, Two Scripts: The Hindi Movement in Nineteenth Century North India*. Bombay: Oxford University Press, 1994.

Liu, Lydia. *Translingual Practice: Literature, Culture, and Translated Modernity, China 1900–1937*. Stanford: Stanford University Press, 1995.

Madan, Indar Nath. *Modern Hindi Literature: A Critical Analysis*. Lahore: Minerva Book Shop, 1939.

Manjhan [Mīr Sayyid Manjhan Rājgīrī]. *Madhumalati: An Indian Sufi Romance*. Translated with introduction and notes by A. Behl and S. Weightman. Oxford: Oxford University Press, 2000.

Masica, Colin P. *The Indo-Aryan Languages*. Cambridge Language Surveys. 1991; Cambridge: Cambridge University Press, 1993.

McGregor, R. S. *Hindi Literature of the Nineteenth and Early Twentieth Centuries*. A History of Indian Literature, vol. VIII, fasc. 2. Edited by Jan Gonda. Wiesbaden: Otto Harrassowitz, 1974.

———. *Hindi Literature from its Beginnings to the Nineteenth Century*. A History of Indian Literature, vol. 8, fasc. 6. Edited by J. Gonda. Wiesbaden: Otto Harrassowitz, 1984.

"Ayodhyāsiṁh Upādhyāy (1865–1947) and his *Priya-pravās*" in *Classics of Modern South Asian Literature*. Edited by Rupert Snell and I. M. P. Raeside. Khoj: A Series of Modern South Asian Studies. Edited by M. Horstmann and A. Asani, vol. 6. Wiesbaden: Harrassowitz Verlag, 1998, 103–117.

Mitra, Pramadā-Dāsa. "Preface" to *The Mirror of Composition, a Treatise on Poetical Criticism, being an English Translation of the Sahitya-Darpana of Viswanatha Kaviraja; the first 128 pages revised from the work of the late Dr. J. R. Ballantyne, and the rest by Pramada-Dasa Mitra*. Calcutta: Baptist Mission Press, 1875.

Mitchell, W. J. T. "Imperial Landscape" in *Landscape and Power*. Edited by W. J. T. Mitchell. Chicago: University of Chicago Press, 1994, 5–34.

Naim, C. M. "Prize-Winning Adab: A Study of Five Books Written in Response to the Allahabad Government Gazzette Notification," in *Moral Conduct and Authority*. Edited by B. Metcalf. Berkeley: University of California Press, 1984, 290–314.

Nanddas. *The Round Dance of Krishna and Uddhav's Message*. R. S. McGregor, trans. London: Luzac, 1973.

Monier-Williams, Monier. *A Sanskrit-English Dictionary: Etymologically and Philologically Arranged with Special Reference to Cognate Indo-European Languages*. New ed., 1899. Reprint, Delhi: Motilal Banarsidass, 1997.

Mukherjee, Meenakshi. *Realism and Reality: The Novel and Society in India*. Delhi: Oxford University Press, 1994.

Nijhawan, Shobhna, ed. *Nationalism in the Vernacular: Hindi, Urdu, and the Literature of Freedom*. Delhi: Permanent Black, 2010.

Orsini, Francesca. *The Hindi Public Sphere, 1920–1940: Language and Literature in the Age of Nationalism*. New Delhi: Oxford University Press, 2002.

———. Introduction to *Love in South Asia: A Cultural History* (F. Orsini, ed.; University of Cambridge Oriental Publications; Cambridge: Cambridge University Press, 2006, 1–42.

Pandey, Gyanendra. *The Construction of Communalism in Colonial North India*. Delhi: Oxford University Press, 1992.

Pauwels, Heidi. "Diptych in Verse: Gender Hybridity, Language Consciousness, and National Identity in Nirālā's 'Jāgo Phir Ek Bār,' " *Journal of the American Oriental Society* 121.3 (2001), 449–81.

Pincott, Frederic. "Preface" to *Khaṛī Bolī ka padya: Poetical Reader of Khaṛī Bolī*. Compiled by Ayodhyā Prasād Khatrī. London: W. H. Allen, 1889.

Pintchman, Tracy. "Prakṛti, Māyā, and Śakti: The Feminine Principle in Philosophical Discourse," Chapter Two of *The Rise of the Goddess in the Hindu Tradition*. Albany: State University of New York Press, 1994.

Platts, John T. *A Dictionary of Urdū, Classical Hindī and English*. Oxford: Clarendon Press, 1884. Reprint, New Delhi: Mushiram Manoharlal, 1997.

Pope, Alexander. *An Essay on Criticism*. London: T. Daniel, et al., 1758.

Prakash, Gyan. *Another Reason: Science and the Imagination of Modern India*. Princeton: Princeton University Press, 1999.

Pritchett, Frances W. *Nets of Awareness: Urdu Poetry and Its Critics*. Berkeley: University of California Press, 1994.

Rai, Alok. *Hindi Nationalism*. Vol. 13, Tracts for the Times. Hyderabad: Orient Longman, 2001.

Rai, Amrit. *A House Divided: The Origin and Development of Hindi/Hindavi*. Delhi: Oxford University Press, 1984.

Ramanujan, A. K. Afterword in *The Interior Landscape: Love Poems from a Classical Tamil Anthology*. Delhi: Oxford University Press, 1967.

Rao, Velcheru Narayana. "Historical After-Essay" in *Hibiscus on the Lake: Twentieth-Century Telugu Poetry from India*. Edited and translated by V. Narayana Rao. Madison: University of Wisconsin Press, 2002.

Ritter, Valerie. "Useful Absences and the Nature of the Modern: Ayodhyāsimh Upādhyāy "Hariaudh" (1865–1947), his *Priyapravās* (1914) and Hindi Poetry." Dissertation, University of Washington, 2001.

———. "The Language of Hariaudh's *Priyapravās*: Notes toward an Archaeology of Modern Standard Hindi," *Journal of the American Oriental Society* 124:3 (July–September 2004), 417–38.

———. "Epiphany in Rādhā's Arbor: Nature and the Reform of Bhakti in Hariaudh's *Priyapravās*," in *Alternative Krishnas: Regional and Vernacular Variations on a Hindu Deit*. Edited by G. Beck. Albany: State University of New York Press, 2005, 177–208.

———. "Networks, Patrons, and Genres, for Late Braj Bhāṣā Poets," in *Hindi and Urdu Before the Divide*. Edited by Francesca Orsini. Delhi: Orient Longman, 2010.

Rosenstein, Ludmila L. *The Devotional Poetry of Svāmī Haridās*. Groningen: Egbert Forsten, 1997.

Rubin, David, trans. *The Return of Sarasvati: Four Hindi Poets*. Delhi: Oxford University Press, 1998.

———. *Of Love and War: A Chayavad Anthology*. Delhi: Oxford University Press, 2005.

Sangari, Kumkum, and S. Vaid, eds. *Recasting Women: Essays in Indian Colonial History*. New Brunswick: Rutgers University Press, 1990.

Schomer, Karine. *Mahadevi Varma and the Chhayavad Age of Modern Hindi Poetry*. Berkeley: University of California Press, 1983.

Sengupta, Sagaree. "Kṛṣṇa the Cruel Beloved: Hariścandra and Urdu." *The Annual of Urdu Studies* 9 (1994), 133–52.

———. *The Indian Subject: The Voices of a Colonial Poet, Bhāratendu Hariścandra (1850–1885)*. Unpublished book manuscript based on author's dissertation. 1994.

Shackle, Christopher, and J. Majeed. Introduction to *Ḥālī's* Musaddas*: The Flow and Ebb of Islam*, Delhi: Oxford University Press, 1997.

Sharma, K. D. "Maithilīśaraṇa Gupta: a literary biography," in *Maithilīśaraṇa Gupta: An Anthology*. Edited by Dr. Nagendra. Contours and Landmarks of Hindi Literature. Delhi: Bansal and Co., 1981, 13–29.

Singh, Nihal, Saint. "The Macaulay Maya" in *Dvivedīabhinandan granth* (Festschrift for Dvivedī). Varanasi: Nāgarī Pracāriṇī Sabhā, 1933, 495–514.

Snell, Rupert. *The Hindi Classical Tradition: A Braj Bhāṣā Reader*. SOAS South Asian Texts 2. New Delhi: Heritage Publishers, 1992.

———, and I. M. P. Raeside. *Classics of Modern South Asian Literature*. Wiesbaden: Harrassowitz, 1998.

Stall, Sylvainus. *What a Young Husband Ought to Know*. Self and Sex series for Men, vol. 3. Philadelphia: Vir Publishing Company, 1897.

Tagore, Rabindranath. *Selected Poems*. Translated and with an introduction by William Radice. London: Penguin, 1994.

———. "The Object and Subject of a Story," *Modern Review*, September 1918. Reprinted in *The English Writings of Rabindranath Tagore*, edited by S. K. Das. New Delhi: Sahitya Akademi, 1994, 737–41.

Trivedi, Harish. "The Progress of Hindi: Part 2" in *Literary Cultures in History: Reconstructions from South Asia*, edited by S. Pollock. Berkeley: University of California Press, 2003, 958–1022.

Varma, Urmila. *Influence of English Poetry on Modern Hindi Poetry, 1900–1940: With Special Reference to Technique, Imagery, Metre, and Diction*. Allahabad: Lokbharti Prakashan, 1980.

Vidyakara. *An Anthology of Sanskrit Court Poetry: Vidyakara's "Subhāṣitaratnakoṣa."* Translated and edited by Daniel H. H. Ingalls. Harvard Oriental Series, vol. 44. Cambridge: Harvard University Press, 1965.

Viswanathan, Gauri. *Masks of Conquest: Literary Study and British Rule in India*. New York: Columbia University Press, 1989.

Wakankar, Milind. "The Moment of Criticism in Indian Nationalist Thought: Ramchandra Shukla and the Poetics of a Hindi Responsibility," *South Atlantic Quarterly* 101:4 (Fall 2002), 987–1014.

Wordsworth, William. Preface to *Lyrical Ballads, with Other Poems*. 2 vols. London: Longman and Rees, 1800.

Yashascandra, Sitamshu. "From Hemachandra to Hind Svaraj: Region and Power in Gujarati Literary Culture" in *Literary Cultures in History: Reconstructions from South Asia*, edited by S. Pollock. Berkeley: University of California Press, 2003, 567–611.

Zysk, Kenneth G. Preface to *Conjugal Love in India:* Ratiśāstra *and* Ratiramaṇa. Sir Henry Wellcome Asian Series, vol. 1. Leiden: Brill, 2002.

Index

www.ingramcontent.com/pod-product-compliance
Lightning Source LLC
LaVergne TN
LVHW090301060926
847296LV00044B/94